Ferruccio Busoni in his study, Berlin, 1911. Photograph by Winifred Burston.

BUSONI AND THE PIANO

The Works, the Writings, and the Recordings

LARRY SITSKY

Contributions to the Study of Music and Dance, Number 7

Greenwood Press
New York • Westport, Connecticut • London

Library of Congress Cataloging in Publication Data

Sitsky, Larry.
   Busoni and the piano.

   (Contributions to the study of music and dance, ISSN
0193-9041   ; no. 7)
   Bibliography: p.
   Discography: p.
   Includes index.
   1. Busoni, Ferruccio, 1866-1924. Piano music.
2. Busoni, Ferruccio, 1866-1924. Piano, orchestra music.
3. Busoni, Ferruccio, 1866-1924.   I. Title.   II. Series.
ML410.B98S57   1986   786.1′092′4   84-3782
ISBN 0-313-23671-2 (lib. bdg.)

Library of Congress Catalog Card Number: 84-3782
ISBN: 0-313-23671-2
ISSN: 0193-9041

First published in 1986

Greenwood Press, Inc.
88 Post Road West
Westport, Connecticut 06881

Printed in the United States of America

10 9 8 7 6 5 4 3 2 1

Copyright Acknowledgments

The author and publisher are grateful for permission to reprint from the following sources.

Edward J. Dent, *Ferruccio Busoni: A Biography* (Oxford: Oxford University Press, 1933). Reprinted by permission of Oxford University Press.

Ferruccio Busoni: Letters to His Wife, trans. Rosamond Ley (London: Edward Arnold, 1938).

Ferruccio Busoni: The Essence of Music and Other Papers, trans. Rosamond Ley (London: Rockliff, 1957). Reprinted by permission of Barrie & Rockliffe, now a part of the Hutchinson Publishing Group.

Music excerpts reprinted by permission of Breitkopf & Haertel, Wiesbaden; Deutsche Staatsbibliothek, Berlin; and Staatsbibliothek Preussischer Kulturbesitz, Berlin.

To Magda

Contents

Preface

> . . . musicians were in a minority and painters, writers, poets, architects, scientists, and a large number of miscellaneous intellectuals were all attracted by the fireworks of his fascinating soliloquy which would go on for an hour or more, before he retired ceremoniously to the inner sanctum, obviously to attend to his creative work proper.
>
> Ernest Krenek

This book may either be used as a reference volume, to look up information relating to a specific work, or be read right through as a complete survey of Ferruccio Busoni's piano music: solo, four hands, two piano, piano and orchestra, arrangements, transcriptions, hybrid works defying neat classification, and unpublished works. Some previously unpublished items are included in the Appendix. The recordings and rolls made by Busoni are discussed in another chapter.

I was extremely fortunate in having as my first piano teacher Winifred Burston (1889-1976) of the N.S.W. State Conservatorium of Music, Sydney, Australia, herself a pupil of Busoni (she is mentioned in Busoni's letters to his wife), and then of Egon Petri, who, apart from his enormous stature as a pianist, was also a close friend and disciple of Busoni for about 30 years. After completing my studies with Burston, I went on to study with Petri himself in California and stayed with him for two years. Apart from the enormous benefits I gained generally from this experience, we spent many hours going through Busoni works and talking about Busoni. The true value of an oral tradition was thus driven home to me, and I have attempted to pass it along in this book.

The lack of appreciation and ignorance of Busoni, even among professional musicians, seemed to me both regrettable and unjust, and this work is a partial attempt to rectify this situation. It is my hope that some day another volume—not necessarily by me—will complete the survey of

Busoni's music by dealing with all the vocal, instrumental, chamber, symphonic, and operatic compositions. Perhaps Busoni's unpublished but enormously readable letters also will be gathered into a collection by someone before they are lost.

Busoni's life and personality were so fascinating and magnetic that the majority of his commentators have succumbed to their lures. I have concerned myself exclusively with Busoni's music; the Bibliography will refer interested readers to studies of his life, an undoubted definitive work among them being Edward J. Dent's marvellously evocative biography. Critical and analytical studies on Busoni have been few and far between. There are, apart from Hans Stuckenschmidt's *Ferruccio Busoni: The Chronicle of a European*, studies in German by Hanspeter Krellmann and Heinz Meyer which are referred to constantly in my text. These, however, each deal only with a specific area of the piano music. There are no Italian writings that I have seen that could be classed as technical by nature.

My orientation—as a pianist and composer—has been primarily practical. My aim has been, therefore, to throw some light on Busoni's thought processes as a composer and performer and to interest pianists in performing Busoni's music. My personal library contains every work for piano that Busoni ever wrote, and the comments to be found in the book are the result of either my concert performances or broadcasts or at the very least a reading at the keyboard of every composition.

ACKNOWLEDGMENTS

to publishers, particularly Breitkopf & Haertel, Wiesbaden, for searching their archives for rare items and arranging photocopies of items no longer available in print; for allowing museum items to be microfilmed;

to libraries for locating rare editions; in particular, the Library of Congress, Washington, D.C., and the British Museum, London;

to the Deutsche Staatsbibliothek, Musikabteilung, Berlin, and the Staatsbibliothek Preussischer Kulturbesitz, Musikabteilung, Berlin, for great cooperation in allowing me to microfilm the relevant items from their Busoni archives, in particular, the works still in manuscript;

to Busoni experts and enthusiasts all over the world: Terence White Gervais in London; Ronald Stevenson in Capetown; John Ogdon in London; Alan Bush in London; Professor Ernest Meyer in East Berlin; and Rosamond Ley in London;

to the International Piano Library, and its Vice President Greg Benko especially, for assistance in hearing the Busoni recordings and piano rolls;

to Denis Condon in Sydney with his magnificent collection of rolls and expression pianos; to Rees Morgan for allowing me to peruse his catalogues of expression rolls;

to various record companies and sound archive organizations for assistance in obtaining copies of Busoni recordings and rolls, Petri recordings, and some other old recordings by pianists from the Busoni circle;

to the Myer Foundation in Melbourne, and the Vaccari Foundation in Melbourne for assistance with the costs of a voluminous research;

to the director of the Canberra School of Music, Ernest Llewellyn CBE, for providing facilities for research;

to Ulla Klesper, Egon Petri's daughter, for the loan of some music from her father's library;

to my teachers Winifred Burston and Egon Petri for introducing me to the world of Busoni and then following this up with very practical assistance in the matter of helping me obtain scores and arranging contacts with the right people;

to Barbara McRae, Warren Bebbington, John C. G. Waterhouse, and Stephen Daw for carefully reading the manuscript and offering helpful and constructive suggestions;

to Stephen Leek for copying the music examples under trying conditions;

to publishers Oxford University Press, Edward Arnold, Barrie & Rockliffe (now part of the Hutchinson Publishing Group) for permission to quote from their books on Busoni;

to Breitkopf & Haertel, Wiesbaden, for permission to quote extensively from Busoni's music and writings; and

to Louise F. Chapman for her patience in typing the manuscript.

Abbreviations

Am. Rec. Guide	The American Record Guide
AMZ	Allgemeine Musikzeitung
Dansk Mus.	Dansk Musiktidsskrift
Diap	The Diapason
Hi Fi/Mus Am	High Fidelity/Musical America
Hi Fi R	Hi Fi Stereo Review
Hud Roz	Hudebni Rozhledy
IMGZ	International Musikgesellschaft Zietschrift
Melos/NZ	Melos/Neue Zeitschrift für Musik
Mens en Mel	Mens en Melodie
MF	Die Musikforschung
MH	Musikhandel
ML	Music & Letters
MM	Modern Music
MQ	The Musical Quarterly
MUS	Musica
Mus & Mus	Music & Musicians
Mus Op	Musical Opinion
Mus Rev	The Music Review
Mus T	The Musical Times
Mus. u. Ges.	Musik und Gesellschaft
Neue ZFM	Neue Zeitschrift für Musik
NMZ	Neue Musikzeitung
Rec. Sound	Recorded Sound

R Ital Mus	*Rivista Italiana di Musicologia*
RMA	*Royal Musical Association Proceedings*
Schweiz. Musikz.	*Schweizerische Musikzeitung*
Soviet Mus.	*Sovietskaya Musika*
ZFM	*Zeitschrift für Musik*

BUSONI
AND THE
PIANO

1

Busoni's Position in the Mainstream of Music History

> The essential touchstone for me was Busoni's prophetic book, *Entwurf einer Neuen Aesthetik der Tonkunst*. This predicts precisely what is happening today in music—that is, if you pass over the whole dodecaphonic development, which in my view represents a sort of hardening of the arteries.
>
> Edgar Varèse

The dangerous thing about cliches is that one tends to forget that so many of them are rooted in fact. If every writer on Busoni has indulged in the cliche about Busoni's tragic duality of character, this does not lessen the truth of such statements. Busoni *was* divided, and that *was* his tragedy; the divisions were in more areas than one and were more numerous than perhaps is commonly known.

There was his political duality. He was born an Italian but lived most of his creative life in Germany. The Italians regarded him as a deserter, the Germans as an interloper. During the First World War, he retired to a neutral country, which did not endear him to either of these countries. The strange thing is that his musical tastes followed his political duality—or was it the other way around? He was always attracted to the German school for its solidity, its sense of form, of organization, and of scholarship, yet he never lost his Latin love of melody. And whereas his earlier works were steeped in the German tradition and dedicated to Brahms, his last period of creativity was almost purely melodic and polyphonic and clearly closer to his Italian origin.

Even as a pianist he was torn between Italian and German styles. Audiences were shocked by his warm cantabile playing of the German Classic and Baroque masters; yet his sense of architecture was indisputable. He left only a small recorded legacy, although many accounts of his playing survive. His style, based on Anton Rubinstein rather than Franz Liszt, has, through pupils and auditors, left a lasting imprint on the history and progress of piano playing. This is a subject in itself, and the bibliography on it is imposing.

But Busoni's status as a pianist, incredibly high though it was, need no longer overshadow other considerations, and it is as a composer that he must now be judged. Whereas in the case of other composer-pianists one career was aided by the other as they vigorously promulgated their own music, in Busoni's case it turned out differently. He made his great pianistic reputation playing the standard repertoire; his own compositions he played less often, especially the more problematical post-1900 works. These he realized were for a later era and for a select audience. In any case, the audience and critics of the day made it amply clear to him that they were not going to take him seriously in a dual role. Bernard Shaw once advised him: "But you should compose under an assumed name. It is incredible that one man could do more than one thing well; and when I heard you play, I said 'It is impossible that he should compose: there is not room enough in a single life for more than one supreme excellence.'"[1] His composing and pianistic careers, far from complementing each other, were in constant opposition.

Not content with dual excellence, Busoni's restless spirit spurred him into activity in other areas as well. As a conductor, years before any ISCM (International Society for Contemporary Music) or other similar bodies existed, Busoni presented series of concerts surveying a wide range of new music, often financed personally because he believed in "the cause." Many young composers owed much to him in their early years. Between 1902 and 1909, he conducted the music of Debussy,[2] Bartók, Elgar, Saint-Saëns, Sinding, Sibelius, Delius, Liszt (first performances), d'Indy, Rimsky-Korsakoff, Beethoven concertos (with Alkan cadenzas), Berlioz, Nielsen, Schenker, Nováček, Pfitzner, Ysaÿe, and Fauré. As an editor, Busoni was responsible for many editions of old music which, in their day, were unusual in their clarity of presentation. Always searching for musical unity in his manifold endeavors, Busoni's life was an almost classical case of dichotomy, of curious contradiction and ambivalence.

His date of birth was unfortunate. I do not speak now of 1 April 1866 when he first saw the light of day, but of the fact that Busoni straddled two centuries. Brought up in a strict tradition, he had to adapt himself to a totally new way of writing music, not because of fashion but from personal necessity and conviction: he thus became a sort of musical Janus, and hence the oft-heard criticism of his eclectic style. The fact that Busoni as a musical thinker had predicted, and even theoretically stipulated, many of the developments of this century in numerous writings, made little difference in the long run, for the discoveries and ideas he had hinted at or only partially developed were soon fully realized by many other composers. As an innovator, Busoni was simply outstripped, and in the race for novelty forgotten, together with the many individual qualities of his own music.

Yet as a theoretician and thinker, Busoni left his mark. Although most of his essays are now available in English, Italian, and German, there are still many letters in manuscript, and, until all his writings are collected from a wide variety of sources (including many contributions to newspapers and periodicals), a complete picture of his wide-ranging ideas will not be known. Even the essays by themselves, however, present an amazing case of musical prophecy and have been read widely all over the world since their publication. Some of the concepts found in these essays include predictions regarding electronic music: mention of the first electronic organ ever built; microtones, serial technique, liberation from dissonance, new notations, and the concept of "Young Classicism." This is not taking into account long and scholarly articles on music of the past, on his own music, on music contemporary to him, and on his libretti (created for him and for other composers).

Of his works, a host of transcriptions—the Bach-Busoni items that graced the programs of every travelling virtuoso—survived for a while. They are now viewed with disfavor, although they are, after Liszt, the highest example of the craft in the piano repertoire. Busoni continued and restored the dignity due to this art and raised it to a new level of achievement.

The many works either based on a fragment by another composer (*Fantasia nach J. S. Bach, Fantasia Contrappuntistica*) or a transmutation of music by other composers (*Kammer-Fantasie über Bizet's Carmen, Duettino Concertante* after the Finale of the *Concerto in F major*, K. 459, of Mozart, *Albumblatt* No. 3—"in the style of a Chorale Prelude"—and Schönberg Op. 11, No. 2—a "concert interpretation") were never understood in their day. Busoni's ideas on the unity of music throw light on these works, but as a philosopher and musician he is known even less than as a composer. Busoni, of course, expected his listeners to know the fragments by other composers, to know the transcribed works in the original, and to be able to appreciate the same work seen through other eyes. In his operas he expected his audience to be able to follow the complex symbolism of the Faust legend and to be familiar with previous Faust dramas, to cope with the swift satire and musical quotations in *Arlecchino*—it may be safely said that he expected too much from his audience, and this, too, was part of his downfall.

But one can say, if these hybrid works are, for the sake of argument, discounted, what about the pure Busoni, the really original works? Here, another paradox confronts us because, at least in the other compositions, even if we objected to the idea of transcription or to the idea of mixing styles or to the writing of a new work around an old fragment by someone else, the very presence of another composer puts us on familiar ground. Busoni's works of early maturity are easy enough to comprehend (*Violin Sonatas* Nos. 1 and 2, *Geharnischte Suite* for orchestra, *Concertstück* for piano and orchestra, and to a certain extent even the *Piano Concerto Op. XXXIX*), but when we arrive at the truly mature compositions (*Elegies* and *Sonatinas* for piano, *Romanza e Scherzoso* for piano and orchestra, the opera *Doktor Faust*, *Nocturne symphonique*, *Berceuse élégiaque* for orchestra, *Nuit de Noël* and *Toccata*, both for piano, and so on), the ground slips away from us. These works seem to move on a plane divorced from reality, from everyday experience.

Busoni's music can be legitimately described as a record of a mystic journey, and as the journey comes to fruition, the message to be deciphered in the record demands an understanding of the mystic vision from the listener. This withdrawal from reality is without doubt the largest single obstacle to the popularization of Busoni's music: it seems conclusive that it can never, by its very nature, appeal to a mass audience.

Here again was dichotomy: the "outsider" type is essentially a lonely man who has to find his own way, yet Busoni, despite such leanings, loved company and indeed built up a brilliant intellectual circle of pupils, friends, and disciples. In his mature years he was not a teacher in the ordinary sense and did not have pupils in the normal way of things but rather disciples, who came to learn about the piano, about composition, or to simply drink in some of the aura of a great man. Whether disciple or friend, they were all influenced by Busoni's personality. He was always excited by the idea of youth, the idea of passing on the torch: the spoken lines in *Doktor Faust* make this desire explicit. Yet apparently he had the happy knack of developing the student's own talents and personality instead of submerging them in his own genius. As such, his monumental intellect has survived into more than one generation, for pupils of pupils continue to pass on the ideas and traditions, and find in them, as Busoni had so fervently hoped, possibilities and hopes for the future.

The more influential of his pupils include: Egon Petri, my own master, who must have taught hundreds of pianists and transmitted the pianistic ideas and an interest in Busoni's music; other pianists in countries all over the world: Natalie Curtis, Maud Allan (the famous dancer), Michael von Zadora, Augusta Cottlow, Leo Kestenberg, Gregor Beklemischeff, Leo Sirota, Edward Steuermann, Rudolf Ganz, Edward Weiss, Theophil Demetriescu, Dimitri Mitropulous, Theodor Szántó, Gino Tagliapietra, and Gottfried Galston; composer-pupils, some of whom have become central figures in the history of twentieth century music: Edgar Varèse, Kurt Weill, Otto Luening, Gisella Selden-Goth, Louis Gruenberg, Stefan Wolpe, Philipp Jarnach, Vladimir Vogel, Guido Guerrini, and Robert Blum; and composers influenced by Busoni: Selim Palmgren, Hans Huber, Arnold Schönberg, Luigi Dallapiccola, Bernard van Dieren, and Dimitri Tiomkin (the film composer). Various performers cite Busoni as a major influence or at least a major inspiration: Joseph Szigeti, Albert Spaulding, Claudio Arrau, Arthur Rubinstein, Alexander Borovsky, Isidor Philipp, and Vianna da Motta. A complete list would be an impossibility; Busoni came into contact with hundreds of musicians. For example, Percy Grainger only studied with him for a few weeks, but regarded himself as a disciple; it is through the avenue of the composer-pupils that no doubt the most lasting effects are felt. The master classes and open house evenings in Berlin were types of powerhouses which left indelible marks upon those fortunate enough to attend such gatherings. No wonder that Busoni's biographers were fascinated with this rich fund of conflict and paradox, and, true as all this is, and important as it may be for the knowledge of the composer, it is symptomatic that Busoni is more often written and talked about than heard. More often than not, the writing is about the man rather than about the music.

Busoni's complete output for piano and piano with orchestra is discussed in comprehensive detail in this book; in consequence, so are his various styles of composition and compositional periods, his creative outlook and methods, and his transcriptions in theory and practice. It seemed appropriate, therefore, to begin this study with some general comments aimed at placing Busoni into perspective in the mainstream of music. The narrow nationalism that plagued Busoni's life is now surely a thing of the past, and we must recognize him as a truly international figure. Stefan Zweig described him during the First World War as "shadowed by sadness," haunted by the thought that his pupils were scattered all over the world: "Perhaps they are shooting at each other right now."[3]

Finally, although the bulk of Busoni's compositions involve the piano, his contributions to chamber, vocal, and orchestral music, and especially the operatic repertoire cannot be ignored.

NOTES

1. Ferruccio Busoni, *Letters to His Wife*, trans. Rosamond Ley (London, Edward Arnold, 1938), p. 289.

2. In those days, Petri had some pretensions to being a composer, a fact that inlater years he liked to conceal "with a dark veil." He had written an orchestral piece that Busoni had programmed for one of his concerts; in rehearsal some problems arose, and Busoni wrote to Petri, who was away on tour, asking him to come to rehearsal to clarify these problems. Petri replied that he could only return on the day of the orchestral concert. Busoni then decided that this was too late and programmed the first two of Debussy's *Nocturnes* instead. This was for a concert on 1 December 1904. A slip was inserted into the program explaining the change. One critic became confused by this and the next day wrote to the effect that "Mr. Petri, while quite a good pianist, should really not tackle composition, as those *Nocturnes* were not much good." Petri, after relating the story, said to me: "And I would have given my right arm to have written *one* of those *Nocturnes*!"

3. Stefan Zweig, *The World of Yesterday* (New York, The Viking Press, 1943), p. 276.

The Shorter and Unpublished Original Works

2

Short Works Unpublished by Busoni

> He always realized his own unique powers. One need only look at the camera portraits made between his first and fifth year to be convinced of this. This may seem a preposterous assertion . . . but a look at the actual photographs will convince all cynics. That as far as his memory reached he always felt the power and direction of his own desires we must believe on his own word. . . . On the evidence collected from the most varied sources one comes to the conclusion that he was aware of his personality long before he was in a position to assert his independence against the masters who trained him to his own precocious satisfaction.
>
> Bernard van Dieren

Fortunately, most of Busoni's earliest compositions and a fine array of his manuscripts in general have been preserved. The collection, known as the *Busoni-Nachlass*, consists of 366 catalogued items (see Catalogue), at present distributed on either side of the Berlin wall. The Stiftung Preussischer Kulturbesitz, Musikabteilung, on the west side holds the manuscript numbers 1-104 which consist of the very early works. The Deutsche Staatsbibliothek, Musikabteilung, on the east side holds numbers 130-176 and 182-366.[1] The latter is by far the more important collection, not only numerically, but also because it includes mature works never published, sketches and alternatives for published works, and Busoni's own corrections, notes, and comments on works already published. During the Second World War, the collection was dispersed for safekeeping. Numbers 177-187 were all concerned with the oratorio *Il Sabato del Villaggio*. Numbers 177 and 178 are the manuscript of the full score and vocal score, respectively, and are to be found in the Stiftung Preussischer Kulturbesitz; numbers 179-181 contained manuscript performance materials but were lost during the war; numbers 105-129 have also not been seen since the war.

I include the contents of the missing manuscripts in the Catalogue in the hope that they may one day come to light; the inclusion of the complete list also makes clearer—albeit only a little—the perplexing situation of Busoni opus numbers. Busoni said concerning this question:

As a child I wrote much and published many things prematurely. Badly advised and inexperienced, I numbered the things which were printed according to the order of their origin instead of according to the sequence of their publication. So the little volume 30-40 was printed with this numbering although those marked 15-29 (21 and 25 excepted), were not yet printed.[2] When I was about seventeen years old, nos. 1-14 and 30-40 among the small compositions had fortunately been published.

At this time—when eighteen years old—the real youthful experiments arose and I began to consider systematising the numbers. At that time Albert Gutmann in Vienna published two songs Op. 15, six studies Op. 16, and another study in variation form Op. 17. The last two were dedicated to Johannes Brahms.

. . . With my next work published by Kistner, I made up my mind to fill out the missing opus numbers in the printed sequence. I finished Op. 18 and soon completed filling out the other numbers (1890). When I compared Op. 30, the work of childhood which bears the number 30, with its successors, I saw the gap which had arisen in the meantime through my development. I could consent no longer to let those "thirties" pass as a continuation of the riper "twenties." I saw that the way out was to compose a new series of "thirties" to which for the sake of distinction I affixed the letter "a." Only the youthful work 37 (twenty-four Preludes), and 40 (four Italian choruses for men with orchestral accompaniment) seemed to me to be of enough value not to require the substitution and in Op. 39 instead of the letter "a" I chose the representation of the number in roman figures in the new series.

The chronological sequence is thus: 1-14, 21, 25, 61, 70, 30-40—childhood; 15, 16, 17, 18, 19, 20, 22, 23, 24, 25, 26, 27, 28, 29 (for the second time)—youth; 30a, 31a, 32a, 33a, 33b, 34a, 35a, 36a, 38 (for the second time), XXXIX, 41—manhood up to 1906. The Elegies should have been 42 but have appeared without an opus number, likewise Kultaselle (Variations for Violoncello).[3]

If this is not sufficiently complex, the question is further confused by yet a third series of opus numbers running through the unpublished works and by missing numbers in various series. An extremely useful thematic-chronological catalogue of Busoni's compositions has been drawn up by Jürgen Kindermann.[4]

Since the dates of composition are the only really reliable guide to Busoni's output, I have adopted a number of procedures in listing the works in Chapters 2 and 3. First, the titles are given exactly as in the manuscripts. Second, if the keys are not given in the title, and a number of works of the same title exist, I have, on occasion, added the key in parenthesis for purposes of identification. Third, the date of composition is standardized into English, but is only given if it is on the manuscript. Likewise, the place of composition is rendered in English, but is only given if it is on the manuscript. Finally, the Staatsbibliothek (SB) number is given for all the manuscript works. Some works will have more than one SB number because Busoni at times recopied a work into another notebook, the "new" version being sometimes given a few extra phrasing and expression marks. I have grouped these early efforts into classes to provide, at a glance, an idea of the young composer's formalistic interests. The more ambitious works are discussed in Chapter 3.

Fuga a 2 voci in stile libero   23 Aug 1875   SB 23

Fuga a 3 voci   2 Sept 1875   SB 25

Fuga per Harmonium-Organo a tre voci   5 Jan 1876   SB 36

Fughetta   9 Sept 1876   Gmunden   SB 54

Fuga in Sol Magg   23 Jan 1877   Vienna   SB 61

Allegro fugato   30 Sept 1877   SB 70

Preludio e Fuga in Do Magg per la mano sinistra sola Op. 15   27 Feb 1878
   Vienna   SB 82

Fuga in stile libero Op. 16   5 Mar 1878   Vienna   SB 83

Fuga   SB 149 No. 54

Preludium & Fuge (D major)   30 Feb 1880   Graz   SB 148

Fuge über das volkslied "O Du Mein Lieber Augustin"   June 1888   SB 195

Preludium & Fuge (a minor)   1 Apr 1881   SB 360

Preludio e Fuga a 2 Pianoff. Op. 32   5 Dec 1878   SB 98

Fuge, G moll Op. 74   Oct 1880   SB 156

Preludium & Fuge (g minor)   (Prelude is a transposed and shortened version of
   SB 213; Fugue is SB 156)   new SB number is 157   Oct 1880

Preludio & Fuge (c minor) *Op. 75*   May 1880   SB 150

* * *

Invenzione   2 Dec 1875   Vienna   SB 31, SB 44, SB 46

Invention (c minor)   31 Dec 1876   Vienna   SB 360

Invenzione   20 June 1877   Gmunden   SB 65

Invention   14 May 1880   SB 149

Invenzione (d minor)   28 July 1885   SB 190

* * *

Preludio per pianoforte Op. 11   Oct 1874   SB 11

Preludio Op. 19   Mar 1875   SB 19

Preludio per pianoforte solo Op. 20   March 1875   SB 21

Preludio   4 Sept 1877   Gmunden   SB 68

Preludio in Fa min Op. 19   5 May 1878   SB 88

Preludio (a minor)   SB 213

* * *

Cadenza; Esercizio Op. 4   Sept 1873   SB 4

Studio Op. 5   Oct 1873   SB 5

Studio in do magg. per pianoforte solo   29 Aug 1875   SB 24

Studio contrappuntato   14 Oct 1875   Vienna   SB 29

Studio   1 Jan 1877   Vienna   SB 59

Studio Op. 12 in Do min.   Feb 1878   Vienna   SB 80

Sechs Kurze Klavierstudien   SB 165   (These are extremely short, more like exercises; No. 6, a canon, is incomplete.)

Klavieretude (C major)   1889   SB 196

Studio (a minor)   SB 166

Etude 15 en forme d'Adagio d'une Sonata   SB 185

Etude 16 (Nocturne)   SB 186

Studio 18 in fa minore   14 Feb 1883   SB 184

*   *   *

Menuetto Op. 17   5 Oct 1873   SB 16, SB 28

Menuetto   3 July 1876   Gmunden   SB 41

Menuetto Op. 4   1 Feb 1878   Vienna   SB 76

*   *   *

Gavotta   26 Sept 1875   Vienna   SB 26

Gavottina Op. 3 No. 3   11 Nov 1876   SB 55, SB 56

*   *   *

Marcia funebre Op. 8   22 Feb 1874   SB 8

Marcia funebre   15 Mar 1876   Vienna   SB 38

*   *   *

Scherzo Op. 14   Oct 1874   SB 13

Scherzo in Si b Magg Op. 15   Feb 1875   SB 15

Scherzo in Si b   11 Feb 1876   Vienna   SB 37

*   *   *

Polka Op. 16   Jan 1875   SB 14

*   *   *

Walzer de Concerto. Momente Musicale   27 Dec 1875   Vienna   SB 35, SB 47

Introduzione; tempo di Walzer; Finale Op. 3   Aug 1873   SB 3

Walzer   SB 149 No. 30

*   *   *

Canzone Op. 1   June 1873   SB 1

La Canzone del cacciatore Op. 10   20 Sept 1874   SB 10

Canzone populare Op. 13   17 Sept 1873   SB 18

* * *

Romanza senza parole Op. 9   24 May 1874   SB 9

Il Dolore; Romanza senza parole   21 June 1876   Gmunden   SB 40

* * *

Inno   28 Sept 1875   Vienna   SB 27

Inno   5 Dec 1875   SB 33, SB 45

Inno-Variato Op. 12   Nov 1874   SB 12

Tema con Variazioni Op. 6   Oct 1873   SB 6

Variationen   SB 149 No. 56

* * *

Capriccio   1 Nov 1875   Vienna   SB 32

Capriccio in Do min.   1 Dec 1875   Vienna   SB 42   (identical to Capriccio, above)

Capriccio per 2 pianoforti Op. 36   21 Feb 1879   Klangenfurt   SB 102

Meditazione   10 Dec 1876   Vienna   SB 57

* * *

Berceuse Op. 2   June 1873   SB 2

Presto   25 Nov 1875   Vienna   SB 30

Mandolinata   25 Dec 1875   Vienna   SB 34

Fantasie-Impromptu   6 June 1876   SB 39

Allegretto   8 Jan 1877   Vienna   SB 60

Toccato Op. 4   17 Feb 1878   Vienna   SB 77

Rapsodie Hongroise Op. 28 (unfinished)   SB 94

Notturni: Prologo (refer to Appendix)   20 May 1918   SB 308

Untitled manuscript piece—rather sketchily written, in d minor   SB 130

Rondo (A major)   Op. 77, altered to Op. 45   July 1880   SB 153

The notebooks containing young Ferruccio's first works are very well preserved. There is, initially, proud parental dating of almost every piece, with touching annotations such as "composed at the age of 7 years and 3 months" found written at the bottom of Busoni's very first composition. (See Figure 2.1.)

Figure 2.1. By kind permission, Berlin, Staatsbibliothek Preussischer Kulturbesitz, Musikabteilung.

The first notebook is labelled *Primi Schizzi Musicali di Ferruccio Weiss-Busoni*, and contains 27 works, dating from between June 1873 and September 1875, that is, between Busoni's eighth and tenth years (SB numbers 1-27). These first years of Busoni's creative life were self-guided, apart from violent lessons from his father and some perhaps more gentle coaching from his mother. Dent notes:

> He was a composer as well as a pianist, and from these earliest years to the end of his life he never wavered in the conviction that composition was his truest form of self-expression. His earliest attempts were copied out, or possibly written down for him, by his father. As might be expected, they are entirely childish in material and expression, but they show a clear and well-defined sense of musical form—the best promise for the future. They show too how his ear must have been perpetually haunted by the sound of his father's clarinet, for some of them have slow sustained melodies, rather after the manner of Concone's vocal studies, with every now and then a wayward flourish such as a clarinet player might have introduced. . . .[5]

Flourishes certainly manifest themselves in these very first pieces, such as the opening warm-up and turn of the *Canzone* SB 1 and the melodic phrases of the *Berceuse* SB 2.

The *Primi Schizzi* is an extraordinary document, not only for the variety of music it contains, but for the palpable progress made by the seven-year-old in the course of the notebook. The *Introduzione, Tempo di Walzer & Finale* SB 3 already shows a rudimentary grasp of structural balance and a virtuosic sense in the *Finale*. The following *Cadenza, Esercizio* SB 4, and *Studio* SB 5 are modelled on Czerny, with the usual sequential patterns shifted from hand to hand: Busoni at this stage obviously equated etudes with uninteresting hours of practice. On the other hand, the following *Tema con Variazioni* SB 6 already contains a much better melodic flow: the crossed-hands effect is musically sound, and, although the variations are just repetitions of the melody with simple embellishments, the chordal Finale once again demonstrates a sense of climax. The *Marcia Funebre* SB 8 has dignity of a sort, but the harmonies are very elementary. Briefly surveying the rest of the notebook:

> In *Romanza senza paroles* SB 9 the melody is still clumsy, but has an unexpected aptness with some decorative twists. The ghost of Ferdinando's clarinet playing haunts these first pages much more so than Anna's more refined tastes.
>
> *La Canzone* SB 10 is light and witty and worthy of a quotation (See Figure 2.2.)
>
> *Preludio* SB 11 contains, for the first time, patterns modelled on the Bach of the first prelude of the "48": this piece is actually the piano part of a *Preludio* for clarinet and piano, SB 17.
>
> *Inno-Variato* SB 12 has a quite surprisingly well balanced theme.
>
> *Polka* SB 14 shows a nice harmonic touch in the trio. (See Figure 2.3.)
>
> *Menuetto* SB 16, SB 28 is quite charming, despite some gaucherie in the trio. (See Figure 2.4.)

Figure 2.2. By kind permission, Berlin, Staatsbibliothek Preussischer Kulturbesitz, Musikabteilung.

Figure 2.3. By kind permission, Berlin, Staatsbibliothek Preussischer Kulturbesitz, Musikabteilung.

Figure 2.4. By kind permission, Berlin, Staatsbibliothek Preussischer Kulturbesitz, Musikabteilung.

The *Canzone popolare* is completely undistinguished (SB 18) and the *Preludio* SB 19
   suffers from bad invertible counterpoint. Finally, the only other piece worth
   mentioning is the *Fuga a 2 voci in stile libero*, which is a first quite commendable
   effort in fugue from the child Busoni: the sequences, instinctively copied from
   Bachian models, "work" (SB 23).

I have written about and quoted from this notebook far more than the
intrinsic worth of the music itself would suggest, but obviously this
document is of some importance, and the basic ingredients of Busoni's styles
and interests are already present. It was Bernard van Dieren who remarked
concerning some photographs of the child Busoni that all the features of the
mature man's face were already present. Similarly, in this first notebook,
one can already discern a sense of form, a performer's theatrical and
virtuosic instinct, a musical intuition (one can hardly, at such an early age,
talk about intentional plagiarism), and a sharp ear assimilating stylistic
turns and quirks in a wide range of music that includes clarinet playing,
Bach, and popular song, as well as a natural sense of contrast and
polyphony. By contrast, the melodies in these pieces are the weakest and
least original of all the traits, and it would probably be fair to say that such
a comment applies equally well to the mature Busoni.

I would like to comment briefly on the rest of the early manuscript pieces,
singling out a few. A *Presto* (SB 30, SB 43) subtitled *Al mio amatissimo
Padre*, and probably, again an imitation of his father's clarinet fantasias,
contains quite effective pianistic figurations in the outer fast sections; the
middle episode is weak, however, with interminable sequences. *Invenzione*
(SB 31, SB 44, and SB 46) and *Fughetta* (SB 54) are both in excellent "Bach
style," and demonstrate Busoni's uncanny ability to absorb the mannerisms
of other composers. *Inno* of 5 December 1875 (SB 33) introduces, for the
first time, the sound of left-hand octaves in the rich bass register of the
piano—the beginnings of the Bach-Busoni doublings. There is a
Mandolinata (SB 34), uninteresting musically, but at least further evidence
of the nine-year-old's technical facility and his ability to transfer the
characteristic repeated notes and phrases of the mandolin onto the
keyboard.

Already the Busonian dichotomy of Italian and German is evident, the
first appearing in the canzones, mandolinatas, and so forth and the second
in all the fugues; pieces of the type of *Inno-Variato* (SB 12) offer some sort
of synthesis. There is quite a difficult virtuoso piece—*Walzer da Concerto*
(SB 35)—with big leaps, testimony to the child-prodigy feats of young
Ferruccio. *Gavottina* (SB 55 and SB 56), although labelled Op. 3 No. 3, and
with the name "Cranz" written on it (the publisher of the piano pieces Op.
3), is not the *Gavotta* eventually used in the printed version. By the time we
reach SB 59, Busoni has transcended his earlier narrow usage of the word
studio, and this one is contrapuntal, in fact a stylish two-part invention,

with Bachian sequences used as a means of modulation. A whole series of quasi-Bach pieces now appear: an *Allegretto* (SB 60), stylistically a baroque gigue; a *Fuga in Sol Magg* (SB 61), with a bad choice of subject which winds round and round with no real point, but nevertheless showing an amazingly Bach-like technique; and a *Toccata* (SB 77) in which it becomes obvious that note spinning is now no problem for the young composer. The *Studio in Do min* (SB 80) branches out into a more chromatic, romantic idiom, Chopinesque at times, with bigger keyboard flourishes. There is a *Preludio e Fuga* for left hand alone (SB 82) which offers a clever technical solution to a difficult problem. The *Fuga in stile libero* (SB 83) contains triplets against quadruplets as a consistent part of its texture. The *Preludio in Fa min* (SB 88) finds a subject more chromatic and widespread, although preludio still means "Bach" to the young composer. A *Rapsodie Hongroise* (SB 94) is incomplete: the slow, gypsy-style introduction is fully written out, and so is the beginning of the traditionally following fast friska-like section, but the manuscript then degenerates into rapidly incomprehensible sketches. SB 98 is *Preludio e Fuga* for two pianos, consisting of a canonically oriented prelude and a double fugue based on two themes from the prelude. (See Figure 2.5.) Given the basic materials, the very respectable length and

Figure 2.5. By kind permission, Berlin, Staatsbibliothek Preussischer Kulturbesitz, Musikabteilung.

workmanship of the fugue, it is a considerable achievement for a 12-year-old. The last work to appear in the notebook before Busoni's studies in Graz is a *Capriccio per 2 pianoforti* (SB 102), written presumably for himself and his mother to perform. This and the preceding *Preludio e Fuga* are the first of a fairly extensive series of works for such a combination since, throughout his life, Busoni was fond of the sound of two pianos and gave many recitals with friends and disciples such as Egon Petri, William Dayas, Ernst Lochbrunner, and José Vianna da Motta. The programs included both his own compositions and works from the standard repertoire. Strangely, the two major influences of Busoni's two-piano style appear here side by side. The *Preludio e Fuga* is Bachian as is to be expected and the sound of the *Fantasia Contrappuntistica* in its two-piano version is embryonically present. The *Capriccio*, on the other hand, after a solemn introduction, breaks into a vivace, and although much of the figuration is still indebted to Bach, the texture has a Mozartian clarity. There is even a cantabile interlude of a directly quasi-Mozartian nature, and much of the general effect of the piece reminds one of the *Duettino Concertante* still many years in the future.

The next group of extant pieces in manuscript relate to Busoni's studies with Dr. Wilhelm Mayer in Graz from late 1879 to early 1881. Mayer, who composed under the pseudonym of W. A. Rémy, also taught notables such as Felix von Weingartner, Wilhelm Kienzl and E. N. von Reznicker: he was able to allow his students to develop their own particular talents while imposing some sort of discipline upon their efforts. There can be no question that Busoni profited from his instruction. The list of works completed under Rémy bespeak a new technical and formal mastery on a scale larger than hitherto met, a much freer approach to modulation, and a more professional presentation of his scores, no doubt due to an insistence on the question of calligraphy by his tutor.

Heinz Meyer offers a bar-by-bar analysis of some of the contrapuntal and sonata works from this period in his *Die Klaviermusik Ferruccio Busonis*; analyses that confirm Busoni's technical expertise without discovering anything greatly original.[6] It should be stated that, in Busoni's case, the works composed under Rémy (see also Chapter 3), necessary and valuable as they were, also entailed a temporary sacrifice of compositional individuality.[7]

It is fascinating today to look over these manuscripts and decipher Rémy's comments, generally approving of his gifted pupil but not fullsome with praise. There are seven works thus completed, apart from the larger compositions: *Preludium & Fuge* (SB 148), unified by the same motive, which can only be described as a slavish imitation of Bach; *Preludio & Fuge* in c minor (SB 150), in which the prelude is more romantic than is usual with Busoni, while the fugue is again very much Bach, including even a cadenza after the traditional diminished 7th pause and ending maestoso. The octave doublings in the left hand now appear perfectly natural, with no ostentatious show of power. A *Rondo* (SB 153) inscribed by Rémy as "very good formally" is precisely that, but very little more. There is a grandiose *Preludio* (SB 213), very much in the Bach-Busoni cast, undated, but which must have been written about this time. According to the manuscript it was meant to be followed by a *Marche Funebre*, but this never eventuated. Instead, the piece was shortened and transposed to act as a preludium to the *Preludium & Fuge* in g minor (SB 157). There is also another manuscript copy of the fugue on its own, numbered SB 156. Rémy had here written "excellent" and "Finis Coronat Opus!" (See Figure 2.6 for the opening of the fugue.) A *Studio* in a minor (SB 166), is full of octaves, 6ths, and octaves with 3rds, all in soon-to-become-approved Bach-Busoni manner. And there is a final confirmation of the style in yet another *Preludium & Fuge* in a minor, dated on Busoni's birthday (1 April 1881), in which the prelude is, again, rather more romantic than Ferruccio's usual style, and the fugue is a Bachian "allegro scherzoso," full of octaves and thick textures generally. (See Figure 2.7.)

It is clear that under Rémy only certain innate traits in Busoni's musical inclinations were allowed to materialize. The Busonian approach to arranging Bach was one of them, and the series of famous transcriptions began to appear only a few years after termination of studies with Rémy.

Only a handful of works remained in manuscript after Busoni's emergence from this short but highly intensive period of formal studies. Already some works had appeared in print, and henceforth almost everything that Busoni composed was published.

Two more Bachian works exist: a *Klavieretude* in C major from 1889 (SB 196), exploring textural problems related to those of the organ transcriptions; and an *Invenzione* (SB 190), the Staatsbibliothek copy enclosed in a printed folder that reads (translated from the Italian): "Facsimile of the composition offered by the illustrious author to the Gorizia Gymnastic Association for their Festival in 1885."

From June 1888 dates a work well worth publishing: *Fuge über das Volkslied "O, du mein lieber Augustin"* (SB 195), a witty fugue in sprightly waltz tempo with the subject treated in a direct as well as mirror fashion followed by a heady coda in 2/4 and finally a gently satiric march ending prestissimo.

Etude 15 en forme d'Adagio d'une Sonata (SB 185) is a passionate, quite lengthy piece, containing the theme in D flat from the slow movement of the *Piano Concerto Op. XXXIX*, but in a much simplified form. Dent gives in his catalogue the date 1892, which I could not find on the manuscript and which seems to me to be too late. A note on the manuscript says, "An Gussy Cottlow"; Augusta Cottlow was a student of Busoni's who first heard him play in Boston when he toured in 1892 and later studied with him in Berlin. Perhaps, as Dent implies, Busoni wished to *publish* the piece with a dedication to Gussy Cottlow in 1892. The other scribbles on the manuscript suggest that Busoni considered including the piece in his *Una Festa di Villaggio*, already published in 1882, and also into his *Il Sabato del Villaggio*, first performed 2 March 1883. *Etude 16* (SB 186) is subtitled *Nocturne*, and is very romantic in style, something quite new in Busoni's manuscript output. *Etude 18* (SB 184) is the only one with a date (14 February 1883) and because of its numbering we must assume that the other two etudes predate it, but probably only just, on the evidence of similarity of style. This last etude is a dance-like essay in 3/2.

Figure 2.6. By kind permission, Deutsche Staatsbibliothek, Berlin.

Figure 2.7. By kind permission, Deutsche Staatsbibliothek, Berlin.

Melodically all three etudes are poor, especially Nos. 16 and 18, and the harmonic flux is awkward, as though just learned. These were the first really romantic works of any ambition attempted by the young composer.

A piece worth mentioning is *Anhang zu Siegfried Ochs "Kommt a Vogerl g'flogen"* (SB 191). It is in an unfinished state in that the pages are unnumbered, and the manuscript does not have that high polish accorded by Busoni to his completed scores. There is no date on the manuscript, but it would seem to be a product of the 1880s. The work is a set of five variations on a song by Siegfried Ochs (1858-1929). The original is not given a piano setting, nor is it clear how the piece was to end and whether there were more variations intended or a restatement of the original theme. Each variation is an amusing pastiche on a different composer and is given a separate title: (1) Schumann, Aus den Kinderszenen "Trotzköpfchen"; (2) Mendelssohn; (3) Chopin, Mazurka; (4) Wagner, Nibelungen; (5) Scarlatti.

Finally, the unpublished manuscripts include a *Prologo* (see Appendix). This was meant for a cycle of pieces titled *Notturni*, which were never completed. The manuscript is dated 20 May 1918; consequently, this little piece does not of course belong to the early group under discussion.

NOTES

1. For the few exceptions to this distribution see Catalogue.

2. The numbers refer to a catalogue of works printed in 1908.

3. Ferruccio Busoni, *The Essence of Music and Other Papers*, trans. Rosamond Ley (London, Rockliff, 1957), pp. 77-78.

4. Jürgen Kindermann, *Thematisch-chronologisches Verzeichnis der musikalischen Werke von Ferruccio B. Busoni* (Regensburg, Gustav Bosse Verlag, 1980).

5. Edward J. Dent, *Ferruccio Busoni: A Biography* (London, Oxford University Press, 1933), p. 17.

6. Heinz Meyer, *Die Klaviermusik Ferruccio Busonis* (Wolfenbüttel, Möseler Verlag, 1969).

7. There also exists a book of technical problems set by Rémy for young Ferruccio to solve (SB 149). The notebook consists of approximately 60 items, covering such aspects of composition as modulation, recapitulation, recitative, orchestration, cantus firmus, fugal exposition, harmonization of chorales, and so forth. The whole is beautifully set out in Busoni's best calligraphy and each item is headed or numbered or both. I found only four works that could be labelled as piano works, and these appear in the lists earlier on, with their appropriate numbering as given by Busoni. (I have not included various items such as harmonized chorales and other workings, which, although set out on two staves, are not true piano pieces.) One of the works, *Gavotte* Op. 70, 11 April 1880, SB 149 No. 31, is identical with the published gavotte bearing the same opus number.

3

Large-Scale Works Unpublished by Busoni

Composing only deserves the name when it busies itself ever with new problems.

Busoni

SOLO LARGE-SCALE WORKS

Sonata   20   August 1875   (SB 22)

In this extremely early essay into sonata form, Busoni, at the age of nine, writes a three-movement piece. Not much need be said about this child-like effort, except that, despite all its expected defects, the elements of the sonata form have been intuitively grasped; the two themes of the first movement are well contrasted, and the first, particularly, is a most characteristic Beethoven-like horn call. In the third movement, a rondo, an interesting major-minor fluctuation makes a number of appearances, a harmonic device that was to become a Busoni signature in later years. (See Figure 3.1.)

Figure 3.1. By kind permission, Berlin, Staatsbibliothek Preussischer Kulturbesitz, Musikabteilung.

Sonata No. 1 in Do magg Op. 7   20 May 1977   (SB 64)

Sonata No. 2 in Re magg Op. 8   5 July 1877   (SB 67)

Sonata No. 3 in Mi magg Op. 9   first movement complete, second movement sketched only   14 Sept 1877   (SB 69)

Sonata fragment Op. 6   Feb 1878   (SB 78)   From a notation on Busoni's score this was meant to be the Sonata No. 4.

Early in 1877, Busoni planned, as shown by his notebooks, an ambitious series of sonatas for the piano. The project petered out after two of the works were written; the third is incomplete and the fourth is only in sketch form. All of the works are very classically oriented and served, like so many other efforts from this period, as apprentice compositions toward the acquisition of technique, without displaying much originality. The *Sonata No. 1*, for instance, begins very badly in con brio tempo with scales in sequence followed by a second subject of classical banality. The menuetto and rondo are competent, but uninteresting. Not much more can be said of the *Sonata No. 2*. *Sonata No. 3* shows evidence of some Haydn studies, but Bachian sequences are still very much in the fore, serving as comforting padding; only the first movement is complete. Sonata No. 4 never got beyond the sketch stage. A scherzo, evidently intended for the E major sonata, was published separately. (See Chapter 4.)

Suite Campestre Op. 18   5 pezzi caratteristici per pianoforte
April 1878   Vienna   (SB 85)[1]

The first piece is subtitled *Canzone Villereccia del Mattino* Op. 5 and is involved principally with the predictable effect of a tolling bell. The second, *La Caccia* Op. 6, is in 6/8, with horn-like calls. The third, *L'Orgia* Op. 7, indulges itself in baroque note spinning. The fourth, *Il Ritorno* Op. 9, is more interesting, a Schumannesque dotted-rhythm march. *Preghiera della Sera*, apparently intended to be the closing piece of the suite, with no opus number, contains the already once attempted (see Sonata SB 22) major-minor fluctuation effect.

The *Suite Campestre* is poor by comparison with the compositions surrounding it chronologically; the romantic program piece or mood piece was generally antipathetic to Busoni's temperament, and although he published a few early examples of the genre (see Chapter 4), his mature output contains hardly any further reference to this style.

Sonate f minor Op. 49   1 Sept 1880   (SB 155)

This first of two f minor sonatas is in an altogether different category from the earliest essays; written under the guidance of Rémy, the Op. 49

sonata exhibits a superb control over the form, an excellent technique with a whirlwind finale. Busoni's interest in the music of Brahms (a short-lived interest) can be first discerned in this sonata, where the march-like progression of sonorous chords in the first movement recalls Brahms's own Op. 1 sonata, as does the second part of the slow movement, the progression showing acquaintance with the older composer's miniatures. (See Figure 3.2.) Young Ferruccio is still, however, most at home in contrapuntal styles. The first movement, after an opening Maestoso, immediately launches into a fugato-like first subject; the contrasting second subject is likewise contrapuntally inclined. The scherzo, in 3/8, cannot avoid the temptation of imitative counterpoint in its main theme; incidentally, it contains two trios. The finale-allegro is undisguisedly fugal. This is the movement that Rémy liked best of all; his remarks can be clearly seen on Busoni's submitted score.

Figure 3.2. By kind permission, Deutsche Staatsbibliothek, Berlin.

Rémy's use of the "48" as a constant model is verified in Busoni's obituary to the composer, published in 1898 in *Die Allgemaine Musikzeitung*:

The undersigned . . . remembers with gratitude and sorrow the immense pleasure that he derived from lessons with Mayer. With his witty and elegant delivery he knew how to hold the attention of his young pupils; his universal erudition enabled him to elucidate, embellish and bring to life points in music and the history of music by drawing upon the entire history of civilization, giving character sketches of the masters where relevant, and making his own highly personal remarks on the side, some factual, some in jest and some poetical. . . . A deep love, an infinite respect, an unshakable faith, were the inspiration of his life . . . his admiration for the genius of Wolfgang Amadeus Mozart. Next in his esteem came Bach; he was inexhaustible . in his continued analysis, elucidation and poetic interpretation of the preludes and fugues of the Well-Tempered Clavier.[2]

Sonate f moll Op. 20, dedicated to Anton Rubinstein   1883   Vienna (SB 187)

Impressive as the sonata SB 155 is, the climax of Busoni's writing in this form is undoubtedly the second f minor sonata, dedicated to Anton Rubinstein. The use of the same key as that of the earlier work is no coincidence. The first movement's second subject is initially identical to that of SB 155; also the finale is largely based on that in the same work. The scherzo, however, is totally excised, and the slow movement now substituted by a shorter one. The first subject idea of the first movement is, germinally, the same as the one used in the first violin sonata, but there the resemblance ends; the developmental process is different, too, from either the violin sonata or SB 155. The first movement is, in fact, very much modelled on the sonatas of Rubinstein himself. The slow interlude leading to the finale has some affinity with the introduction to the fugue in the *Hammerclavier* sonata, and much of the fugal last movement is also reminiscent, in more than just general approach, of the Beethovian model.[3] The storm of the *Appassionata* (and some of the refreshing coolness of the rondo of the *Waldstein*, the crossed-hands figure in particular) is present here too in the exciting, propulsive finale. The fugue appears in inversion, and at the very end, the first subject idea from the first movement is thundered out. The last pages of the sonata also include a cadenza in parallel motion before the last statement in a triumphant major, which is exactly what Rubinstein does in his sonata Op. 12, whose basic key is e minor.

The sonata is well worth publishing and performing; although not an undiscovered masterpiece, it is an extremely solid, able, and pleasurable work. It is unique in Busoni's output in that he never again returned to strict sonata forms, and it represents a peak of achievement of his early studies.

WORKS FOR PIANO AND ORCHESTRA

Concerto per pianoforte accompagnamente di quartetto ad arco
Op. 17   March 1878   Vienna   (SB 84)

Unlike most of Busoni's other manuscripts, this concerto presents a somewhat unfinished appearance. The score is almost totally devoid of any expression marks. The string parts have some indications, but many of them are contradictory: there are discrepancies in the dynamics, some note values do not correspond with other parts or the score where they should correspond, for example, in chords; the phrases or slurs in the string parts are not necessarily bowing marks, but rather marks inserted by a young— albeit extremely precocious—pianist-composer. There is also the question of whether the work is a chamber work or an orchestral piece. Unquestionably, some of the texture and style of both the piano and the strings suggests chamber music. On the other hand, there are tutti and divisi indications in the music, which suggest the opposite. I would personally propose a small string orchestra as the ideal solution; as well, as was common in those days, I would double the cello parts with the string bass.

The sound world of this composition reminds us of Field, Hummel, early Chopin and—in the third movement—Beethoven. The dotted rhythms of the first movement and some of the piano figurations tell us that the young composer had also studied Bach.

The first movement features a dotted figure with a four-square rhythm. Scalar sequential figures form a large part of the piano figuration; the texture is clean and uncluttered, imitative by nature. The piano at times provides a decorative background for the dotted patterns via scale runs. In the second movement, a ground bass foundation of chords is laid at the very start, somewhat like the middle movement of Bach's d minor piano concerto. The piano phrases are built around this ground bass. The third movement, a Beethoven-like scherzo, is in a joyous 3/4. The fourth opens with a Mendelssohnian flourish. (See Figure 3.3.)

Figure 3.3. By kind permission, Berlin, Staatsbibliothek Preussischer Kulturbesitz, Musikabteilung.

This is a most unusual piece for a child prodigy to want to write; there is a general lack of bravura, the piano writing is well integrated with the strings, and the primary concern of the composer seems to have been a tight formal structuring rather than a display of pianistic technique. I find this concerto no less amazing than works at the same age by composers such as Mendelssohn. A performing edition of this work should be contemplated for more than just curiosity value.

Introduction et Scherzo pour Piano et Orchestra   October 1882
Empoli   (SB 182)

On 21 September 1884—according to Dent—Busoni was informed by the Philharmonic committee in Vienna that the orchestra, under Hans Richter, would try out his *Suite for Orchestra* Op. 25 and also his "concert piece for pianoforte and orchestra." The suite was played through, behind closed doors, on 4 October, and the orchestra voted by a majority of one not to perform it publicly, much to Busoni's bitter disappointment. Apparently the "concert piece" was never even given a preliminary hearing. Dent does not mention the work again, and it is difficult now to establish clearly which composition was referred to. The *Concert-Fantasie* Op. 29 was not yet written (see below) and the only work that fits chronologically into this time is the *Introduction and Scherzo* for piano and orchestra. At the time of Busoni's first approaches to Richter and the Vienna Philharmonic (October 1883), the *Introduction and Scherzo* would have been only a year old and unperformed. This assumption is strengthened by a notation on the score that gives August 1884 as a date of "revision," ostensibly in preparation for the audition by Richter and his orchestra.

The manuscript consists of 124 pages of full score; therefore, like the early Bartók *Scherzo* which was in reality a substantial composition and not a short light piece as its title seems to imply, the Busoni work is almost a fully fledged concerto in the Lisztian one-movement mold. Like the very early *Concerto for Piano and Strings* (SB 84), the *Introduction and Scherzo* is greatly concerned with symmetry of form. Here is the layout of the work:

INTRODUCTION

(1)   Soft opening, with a piano pattern bubbling up and down; (see Figure 3.4)

(2)   Più mosso: the piano figure is covered by a broad melodic line in the brass and wind;

(3)   Variation is obtained by Lisztian configurations, reminiscent of the A major concerto (among many other possible models);

(4)   A big statement of the main theme;

(5)   Opening piano patterns reiterated.

SCHERZO

(1)   Scherzo I

(2)   Trio I

(3)   Scherzo II

(4)   Trio II

(5)   Scherzo I and coda

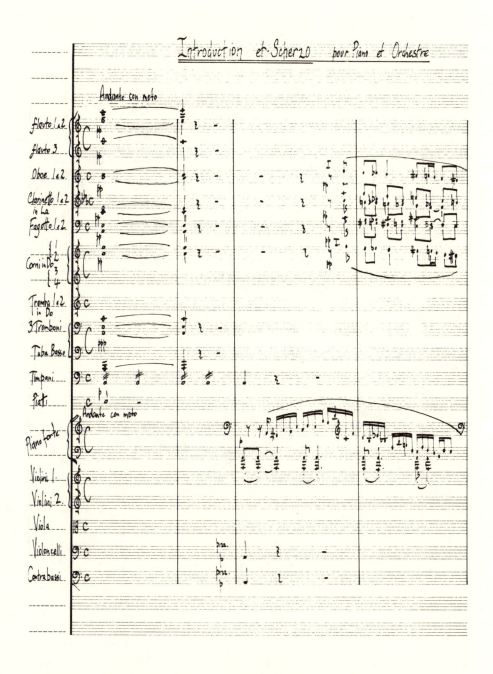

Figure 3.4. By kind permission, Deutsche Staatsbibliothek, Berlin.

Figure 3.4 *continued*

The trios are written in lento tempo and provide relief from the presto of the scherzi, a presto, it must be said, which is often rather repetitive. The theme of the scherzo is a transformation of the main idea of the introduction. The general technique is Lisztian, not only in the use of an *idée fixe*, but likewise in the distribution of parts wherein the piano often gives out the theme first, which then passes to the wind, with the solo instrument playing background figures derived from that same theme. The lento themes are, again, transformations of the same idea. What is more fundamental and important is the careful symmetry apparent in the layout of the work, a symmetry that is to find its full flowering in the *Concerto Op. XXXIX* (see Chapter 7); and the advances evident in the style of the still teenage composer since the *Concerto for Piano and Strings*. With Busoni it is not just a matter of his becoming acquainted with a style, but with his mastery of it. Between the *Concerto* and the *Introduction and Scherzo* lie the years of mastering the romantic idiom, which came to Busoni later, after his working in a contrapuntal language.

Concert-Fantasie Op. 29 für Orchester mit Obliggato pianoforte also
titled *Symphonisches Concertstück für pianoforte mit orchester*
Dec 1888-1889   Helsingfors   (SB 197)

This composition is a work in progress of what finally appeared in print as *Symphonisches Tongedicht* Op. 32a (Breitkopf & Haertel, Score No. 1666). Nevertheless, it exists in perfectly finished form, the full score of which takes 97 numbered pages. The final product is much more than just a rescored version of the *Concert-Fantasie*, although certainly there are stretches of the work that are more or less identical in both versions, the piano part redistributed for harp and other instruments. Op. 29 is in one continuous movement, *Symphonisches Tongedicht* has three numbered sections, but this is a purely external difference, as the layout of both works is much the same. The first section compares fairly closely apart from rescoring, the ending being much more extended in the *Symphonisches Tongedicht*; the final version has also a much richer and fuller scoring in lieu of the piano part. The second and third sections differ considerably, the *Concert-Fantasie* containing much cadenza-like material, most of which is excised in the *Symphonisches Tongedicht*. The *Concert-Fantasie* has thus strong affiliations with the *Indian Fantasy* and the *Concertstück* (see Chapter 8) in that there is a great deal for solo piano, and the pianist and orchestra work not so much together as alternately.

The decision to rework and rescore the *Concert-Fantasie* was undoubtedly the correct one, for the following reasons:

1.   The piano part of the *Concert-Fantasie* is at times "orchestral," and meant to blend rather than stand out. The *Symphonisches Tongedicht* achieves this same end with simpler and more effective means.

2. The piano figurations are often busy for their own sake and detract from the basic stillness of the piece; this defect is absent in the final version.

3. Apart from the figurations, the numerous cadenzas tend to lend a conventional air to a piece not really conventional for its time.

4. The cadenzas contain some padding: chromatic runs in thirds, many sequences and repetitions of patterns in different octaves. These are all excised from the *Symphonisches Tongedicht*.

5. The *Concert-Fantasie* is thus too long for its basic materials, a conclusion that must have been reached by the composer himself.

Even the ending is different: the *Concert-Fantasie* ends loudly with a conventional flourish; the *Symphonisches Tongedicht* fades into a pianissimo.

Busoni knew and admired the early symphonic poems of Richard Strauss, and the *Symphonisches Tongedicht* pays some homage to this influence; the score is prefaced by quotations from Nikolaus Lenau and Giacomo Leopardi and hints at a hidden program. As well as the chromaticism of Strauss, canonic procedures from Bach are apparent, and the whole is permeated by a Sibelius-like atmosphere—long pedal points, an expansiveness, and themes mostly scalar in character, a very typical Sibelius trademark—the whole brooding and sombre but not without some Italian flashes, as in a burst of march music in the third section. There can be of course no question of Sibelius's "influence"; most of the Finnish master's music was yet to come.

A summation of the early manuscripts of Busoni brings to mind the following observations:

1. The very great importance of polyphony generally, and J. S. Bach particularly, in his first pieces, with the unusual result that contrapuntal thinking was far more natural to Busoni than harmonic orientation.

2. The classical, and then later, romantic styles, evident after the baroque style. Some of the early romantic pieces demonstrate how awkward the idiom proved to be at first handling.

3. Busoni's technical fluency and formal command at a very early age. When most composers were taking their first halting steps he had at his disposal a complete vocabulary. This may well account for the relatively late appearance of his really individual music.

4. The presence of the seeds of the Bach-Busoni textures in these early student works, which therefore represent a very early aspect of his pianistic style; ironically, he was to become best known for these transcriptions.

At this writing there are plans to publish some of the works described in this and the previous chapter.

NOTES

1. Published by Breitkopf & Haertel, Wiesbaden, in 1982-1983, EB 8127.

2. H. H. Stuckenschmidt, *Ferruccio Busoni: Chronicle of a European*, trans. Sandra Morris (London, Calder & Boyars, 1970), p. 21. The finale of the sonata in question, however, is based on Beethoven, not Bach. See sonata SB 187.

3. This is in no way surprising. The seventeen-year-old, during the same year, was giving recitals with programs such as Beethoven, *Sonata* Op. 111; Bach, *Italian Concerto*; Schumann, *Etudes Symphoniques*; Chopin, *Andante Spianato and Polonaise Brillante*; Mendelssohn/Liszt, transcription from *Midsummer Night's Dream*; Busoni, *Variations* and *Scherzo* for piano trio; Busoni, *Serenade* for cello and piano; and Busoni, two etudes for piano solo.

4

Early Published Works

> . . . whatever the ultimate value of Busoni's music may prove to be, at
> least the significance of his historic role as the prophet and pioneer of a
> new classicism in music cannot be questioned.
>
> Cecil Gray

Busoni's early published output is voluminous. He thought in later years
that much of what he allowed to go into print was ill advised and hasty;
certainly, in the sense that the line of demarcation between what is a student
effort and what is a published piece is often difficult to define, he was
correct. The published works, which begin in his twelfth year, continue and
solidify the technical expertise arrived at so swiftly in his manuscript works,
and they extend his horizons of study to include certain romantic forms.
However, the natural inclination toward contrapuntal styles continues,
sometimes producing curious hybrid pieces, such as the *Racconti Fantastici*.

A parallel should be drawn here with Max Reger, another composer with
vast contrapuntal mastery. Reger was in the final analysis much closer
spiritually to the neo-classicists than Busoni, in that he consistently used the
established frameworks of baroque-classical forms, but, having considerably weakened the unifying force of tonality in many of his compositions,
he did not alter the skeleton of his structures. This seems to me to be the
fundamental weakness of much of not only Reger's music, but the neo-
classic movement's as well. Busoni could well have developed in this sterile
manner, given the great temptation of an early established technique.

Some of the first published works went through a number of hands. Most
notably, Ricordi & Co. reissued some of the Lucca publications and some
other double issues exist. Most of this music is now out of print and
unobtainable. The sheer volume of the early published music precludes a
detailed examination.[1] Heinz Meyer (in *Die Klaviermusik Ferruccio
Busonis*) gives analyses of some of these works. The music naturally falls

into classes, and I have grouped the pieces according to these classes, insofar as this is at all possible, rather than chronologically.

"CHARACTER" PIECES

Busoni felt uneasy in the realms of program music and "character pieces": his output has few such examples, and almost all of them are very early. In his formative years, the antipathy may have been due to his preference for the larger forms; in later years his objections would have been on aesthetic grounds. Nevertheless, some of Busoni's most successful early works appeared in this genre: it did teach him economy of means and durations, and without this training, the *Elegies* and subsequent mature works would not have been possible. It is, in effect, the successful marriage of formality and elusiveness that give his works their own particular flavor.

RACCONTI FANTASTICI *3 pezzi caratteristici per Pianoforte* Op. 12 Bologna Edizioni Trebbi 1882 Cat. Nos. 1571-73 Also Wiesbaden Breitkopf & Haertel 1982-1983 EB 8128 Composed in 1878

1. *Duello*
2. *Klein Zaches* (vedi la novella fantastica di E. T. A. Hoffmann)
3. *La Caverna di Steenfoll* (vedi il racconto fantastico di G. Hauff)

The path from these first excursions into the magical to the fruition to be found in *Brautwahl* and *Doktor Faust* is a long one, but the beginning is made. Raw technique is, at this stage of Busoni's career, almost an impediment. *Duello*, for example, turns out to be a fairly dry fugato and can only be saved by a quick and breathless tempo. The Hoffmann piece is again imitative, its only mystic features being a fluctuation between major and minor, and some 2/8 and 2/4 bars inserted into a basic 3/4 flow. The third piece is far too long and ordinary, leaning heavily on diminished 7th rumbles to provide atmosphere. Its one redeeming feature is an F major episode consisting of semiquaver scalar figures in the left hand and chords in the right, creating a successful two-plane effect. (See Figure 4.1.) It is typical of later Busoni that all three pieces are very fast: unlike most composers delving into the magical, or other-dimensional, who tend to establish "presence" by static, slowly unfolding structures, Busoni is concerned, as he makes clear in *Doktor Faust*, with the "speed of human thought" necessary to induce such states.

DANZA NOTTURNA Op. 13 Bologna Edizioni Trebbi 1882 Cat. No. 1574 Composed in 1878

Like the *Racconti*, this *Danza* is but a humble beginning destined to lead to the true "night music" pieces of later years; there is quite an interesting

Figure 4.1

progression at the very opening (see Figure 4.2) which serves to soften the focus; against this, there are moments full of terrible cliches and the *Danza* is simply too long. (See Chapter 5 for some comments on Busoni's dance music.)

My copy bears the wrong opus number: 12.

Figure 4.2

UNA FESTA DI VILLAGGIO *6 pezzi caratteristici* Op. 9   Milano
Lucca   1882   Cat. Nos. 36744-49, 36750 for the set   Milano
G. Ricordi   1882   Cat. Nos. 64482-87   Also Milano   G. Ricordi
1926   ER 650   The first three pieces were also published in
G. Tagliapietra, *Anthologie alter und neuer Musik für Klavier*   Milano
G. Ricordi   1934   ER 1678

No. 1   *Preparazioni alla Festa*   Cat. No. 64482

No. 2   *Marcia trionfale*   Cat. No. 64483

No. 3   *In Chiesa*   Cat. No. 64484

No. 4   *La Fiera*   Cat. No. 64485

No. 5   *Danza*   Cat. No. 64486

No. 6   *Notte*   Cat. No. 64487

Cat. No. for complete edition: 64488   Composed in 1881.

By a strange coincidence, the opus number of *Una Festa* is the same as
that of the Schumann *Carnaval*. Is this deliberate on the young composer's
part, for Busoni's Op. 9 is modelled on Schumann? The whole poetic idea of
the *Festa*, the bell-like chords of the opening, and at the end of the carnival,
the rhythms and turns of phrase, all point to Schumann. Working on this
premise, I subjected the Busoni cycle to a Reti-style analysis to see if the six
pieces have inner links, and did indeed discover that various thematic cells
reappear in all the pieces. Whether this is unconscious on Busoni's part or a
cultivated technique it is now impossible to say. The subtitle of Schumann's
Carnaval makes clear the derivation of the cycle from four notes, and this
fact Busoni would have known and probably analyzed. Much of *Una Festa*
is also based on a four-note cell in various permutations.

No. 1 begins with the tolling of bells, and very Schumannesque dotted
rhythms. A harmonic audacity makes an unexpected appearance, as the
bells become almost bitonal: A major and F major simultaneously.
Constant tempo changes occur. No. 2 is a march, in a related dotted
rhythm, again of the type that Schumann often wrote. No. 3 is a rather
theatrical piece, almost like an overture to an Italian opera, with orchestral-
like, dramatic (or melodramatic) tremolos and flourishes. No. 4 is a
montage (the fair scene from *Petrouchka* springs to mind), with character
sketches paraded before the listener and explicitly labelled: *Mercato,
Zingari, Musette, Mago, Pagliaccio*. A number of jolts are again
administered: quasi-bitonality and a 2/8 bar in a 3/8 section. Here, as in the
Op. 32 *Marcia* (see below), Busoni momentarily transcends his extreme
youth, and manages a glimpse into the future of his own style. No. 5 is a
slow waltz, a cross between Schumann and Johann Strauss. This sort of
dual allegiance in the realms of the waltz will reappear in many later pieces,
as in the *Tanzwalzer* for orchestra and some of the *Balletscenes*. The
Tanswalzer is dedicated to the memory of Johann Strauss, to some minds a

curious homage from an intellectual composer. No. 6 has transformed reminiscences of the opening piece. The atmosphere is somewhat like the ending of *Papillons*.

MARCIA DI PAESANI E CONTADINE Op. 32   Trieste   Schmidl-Vicentini   1883   Cat. No. C. 6 Sch.

This march was composed as an additional piece for Op. 9. The opus numbers are deceptive as only a few months separate the composition of the two works. Exactly at what point in the cycle the march was to be inserted is not made clear; because of its exciting nature, I would have thought somewhere near the end of the set, perhaps just before the final piece. Two examples of advanced harmonic effect occur: in the principal march section a strong timpani-like C tonality is established as a pedal point; the right hand then gradually moves away from this tonal center, although the left hand continues pounding away at the C bass. In the trio, most of the music is built on the unresolved discord: G flat, B flat, D flat, F in various inversions. The result is disturbing and reminds one of Charles-Valentin Alkan. A commonplace, even banal phrase is taken and gradually, by dint of constant repetition and slight fluctuation, the phrase acquires sinister overtones. The Op. 9/32 is one of Busoni's most successful early works; it rises above mere technical brilliance, or academic imitation, and seems to me worth occasional revival.

MACHIETTE MEDIOEVALI Op. 33   Bologna   Edizioni Trebbi 1883   Also Wiesbaden   Breitkopf & Haertel   1982-1983   EB 8129

1. *Dama*   Cat. No. 1655
2. *Cavaliere*   Cat. No. 1656
3. *Paggio*   Cat. No. 1657
4. *Guerriero*   Cat. No. 1658
5. *Astrologo*   Cat. No. 1659
6. *Trovatore*   Cat. No. 1660

Cat. No. for complete set: 1661.

Dent gives no opus number for this publication; this is untypical of Busoni at this time and my copy has Op. 33 very prominently upon it. This means that there are four compositions so numbered: two Op. 33s, an Op. 33a and an Op. 33b (see Chapter 5).

These are quite charming miniatures, and the few uneasy and obvious moments are counterbalanced by interesting harmonic turns, such as from *Paggio* (see Figure 4.3) and from *Astrologo* (see Figure 4.4). *Trovatore* is marked by widely separated textures, with the melodies given in single notes rather than octaves, which would be possible and normal in this

Figure 4.3

Figure 4.4

idiom—creating in this way a purer line. The complete cycle contains many delicate and muted trumpet sounds: the pieces are all short and therefore not subject to the temptations of formal aggrandizement which mar much of the early published output. The size of Busoni's hands is already evident from demands in *Guerriero*. (See Figure 4.5.)

Figure 4.5

"BAROQUE-CLASSICAL" PIECES

Dealing with these imitations, we must remind ourselves that this is music written by a boy of between 11 and 17, and while it is possible to marvel at their technical expertise, one must also make due allowance for lack of originality. They are truly student pieces, in the very good meaning of that word, but now and then a composition appears that is out of the ordinary and worth reviving. What is amply clear is that Busoni had, by accident or inclination, mastered the neo-classic technique years before the historical appearance of the neo-classic movement proper.

It is important at this stage to define Busoni's concept of this historic tendency. Busoni's own "Young Classicism" was imbued with the notion that knowledge of tradition leads to new traditions; one studies the past, but always looks to the future with all its mysteries as yet undiscovered, mysteries that one must always attempt to unravel.

The true "Young Classicist," therefore, was aware of the past and, more than that, had studied the techniques of the past. Such techniques were always available to be used again and also in the future but not in a sterile manner, not in the "wrong note" technique displayed in much European and American music of the time masquerading as new music, nor in the manner of arch pastiche, the latter a technique that Busoni had mastered as a youngster. The seeds of the future are in the past, and this is how Busoni studied the classics (and performed them). Moreover, "Young Classicism" does not only build on the past, but is ever alert to the new and the fresh in conjunction with the old. Here again, Busoni was strongly against novelty for its own sake and said so, although he regarded sensible experimentation as the basis of his art. His studies of the old masters led him to try to emulate that repository of standards and yet to avoid the unlimited pillaging of that repository, which the Les Six tended to do.

The history books correctly ascribe much of the impetus of the neo-classic movement to Busoni, but it is ironic that he was not in sympathy with most of that movement's direction—his own idealistic vision of what the "Young Classicism" was can best be gleaned from his own writings.

CINQ PIÈCES POUR PIANO Op. 3 Leipzig Aug. Cranz 1877
Cat. Nos. 24541-45 *Preludio, Menuetto, Gavotta, Etude,* and *Gigue*

The Op. 3 is Busoni's earliest published piano work. Understandably, it lacks overall unity. The *Preludio* is Bachian, and contains a four-note figure (see Figure 4.6) very much like an important motive in the late *Sonatina nach Bach* (see Chaper 11). The *Menuetto* and *Gavotta* are both extremely classical, and, since Busoni had no difficulty in turning out historical models such as this in his twelfth year, it is little wonder that when the real neo-classic movement came along, he was already bored by such procedures. The *Etude* is Cramer-like with a dash, once more, of Bach; the

Figure 4.6

Gigue, also paying homage to Bach, has a certain amount of major-minor fluctuation, already noted in the manuscript pieces.

SCHERZO TRATTO DALLA SONATA OP. 8 IN MI MAGGIORE
Milano   Lucca   1882   Cat. No. 35468   Composed in 1877

This is the only published survivor of a series of sonatas planned early in 1877 (see Chapter 3). The *Sonata in Mi Maggiore,* incidentally, was labelled "Op. 9." The Op. 8 sonata was in "Re Maggiore." Busoni tangled his own opus numbers very early in life.

This extremely early piece shows the combined influences of Bach and Beethoven; the first in the contrapuntal technique, the second in form and in a certain aggressive style.

PRELUDIO e FUGA Op. 21   Milano   Lucca   1880   Cat. No. 35470
Also published together with PRELUDIO e FUGA Op. 36   Milano
G. Ricordi   1926   ER 654   Composed in 1878

The prelude runs straight into the fugue and is a further confirmation of Busoni's Bach studies; the subject of the fugue is reminiscent of Bach's *Capriccio* from the *Partita* in c minor (the same key as the Busoni piece) in that both works make the leap of a tenth their principal feature.

GAVOTTA PER PIANOFORTE Op. 25

There are three publications bearing the imprint Op. 25:

1. A piano piece titled GAVOTTA PER PIANOFORTE   Milano   Lucca 1882   Cat. No. 35471   Also, together with the MINUETTO Op. 14 Milano   G. Ricordi   1926   ER 653   Composed in 1878
2. An orchestral work, SYMPHONISCHE SUITE, consisting of *Präludium, Gavotte, Gigue, Langsames Intermezzo,* and *Alla breve (Allegro fugato).* This is a later work, published by C. F. Kahnt in Leipzig in 1888   Cat. No. 2920, and later Breitkopf & Haertel   Score No. 2498.

3. Busoni also arranged the *Gavotte* from this symphonic suite for piano.
   This arrangement was published by Breitkopf & Haertel in 1888. I have
   been unable to find a copy of it.

The Lucca publication is of work dating from Busoni's thirteenth year
and is, almost predictably, contrapuntally oriented.

MENUETTO CAPRICCIOSO Op. 61   Hamburg   Aug. Cranz and
Wien Spina 1880 Cat. No. 25134   Cranz published this work
together with the GAVOTTE Op. 70   (see below)

This is a tightly knit, almost scherzo-like, Beethovenian piece, with a
characteristic opening figure (see Figure 4.7) that is the basis for both the
minuet and its trio. Spans of major and minor tenths are quite common,
with held inner notes as well.

Figure 4.7

GAVOTTE Op. 70 Hamburg Aug. Cranz and Wien Spina 1880
Cat. No. 25135 Cranz published this work together with the MEN-
UETTO CAPRICCIOSO Op. 61 (see above) Composed in 1880

Like Op. 61, this is thematically closely controlled by having the trio, in
the tonic major, constructed almost like a variation of the f minor gavotte,
the models seem to be Beethoven and the Bach of the solo violin sonatas.

PRELUDIO e FUGA Op. 36 Milano Lucca 1882 Cat. No. 36962
G. Ricordi 1926 ER 654 (see Op. 21 above)

Heinz Meyer gives an analysis of this piece.[2]

It is a grandiose but unoriginal double fugue, with a magisterial dominant pedal point inspired by organ sounds, well worth playing, but unrepresentative of Busoni.

TRE PEZZI NELLO STILE ANTICO Op. 10   Milano   Lucca and Milano   Ricordi   1882

	LUCCA NOS.	RICORDI NOS.
No. 1 *Minuetto*	Cat. No. 36967	Cat. No. 64489
No. 2 *Sonatina*	Cat. No. 36968	Cat. No. 64490
No. 3 *Gigue*	Cat. No. 36969	Cat. No. 64491

Also G. Ricordi   1926   ER 651   Composed in 1880

No. 1 is classical, No. 2 is based on Clementi, and No. 3 on Bach. The second half of the *Gigue* is treated in inverso.

DANZE ANTICHE Op. 11   Milano   Lucca   1882

No. 1 *Minuetto*	Cat. No. 36963
No. 2 *Gavotte*	Cat. No. 36964
No. 3 *Giga*	Cat. No. 36965
No. 4 *Boureé*	Cat. No. 36966

Also G. Ricordi   1926   ER 652

The *Gavotte* has a Prokofievan vitality and wit. (See Figure 4.8.) A number of these classically oriented Busoni dances strongly prefigure the Russian master, although none of them contain the sometimes savage irony of which Prokofiev was capable.

Figure 4.8

MINUETTO Op. 14   Milano   Lucca   1882   Cat. No. 35469
Milano   G. Ricordi   1882   Cat. No. 64496   Also G. Ricordi
1926   ER 653 and in G. Tagliapietra *Anthologie alter und neuer
Musik für Klavier*   1934   ER 1678   Composed in 1878

The model here is Beethoven; there is some resemblance to the scherzo
from the Op. 26 *Sonata*.

TROIS MORCEAUX Op. 4, 5, and 6   Wien   EM Wetzler   1884
Cat. Nos. E. 118 W, E. 119 W, and E. 747³ W   (The title pages of Op.
4 and Op. 5 give a Cat. No. of E. 120 W for Op. 6; this was evidently
altered by the time Op. 6 went into print)   Also Wien-Münich
L. Doblinger   1976   D. 953

Scherzo Op. 4: The model for this scherzo is Beethoven, particularly in
the trio and coda. It opens with a figure that lends itself immediately and
suggestively to contrapuntal treatment. The trio becomes exuberant, in a
style more reminiscent of Italian folksong than the classic sonata. (See
Figure 4.9.)

Figure 4.9

The *Prélude et Fugue* Op. 5 (inside, the titles appear as *Praeludium* and
Fuge): the Prélude is distilled Bach, moving rapidly in alla breve time in a
predominantly two-voiced texture; both the *Prélude* and *Fugue* are dance-
like. It is hard to think of Busoni as a ballet composer, yet it is a fact that not
only has he written a series of pieces explicitly titled *Balletszenen* (Chapter
5), but much of his pianistic output is concerned with dance forms and their
gradual evolution from mere historical models to something quite personal
and often sinister. The operas contain much dance or dance-like music, and
Lawrence Durrell, in *Tunc*, writes about "the stripes and bars of Busoni's
music," a reference to the propulsive quality of much of the mature output,

whether vocal, orchestral or pianistic.[3] Much of this feeling of perpetual motion probably comes from Bach.

Scéne de Ballet Op. 6: see Chapter 5 for discussion on the whole cycle of ballet pieces.

"FORMAL-ROMANTIC" PIECES

Busoni's constant search for logic and structural perfection already led him to group his character pieces into suites; it was inevitable that the more tightly knit models such as the Chopin *Preludes* and the Brahms variation sets would attract him.

24 PRÉLUDES Op. 37 Milano Lucca 1881 Cat. Nos. 36641-44
Milano G. Ricordi 1881 Cat. Nos. 64500-4 Also Milano
G. Ricordi 1927 ER 694-95 PRELUDES Nos. 1, 6, and 10 were
also published in G. Tagliapietra *Anthologie alter und neuer Musik
für Klavier* Milano G. Ricordi 1934 ER 1678

If some of Busoni's early published works (see below) were written under the umbrella of Brahms, the very early *Préludes* are the result of an interest in Schumann and Chopin; the scheme of *24 Préludes* is taken directly from Chopin, and the same sequence of keys is used.

Heinz Meyer devotes 12 pages to rather detailed comment on these *Préludes*, perhaps more than they deserve; we are still dealing with the work of a teenager, although a greatly precocious one.[4] Meyer sees much of future Busoni in these *Préludes*. If one compares these pieces with those of the more German romantic type, it certainly does emerge that the textures are cleaner, the writing more idiomatic and individual; this is the romantic miniature seen through Italian eyes, and, with that vision, much of the music is of the dance. Busoni's own personality provides the usual dose of neo-classic and neo-baroque pieces; many of the endings are quiet, which comes as much from the "standard" romantic miniature as, possibly, from future Busoni, and the bombast of the later Brahms-like pieces is entirely missing. The virtuoso element is not ignored, and, particularly toward the end of the series, considerable demands are made on the pianist. A variety of styles is encompassed—perhaps too large a variety: a chromatic chorale (No. 6), an orchestrally conceived funeral march (No. 14), a Bachian gigue (No. 7),[5] 5/4 time (No. 13), an offspring of Schumann's *In der Nacht* (No. 18), an Italian descendant of the Chopin d minor *Prelude* (No. 2), a neo-classic contrapuntally developed minuet (No. 21), and an Italianate dance (No. 4). Some of the *Préludes* have rhythmic interest, such as No. 1, with the same syncopated rhythm as the last movement of the Bartók *Suite* Op. 14, and No. 5. (See Figure 4.10.)

Figure 4.10

Some of the Préludes are retrospective: No. 9 is like the "fireworks" from *Una Festa di Villaggio*; some continue established practices: No. 8 vacillates between major and minor, a tendency already noted before that will emerge fully fledged later on. It is quite clearly a compositional development, not a cerebral exercise. Some move forward: No. 22's fugato is quite elusive and unstable, positively advanced compared to the academic fugues of earlier years. (See Figure 4.11.) Finally, some look a long way ahead, No. 10 ends on a long pedal and widespread sonorities faintly reminiscent of the *Berceuse* from the *Elegies*. In sum, these *Préludes* are not really original, but do deserve to appear now and then in recital programs, their technical finish is beyond doubt even if, as a cycle, they falter compositionally.

Figure 4.11

6 ETUDES POUR LE PIANO Op. 16   Wien   Albert J. Gutmann 1883   Cat. No. A.J.G. 614   Gutmann also issued No. 5 separately in 1884 (A. J. G. 530)   Breitkopf & Haertel in Leipzig published the ETUDES under the title *Sechs Etüden für Klavier*   1886   EB 5079 Finally, Breitkopf & Haertel also issued No. 5 separately in 1886

ETUDE EN FORME DE VARIATIONS Op. 17   Wien   Albert J.
Gutmann   1884   Cat. No. A. J. G. 531   Also published by
Breitkopf & Haertel in Leipzig in 1884 under the title *Etude. Tema
e Variazioni* Op. 17   Klav. Bibl. 28469

Both of these opus numbers are dedicated to Brahms (see Chapter 14).
Predictably, these are probably the most Germanic pieces that Busoni ever
wrote, together with the *Variationen und Fuge in frier Form über Fr.
Chopins c-moll Präludium*, from the same time. The modelling is on
Brahms's keyboard textures, particularly in Op. 17, which seems to me to
be a slightly earlier piece.

Of the Op. 16 *Etudes*, the first two are pure Brahms. No. 3 has an ending
more typical of later Busoni in that it dies away on a furtive chromatic
rumble, but the rest of the piece is again Brahms. No. 4 has some rather
sinister left-hand scales, rising and falling, and is generally a little more
individual, particularly when we realize that these scales, with their
insistence on quasi-oriental augmented seconds, are a foreshadowing of
Busoni's systematic investigations into unusual scale formations in the
Sketch of a New Aesthetic of Music more than 20 years later. No. 5 is a
fugue modelled on the one from the Brahms-Handel *Variations*; and,
finally, No. 6, though textually owing much to Brahms, indulges in some
interesting rhythmic instabilities: in one passage, for example, the sequence
of bars, within two lines, includes 3/2, 4/4, 5/4, 3/2, 5/4, 4/4.

Busoni evidently set out to write 24 etudes, one in each key, in the same
sequence of tonalities as the *Préludes*: these first six *Etudes* are in just this
sequence: C major, a minor, G major, e minor, D major, b minor. Three
more etudes exist in manuscript form, probably meant to be part of the
complete set, since the dates of composition fall into the same time span (see
Chapter 2).

ZWEITE BALLETTSZENE Op. 20   (see Chapter 5)

VARIATIONEN UND FUGE IN FREIER FORM ÜBER FR. CHOPIN
C-MOLL PRÄLUDIUM Op. 22   (see Chapter 5 for comparison of the
two versions of this work)

NOTES

1. In what follows, dates of composition, as distinct from dates of publication, are
only given if the relevant Busoni manuscripts are still in existence.

2. Heinz Meyer, *Die Klaviermusik Ferruccio Busonis, eine stilkritische Untersuchung* (Zürich, Möseler Verlag Wolfenbüttel, 1969), p. 43

3. Lawrence Durrell, *Tunc* (London, Faber & Faber, 1968), p. 181.

4. Meyer, *Die Klaviermusik*, pp. 61–72.

5. Tagliapietra makes the comment here that "a touch constantly non-legato is better adapted to the harpsichord character of this composition. The composer himself, in the years of his maturity, preferred this way of execution, therefore the editor, without changing the original indication of the text thinks well to advise the same to the executant." Busoni; 24 Preludi Op. 37 per pianoforte. (Ed. Tagliapietra); G. Ricordi, ER 694, Milano, 1927. Quote is on p. 18. Tagliapietra is here referring to Busoni's style of performing Bach; the composer in his later years was disdainful of these youthful compositions and certainly never played them.

5

Miscellaneous Published Works

Busoni the pianist is bound to become a legend—it cannot be otherwise, but his original compositions, for many years to come, can still point our way towards the future.

Edward Dent

WORKS STILL IN ROMANTIC STYLE

FINNLAENDISCHE VOLKWEISEN Op. 27   Leipzig   C. F. Peters
1889   P 2448   Also Frankfurt   C. F. Peters   1953   P 2448

This is in the nature of a divertimento: a work in two movements, in which the first is predominantly fast, treating a number of folktunes, and the second doubles up as a slow movement and a vivace finale. The work has some affinities with Busoni's early setting for piano four hands of *O, du mein lieber Augustin* (Chapter 2) in its light and witty treatment of the Finnish folktunes, which, incidentally, are not particularly distinguished. The melodies are treated contrapuntally at times, but the technical demands on the players are modest. The settings also look forward to the more ambitious treatment of folk materials in the *Indian Fantasy* and *Indian Diary*, in that some unexpected and darkly colored key shifts make fleeting appearances.

Busoni used Finnish materials again in the *Finnish Ballade*, from Op. 33b. Folk melodies to Busoni, whether English, German, Russian, Finnish, or American Indian, had little ethnic significance: he was simply interested in them as raw materials for his own mill, to be transformed into his personal idiom. He treated them as ruthlessly as he treated materials from other composers. It was always the personal vision of an object that was of paramount importance to him.

SECHS STÜCKE FÜR PIANOFORTE Op. 33b   Leipzig   C.F. Peters
1896

SERIES I. CAT. NO. 2838a

1. *Schwermuth*

2. *Frohsinn*

3. *Scherzino*

SERIES II. CAT. NO. 2838b

4. *Fantasia in modo antico*

5. *Finnische Ballade*

6. *Exuent Omnes*

These are the last pieces for solo piano before the epoch-making *Elegies;* there was thus a gap of 12 years before Busoni embarked upon his drastic change of approach to the keyboard. The Op. 33b pieces already partake to a limited extent of the forthcoming change. In some ways, the dedication of the first series to Max Reger is quite inappropriate, for the last vestiges of the thick textures that Reger loved—and that Busoni partially approached in some of his earlier music—are here being excised.

No. 1 *Schwermuth* (Melancholy) is a nostalgic piece, in Italian dotted rhythm, a little like the Italian Liszt of the *Venezia e Napoli;* it has some premonitions of the nationalistic moments in the *Piano Concerto.* The "three hand" distribution is taken from Liszt; the morbidezza is the beginning of Busoni's true appreciation of Latin melody. The key is an elusive b minor: the piece begins and ends on the dominant triad and keeps away from the tonic.

No. 2 *Frohsinn* (Gaiety) is yet another of Busoni's concert waltzes. The hand distribution is somewhat like the coming *All' Italia!* in the *Elegies.* The melody, in a strong F major, is often doubled in thirds in true Italian style.

No. 3 *Scherzino,* also in an undoubted key (C major), is not a distinguished piece; based on very quick repeated notes, there are far too many basic triadic patterns for sustained interest.

No. 4 *Fantasia in modo antico* seems based on the Bach *Fantasie and Fugue* in a minor, which Busoni loved and edited. The layout is very similar: a chordal opening section; fugato on subject A; fugato on subject B (a dropping chromatic subject, almost identical to the Bach); fugato on A and B combined; chordal section recapitulated. This moves away from the Bach-Busoni of the first organ transcriptions: the lines are purer, the texture cleaner, there is more staccato and transparency—Busoni preferred to play Bach in this fashion as he grew older.

No. 5 *Finnische Ballade* is also quite formal in its layout: (1) andante, giving Finnish folksong;[1] (2) un poco più mosso, an agitated staccato section on a C pedal (some reference to 1); (3) molto tranquillo—a contrapuntal section, based on a folk-like theme with intervallic resemblance to 1 (some direct reference to 1); (4) andantino, melody over a sparse arpeggio left hand, in the style of late Liszt; melodic line has some affinity with 1; (5) abbreviated-modified return of 1; (6) abbreviated-modified return of 3; (7) abbreviated-modified return of 2; (8) coda, pianissimo, a strangely wan, subdued progression that almost acquires the nebulosity of later Busoni. (The melody here also has intervallic affinities with 1.)

No. 6 *Exuent Omnes* is a Schumann-like march (in 3/4 dotted rhythm) with a short E flat major interlude, the tonality of which may have irresistibly reminded the composer of the *Emperor* concerto, for we have here a series of scales very like the end of the piano part in the Beethoven.

Op. 33b, therefore, is on the way to the clarity of later Busoni; the Italian vein is emerging, the rhythms are more vital and dance-like. Still extremely tonal, the chains are beginning to weaken.

THE BALLET-SCENE WORKS
Scène de ballet Op 6   Wien   E. M. Wetzler   1884   E. 747[3] Part of *Trois Morceaux pour piano*   (see Chapter 4)

ZWEITE BALLET-SCENE Op. 20   Leipzig   Breitkopf & Haertel 1885   Klav. Bibl. 17065

Kleine (III.) Ballet-Scene Op. 30a   Hamburg   D. Rahter   1890 and 1914   see details below

VIERTE BALLET-SCENE Op. 33a   Leipzig   Breitkopf & Haertel 1894 and 1913   see details below

The importance of dance music in Busoni's output cannot be overestimated; the operas are full of stylized dances, many of them explicitly labelled as such; a large percentage of the piano output is oriented toward dance forms of one kind or another. This tendency has already been noted in the very early manuscript pieces. The progression over the creative span of Busoni's life is from recreations of classical and baroque dance forms to extremely individual utterances such as the powerful *Sarabande and Cortège* Op. 51 (two studies for *Doktor Faust*) for orchestra or the *Scherzoso* from Op. 54 for piano and orchestra, as well as the solo form of this movement, the *Perpetuum Mobile*.

The ballet scenes derive from the genre of the Liszt *Mephisto Waltzes* and *Forgotten Waltzes*; they have very little in common with what was called ballet music in the late nineteenth century, and are in reality highly stylized romantic pieces that have transcended their models. In Liszt, the diabolic is often predominant; in Busoni, the music is often disturbed or dislocated from reality. Busoni never composed a real ballet, although letters to his wife outline some fascinating plans for one.

Scène de ballet Op. 6, the first in the series, features undistinguished and weakly constructed melodies, including a pentatonic tune for the black notes of the piano. The middle section is parent to some passages in the *Piano Concerto* (and *All' Italia!* of the *Elegies*, a related piece). Technically, the idiom is already quite formidable. (See Figure 5.1.)

Figure 5.1

Zweite Ballet-Scene Op. 20: A year later a marked advance is obvious. The aroma of late Liszt, with his parallel augmented chords, permeates the piece. The shift from a 3/4 waltz to a more frenetic 2/4 interlude is a device more successfully achieved in the last of the series. As opposed to the fairly obvious construction of the first scene, this one manages to evolve quite an elegant structure:

A   Introduction   veloce   (augmented chords)_____i
       Valse I, con grazia, F major_____ii
            Trio I, staccato, C pedal_____iii
       Valse I reprise, cadence in F major_____ii
       Intro. figures_____i

B   Quasi presto (the sort of propulsive dance to_____iv
            reach its epitome in the Galopp of
            scene No. 4); e minor/E major;
            perhaps a trifle too long (too many
            sequences); many augmented chords_____i

Rhythm moves in 2/4 ♩♪♪♪ with ♪♪♪ (3)
interrupting, finally moving back to

```
      ┌─────────────────────────────┐
A  Intro. figures and valse I (altered, more        i
        brilliant, some recit. figurations)_____ii
    ┌──────────────────────────────────────── iii
    Trio I has motive from quasi presto
        combined with it   └─────────────────────────iv
     Instead of valse I, an exciting coda, using
   intro. material
      └─────────────────────────────┘
                                      i
```

Although adhering to ABA, some unexpected cross-relationships occur, leading to quite involved ternary structures. The *Concerto Op. XXXIX* is a prime example of Busoni's flexibility within rigid forms.

BALLET-SCENE WORKS IN TWO VERSIONS

ZWEI CLAVIERSTÜCKE. Op. 30a (1)*Contrapunctisches Tanzstück* (2) *Kleine (III.) Ballet-Scene* Hamburg D. Rahter 1891 Cat. Nos. 1392, 1393 Awarded the Rubinstein prize for composition in 1890, this work was also included in an anthology *Moderne Klaviermeister. Album moderner Klavierstücke für Piano solo* Wien Universal-Edition 1908

Rahter also published a new revised edition of this work in 1914, with the same catalogue and opus numbers. The titles of the two pieces were altered to No. 1, *Waffentanz*, and No. 2, *Friedenstanz*. The work was renamed *Zwei Tanzstücke*. Breitkopf & Haertel also issued this version in 1914 (EB 5078). The following list details the changes made in the later version of Op. 30a.

1890 Rahter	1914 Rahter (and Breitkopf & Haertel)
	NO. 1 (3/4)
Contrapunctisches Tanzstück, Quasi tempo di valse	*Waffentanz* Allegro giusto Slight harmonic adjustments; sharper dynamics; faster tempo; a few inner voices added; some bass added. Pedal points in middle section; 4/4 bar inserted; more fleeting, staccato style, octave displacements; some semitonal alterations. Ending: new material, longer, more elusive. Final dynamic: piano instead of fortissimo, and up an octave.

NO. 2 (3/2)

Kleine (III.) Ballet-Scene

Friedenstanz

Pianistic lightening; breaking up of some of the vamping bass into woodwind-like arpeggios; some rearrangement and octave displacement; 4/2 bar inserted.

Many block figures replaced by angular and tenuous staccato patterns.

Cadenza added before final section, now marked "Tranquillo e con grazia," phrased differently; whole last section quite new, much more shadowy, both pianistically and harmonically.

VIERTE BALLET-SCENE IN FORM EINES CONCERT-WALZERS
Op. 33a   Leipzig   Breitkopf & Haertel   1894   Cat. No. 20389

The second version of this opus was completed and published in 1913 by Breitkopf & Haertel as *Vierte Ballett-Szene (Walzer und Galopp)* EB 3880. That Busoni continued to be interested in these pieces is self-evident, since he took the trouble to revise and rewrite them. (The beginnings of a *5ᵉ Scène de Ballet* are contained in the Busoni-Nachlass SB 222.) Here is a list comparing the two versions of Op. 33a.

BALLET-SCENE OP. 33a

1892 (98 bars) *In Form eines Concert-Walzers*	1913 (126 bars) *Walzer und Galopp*
Intro.: moderato grazioso	Almost the same—some polyphony added in left hand; transition chords more chromatic.
1. Tempo di valse moderato, elegantemente (repeated), D major	Repeat no longer the same—some abrupt side slips of key, more demonic character.
Link	Link
2. D flat major A flat pedal	Same.
Link	Link slightly altered.
3. C major, chromatic, moving to a minor	More chromatic-semitonal changes, pianistic rearrangement—a little shorter.
Link	Link more precipitato.
4. D major opening (1), then new material	Much more sinister, with chromatic runs taken from (3); new material.
5. Tranquillo	Cut.
6. Intermezzo (A flat major)	Cut.
7. C major	Cut.

8. A flat major-deciso	Cut.
9. Ripresa	Cut.
10. D major	Mostly used (11 bars cut at opening of section); more chromatic; flourish before stretto more headlong.
11. Stretta quasi presto	Pianistically rearranged; octave displacements; longer; semitonal adjustment to create out of focus effects. Galopp becomes much more important.

If the ancestors of this work are the Schubert/Liszt *Siorées de Vienne*, and the Liszt *Forgotten* and *Mephisto Waltzes*, a descendant must be the Ravel *La Valse* (1920). Busoni here creates a sort of disintegration of the waltz.

OTHER WORKS IN TWO VERSIONS

VARIATIONEN UND FUGE IN FREIER FORM ÜBER FR. CHOPINS C—MOLL PRÄLUDIUM. Op. 22 Leipzig Breitkopf & Haertel 1885 EB 3841

ZEHN VARIATIONEN ÜBER EIN PRÄLUDIUM VON CHOPIN Leipzig
Breitkopf & Haertel 1922 EB 5225 This version also appears in *Klavierübung* 1st ed. book 5 slightly altered in *Klavierübung* 2d ed. book 8 1925

Here are charts comparing the two versions of this important set of variations; the first is one of a set of pieces inspired by Brahms (see Chapters 4 and 14); the second dates from his last years. Even the dedication is altered from one to the Leipzig composer and teacher Carl Reinecke (1824-1910) in 1884 to the composer Gino Tagliapietra (1887-1954), in 1922.

VARIATIONEN UND FUGE IN FREIER FORM, OP. 22	10 VARIATIONEN
1884	1922
ded. Dr. Carl Reinecke	ded. Gino Tagliapietra
Original Chopin prelude given	4 bars intro.; prelude melody treated canonically; original Chopin given; slightly different chord voicings and dynamics.
Var. I: grave, lugubre, 3/2 (reused in 1922)	(1) Sostenuto, alla breve; written in double values; a fraction shorter, but substantially the same as I.

Var. II: Più mosso, scherzoso (reused in 1922)

(2) Poco più vivo, leggiero scherzoso; double values, texture reduced; slightly shortened; new link to (3); new arrangement of alternating hands generates (3); substantially the same as II.

Var. III: calmo e legato

(3) En carillon; totally new; alternating hands, heavily veiled (pedalled) variation.

Var. IV: deciso e marcato

(4) Based on XIV; shifts of key (not as in XIV), stable c minor; substantially the same except for side slips; moves directly into (5).

Var. V: semplice, moderato

(5) Sotto voce e poi sempre aumentando; based on XVI, barred differently; solemn quote in XVI here becomes dancelike; some octave shifts upwards, slightly altered only; moves directly into (6).

Var. VI: sostenuto

(6) Based on X; wider separation of hands; some new material; middle section lightened; ending on C major chord.

Var. VII: più mosso, molto energico

(7) Fantasia; based on IX; first bar omitted, left hand up minor 3rd, free bars written out, quote (part of the Chopin prelude) altered; chordal middle part lightened considerably, quote left in, final burst lightened. This section is left out in the final version of this work in the second edition of the Klavierübung (1925).

Var. VIII: listesso tempo

(8) Very short allegro deciso variation really an introduction into (9), establishing rhythmic pattern.

Var. IX: quasi fantasia (reused in 1922)

(9) Scherzo finale. Based on Fuga in a very free way: exposition on same pitch succession (see first 22 bars). Almost a mocking reference to the working out section of fugue.

Var. X: allegro (reused in 1922)

(10) Hommage à Chopin: tempo di valse, tranquillo moderato. New material.

Var. XI: vivace, ben ritmato

(11) Continuation of scherzo—light, witty conclusion.

Var. XII. Più calmo, con eleganza

Var. XIII: vivace, con fuoco

Var. XIV: andante con moto (reused in 1922)

Var. XV: moderato, scherzoso

Var. XVI: allegro con fuoco (reused in 1922)

Var. XVII: andantino, dolce ed espressivo

Var. XVIII: energico ed appassionato

Fuga: (partly and extremely freely reused in 1922)

Alterations to the earlier work include attenuation of texture, accent toward polyphony; sudden side slips of key; continuity of development rather than boxed-in variation structure; disinterest in strict fugue, almost a burlesque of it presented; and hommage to Chopin, rather than to Brahms. Despite all this, Op. 22 is still a very solid and worthwhile work in its own right.

IMPROVISATION ÜBER BACHSCHE CHORALLIED "WIE WOHL IST MIR, O FREUND DER SEELE, WENN ICH IN DEINER LIEBE RUH" FÜR ZWEI KLAVIERE LEIPZIG BREITKOPF & HAERTEL 1917 EB 4941 Composed in 1916 Also in volume 7 of the Bach-Busoni Ausgabe, Breitkopf & Haertel 1920 (see Chapter 11)

This is yet another of the early works that Busoni later revised. The original version is contained in the Second Sonata for Violin and Piano, Op. 36a, which dates from 1898. The last movement of the sonata is a set of variations on the Bach chorale *Wie wohl ist mir* (BWV 517). The material is set out thus:

Introduction: andante, piuttosto grave. (Some material not related to the chorale is given here; it had already appeared earlier in the sonata.)

Theme: chorale—andante con moto.

Variation I: poco più andante.

Variation II: alla marcia, vivace.

Variation III: lo stesso movimento.

Variation IV: andante.

Variation V: tranquillo assai.

Variation VI: allegro deciso, un poco maestoso, leading into an extended coda.

Coda: includes a con fuoco reference to the introduction, a settling down process and another reference to the introduction, this time più tranquillo, apoteotico.

The *Improvisation* of 18 years later:

1. Molto sostenuto. Material from introduction, followed by transfigured material from variation IV.

2. Presto, piano sempre. A new variation, in fugato style. The rhythm has some allegiance to variation II.

3. Lo stesso. Material from variation III.

4. Sostenuto, non forte. New variation, leading up to theme.

5. Theme. Chorale. Andante con moto. Broadly similar harmonization as in 1898.

6. Theme interrupted by part of variation I in modified form.

6a. Second half of theme given out.

6b. Second part of variation I given out.

7. Andando, ma molto tranquillo. This is a quote from an earlier part of the violin-piano sonata on pages 10-11 of the piano score. The bass has the same motive as the introduction in augmentation: piano 2 adds motives from chorale. Then another reference to variation IV.

8. Tranquillo assai. Material from variation V. Sotto voce reference to variation IV in bass.

9. Con dignita. New variation; with variation IV motive appearing again, surrounded by decorative runs in alternate hand octaves.

10. Allegro con fuoco, ma fermamente. Material from coda (con fuoco) variation IV motive again given out in bass.

11. Molto meno, calmato. Material from coda (più tranquillo, apoteotico) ending with reference to further material from variation IV.

This is the most drastic reworking of all the old pieces. It is partly the result of changing the instrumental combination, two pianos demanding a quite different treatment from a violin and piano. Some of the original material must have been considered useless in the two-piano setting, and therefore new material was composed. The tendencies already noted in the other reworkings—semitonal shifts away from the established key and other refinements—all appear here as well; but what is particularly interesting is the structural reworking. I have given the sequence of events in the two pieces, so that it can be clearly perceived. In the 1898 version, the theme and variations are set out in conventionally accepted style; but in 1916, the chorale appears in the middle of the piece when part of the variation process has already taken place. Busoni presents here a demonstration of his idea that a work of art does not have to exist only in one state, and is capable of numerous solutions. This has some affinity with the more recent phenomenon of aleatoric structure; basically, if I may be allowed a gross oversimplification, the second work is the same as the first, but in a different order.

WORKS IN NEW STYLE

ELEGIEN 6 NEUE KLAVIERSTÜCKE Leipzig Breitkopf &
Haertel 1908 Klav. Bibl. 26042-46 and 26052 Composed in 1907
A seventh elegy (*Berceuse*) was added to the set, which was then
published as *Elegien: 7 neue Klavierstücke* Leipzig Breitkopf
& Haertel 1909 EB 5214

1. *Nach der Wendung* Recueillement
2. *All' Italia! In modo napolitano* (also published separately EB 2907)
3. *Meine Seele bangt und hofft zu Dir.* Choralvorspiel
4. *Turandots Frauengemach* Intermezzo (also published separately EB 2908)
5. *Die Nächtlichen* Walzer
6. *Erscheinung* Notturno
7. *Berceuse* (also published separately EB 3053)

Although these were publicized in the Breitkopf catalogue as "Sieben neue Klavierstücke," most of the *Elegies* stem from other, older compositions: No. 2 is based on material from the massive *Piano Concerto* (see Chapter 7); No. 3 is one of the germinal pieces to later constitute the *Fantasia Contrappuntistica* (see Chapter 9); No. 4 comes from *Turandot* (see the score of *Turandot Suite*, p. 75, and the vocal score, p. 88); No. 5 is also from *Turandot* (see *Turandot Suite*, pp. 99 and 124, also the vocal score, p. 98); and No. 6 uses an important motive from *Die Brautwahl* as its origin (see the vocal score pp. 54-55, 309, and 312).

In the original set of six *Elegies*, No. 6 has an alternative ending, quoting the first three bars of No. 1 with a suggestion to the performer that this be used if the six are played as a cycle. Otherwise, there is no connection— other than general style—between the *Elegies*. What distinguishes these *Elegies* from what came before? A new and daring use of the pedal to further blend an already extended harmonic language: unrelated triads placed next to and above each other; and chords built up from intervals other than 3rds. Melodies in which whole and half steps predominate add to this disturbing effect, as well as isolated "sighs" that move melodically and/or harmonically by semitone. Soft chromatic runs in single and double notes are also used to saturate the harmonic field in addition to various new scale patterns invented by Busoni, which are often in contradiction to the harmony surrounding them.

The borrowings from other works (the tarantella and neopolitan song from the *Concerto*, the waltz from *Turandot*, the *Frauengemach* from *Turandot*, and the *Notturno* from *Brautwahl*) are all much more than kleptomania by an impoverished composer. The language of all these earlier pieces is subtly altered to conform to Busoni's new outlook on music; tonality is generally weakened and a deliberately diffuse bitonality appears. The variants from the originals also incorporate extra introductory bars, connecting bridge passages, transpositions, the repetition of phrases in differing contexts, and harmonic enrichments. Thus, the *Elegies*, like Busoni himself, partake of the past as well as the future. They are very important pieces in his growth, and Busoni recognized this fact: "My entire personal vision I put down at last and for the first time in the *Elegies*."[2] After composing Nos. 2-6, it became clear to Busoni that he was entering a totally new era; so that, when he wrote No. 1, he put at its head *Nach der Wendung*—literally, "after the turning" or "turning-point"—and added *Recueillement*, which could be taken to mean self-communion or self-realization. The first *Elegy* alone would have been sufficient to announce the drastic change in his outlook. Stemming from the late Liszt pieces (from which Bartók, a few years later, was to draw inspiration) this first *Elegy* immediately brings us into the spectral, half-lit world of the mature Busoni, where the chromatic rather than the diatonic scale is the medium and where the pedal is used to cloud and merge sonority. But it is characteristic of Busoni that he builds the new on the old, and the *Elegies* are a musical demonstration of this principle.

All' Italia! takes its title from the fourth movement of the *Piano Concerto* (there the title is *All' Italiana*), although the material used does not come only from that movement. Indeed, the most striking effect of this *Elegy*—the superimposed major-minor arpeggios—comes from the second movement of the concerto, the section given as "in modo napolitano." Busoni uses the basic material purely as a starting point, there is no question here of arranging or even transcribing: the material is subjected to a new setting, as for instance, the glittering, exotic scales now combined with the Neapolitan melody. From the fourth movement of the concerto, Busoni addresses himself to the section subtitled "in tono populare," and builds the middle portion of the *Elegy* from it. A three-hand effect is achieved (not, of course, an invention of Busoni's) by the crossing of hands and, once more, the material is not taken from the concerto, but reworked. There is then a return to the pedalled major-minor effect, but in the last section of the *Elegy* Busoni also quotes a theme from the third movement of the concerto (see p. 68 of the two-piano reduction) in a soft and heavily pedalled version.

To understand this *Elegy*, one has to be familiar with the *Piano Concerto*. Busoni made very clear how he saw the connection between a number of the themes and movements; a disciple, too, would appreciate the transformation that had been wrought upon familiar material. To the uninitiated, some of the point of the exercise would have been lost; indeed, an outsider may well be puzzled at this sort of seemingly indiscriminate use of material from widely separated sections of the concerto. The ending of *All' Italia!* dissatisfied Busoni, and he devised an alternative, passed on to me by Egon Petri, written down for the first time here (see Appendix). There is an "in" joke that Busoni perpetrated in this piece. Harmonically, the *Elegy* basically consists of a tug-of-war between the tonal centers B or B flat and F sharp. B and F are Busoni's initials. Petri pointed this out to me, and it would be precisely the sort of hidden jest that Busoni would find amusing, and that only his close associates would be told about.

The third *Elegy* corresponds very closely with the first 10 pages of the 1910 version of the *Fantasia Contrappuntistica*. Significant alterations are only made in the very beginning and in the "ansioso" section, where the *Elegy* is only able to suggest what Busoni finally achieves in the *Fantasia* by a very clever redistribution of hands, allowing a rhythmic variant of the chorale melody to be added to the already agitated texture. But the bitonal section near the opening (A major chorale against an E flat pedal), stressing the interval of the tritone, is a genuine aural discovery and remains unchanged in the later editions of the *Fantasia* (See also Chapter 9.)

An amusing circumstance surrounds the fourth *Elegy*. According to Petri, someone had shown Busoni the melody *Greensleeves*, and had convinced him, or else Busoni had assumed, that it was an oriental tune. At any rate, *Greensleeves* makes its appearance in *Turandot* and in due course in these *Elegies*. Three separate settings of *Greensleeves* exist. Both in the pre-*Elegy* *Turandot Suite* and in the post-*Elegy* *Turandot* (the opera), the melody appears as a fairly short number (in the opera, the tune is sung "la-la-la" by a chorus and solo voice). The *Elegy* setting, which came in between these two, is more substantial. It follows the *Suite* rather closely in that the basic harmonic scheme is to establish G major—then to play *Greensleeves* in e minor—and finally to close in G major. This ambiguity is partly negated in the opera, which also advocates a slower tempo. In the *Elegy*, at the very end, an E major chord abruptly ends the piece. Dynamics are restrained, and the melody is constantly surrounded with light, staccato decorations, which also serve to blur the tonality with notes distant from the expected harmony.

The same basic considerations apply to the fifth *Elegy*, preceded by No. 7 from the *Turandot Suite* and by an *Intermezzo* from the opera. What began fortissimo in the *Suite* and was marked, "Düster, kraftvoll und bewegt," becomes in the *Elegy*, "Rapido, fuggevole e velato," marked down to a piano. The opera simply asks for "Molto tranquillo (alla breve)," and drops the dynamic even further down to a pianissimo. Similar to the previous *Elegy*, the original music is used purely as a beginning, at times as a rough sketch. Even when the original music is harmonically unchanged, the regular waltz beat is transformed into fast and fleeting triplet figures, but much of the original is greatly changed by means already described. A levelling out of tempo occurs over the three versions. In the *Suite*, the middle section is marked "molto più tranquillo"; in the *Elegy*, "Un poco più tranquillo"; in the opera the tempo remains the same throughout.

The peculiarly personal, mystical vision of Busoni is best seen in the first, sixth, and seventh *Elegies*. *Elegy* No. 6 is really an operatic fantasia in miniature; there is a strong Lisztian flavor in the runs, chords, and tremolos that permeate Busoni's treatment of his own melodic line, though, as with the other *Elegies*, the dynamics are held back, and various harmonic audacities are apparent. Quite often the runs surrounding a melody and its harmonization seem deliberately to avoid the repetition of the same notes, creating a chromatically saturated effect; the motive from *Brautwahl* is in itself highly chromatic and unstable, and the result is a shimmering, other-worldly character. Schönberg was much attracted to the seventh *Elegy* in its orchestral guise and arranged it for small chamber ensemble (see Chapter 14).

A comparison of the *Berceuse élégiaque* with its pianistic partner, the *Berceuse* (*Elegy* No. 7), reveals that Busoni did not simply orchestrate the piano work.[3] The orchestral version is longer (118 bars compared to 81), because the quite magical changes of color that Busoni achieved with his chamber orchestra cannot be matched by the piano. More significant, however, is the reworking of the middle, bitonal section. In the orchestral version, pairs of keys appear next to each other, arranged in such a fashion that the tritone is often predominating, and the third made ambiguous, thus creating an a-tonal effect: F major/a flat minor, E flat major/f sharp minor, C major/e flat minor, D major/f minor, and so on. In the piano version, this section is marked "sempre i due Pedali tenuti," and the chords are thus effectively blurred into a resultant cluster: quite an extraordinary sound. The progression of bass pedals and harmonies is altered as well. In brief, the orchestral version is more chromatic in this respect, but gravitates safely back to its original F at the end. The piano version tends to maintain its long F pedals in a much more stable manner throughout: how much more unsettling, then, is the end, where, totally unexpectedly, the piece comes to an uneasy rest on a C bass, with the seventh sounding above it. The orchestral version contains some ideas that are pianistically impossible,

such as the superimposition of   ♫♫♫   over   ♩♩♩ ;

however, Busoni makes up for this in many fine points of detail in the piano score as well as by his familiar technique of semitone side slips to accentuate an already unstable harmony.

Apart from many such minute differences (although not minute in their totality), the piano sound seems to achieve more closely and successfully that remoteness that Busoni was striving for against a beautiful crystallinity of orchestral sound—with some affinity to Anton Webern—which nevertheless retains some remnants of a romantic lushness about it. The *Berceuse* achieves effects that lead Busoni quite naturally to his next orchestral work, the *Nocturne Symphonique* Op. 43. In these *Elegies*, in the sonatinas *1910* and *Seconda*, Busoni is very close to the Second Viennese School and its directions; and his best works between the *Elegies* and his death must be added to that fascinating list of pioneering compositions before the advent of strict 12-tone dogma. As such, the *Elegies* are studies in expression rather than form, a comment applicable to many of Busoni's later piano works.

AN DIE JUGEND   Leipzig   J. H. Zimmermann   1909   Published separately in four books   Composed in 1909

1. *Preludietto, Fughetta ed Esercizio*   Z 4755
2. *Preludio, Fuga e Fuga figurata (nach J. S. Bach)*   Z 4756
3. *Giga, Bolero e Variazione (nach Mozart)*   Z 4757
4. *Introduzione, Capriccio (Paganinesco) & Epilogo*   Z 4781

(Also Leipzig: Breitkopf & Haertel   EB 4944, EB 4945, EB 4946, and EB 4947)

For discussion of No. 2 see Chapter 11. For discussion of No. 3 see Chapter 13. For discussion of No. 4—the first two movements—see Chapter 14.

This collection continues the new paths first explored in the *Elegies*. The title is yet again a little joke on Busoni's part at everyone's expense, for it led the unwary to believe that he had composed a piano primer. If the title, apart from its possibly sarcastic connotations, had any intention, surely it was to suggest that the coming new music was for the young at heart, ever ready to push the possibilities of music further afield; at the same time, in all these pieces, Busoni underlines the value of tradition, and in a most practical manner. The works based on Bach and Mozart suggest ways in which their language could be extended. The work based on Mozart contains a chromatic-rhythmic variant of the little *Gigue* K. 574; that based on Bach combines a prelude with its associated fugue, demonstrating Busoni's belief in the unity underlying Bach's music. The piece after Paganini suggests pianistic extension, perhaps based on the Alkan studies for a single hand. But the most significant forward leap is contained in the first book, and the *Epilogo* of the last: for these four sections constitute between them the first version of the *Sonatina*, also published by J. H. Zimmermann (Leipzig, 1910, Z 4951), thus inaugurating the series of works that contain some of the most original and personal contributions to piano literature in the early part of this century. (See Chapter 6.) The *Preludietto*, *Fughetta*, *Esercizio*, and *Epilogo* are four obviously related pieces, already constituting a formal entity, a set of variations without a theme. What Busoni did in the *Sonatina* was to write short links giving the very basic thematic origins of the four pieces and welding them into one continuous whole. I think the *Epilogo* was separated from its three companion pieces and published at the very end of *An die Jugend* simply to round off the collection of pieces.

NUIT DE NOËL (1908)   Esquisse pour le Piano   Paris   A. Durand & Fils   1909   Cat. No. 7298

In the *Essence of Music*, Busoni says this concerning Debussy:

. . . this made it all the more surprising to me to read of my work being taken for the art of the Frenchman Debussy. I want to correct this error firmly.

Debussy's art propels his personal and clearly defined feeling out of his own nature, into the outer world. I endeavour to draw upon the Infinite which surrounds mankind and to give it back its created form.

Debussy's art implies a limitation which strikes many letters out of the alphabet and follows the example of a scholastic poetic pastime, of writing poems in which the A's and R's are omitted. I strive for the enrichment, the enlargement, and the expansion of all means and forms of expression.

Debussy's music interprets the most varied feelings and situations with similar sounding formulas; for every subject I have endeavoured to find different and suitable sounds. Debussy's tone pictures are parallel and homophonic; I wish mine to be polyphonic and "multi-versal." In Debussy's music we find the chord of the dominant ninth as a harmonic foundation and the whole tone as a melodic principle, without their merging together. I try to avoid every system, and to turn harmony and melody into indissoluble unity. He separates consonance and dissonance; I teach the denial of this difference. I "try," I "want," I "have endeavoured"—not that I have ever done it wholly or comprehensively, for I feel I am making a beginning whereas Debussy has reached an end.[4]

This tells us more about Busoni than about Debussy, of course. In Busoni's defense too, it must be said that the article from which this quotation is taken was written in 1911, before Debussy's late works emerged. The early impressionist movement must have seemed to Busoni to have lapsed into mannerism. The *Nuit de Noël*, one of Busoni's impressionist pieces (and there are very few of his works which can be so labelled) is colder than Debussy and less romantic. As though through a veil, created by the two pedals kept down much of the time, a disembodied, faraway tarantella is heard, unfolding in slow motion, andantino, its melody having some affinity with the tarantella from *All' Italia!* A middle section (un peu vivement sans Pédale) follows, with the folk elements of Italian dance and then song, more clearly heard (pages 3-4); then the veil descends again, and the pedals cloud the remainder of the composition.

DREI ALBUMBLÄTTER   Leipzig   Breitkopf & Haertel   1921
EB 5193   No. 1 composed in 1917; Nos. 2 and 3 in 1921   No. 1 was

also published separately (Leipzig   Breitkopf & Haertel   1918
EB 5056). It was originally written for flute or violin and piano
(Leipzig   Breitkopf & Haertel   1917   EB 4943)   A version for viola
or cello and piano appeared in the same year (EB 5023)[5]

These are three tiny gems, in their own way a summation of some of
Busoni's mature traits.

In No. 1, over a light staccato accompaniment, a pure Italian-like
cantilena unfolds, with a free contrapuntal part in the bass. It is refined,
dignified, and classical. Although no really complex harmonies are used,
quick successions of traditionally unrelated chords are a feature of this little
piece. No. 2 is purely linear, based on a chromatically unstable theme, full
of semitones treated imitatively. No. 3 is subtitled *In der Art eines
Choralvorspiels*, based on a Bach chorale (see Chapter 11).

TOCCATA   *Preludio—Fantasia—Ciaccona*   First published as a
supplement in the *Musikblätter des Anbruch* in a special issue devoted
to Busoni in January 1921   Wien   Universal Edition   Also Leipzig
Breitkopf & Haertel   1922   EB 5187

This is Busoni's last major work for solo piano. Prefaced by an ironic
quotation from Girolamo Frescobaldi ("Non è senza difficoltà che si arriva
al fine"), the *Toccata* is one of Busoni's most advanced pieces, both
musically and technically. Powerful, darkly colored, often gloomy,
rotating round the key of a flat minor, with little pedal in fast passages and
much staccato, it embodies the style of Busoni's last period of piano
playing.

The concept of the *Toccata* is the old one, there are no fugal sections
(apart from a hint of fugato in the andante tranquillo section, and the
Ciaccona opening) and it is a demonstration piece for the accomplished
virtuoso. It is also Busoni's final statement concerning the possibilities of the
true neo-classicism; old and new are successfully wedded here, the seams
are invisible and the potentialities for the future are given. Often, common
chords are amalgamated to create totally new combinations. The inexorable
logic of the piece, all of which grows from a minor third and a dotted
rhythm heard at the onset (somewhat like a chord progression in Liszt's b
minor *Sonata*), reminds us of the neo-classic Bartók yet to come.

PRÉLUDE ET ETUDE *en Arpèges*   Paris   Heugel   1923   H 28,336
(28,194)   Also published as part of *École des Arpèges, Suivie de deux
études originales de Ferruccio Busoni* par I. Phillipp,   Paris   Heugel
1923   Part of a series titled *Enseignement du Piano*

The pianist Isidor Philipp (1863-1958) was a close friend of Busoni. The
Prélude et Etude was written at his request for a manual on arpeggio

playing. This was probably Busoni's last work for piano solo. The *Prélude* is subtitled *Arioso*, and the performing direction is "volante ma tranquillo." It consists of glittering arpeggios surrounding a melodic line in which steps and half steps are the predominant intervals. Both the *Prélude* and the following *Etude*, which are thematically linked and meant to be played as one piece, exploit the arpeggio of the fairly ordinary type; but the juxtaposition of these, and their layering over and next to each other and onto melodic lines, allows this last work to transcend mere etude writing. Technically, it is extremely difficult to bring off, involving great delicacy and clarity with speed. Texturally, the pianist is either asked to play with no pedal or else with both pedals down. This is again a demonstration of how Busoni's impressionism differs from Debussy's.

Mere mention of the performing indications should give some idea of the flavor of the music: apart from the volante ma tranquillo in the *Prélude*, the pianist is also asked to play "sommessamente" and "con dolce estasi." In the *Etude*, the opening arpeggios are marked "violinisticamente articolato." There is a big, con fuoco moment, related to a more earthy virtuosity, but immediately after it come "sotto voce," "occultamente," "velato," "egualmente possibile," and we are plunged again into Busoni's mystical visionary world, where emotion is transcended, all is seen in a dazzling light, and moves at great speed. A second con fuoco, and the *Etude* ends on a shimmering C major; there are seven bars of 3/2 with the pedal left down, consisting of nothing but C major arpeggios.

PERPETUUM MOBILE   (see Chapter 8)

SIEBEN KURZE STÜCKE ZUR PFLEGE DES POLYPHONEN SPIELS
(see Chapter 10)

INDIANISCHES TAGEBUCH   (see Chapter 8)

NOTES

1. The same theme is treated in *Kultaselle*: 10 variations for violoncello and pianoforte.

2. Ferruccio Busoni, *The Essence of Music and Other Papers*, trans. Rosamond Ley (London, Rockliff, 1957), p. 78.

3. The autographs of the *Berceuse* and the *Berceuse élégiaque* are dated 5 June 1909 and 27 October 1909, respectively.

4. Busoni, *The Essence of Music*, p. 49.

5. Furthermore, to be absolutely precise, both the instrumental and piano versions of this first *Albumblatt* can be found in the *Arioso* from the second act of *Turandot* (see p. 114 of the vocal score; the *Arioso* does not appear in the *Turandot Orchestersuite* Op. 41). It should also be made clear that Busoni only created the version for flute or violin and piano. The viola and cello versions were done, presumably with Busoni's blessings, by Paul Klengel.

The Major Original Works

6

The Six Sonatinas

. . . that profoundly enigmatic and disturbing genius, Ferruccio Busoni.
Kaikhosru Sorabji

The sonatinas for piano all belong to Busoni's last period and were composed between 1910 and 1921. The writers who describe him as one of the few real mystics among composers must have had these works in mind and, in particular, the *Sonatina seconda*, musically and technically the culmination of the series. Despite their varying procedures and differing origins, all the sonatinas have certain traits in common: they are all predominantly quiet, contemplative works; they all end softly, and with the exception of the *Sonatina super Carmen*, they also begin softly or simply or both. This is not to give the impression that they lack fast-moving sections or contrasts—there are moments of great exaltation, speed, and technical difficulty in almost all the sonatinas. Yet the overriding mood of these works is very personal—one is almost tempted to say autobiographical in a spiritual sense, and they refute once and for all the strange notion propagated by so many critics, that Busoni did not have a style of his own. The sonatinas as a body are unique in the annals of piano literature; the other-worldliness, the elusiveness, the sinister qualities of Busoni's approach to the keyboard are all highlighted here in a most memorable way.

Was the title "sonatina" a form of modesty on Busoni's part? It really does not describe the works we are about to consider. Some are too long and serious for such a title, some are not in sonata form. There is a body of opinion that puts forward the view that the sonatinas were works in transit, aimed at some gigantic work to come—to which they were only stepping stones. This point of view seems to imply some incompleteness, some sense of experimentation in the sonatinas, which is difficult to reconcile with a study of the works. It seems more likely that the word *sonatina* is used in its older sense as meaning not allied to any of the forms traditionally linked with it; but knowing something about Busoni himself, it seems most likely it was simply a quiet joke on the composer's part. Busoni would have been more interested in the music—the title was of secondary importance, and here was yet another opportunity to scandalize the critics.

The six sonatinas group themselves very conveniently into three subgroups: (1) *Sonatina brevis* (based on Bach) and *Sonatina super Carmen*, which illustrate Busoni's manner of manipulating material by other composers; (2) *Sonatina ad usum infantis* and *Sonatina 1917*; and (3) *Sonatina* (1910) and *Sonatina seconda*. Subgroups 2 and 3 have similar musical aims, subgroup 2 being simpler in content and more lyrical by nature.

It will be convenient to examine the works in these groups. We will be chronologically out of order, but this will hardly matter, since all six sonatinas were written in the span of 11 years and belong to the same creative period of Busoni's life.

SONATINA BREVIS IN SIGNO JOANNIS SEBASTIANI MAGNI
Leipzig   Breitkopf & Haertel   1919   EB 5093   Composed in 1918
Also in volume 7 of the Bach-Busoni Ausgabe   Breitkopf & Haertel
1920   wherein the title was extended to read *Sonatina brevis.   In Signo Joannis Sebastiani Magni.   In freier Nachdichtung von Bachs Kleiner Fantasie und Fuge D moll*

If we were to look at volume XVI of the Bach *Klavierwerke* (edited by Busoni), as well as volume 7 of the Bach-Busoni edition, we would find a work titled *Fantasie, Fuge, Andante und Scherzo*. There is, of course, no such work by Bach.[1] Following his established procedure, Busoni assembled in this edition three separate works into one "sonatina." His excuse was that "the editor feels that there is a connection between them, as a result both of common and related keys. The three little works (four pieces) appear in this connection as a suggestive small concert number (especially at pupil's concerts) which contain a various scale of technical and mental problems in miniature." (The rather quaint English is quoted verbatim from the Breitkopf & Haertel edition, p. 3.) The first of these pieces is the *Fantasie und Fuge* in d minor, BWV 905, which obviously held a special interest for Busoni, for it is the basis of his *Sonatina brevis*. A comment relating to the countersubject of the fugue, therefore, is not unexpected: "The countersubject appears as a fragment of an obvious canonical leading which has not been developed." A suggested solution follows, and this is fully exploited in the *Sonatina brevis* itself, where Busoni felt no compulsion to restrict himself to Bachian harmony. A technical device employed elsewhere is here put to good use: Busoni invents what might be termed a binding motive and uses it to coalesce disparate elements into a whole.[2] Thus, in the *Sonatina brevis* the binding motive consists of a drooping figure of diminished sevenths. The first section of the work (andante, espressivo e sostenuto) begins and ends with this motive; in between, the material is based on, and not too far removed from, the original Bach *Fantasie*. The second section is based on the Bach fugue; it is marked poco più mosso, ma tranquillo; the suggestions for a more interesting countersubject are here so far carried out that the very exposition is different. A few bars later, much to the confusion and bewilderment of academic musicians, we have the strange sound of impressionistic harmony in a Bach fugue. The harmony, however, is arrived at by logical contrapuntal extension of the ideas in the exposition, rather than by harmonic process; the tonality is vague in the extreme. (See Figure 6.1.) The

Figure 6.1. By kind permission, Breitkopf & Haertel, Wiesbaden.

binding motive is heard again, and this time introduces the third section of the sonatina wherein the subjects of the *Fuge* and the opening *Andante* are combined. This is quite an extensive section and works up to its climax by combining the three main motives of the work: the theme of the *Andante*, the fugue subject, and the binding motive. The final fourth section is a serene coda using mostly ideas based on the binding motive. Thus, the purpose of the motive is now seen as a catalytic agent, the key to the possibilities of contrapuntal combination of themes from the *Fantasie und Fuge* of Bach. A further question may now be asked: where did the binding motive come from? It was probably suggested by some falling figures in bars 6-14 of the original Bach *Fantasie*; and the opening of the Bach *Andante* (the second movement of the "sonatina" concocted by Busoni), which begins with a figure to some extent coincidental with the four-note figure of Busoni; even the main subject of the *Scherzo* contains a similar outline. (See Figure 6.2.)

Whether such connections are real and subconsciously linked in Busoni's mind or in the imagination of the writer, is impossible to resolve.[3] The chromatic bass in octaves accompanying this motive in its later appearances was derived from the subject of the *Fuge*. (See Figure 6.3.)

The *Sonatina brevis* is, of course, not a transcription: it is too far removed from the original Bach to be considered as such. Busoni was

Figure 6.2

Figure 6.3

always searching for order: much of his Bach editing tries to underline such order, but contrapuntal thinking was completely natural to him, so it is not surprising to find him investigating combinatorial possibilities of various themes and eventually building new works out of such possibilities. The immense *Fantasia Contrappuntistica* is the result of just such curiosity, and the demonstration of Busoni's contrapuntal technique in that piece is nothing short of awe inspiring. One of Busoni's most original gifts as a creative artist was his ability to see in the music of Bach both definitive and creatively potent materials. This ability, although it followed naturally from Busoni's own personality and originality, also recalls the parody techniques of music composed between Machaut and Mozart; significantly, the same approach has since been demonstrated to exist in many of Bach's own compositions. There is thus the strange effect of looking around a corner, of seeing a familiar object in a mysterious and not always bright light.

KAMMER-FANTASIE ÜBER CARMEN (Also known as *Sonatina super Carmen*) Leipzig Breitkopf & Haertel 1921 EB 5186 Composed in 1920[4]

This sonatina is a lineal descendant of the Lisztian operatic paraphrase. I should clarify my statement: the musically successful Liszt opera fantasia-paraphrase did much more than just present a potpourri of more memorable melodies from an opera, combined with glittering display material for the pianist—certainly, the host of Liszt imitators did only that—the successful Liszt paraphrase was, in effect, a drama in compressed form. The melodies were often subject to variation, combination with one another, and re-harmonization (this last not so often). Busoni, by the time he wrote the *Sonatina super Carmen*, was no longer interested in superficial virtuosity, indeed, he had passed that stage long before. What we have here is a great artist commenting on an opera he had just seen. Busoni comes home and broods at the piano; what emerges is *Carmen* seen through his mystic vision. The familiar melodies acquire strange colors, as though distorted by a camera lens.

The *Sonatina* falls naturally into five sections: (1) brilliant octave and canonic treatment of the chorus from act 4; (2) The *Flower Song* from act 2, scene 2, in free paraphrase, the melody in the middle "third" hand, surrounded by chords in the bass and florid ornamentation in the right hand. Up to this point, except for some unexpected harmonic turns and predominantly linear writing, the *Sonatina* is Lisztian. But in section 3, something that is typical Busoni happens: (3) the *Habanera* from the first act becomes a foreshadowing of the final tragedy, an articulate death wish. This spectral treatment is pursued through a number of transformations, one of them marked "fantastico" (see Figure 6.4); (4) the *Prelude* to act 1 is

Figure 6.4. By kind permission, Breitkopf & Haertel, Wiesbaden.

now heard as a relief from the preceding section, but even this infectious melody is darker at times than one expects, until it leads to the magical last page; (5) "andante visionario"—the theme of fate, already heard at the end of the second section is here set in full and finally sobs itself into silence. Like all of Busoni's sonatinas, this one too ends softly. (See Figure 6.5.)

Figure 6.5. By kind permission, Breitkopf & Haertel, Wiesbaden.

The term *visionario* is appropriate to much of Busoni's music. The muted dynamics that occur so often, particularly in these sonatinas, are not to be confused with the half-defined world of the impressionist. With Busoni, the mystic vision, the glimpse into another world, is the key to understanding. Kaikhosru Sorabji, critic and composer, wrote:

The last great Master to be considered is that profoundly enigmatic and disturbing genius, Ferruccio Busoni. In his work I feel the metapsychic element to be present to a degree and intensity unparalleled in music. Every bar of his mature work seems to me permeated with it. . . . Busoni's overshadowing power is as great as, and even greater than, Liszt's, for he not only speaks *through* the other composer but melts, dissolves the other composer's thoughts into his own while preserving intact and fully recognizable all the original outer lineaments. Power such as this is rather terrifying. . . . Another conspicuous example . . . is the *Fantasia da Camera* upon motives from Bizet's *Carmen*. The gay and occasionally rather trivial Bizet tunes become indescribably "charged" and even sinister, undergoing a sort of dissolution and transformation in a manner that is . . . fascinating and haunting to the mind of the suitably "attuned" listener, so that at the end of the process one almost says to oneself—such is the impression of the ineluctable and immense power behind the whole business—this is a psychical invasion in musical terms.[5]

SONATINA AD USUM INFANTIS MADELINE M* AMERICANAE PRO CLAVICIMBALO [sic] COMPOSITA   Leipzig   Breitkopf & Haertel   1916   EB 4836   The third movement of this sonatina also appears in *Silhouetten   Tanzbilder aus alter und neuer Zeit für Klavier*   (Leipzig   Breitkopf & Haertel   1969)

This is at once the least integrated of the series and the most conventional: possibly, in Busoni's case, the two factors interact upon each other. The direction "pro Clavicimbalo" has up to now been ignored even by Busoni lovers, and the work is played on the piano probably to its detriment; the lines are too tenuous, the resonance and sweep too limited, and the expressive range of the thematic materials too restrictive for the modern piano. On the other hand, much of the distribution of the material is pianistic in character.[6] It would be an interesting experiment to hear the work performed on a piano and harpsichord in succession.

However, the compositional procedures are more interesting. The work is in five short separate movements, and is the only sonatina to be subdivided into numbered movements by the composer: (1) molto tranquillo; (2) andantino melancolico; (3) vivace (alla marcia); (4) molto tranquillo; (5) Polonaise (un poco cerimonioso).

The fourth movement is related to the first, using the same materials in a different and more compressed fashion. The last movement is based on the one-act opera *Arlecchino*, in which, strangely enough, the marking is "Tempo di minuetto sostenuto" and not *Polonaise*. This discrepancy need not really concern us here: in context, the music meets operatic needs; in the sonatina, the music has no such obligation. The fact that this movement comes from *Arlecchino*, although typical of much of Busoni's compositional procedures, is not essential to its understanding—there is certainly no programmatic or epigrammatic intent.

Busoni often used the same materials and ideas in a number of different works; usually these were written at the same time, but in certain instances ideas put down in youth reappear in mature works. Liszt often did this too: the three versions of the *Transcendental Studies* are a fine illustration of growth from the humblest origins. Petri told me that after Busoni's death in 1924, he was invited by the composer's widow to look through Busoni's papers and manuscripts with a view to posthumous publication. Among many other items (most of them still unpublished today) a youthful study in D flat major was found. Petri was touched to find it the ancestor of the slow movement of the mammoth *Piano Concerto*. Detractors of Busoni constantly underline this tendency in him to re-use material as evidence of a basic poverty; this can be proven arrant nonsense by a quick look at a score such as *Doktor Faust* or *Die Brautwahl*, where one new invention crowds another on every page. It was simply that Busoni became obsessed with certain ideas and had to re-use them until their potential was exhausted, or else he consciously reworked things, looking at them from a new angle, and developing a different facet.

But to return to the *Sonatina ad usum infantis* and its last movement. The curious reader need only turn to scenes 5a, 5b, and 9 from *Arlecchino* to find direct and lengthy correspondences. Thematic connections will be found with other parts of the opera; but this is hardly surprising in view of the fact that *Arlecchino*, like almost all mature Busoni, is tightly integrated and is largely based on the "row" which appears as a fanfare at the commencement of the opera.

The first four bars of the *Sonatina ad usum infantis* contain in basic form all the materials of the work. (See Figure 6.6.) Figure 6.7 shows the four

fundamental cells announced in Figure 6.6. These are subjected throughout
the sonatina to inversion, augmentation, and rhythmic alteration, in fact all

Figure 6.6. By kind permission, Breitkopf & Haertel, Wiesbaden.

Figure 6.7

the procedures known to the old masters, used so brilliantly by Beethoven,
and described in more recent times as cellular techniques. What is
interesting in the case of Busoni is that although usually classified as a
romantic, he uses, after 1900, a technique that is really prophetic of the
post-Second World War period: a pure polyphony, combined with this so-
called cellular technique. He was aware of what was to come, and wrote:

Absolute Melody: A row of repeated ascending and descending intervals, which are
organized and move rhythmically. It contains in itself a latent harmony, reflects a
mood of feeling. It can exist without depending on words for expression and without
accompanying voices. When performed, the choice of pitch or of instrument makes
no alteration to the nature of its being.

Melody, independent at first, joined the accompanying harmony subsequently,
and later melted into inseparable unity with it. Recently, it has been the aim of
polyphonic music, which is always progressing, to free itself from this unity.

In contradiction to points of view which are deeply rooted, it must be maintained
here that melody has expanded continuously, that it has grown in line and capacity
for expression and that in the end it must succeed in becoming the most powerful
thing in composition.[7]

By "Young Classicism" I mean the mastery, the sifting and the turning to account
of all the gains of previous experiments and their inclusion in strong and beautiful
forms.

This art will be old and new at the same time at first. We are steering in that
direction, luckily, consciously or unconsciously, willingly or unwillingly. . . .

With "Young Classicism" I include the definite departure from what is thematic and the return to melody again as the ruler of all voices and all emotions (not in the sense of a pleasing motive) and as the bearer of the idea and the begetter of harmony, in short, the most highly developed (not the most complicated) polyphony.[8]

If we return now to consideration of the opening of the *Sonatina ad usum infantis*, we find that the second half of the first subject is really derived from the first half, with an interpolated sixth, and the cell B in mirror image. The left hand reflects this cell in quavers, and stresses the interpolated sixth. The second subject, moving serenely over a semiquaver accompaniment, uses an ostinato figure (see Figure 6.8) which is derived from A plus B, consists of a new usage of cells D, B, and C. No more new materials are introduced. The ostinato figure fluctuates in its intervals but persists to the end of the movement, working its way down the keyboard.

Figure 6.8

The second movement again involves three principal ideas. The first uses A in canon and fugato; again, the accompaniment figure is extracted from the theme, in which C now appears with a minor third instead of a perfect fourth. (See Figure 6.9.) The second subject is related to the second subject from the first movement, using C, D, and B.

Figure 6.9. By kind permission, Breitkopf & Haertel, Wiesbaden.

The third movement is a march using permutations of C. (See Figure 6.10.) It ends with a mocking fanfare, a reference to the last movement and to arpeggio-like figures heard under the march tune.

Figure 6.10

The fourth movement uses no new material.

The last movement is closely linked with the third in its use of C, and the fanfare idea. A second melody uses D and, to a lesser extent, B, but the overall result here, and in the sonatina in general, is lacking in the strong cohesion that characterizes the *Sonatina* (1910) and the *Sonatina seconda*, especially. It is interesting to note that harmonic analysis yields little of interest in the case of these sonatinas, but analysis of cells is fruitful, and shows the principle of endless variation of the one idea at work in Busoni.

SONATINA IN DIEM NATIVITATIS CHRISTI MCMXVII
Leipzig   Breitkopf & Haertel   1918   EB 5071   Composed in 1917

This is the first sonatina in which thematic economy is shown to advantage. In the opening bars (see Figure 6.11), the top-line theme contains

Figure 6.11. By kind permission, Breitkopf & Haertel, Wiesbaden.

many steps and half steps; the second half of the theme is an extension of the first, by addition of a suspension; and the intervals of the third and fourth are prominent. The triplet in the inner part is used only once, and therefore underlined: it will assume importance later. The left-hand figure becomes a secondary motive, used almost immediately in diminution and inversion. Note that C is a simplified version of the main theme, and is contained in embryo in the triplet of the first bar.

From this simple beginning, the sonatina unfolds. The intervallic constituents of the theme appear in numerous transformations. (See Figure 6.12.) It is combined in various ingenious ways with the other cells, and finally, at the end of the sonatina, with itself in stretto, augmentation, and rhythmic transformation.

Figure 6.12

The sonatina is made up of six main sections which, in textbook fashion, may be made to conform to the movements of a sonata, or in a broad way to the shape of the sonata first movement form: (1) exposition, (2) development, (3) slow movement (with some extraordinary pedal effects), (4) scherzo,[9] (5) bridge (composed of reference to slow movement), and (6) recapitulation. Thus, the sonatina can be likened to a compressed but complete sonata which, in a clever way, encompasses a slow and scherzo movement within the scope of a continuous first movement form. But such a point of view tells us little of the work, and does not explain our sense of completeness on hearing it. This, too, is symptomatic of the Busoni sonatinas: analysis of form is not instructive, and the case to be made out for it is weak. Broadly, the four sonatinas based on original material are polyphonic in technique; all use cellular materials in constant variation. All the sonatinas can be made to fit into some form or another—but the fitting is ungainly.

SONATINA Leipzig J. H. Zimmermann 1910 Z. 4951 Also
Leipzig Breitkopf & Haertel EB 4948 Composed in 1910

This is the first of the two "big" sonatinas; it is based on music written earlier, a series of pieces titled *An die Jugend* (see Chapter 5). Like some other piano works such as the *Elegies*, the *An die Jugend* is a turning point in Busoni's style and language, and is one of the first works of its kind, which owes little or nothing to the super-chromaticism of the post-Wagnerians or the misty world of the impressionists. The first part of *An die Jugend* was titled *Preludietto, Fughetta ed Esercizio*. These three related pieces are to be found, substantially the same, in the *Sonatina* (1910). From the fourth part of *An die Jugend* (*Introduzione, Capriccio & Epilogo*) came the *Epilogo* in this sonatina.

It may be asked: How was it aesthetically justifiable to take four different pieces and combine them to form one new one? The answer is that these sections of *An die Jugend* are related, based on a Paganini *Caprice*; Busoni simply took four thematically related pieces, integrated them into one continuous whole, rewrote sections as necessary, and, notably, provided a new beginning. The result is that whereas *An die Jugend* is only sketched, or suggested, the *Sonatina* is a complete and satisfying unity.

For want of a better description, it would be quite accurate to say that the *Sonatina* consists of eight sections, set out as a theme with seven variations. Of these, variation 4 is the most extensive; it is flanked by variations 3 and 5, which are fairly extensive though less turbulent, and these in turn are rounded off by the theme and variations 1 and 2 on one end, and variations 6 and 7 on the other, which are fairly short and calm. The *Sonatina* is therefore in arch form, with the extraordinary fourth variation fulfilling duty as the keystone.

The theme is treated very freely; for the variations are neither melodic nor harmonic: they seize upon particular intervals and rhythms, and develop these separately. The actual theme is repeated once near the beginning with a different accompaniment and once more near the end, this time as a reminiscence, as though to remind the listener that, no matter how far the variations appear to have branched out, the basic material is still the same. Busoni follows a procedure by now familiar: a melody usually of quite simple nature, is stated at the onset of the work; it is seen to contain in essence all that is to follow. The actual melody itself is not necessarily of any importance, and tends to be naive, almost folksong-like in character. This is especially true of the opening of the *Sonatina*. (See Figure 6.13.)

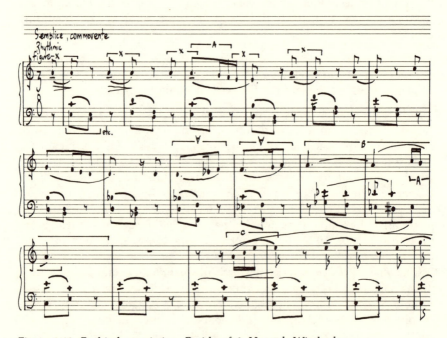

Figure 6.13. By kind permission, Breitkopf & Haertel, Wiesbaden.

We note the predominance of the interval of a 3rd both in B and in the accompaniment; the rhythmic figure X; and A and A in mirror image, with the major or minor 3rd also in prominence. B is, of course, an extension of A. C is a subsidiary cell used mostly for fantastic decorative work; note also that it is constructed from piled-up 3rds. The fact that A is used in both its three-note and four-note versions has rhythmic significance later: Busoni uses just such cross rhythms at the climax of the sonatina, in variation 4, and in some figurations, sequences of three notes are written out in groups of four. The general implication of four (or two) against three, is also used in other variations: in 1 it forms a new rhythm, in 2 it is combined with the 3/8 of the theme. Variations 1 and 2 are used mostly to play off the theme against an ever-increasing complexity of rhythm. B is heard as a melody. (See Figure 6.14.)

Figure 6.14. By kind permission, Breitkopf & Haertel, Wiesbaden.

Variation 3 is a fugato based on B and rhythm X, più tranquillo.

Variation 4 is again a cross rhythm, this time wild, whole-tonish transformation of the mirrored A is used, with B, in a perpetual swirl of quavers. B augmented is heard against this, plus the rhythm of the opening of the *Sonatina*. The quaver passages gradually thicken, strident cadenzas interrupt but do not lessen the tension. Finally, this extended variation ends in a florid vortex of notes based on primary shapes stretched and distorted. In sheer ecstasy of sound this variation presages Messiaen. A short reminder of the theme follows to bring us back to reality. Variation 5 is a quasi cadenza; A is used both in its three- and four-note form and later with B in a "fantastico" passage. Rhythm X is heard again. Variations 6 and 7, like 1 and 2, are merged into each other, and of similar character, but octave extensions are now used in the representation of B in left-hand octaves. (See Figure 6.15.) Finally, all cells and rhythms—A, B, C, and X—are combined

Figure 6.15

and manipulated in a new way in the final variation, "molto sostenuto."

It is impossible without recourse to a score of the *Sonatina* to describe adequately or represent the ingenuity and economy of the use of the basic cells. Here is a true precursor of serial technique. Busoni surpasses this work in only one other of the sonatinas: it is the last one we are to consider, the crown of all the sonatinas.

SONATINA SECONDA   Leipzig   Breitkopf & Haertel   1912
EB 3828   Composed in 1912

We have now traced through five sonatinas, and seen examples of loosely bound paraphrase (*Sonatina super Carmen*); an artificially created unity among the disparate elements of another composer combined by Busoni (*Sonatina brevis*); an almost traditional division into movements (*Sonatina ad usum infantis*); a tighter organization into a sort of compressed sonata (*Sonatina (1917)*); and a free variation form (*Sonatina (1910)*). With the *Sonatina seconda* we come to an example of extremely free constant variation. We have also observed that, despite fairly economical usage of cells, Busoni invariably has hidden these cells within melodies; in the *Sonatina seconda* there is no such melody: the basic raw material of the work is announced in parlando fashion in a row-like succession of notes. Tonal centers, already difficult to identify in passages from some of the other sonatinas, are missing here altogether. The notation is prophetic in two respects: (1) accidentals apply only once, thus there is no necessity for natural signs. This convention has only recently been adopted among progressive composers; (2) a tendency noticeable in other sonatinas, the writing of free bars of irregular length, is here taken to its extreme. There is no time signature at all; the bar lines act more like phrase divisions than anything else; their use is similar to that of contemporary composers.

The application of the term *row* to the opening series of notes is, of course, a description that is not to be taken too literally; nowhere is there a Schönbergian use of a strict row—Busoni was too free for that to occur in his music, even had Schönberg by then already formulated the laws of 12-tone composition. It is ironic that what was criticized by the dodecaphonic disciples as falling short of realization of row technique should now be recognized as being ahead of its time: the free application of a row, with due regard to the intervals comprising it, and its subdivision into cells, separately developed. Certainly, because of such a procedure, Busoni's music looks both ways: it is prophetic and yet tied strongly to the past. In this sonatina, despite the irregular barlines, some rhythms are regular; sequences are used; and there is some repetition. Nevertheless, the composition is an extraordinary achievement. Figure 6.16 shows the row with which the work begins. A number of interesting facts arise from perusal of the row:

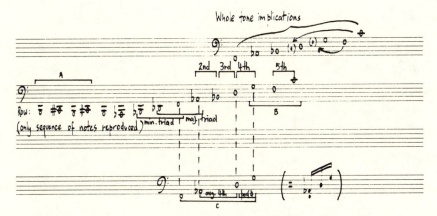

Figure 6.16

1. The basic shape of the row is a spiral. It consists of intervals expanding from a major 2nd to a perfect 5th.

2. The row contains a major triad.

3. The row contains a minor triad.

4. The row has whole-tone implications.

5. The perfect and augmented 4ths hidden in the row are used to build up chords.

6. Cell A is the most important of the work, and it becomes clear when we hear or play the sonatina why the first two notes of the row had to be repeated at the very start: they form an easily audible cell of four notes, which are heard right after the row surrounded by broken chords of the types described in no. 5. The four-note cell is gradually transformed into other cells of four notes with varying intervals. They deviate widely. (See Figure 6.17.)

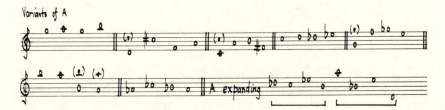

Figure 6.17

6a. The rhythm of A—short-long, short-long—is also to become a characteristic feature of this cell throughout the sonatina.

6b. Later in the piece, by adding an augmented 4th to the front of the cell, a new mutant of A emerges; A is also capable of reproducing itself, as it were. (See Figure 6.18.)

Figure 6.18

7. B is used rarely, possibly because traditional cadential associations are too strong in such a series of notes.

8. The expanding tendency of the row is utilized in passages over and over again: without aping the exact row, the aural sensation of opening out is used as an effect in the most varied contexts.

9. The chords forming C are used twice in extraordinary canons. (See Figure 6.19.)

Figure 6.19. By kind permission, Breitkopf & Haertel, Wiesbaden.

A more detailed analysis of the *Sonatina seconda* without the score would be pointless. The reader can now, having been given the key, unravel the compositional procedures bar by bar, and indeed be satisfied that in this amazing work prophecy and a technical tour de force have been combined. The *Sonatina seconda* is a major landmark in Busoni's output and still one of the most interesting and significant compositions of its time. Perhaps the best description of the work can be given by simply quoting Busoni's performance mark at the beginning: "Il tutto vivace, fantastico, con energia, capriccio e sentimento."

Parts of this sonatina were later used by Busoni in heavily altered form in the first prologue to his opera *Doktor Faust*; for Faust is Busoni—the seeker after Truth. And in this last great work, Busoni revealed perhaps more of himself than even he realized. In the verses (Busoni wrote his own libretto) preceding the score we find evidence of Busoni's hope that his work would be carried on in the future:

> Still unexhausted all the symbols wait
> That in this work are hidden and conceal'd;
> Their germs a later school shall procreate
> Whose fruits to those unborn shall be reveal'd;
> Let each take what he finds appropriate;
> The seed is sown, others may reap the field.
> So, rising on the shoulders of the past,
> The soul of man shall reach his heaven at last.[10]

NOTES

1. The relevant Schmieder nos. are *Fantasie und Fuge* (BWV 905), *Andante* (BWV 969), and *Scherzo* (BWV 844). It should be pointed out here that the *Fantasie und Fuge* (BWV 905) is now considered to be spurious.

2. Notably in the *Albumblatt* No. 3 for piano, *In der Art des Choralvorspiel*, based on the Bach chorale *Christ lag in Todesbanden*. (See Chapter 11.)

3. If one compares the left-hand bass entry and the right-hand entry—lines 3 and 4, page 7—of the *Sonatina brevis*, with the *Andante* subject and Busoni's suggested bass doubling near the end, such speculations perhaps become more plausible.

4. But as early as in 1917, Busoni must have at least considered such a project. In his essay "Mozart's *Don Giovanni* and Liszt's *Don Juan Fantasy*," printed as a preface to his edition of the Liszt work, he writes " . . . if it were a question of the paraphrase of *Carmen*, the transcriber, following Liszt's example, would begin with the suggestive scene in the market place in Act IV, and in the introduction as contrast to this, would join the pathetic 'Carmen' theme built on the gipsy scale. The middle section would be composed of the Habanera (followed by variations), the Finale, the bull-ring music. . . ." Ferruccio Busoni, *The Essence of Music and Other Papers*, trans. Rosamond Ley (London, Rockliff, 1957), p. 93, n.1.

5. Kaikhosru Sorabji, *Mi Contra Fa* (London, Porcupine Press, 1947), pp. 213-15.

6. We do not know how seriously Busoni took the directive "pro Clavicimbalo." He played the work on the piano in Zürich in 1917; perhaps there was no harpsichord available. Egon Petri recorded it on the piano—all lesser Busoni interpreters followed suit.

7. Ferruccio Busoni, *Letters to His Wife*, trans. Rosamond Ley (London, Edward Arnold, 1938), pp. 228-29.

8. From "Young Classicism," a letter to Paul Bekker which arose out of controversy between Pfitzner and Busoni. First published in the *Frankfurter Allgemeine Zeitung*, 7 February 1920, and then printed in the Busoni number of *Musikblätter des Anbruch*, 1921. See Busoni, *The Essence of Music*, pp. 20-21.

9. The only violent section in the sonatina—endlessly repeated fanfares, persistent rhythms: is this a statement about the hollowness of war? Busoni wrote

the sonatina while in Zürich; he had retired there during the war, refusing to take part in any way whatsoever in the madness that had enveloped the world. The very title of the sonatina seems a mocking reference to such madness. *Arlecchino*, written at the same time, is also a satire on, among other things, war and human failings.

10. English translation of *Doktor Faust* by Edward J. Dent, published by the BBC in the program of a concert performance of the work on 17 March 1937.

The Piano Concerto

Busoni was not a religious man in the conventional sense. He visited churches for aesthetic rather than religious reasons; and on the question of education, he never mentioned God. But he was a man, who by reason of his spiritual make-up was constantly aware of religious and mythical ideas. His religion was an intellectual one, concerned with goodness and peace. He knew about the secrets of the supernatural; both his music and his writing testify most convincingly to the beneficent and daemonic powers that, he believed, operate beneath the surface of everyday life.

H. H. Stuckenschmidt

CONCERTO PER UN PIANOFORTE PRINCIPALE E DIVERSE STRUMENTI AD ARCO A FIATO ED A PERCUSSIONE AGGIUNTOVI UN CORO FINALE PER VOCI D'UOMINI A SEI PARTI   LE PAROLE ALEMANNE DEL POETA OEHLENSCHLAEGER DANESE   LA MUSICA DI FERRUCCIO BUSONI DA EMPOLI ANNO MCMIV   OPERA XXXIX   Leipzig Breitkopf & Haertel   1906   Part. B.   1949   Composed in 1904 The two-piano reduction by Egon Petri appeared in 1909 Leipzig   Breitkopf & Haertel   1909   EB 2861

We first hear of a planned concerto from Busoni in February 1902, in letters written from London, during a typical and exhausting tour:

I have thought it out and decided not to use Oehlenschläger's Aladdin for an opera, but to write a composition in which drama, music, dancing and magic are combined—cut down for one evening's performance if possible. It is my old idea of a play with music *where it is necessary*, without hampering the dialogue. As a spectacle and as a deep symbolic work it might be somewhat similar to the Magic

Flute; at the same time it would have a better meaning and an indestructible subject. Besides this, I have planned 6 works for the summer, the principal one being the pianoforte Concerto.[1]

Shades of Scriabin and his *Mysterium*. Fortunately, Busoni never attempted anything like this; and he was not to know then that the *Concerto*, far from being a summer's work (with five other compositions!) was to take up to two-and-a-half years; nor that *Aladdin* and the *Concerto* were to become inextricably united in one piece of music. The name *Aladdin* has most unfortunate associations to the English reader; of course, it has nothing to do with the Christmas pantomime. In Arabic the name *Aladdin* means "The Sublimity of Religion"; Oehlenschläger's poem-drama, attractive to Busoni because of its close links with Goethe's *Faust* and Mozart's *Magic Flute*, was mystical, romantic, magical; the chorus from *Aladdin* that Busoni set and used in the last movement of his *Concerto* is a hymn to Allah, possible inspired by the *Chorus Mysticus* which ends the second part of Goethe's *Faust*.

True to his word, that summer Busoni set to work on the *Concerto*. A curious letter is sent to Gerda:

This drawing enclosed is crude and clumsy, but not ridiculous. I have a little weakness for it. It is the idea of my piano Concerto in one picture and it is represented by architecture, landscape, and symbolism. The three buildings are the first, third and fifth movements. In between come the two "lively" ones; Scherzo, and Tarantelle; the first represented by a miraculous flower and birds, freaks of nature; the second by Vesuvius and cypress trees. The sun rises over the *entrance*; a seal is fastened to the door of the end building. The winged being quite at the end is taken from Oehlenschläger's chorus and represents mysticism in nature. . . .

(21 and 22 July 1902)[2]

This sketch was later used as the basis for a more professional drawing by Heinrich Vogeler and reproduced on the frontispiece of the published work.

It is evident from all this that at least the overall conception of the work was perfectly clear in Busoni's mind at this time; I make the point because some Italian writers (notably Guido Guerrini) claim that the final chorus was added as an afterthought, and that it spoils the essentially Italian character of the *Concerto*.[3] Dent, on the other hand, asserts that the chorus setting was written before the *Concerto* was begun. Both were wrong. For the moment, we return to the summer of 1902. Busoni worked at the *Concerto* right through until autumn, when he had to abandon it for yet another concert tour. How much was actually written we do not know; letters to Gerda suggest that most of Busoni's effort went into the *Tarantelle*. We have a first sketch of the work dated simply 1903; this must represent some of the work done during the summer of 1902, possibly carried on spasmodically during tours (as was Busoni's habit), and finally

PER VN·PIANOFORTE·PRINCIPALE·E
DIVERSI·STRVMENTI·AD·ARCO · A···
FIATO·ED·A·PERCVSSIONE · · Ag.
GIVNTOVI·VN·CORO·FINALE·PER
VOCI·D'VOMINI·A·SEI·PARTI · Le
PAROLE·ALEMANNE·DEL·POETA
Oehlenschlaeger·Danese · ·
LA·Mvsica·di·
Ferrvccio·Bvsoni·da·Empoli
ANNO·Mcmiv· · OPERA · XXXIX

Reprinted by kind permission, Breitkopf & Haertel, Wiesbaden.

completed on 15 July 1903: "The Concerto is rounded off to my complete
satisfaction, I have 'dotted all the i's. . . .'"[4] Three days prior to this he had
written: "I make daily progress with the big sketch for the Concerto. And to
make it perfect, I also work at the details every day."[5] Evidently, Busoni
worked at a rough sketch and a more detailed sketch simultaneously.
Having completed his preliminary sketch, with much detail clearly still
carried in his head, Busoni, with the prospect of more concerts, became
worried:

You must forgive me for what I did to-day. I cancelled both concerts in London on
the 17th and 21st. That sounds short and dry, but I went through several bad days
before things reached this pass. I have never noticed this kind of nervousness in me
before. What I was most concerned about was the interruption whilst I am writing
down the concerto. I felt that it would never be completed if once I were interrupted;

(nobody could understand the sketch made in pencil) and I thought, too, that the distraction would make me forget all the important details not yet written down. . . . Finally, I decided that I *really* ran the risk of not finishing the Concerto if I don't work at the sketch again until the end of July. Owing to this excitement (and, having to practise the piano again) I have lost four days. . . .

(16 July 1903)[6]

The decision to continue work proved to be the correct one; that summer of 1903 was one of singular fluency and productivity, even for Busoni, accustomed to working at great speed and pressure. The second sketch of the work, marked *Secondo abbozzo, in esteso,* contains the solo part complete with the orchestral accompaniment sketched in. This is dated 18 August 1903. On 11 September 1903 Busoni wrote to his wife, "I have begun the instrumentation . . ." and the scoring took him approximately another year; the word "finis" appears on the full score on 3 August 1904.

Busoni wrote about the *Concerto* in the program notes to the first performance:

The title "concerto" is used here in its original sense, signifying a co-operation of different means of producing sound.

With the rise of virtuosity the word became restricted to the meaning which it still commonly has—a *bravura* piece for a single instrument, for the greater glory of which the orchestra, the most perfect and powerful musical medium, is subordinated.

For the sake of respectability these *morceaux d'occasion* were given the outward shape of a symphony; its first movement put on the mask of a certain dignity, but in the following movements the mask was gradually dropped, until the finale brazenly displayed the grimace of an acrobat.

The orchestra usually did not enter with its full power until the soloist had come to a stop, thus giving the conventional form of the *tutti;* otherwise the orchestra, like a discreet lion, drew in its claws and followed its dandified ringmaster.

Virtuosity is now on the down grade, and thus that caricature of a symphony called a concerto loses its claim to existence.

Absurd as this framework was, Beethoven, Brahms and Liszt could not help creating works of beauty and value within it. They instinctively revolted against it, but they could not break away from the convention of their day. The orchestra still remained timid, and the soloist aggressive. These composers forced themselves to restrain their symphonic impulses and to work in superfluous flourishes such as one never finds in their other works.

The pianoforte of today is more powerful and richer in colour than that of our forefathers, owing both to its construction and to the way in which it is played. It is now able to do battle with the untamed orchestra and also to unite with it and give it colour of its own. The union of these two forces takes on a new significance, and the concerto can assume a more perfect form. But since that is only made possible by the achievements of modern pianoforte-playing, the concerto of the future will always throw a severe task on the soloist, for although the solo instrument no longer stands at the head of the orchestra, we must not allow it to be dragged at its tail.

The present Concerto differs from its predecessors first by its outward form, which for the first time is extended to five movements. The first to be composed were nos. 1, 3 and 5, which are all tranquil in general feeling. Nos. 2 and 4 naturally supplied livelier rhythms; and of these no. 2 illustrates liveliness of imagination, and no. 4 liveliness of temperament, and this reaches so high a degree of energy that the fundamental spirit of the work would have been destroyed without the fifth movement to restore it. The fifth movement is, therefore, indispensable; it completes the circle through which we have traveled, and joins the end to the beginning. And the music has taken us through so manifold a variety of human feelings that the words of a poet are necessary to sum them up in conclusion.

The addition of a male voice choir is the second novelty of this work. The chorus does not break away from the previous mood to the opposite extreme of feeling, as it does in the Ninth Symphony; it resembles rather some original inborn quality of a person which in the course of years comes out again in him purified and matured as he reaches the last phase of his transformations.

A third characteristic of this work is the insistence on the melodies and rhythms of Italy. Besides three actual Italian folk-songs there are many turns of phrase that are definitely Italian. The fourth movement—a sort of Neapolitan carnival—is a highly developed form of tarantella.[7]

A version without final chorus was apparently intended for the 1906 edition, but was mercifully omitted. The original plates of the *Concerto* were destroyed during World War II.

The first performance of the *Concerto* took place in Berlin on 10 November 1904 in the Beethoven-Saal. The work was roundly abused by almost all the press. The German critics were scandalized by Busoni's insistence that the title of the *Concerto* be printed in Italian and the opus number given in Roman numerals, that Italian street songs were used in a work of this nature (premiered in a hall "sacred to the name of Beethoven" as one critic put it), and that even the subtitles of the movements and all musical directions were in Italian. Many found the second and fourth movements cacophonous and the inclusion of a choir into a piano concerto caused an additional outcry. It is doubly amusing to read Italian critics on the *Concerto*, who complain that this essentially Italian work is spoiled by its German elements, by German words in the choral movement (even though the original verses were in Danish), by the Wagnerian style of the third movement, by the lack of transparency in the scoring, and by its heavy Teutonic mood. All this nationalistic self-righteousness is farcical in retrospect; in music at least, we have ceased to be patriotic, or one hopes so. But no doubt everyone felt very strongly about such principles in 1904. The Italo-German controversy apart, critics also complained about the length of the *Concerto*, accused Busoni of having written, like Brahms, a symphony with piano obbligato, and pointed out stylistic discrepancies and clashes.

When Egon Petri played the *Concerto* for the first time in England on 22 October 1909 (with the London Symphony Orchestra, Busoni conducting), he felt compelled to write this defensive program note:

The work before us is not a "piano-concerto" in the ordinary traditional sense. Formerly, and indeed (in spite of Liszt's revolutionary innovations) today also, to the concert-going classically educated public the term "piano-concerto" signifies a collection of three or four movements—perhaps an Allegro in Sonata-form, a melodious Adagio, a lively Scherzo in 3/4, and a final Presto;—generally speaking, in all these movements there are alternate "Soli" and "Tutti"; the former afford opportunity to the soloist to display his technique, the latter, besides allowing him to take an occasional rest, being necessary to give relief in the matter of tone-colour; in short, the relation between the two is that of figure and background. But we have in this work an entirely different conception. There are five movements; its performance lasts more than an hour; there is no break between the movements; and at the end appears a choir. It might be asked, as indeed it has been done, "but what on earth is a chorus doing in a piano-concerto?" An attempt to explain this will be made in the next paragraph. With the examples of Beethoven's Ninth Symphony and Choral Fantasia with piano, not to mention more recent compositions, no charge of unheard-of innovation can be sustained. The step from a Symphony with chorus to a piano-concerto with chorus is not so great as it appears, if one considers that the modern piano-concerto has taken more and more the shape of a symphony. And as far as the piano-soloist is concerned, an examination of the score would most likely surprise him with the facts, that there are no defined "Soli" (excepting perhaps in the first movement, which is, of all five, the nearest in approach to the accepted form) that the orchestra often covers the piano, that, in the "Cantico" the piano is reduced to the level of an accompanying instrument, and that, on the whole his task is no thankful one. To all this the reply is, that neither listeners nor would-be performers can hope to form a just opinion of this work, unless they detach themselves from all prejudicial opinion.

The only fair way to judge *any* new work of art is to consider it from its own point of view, and to follow the development of itself from its innate laws and intentions. Such consideration, given to the present work, should lead to the perception, that the composer had in this case one prominent idea, mainly, to translate into sound the various phases of an artistic "inner life" as they were reflected in his own soul—that from this there sprang the thought of concentrating in a great solemn, slow movement, as the axis of the whole work, the struggle of opposing forces in that soul—that, round this "Andante," the slow movements of fantasy and worldly enjoyment grouped themselves, as a contrast, in harmonious symmetry—that a Prologue, forming an introduction, demanded an Epilogue, as a conclusion and completion of itself—that in order to obtain the highest possibilities of personal expression and of floating sound which would be capable of reproducing every dark and mystic emotion of the human heart, then arose the notion of the orchestra combined with the modern concert-grand piano—and that, finally, the feeling, that the inward growth and maturity should have a clear form of expression, compelled the musician to call to the poet for assistance; the words of the latter now stand forth as a symbol of the whole work; sprung from it, these words on the other hand carry the germ of the work in themselves, just as a plant contains in it the seed from which it has grown.

This program note was written while Petri was completely under Busoni's influence; he confessed to me that he was so imbued, so carried away by the whole idea, that he felt it his duty to play the work whenever possible. And, of course, he proved to be its greatest protagonist, and may have saved it from oblivion after Busoni's death. He once said to me: "Busoni wanted to write a concerto to end all concerti . . . and, you know, he almost succeeded! . . . But I still like it very much, despite everything: it's so beautifully written. . . ."

By 1912 Busoni had realized that the *Concerto* was the end of an epoch, not the beginning of a new one: that he had almost succeeded in writing that last concerto. For, in truth, the *Op. XXXIX* is the summation of the romantic concerto, and the last work in his nineteenth-century style:

The Concerto for Pianoforte, Orchestra and Men's Choir formed the third and last item on the programme. I endeavoured with this work to gather together the results of my first period of manhood, and it represents the actual conclusion of it.

Like every work which falls into such periods of development, it is ripe through experience gained and supported by tradition.

It does not know about the future at all, but represents the present at the time of its origin. The proportions and the contrasts are carefully distributed and, in order that the plan should be firmly established before putting it into execution, nothing in it is accidental.

The old does not yield to the new but to the better. We have this advantage over the academicians in that we hope for the new whilst we honour the old; that we can suffer and enjoy at the same time; that we willingly humble ourselves without remaining inactive.[8]

We are no longer disturbed by Italian and German elements mixed in one work; the discordant parts no longer sound modern although the mixture of styles may still disturb some listeners. But why can't one have a counterpoint of styles just as one approves of a counterpoint of themes? Busoni was unconcerned by considerations such as these, and even though a hymn to Allah and a Neapolitan tarantella may sound incongruous, there is no real reason why the two cannot appear in the same composition. Perhaps the title "Concerto" is inappropriate, but does this really matter? While performing the *Concerto* recently, I was struck by the fact that it had become a classic, and one listened to it and accepted it as part of musical history. Despite debts to composers like Liszt, Beethoven, Berlioz (and what composer is not indebted to another?), my overwhelming stylistic association of this concerto was with Gustav Mahler. There was the same vast conception on a symphonic scale, the use of voices, much of the actual orchestral sonority, the choice of words, the nostalgia, brought on both by original and folk themes, the latter often used as a foil to the sophistication of the original themes, the physical duration of the work. The *Op. XXXIX* really is a symphony; some of the critics were quite right. The piano part is Busoni himself, involved with the orchestral drama around him, and it is in this way that we must hear the *Concerto*. Like the Mahler symphonies, the

Busoni *Op. XXXIX* has faults, but it is a remarkable achievement nonetheless.

We are now ready to consider the *Concerto* in detail, movement by movement. All pages quoted in this analysis come from the two-piano reduction; number references (always given as, for example, No. 65) apply both to the two-piano and to the orchestral scores.

I. Prologo e Introito

"Since deciding not to travel I have worked magnificently; *I have written out the first movement in detail in three days!*" (19 July 1903).[9] Thus Busoni heralds start of work on the second detailed sketch.

The first movement is in the fairly traditional mold with a long orchestral tutti, in the course of which three themes are introduced. (See Figure 7.1.)

Figure 7.1. By kind permission, Breitkopf & Haertel, Wiesbaden.

The piano then enters, as Dent says, "with a very massive treatment of a new theme."[10] (See Figure 7.2.) This is heard soon after in diminution on the woodwind. (See Figure 7.3.) There is also another motive that assumes considerable importance here and in other movements. (See Figure 7.4.) The movement ends on a pedal C, with various thematic fragments above it, in a sort of soft reminiscence.

Figure 7.2. By kind permission, Breitkopf & Haertel, Wiesbaden.

Figure 7.3. By kind permission, Breitkopf & Haertel, Wiesbaden.

Figure 7.4. By kind permission, Breitkopf & Haertel, Wiesbaden.

I have deliberately given the themes in a concert-program type of context, in the manner in which they are usually presented, even by learned commentators such as Edward Dent and Denis Stevens. But these ideas can be considered in a different way. (See Figure 7.5.) It becomes immediately

Figure 7.5. By kind permission, Breitkopf & Haertel, Wiesbaden.

obvious that the themes are related far more closely than one might initially suspect. The fourth is not a new theme but a transformation, a re-blending of old material; the fifth is a harmonic version of A. Viewed in such a light, it is clear that when the piano enters it is really ushering in the beginning of a development process, which in technical terms consists of re-assembling

and rhythmically transforming the basic cellular motives. For example, B
undergoes metamorphoses such as shown in Figure 7.6. E is heard in
pianistic bravura passages (see Figure 7.7) and also in octaves, in similar
context. C is heard in a form that assumes great importance later in the
Concerto. (See Figure 7.8.)

Figure 7.6. By kind permission, Breitkopf & Haertel, Wiesbaden.

Figure 7.7. By kind permission, Breitkopf & Haertel, Wiesbaden.

Figure 7.8. By kind permission, Breitkopf & Haertel, Wiesbaden.

The development could also be said to commence after the piano entry,
when the key moves away from C major. Arguments about this, however,
have academic interest only. I have gone into a reasonable (or perhaps an
unreasonable) amount of detail in the presentation of this movement to
show, apart from other things, that the mantle of a classical sonata form sits
most uneasily on this movement's shoulders. We can always work the
sonata principle in, but it is not convincing. The themes are not distinct
enough in character; they all have a broad, epic-heroic sweep about them,
there are too many of them for a well-defined sonata and their general
treatment is not that of a sonata, if the word is to be understood in any sort
of traditional way. The "re-capitulation" is not, aurally, well defined,
although on paper it can certainly be shown to exist. The ear tells us one
thing only: that the movement has an arch form, starts softly, swells to an
imposing and leisurely climax, and sinks back to a quiet ending. If there is a
clear-cut exposition, it is only because the thematic materials have to be
presented somehow at the beginning, and does not necessarily imply that
such an exposition is followed by sonata procedures.

The key relationships disclose an interesting fact: just as the themes
showed a preference for certain intervals (see thematic diagram and Chart 1),

so the fluctuations of key follow the same intervallic pattern. In case this appears to be a coincidence, we shall find similar key relationships and key centers stressed in all other movements as well.

The technique is that of re-combination of the various motives making up the themes rather than variation of the themes themselves. Often motives are blended into each other. (See Figure 7.9.) In this way Busoni achieves a

Figure 7.9. By kind permission, Breitkopf & Haertel, Wiesbaden.

unity otherwise impossible in a work of such length and with so many themes.

At this point we refer back to the question of the choral ending having been written first (see above). 4a, or rather 4, is, in fact, used in the fifth movement, but this does not prove what Dent tries to make it prove. We know now that 4 is a derivative of 1, so that it could not have been written first, but is an outcome of the first theme of the *Concerto*; therefore, the choral setting could not have been written earlier and artificially grafted onto the body of the *Concerto*.[11] Finally, we should note that the piano plays an almost exclusively decorative function. This, too, is typical of the whole work; the important themes are most usually heard in the orchestral part.

Busoni's marking for the movement—Allegro, dolce e solenne—is a perfect description of it, moving unhurriedly through its delicate and morbid moments, as also through its solemn and heroic climax. By its title we know it to be a curtain raiser for the vast drama that is to unfold. My purpose is to suggest that in matters of technique, construction, key, balance of piano and orchestra, and overall mood, this movement sets the pattern for what is to come.

II. Pezzo giocoso

Unlike the *Prologo*, the *Pezzo giocoso* uses an extremely limited amount of basic materials: two themes and a characteristic rhythm. (See Figure 7.10.) The folk-song is closely related to a melody used by Liszt in *Venezia e Napoli*, but what interests us more is a possible link with themes from the first movement. (See Figure 7.11.) Is this far-fetched? Possibly. The melody was selected for its own intrinsic beauty, I am sure; if there were links of the kind I have indicated they were probably unconsciously perceived. But there is no doubt as to the origin of 7. (See Figure 7.12.) Chart 2 presents a formal summary of this movement, though in less detail.

Chart 1
Prologo e Introito

I. Exposition	1	C major (short shift to A)	Tonic
			3d down
	2 at No. 2, B used canonically	C major	Tonic
bridge	Tempo moderato, parts of 1 used	Shift to E flat minor, on B flat pedal	3d up
		B pedal, used as first inversion of the dominant of C.	
	3 at No. 4	G pedal (shift to F)	Dominant
		C major (used with B flat, A flat, F sharp, E flat)	Tonic
bridge	Using 2, preparing for piano entry		
II. Development	Piano enters with 4, at No. 5	C major (short shift to A)	Tonic
	Orchestra gradually creeps in with C1	D flat major	semitone up
	Piano takes over C1, orchestra plays G	Vaccillation between D flat major, D major/minor	semitone, tone up
	At No. 8, orchestra plays 3, piano is decorative	E major	3d up
	Piano has staccato chord version of E Woodwind play 4a		
	At No. 9, 4a in bass (in rhythm only) various fragments in flux	(short departures)	
	At No. 10, 5 and C1 are combined		
	Piano cadenza, using B1, then E in octaves		

III. Recapitulation	Tempo I, soft piano cadenza, decorative figures round 1, on oboe		
	At No. 12, 1 pizz, then in other instruments B2 in piano and orchestra	C major (shift to D flat) B major	tonic semitone down
	1 in orchestra, p. 34. Piano cadenza, ending in trills based on B3 and mirrored B	Gradual working back to C major	
	At No. 14, 2 (used as dominant pedal)	G pedal	Dominant
	At No. 15, a sense of rest, 3 At No. 16, 1, 2; F in woodwind, tonic pedal	C major	Tonic

Figure 7.10. By kind permission, Breitkopf & Haertel, Wiesbaden.

Figure 7.11. By kind permission, Breitkopf & Haertel, Wiesbaden.

Figure 7.12. By kind permission, Breitkopf & Haertel, Wiesbaden.

Trio II and Scherzo III, both short, are in the nature of a Coda and counterbalance the Introduction; thus, formally, the structure of this movement is explicit: Introduction, Scherzo-Trio-Scherzo, Coda. An arch form within an arch.

The key centers are far more elusive than in the *Prologo*, but, when definable, follow the pattern suggested above; keys are mostly semitone-

Chart 2
Pezzo Giocoso

Introduction	Rhythm 6, fragment of 7, fragment of 8	C pedal (A major, E minor, B flat minor)
Scherzo I	Movement proper begins on p. 47 Based on 7; transformation of rhythm leads to p. 53.	E major (ends in E major/minor)
Trio I	Based on 8, p. 53	B flat minor, F sharp major/minor (short)
	Short piano cadenza leads to:	B flat major, Cadenza pedal on F sharp
Scherzo II	P. 57; many new variants of 7. Reminiscence of plucked guitar-like chords from Trio I lead to:	Pedal on A; F sharp major; pedals on D, E; E major; E, D, C, B flat: major/minor
Trio II	Further variants and elaborations of 8 (p. 65) (Very short)	D major/minor
Scherzo III	No. 30; also very short. "Spectrale" version of 7.	F sharp pedal (D major); ends on 6/4 chord

tone, and 3rd above and below C; there is much mixing of major and minor; the F sharp forming a tritone with C keeps much of the tonality vague; the style is extremely chromatic, and contains much startling reference to Busoni's later "fantastico" style.

The movement partakes of the nature of an Intermezzo-Scherzo: the music fluctuates between the languorous sensuality of 8 and the witty agile effervescence of 7, especially in the piano part, which is often diabolically difficult. (See Figure 7.13.) Once more, the piano constantly decorates, dazzles and comments, but very rarely plays any thematically important passage.

III. Pezzo serioso

In the burst of creativity that precipitated the second sketch of the *Concerto*, the third movement was no exception: it was written in a matter of days.[12]

Figure 7.13. By kind permission, Breitkopf & Haertel, Wiesbaden.

The *Pezzo serioso* is the most complex of the five movements of the
Concerto; it is also meant to be the most important, and around it the other
four revolve like satellites. Ingenious in its thematic developments, richly
woven, with sumptuous and extended themes, stirring in the lyrical and
tragic parts; a solid symphonic piece, yet it contains some curious
contradictions. These stem from Busoni's use of music he wrote in his
youth: material from the unfinished opera *Sigune* and from an *Etude* for
piano, both unpublished. Even Busoni's skill in mixing styles cannot quite
overcome the dichotomy thus created; parts of the movement sound old-
fashioned (not in itself a fault) in relation to other parts; taken *in toto*,
Guido Guerrini is quite correct when he describes the *Pezzo serioso* as "the
only example of an almost Wagnerian Busoni, or more correctly, a Busoni
derived from that Liszt which Wagner plagiarized."[13]

Not that Busoni bodily inserts excerpts from earlier compositions: only
themes are used, and even these are chromaticized to blend them more into
the general style of the *Concerto*, but the very profusion of themes is
confusing to the listener and obscures the construction of the movement.[14]
Busoni divided the *Pezzo serioso* into four parts: *Introductio*, *Prima Pars*,
Altera Pars and *Ultima Pars*. We first hear a passacaglia-like bass. (See
Figure 7.14.) Over it is a recitando theme. (See Figure 7.15.) Figure H seems

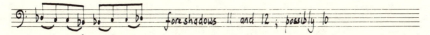

Figure 7.14. By kind permission, Breitkopf & Haertel, Wiesbaden.

Figure 7.15. By kind permission, Breitkopf & Haertel, Wiesbaden.

to generate a new idea, and two more themes appear in quick succession. (See Figure 7.16.) That H is an actual common factor to the two themes can be confirmed by the reader on pages 86-87, where H is played in the basic rhythm of 10. (See Figure 7.17.)

Figure 7.16. By kind permission, Breitkopf & Haertel, Wiesbaden.

Figure 7.17. By kind permission, Breitkopf & Haertel, Wiesbaden.

The *Introductio* ends with a foreshadowing of the main theme of *Prima Pars*, and, indeed, of the whole movement, with an altered form of 11 against it. (See Figure 7.18.) *Prima Pars* commences quite simply, with the pianist playing the theme taken from the old *Etude*. (See Figure 7.19.) This is followed at once by a sort of augmentation, both rhythmic and intervallic. (See Figure 7.20.) Both forms of 12 are used; there is also heard what Dent numbers as a new theme, but which is actually a melodic version of 11a. (See Figure 7.21.)

Figure 7.18. By kind permission, Breitkopf & Haertel, Wiesbaden.

Figure 7.19. By kind permission, Breitkopf & Haertel, Wiesbaden.

Figure 7.20. By kind permission, Breitkopf & Haertel, Wiesbaden.

Figure 7.21. By kind permission, Breitkopf & Haertel, Wiesbaden.

With the advent of *Altera Pars*, we return to familiar territory. 6 is used extensively; Dent's "new subject" is really old material in disguise. (See Figure 7.22.) The music develops through a long section to an enormous climax.[15] We hear 13 in a more dramatic form (see Figure 7.23) as well as many other previous themes (see Chart 3). At the *Ultima Pars*, a sort of tragic disintegration of 13 is heard (see Figure 7.24), after which the movement comes to a close on a long (Guerrini says "too long") D flat pedal point. These are the raw materials of the *Pezzo serioso*. In Chart 3 is shown what happens schematically.

Figure 7.22. By kind permission, Breitkopf & Haertel, Wiesbaden.

Figure 7.23. By kind permission, Breitkopf & Haertel, Wiesbaden.

Figure 7.24. By kind permission, Breitkopf & Haertel, Wiesbaden.

The most important consequence of this consideration is my proposed division of the movement into five parts; the argument is based on, first of all, the aural feeling of having arrived at a perfect cadence at the *Come da principio*, just after No. 45; the ear has a sense of repose after the vast climax of the *Altera Pars*. Furthermore, after the perfect cadence (in A flat, the dominant), the key, after some fluctuations, arrives very definitely at D flat major (No. 47), strengthening this feeling of having turned full circle. From the chart it is obvious, too, that the relative length of the five section forms a perfect archsymmetry: *Introductio* (short), *Prima Pars* (moderate length), *Altera Pars* (long), *Come da principio* (moderate length), *Ultima Pars* (short). The *Ultima Pars* thus becomes a form of coda, an emotional summary of the movement. The tragic undertones of the *Pezzo serioso* here burst out unrestrained, and then merge into the aloof romanticism that is more generally characteristic of the movement.

So, once more, we see the patterns set by the *Prologo* repeated here: the archstructure, the key centers, the role of the piano, links with previous themes, and similar methods of transformation. We also note that the *Introductio* and *Prima Pars* are stylistically separated from the rest of the movement. From the *Altera Pars* on, the music is not only directly related to other movements of the *Concerto*, but is in a more advanced chromatic language. This can be classed as a fault; it certainly creates a fissure in the flow of the movement. It is possible, of course, that it was deliberate.

IV. All' Italiana

We know from Busoni's letters that this movement, which he refers to as a *Tarantelle* in correspondence, caused him more labor than any of the others. At first, working on the rough sketch, he seems to be swept along by the impetus and frenzy of the music: "There is a night of love, with a Serenade, in the Tarantelle, and a Vesuvius eruption too. It is getting on well . . ." (22 July 1902).[16] But only a few days later he writes: "The Tarantelle will be Naples itself; only the score will be rather cleaner, nevertheless not so clean as the other movements. At the moment it still

Chart 3
Pezzo Serioso

Introduction	quite short; used to introduce 9, 10, 11, and 12, in part.	Introduction and prima pars principally in D flat, only briefly touching A flat, E, and F.
Prima Pars	12 in full, 11b once. Quite extensive development. Moderate length section.	
Altera Pars	6 and 13; extensive development of this combination, especially 6 with D and E portions of 13. 13a climax, in combination with 12 and 10 9 with piano cadenza based on introductory figure. 9 transformed, with H prominently singled out. 10 in bass, and also in fragmentary style. 9 in canon. 10 in low register of piano with arpeggios, then in orchestra. Lengthy section.	Avoids D flat Keys quickly fluctuate; C major (B major-short), C major. B flat pedal then B, G; C minor, B minor, E flat major; G minor, G pedal, G major; B major, E flat major.
(Come da principio)	Just after No. 45, a feeling of rest; sense of recapitulation: introductory bass heard again; combined with parts of 10. 12 heard again; rhythm 6, and 11b. 10 in epic style. Moderate length.	Soon after Come da principio, where key is vague, D flat firmly established (at No. 47) D flat until Ultima Pars.
Ultima Pars	Tragic character: 13b Long pedal to end. Quite short section.	F sharp minor at first on C sharp pedal, then long D flat pedal.

contains *too much*, and must be cleared up again. But the conception of the whole thing is there. . . ." (1 August 1902).[17]

This process of pruning went on for quite a time; on 29 July 1903 he had complained that "the Tarantelle will . . . give me many a nut to 'crack.'" On 3 August he reported performing "two little operations" on the *Tarantelle*, apparently shortening the movement. It is not until 6 August that we learn: "I have gone ahead again and the nuts I was afraid of in the Tarantelle have been successfully cracked; (without nutcrackers—with my own teeth; nothing but the nuts broken). Everything seems to be succeeding and you will be pleased. . . ."[18]

We should not take Busoni's pictorial descriptions of this movement seriously; he was only attempting to convey a general emotional sensation. The idea of Busoni describing the eruption of Mt. Vesuvius is ridiculous—he was not attracted to this type of programmatic writing. But what he was attempting to do here was to use Italian themes (his own, or popular folktunes) and rhythms (mostly the *Tarantelle*) to write a whirlwind of a movement, as full of color and excitement as he could manage. The problem, no doubt, was the molding of all this exuberance into some sort of disciplined shape, the avoidance of repetition and excessive duration, the ability to keep up a form of perpetual motion (all dance-like and most of it in 6/8) without flagging.

A large number of melodies appear, many of them related to each other by variation and transformation. The most important are shown in Figure 7.25. We notice at once that 14 and 16 have many resemblances, that 8a is the bare framework of the by now familiar theme from the second movement, heard in full, though still in expanded time values, at No. 74. (See Figure 7.26.) 17 is an old marching song of the Bersaglieri:

E sì, e sì, e sì che la portemero
la piuma sul cappello
avanti al colonello
giuriam la fedeltà
La dis, la dis, la dis che l'è malata. . . .

18 has some relationships with 8. (See Chart 4.)

The division of the movement into three main sections is mine, not Busoni's; also, I must take the responsibility for the subdivision of each section into three further parts. However, these divisions are not academically forced to comply with a prearranged scheme, but are quite clear in the music; the end of I (see Chart 4) is a very strong statement of 6, pulling everything, quite unmistakably, to a complete halt; the end of II is signalled, also very clearly, by the commencement of the piano cadenza. The smaller divisions are not so obvious as these, but are nevertheless aurally clear. The three-by-three structure may give the impression, on

Figure 7.25. By kind permission, Breitkopf & Haertel, Wiesbaden.

Figure 7.26. By kind permission, Breitkopf & Haertel, Wiesbaden.

paper, that the sections are of comparable length. This is in reality not so, as the first section is much longer than the following two. A form of tele-scoping occurs, with each section shorter than the one before it; possibly this is caused by the incredible impetus of the music.

Key changes are fast and furious, and very often too fleeting to establish any feeling of tonality. I have noted only the main keys here, to demonstrate that Busoni is still adhering to his cycle of keys, but it must be explained that within these keys there is an enormous amount of harmonic-chromatic flux.

All' Italiana is often criticized for being too long and too confused, for flagging invention, for unmemorable and undifferentiated themes, and for vulgarity, especially in the appearances of 17.

Chart 4
All' Italiana

I.	(a)	Vivace: using 14, from opening to No. 59; much variation of theme. At No. 59, 15 appears and is developed.	*C sharp minor*; F minor (short) *A minor* (long); C minor, C major
	(b)	Un poco gravemente: after No. 63. 8a used, up to just before No. 66	F minor going to C minor/major
	(c)	Tempo primo: 16 appears; used up to No. 69. At No. 69, we hear 17 for the first time. Tempo becomes even more frantic, is suddenly pulled up by a fortissimo appearance of 6.	B flat minor, B major, C major, *E major*, A flat major, C minor/major
II.	(a)	"La Stretta" commences using 18 as an accumulative factor.	
	(b)	Short interruption; time changes to 2/4. 17 is heard.	C major
	(c)	Return to stretto 6/8 (pulled up suddenly by commencement of Cadenza, soon after No. 81)	
III.	Cadenza:		
	(a)	Commences in 12/8, with a florid version of 13.	C major (very chromatic)
	(b)	Middle section of cadenza has violent interjections from the orchestra, blaring out 16.	A flat major, A major
	(c)	Cadenza continues solo, with a florid variant of motive A, as heard previously in 13b. Orchestra joins in at the very end with another powerful statement of 6.	B major, E flat major, C major

---

One must note also that 6 and 5 appear at various points throughout the movement; another rhythm very favored is of course the tarantella rhythm ♩ ♪❙ ♪ often repeated almost obsessively, and sometimes in combination with a characteristic melodic descent (stepwise).
Variation is incredibly rich and fertile so that it is impossible to present in an analysis details of such variation, indeed, almost undesirable, since the main outlines would then be obscured.

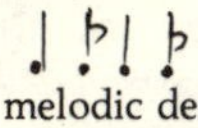

Two Versions of the Cadenza in "All' Italiana"

The first version of this candenza was published in the orchestral score. Busoni was dissatisfied with it from the start, and, according to Petri, was varying it even in the first performance of the *Concerto*. By the time the two-piano score of the *Concerto* appeared, Busoni had written this second version down, and it was published at the back of this edition as *Versione amplificata della Cadenza che occorre nel quarto movimento del Concerto*. It is this second version that Busoni and Petri always played; pianistically it is more effective while musically it establishes closer links with other movements by its quotation of 13.

The amplification is not at all drastic. Section (a) is 33 bars compared to 28, (b) is 17 compared to 16, and in (c) both versions have a prestissimo B major section of 33 bars. The early version then joins up to a tutti statement of 6 via a 3-bar link. The later version has a 17-bar link, which anticipates 6 in E flat major before we hear it triumphantly asserted in C major.

V. Cantico

This fifth epilogue-like movement looks back at materials previously heard, and although it does exploit some new combinations of motives, is not really a developmental, but rather a nostalgic-mystic, movement. The choral setting is chant-like, or chorale-like, in blocks of sound, with the male choir divided at times into six parts. Busoni stipulates in the score that the choir is to be invisible, a direction difficult to fulfill in performance; the choir is used as a section of the orchestra ("to add a new register to the sonorities which precede it," according to Busoni). Oehlenschläger's words are not as important, perhaps, as the effect they create:

> *"The Pillars of Rock Begin to Take Soft and Gentle Music"*[19]
> Lift up your hearts to the Power Eternal,
> Draw ye to Allah nigh, witness his work.
> Earth has its share of rejoicing and sorrow.
> Firm the foundations that hold up the world.
> Thousands and thousands of years march relentlessly,
> Show forth in silence his glory, his might,
> Flashing immaculate, splendid and fast they stand,
> Time cannot shake them, yea time without end.
>
> Hearts flamed in ecstasy, hearts turned to dust again,
> Playfully life and death stakes each his claim,
> Yet in mute readiness patiently tarring,
> Splendid and mighty both, for evermore.
> Lift up your hearts to the Power Eternal,
> Draw ye to Allah nigh, witness his work.
> Fully regenerate now is the world of yore,
> Praising its Maker e'er unto the end.[20]

We need notate only three ideas; the first two are heard in the orchestral introduction (see Figure 7.27), and the third is the theme sung by the choir at its first entry. (See Figure 7.28.) A summary of this last movement is shown in Chart 5.

Figure 7.27. By kind permission, Breitkopf & Haertel, Wiesbaden.

Figure 7.28. By kind permission, Breitkopf & Haertel, Wiesbaden.

Once again we are faced with a movement in three parts. This time the choral section makes a very clear division; this middle part is naturally the most important both in length and substance. Except for the final allegro con fuoco, the piano part is literally an accompanying instrument to the choir. We note also Busoni's final consistency in the use of keys; the predictions, musically made in the first movement, have been fulfilled. Guerrini says that the *Cantico* "does not possess a definite tonality, which is its greatest fascination."[21] It seems to me, on the contrary, that this is tonally perhaps the most stable movement of all. Note the preponderance of long pedal points: it is they that give the *Cantico* a firm foundation on which the mystical serenity that Busoni strives to convey is based. The nostalgic elements are supplied by the piano and orchestra, in their use of themes and motives from previous movements, in remembered sounds; the choral use of old themes is nevertheless so startling on first hearing that one tends to miss the links.

The choral climax is arrived at by purely musical intensification rather than a rise in sonority, as befits a mystical mood, a form of inner exaltation. Petri wondered whether the traditional upbringing in Busoni prohibited him from ending the whole *Concerto* softly (see also my comments regarding the ending of the *Indian Fantasy*), whether the formal, brilliant gesture of the C major affirmation at the end was extraneous to what had been achieved. But then this is only conjecture. One could reason just as well that the triumphant affirmation was necessary.

Chart 5
Cantico

Orchestral Introduction	Use of K and mirrored B, E. 6 is also heard.	E minor on B pedal; changing to E major, still on B pedal.
Choral Section	Entry on transformation of 4; orchestral accompaniment based on C1	E major
	At the six-bar orchestral interlude just before No. 89, the C1 motive is played almost exactly as it was heard in the Prologo, with 5 over it	B major
	Further choral transformation of 4, involving motives D, F, and A (i.e., 3rds, 4ths, and semitonal shifts)	B flat minor
	At No. 90, melodic use of a form of 3 (with relations to C1 as well, in the rhythm)	E major (long B pedal)
	P. 170: 6 in orchestra; 13 in choir, more orchestral melodic use of 4ths, 3rds, and E	C major (rhythmic and tonic pedal)
	No. 92: choir sings C in rising form, exalted	Transitional harmonies
	No. 94: 10 is heard in orchestra, in epic form	C minor (sometimes with F sharp forming a diminished 7th)
Orchestral Conclusion (largamente)	P. 177: figure played by piano close to first entry in Prologo; orchestra plays a figure in rising form of C or C1, making explicit the connection between C1 and 8.	
(allegro con fuoco)	Piano plays version in alternating hands of B2-B3, also from the Prologo. Ending consists of some conventional but brilliantly scored flourishes in C major.	C major

In surveying the *Concerto* as a whole, a most satisfying overall symmetry emerges, as shown in Chart 6.

Chart 6

I. Exposition Development Recapitulation	3 parts	C major through E major to C major
II. Introduction Scherzo-Trio-Scherzo (3 parts) Coda (Trio-Scherzo)	3 parts, could also be viewed as 5 parts	C major through to D major
III. Introduction Prima Pars Altera Pars Come da principio Ultima Pars	5 parts, with longest part in the middle	D flat major through variety of keys in Altera Pars to D flat major (enharmonic change to)
IV. Vivace Stretta Cadenza	3 parts, each divisible into 3 further parts	C sharp minor to C major
V. Introduction Choral Part Finale	3 parts	E minor/major through B and B flat to C major

Note the symmetrical structure. I-V: all arch forms, simple and compound. I and V related in form, length, and mood; also thematically. II and IV similarly related; both compound forms. III: keystone and emotional highlight of concerto. Five-part division of the Pezzo Serioso with Altera Pars as keystone reflected in the five-movement concerto and Pezzo Serioso as keystone. Key fluctuations also show inter-movement relationships; II and IV are the most unstable harmonically.

Two final general observations: even though the piano part of the *Concerto* is of the greatest difficulty, requiring of the pianist not only strength and agility but great endurance as well, the soloist does not have the opportunity for much real virtuoso display. The piano, with very rare exceptions, has an integrating role; it is an important orchestral instrument most of the time, supplying new textures, commenting and elaborating. This decorative function is at times almost removed from the basic musical argument going on in the orchestra, so that the piano part almost takes on an autonomous life of its own, a simultaneous rather than a functional role. Because of this few have played the work; it is pianistically ungrateful.

Technically speaking, the piano part is Lisztian in its origins, although Busoni develops simple Lisztian figures to their complex extreme and at great length; pianistically, the *Concerto* is the apex of Busoni's output as performer-composer, in that it poses and resolves an enormous quantity of keyboard problems, exploits an infinite amount of technical combinations, and seems inexhaustible in its invention.

Alternate Ending without Choir

Among the Busoni-Nachlass folders in the Berlin Staatsbibliothek one comes across a rather voluminous one (SB 233), labelled simply "Busoni Concerto," and with the crest Breitkopf & Haertel stamped upon it. On the top right hand corner there are some scribbles with the date 1906 clearly legible. The folder contains orchestral parts but no score. Each part is labelled *Concerto. Coda supplementaria. F. Busoni.*

Petri told me of the existence of a version without choir, but he knew nothing else; it had never been performed to his knowledge, nor to mine, although the parts bear Nos. 83 and 84 in pencil to orient the *Coda* with the numbers in the full score.

Busoni must have eliminated the choir purely as a concession to expediency, possibly at the suggestion of his publishers, to try to promote more performances of the rarely attempted *Concerto*. Whatever the reason, this alternative was never put into print, and the full score of the *Coda supplementaria* was lost during World War II.

Fortunately, a copy of the score has been preserved in Leipzig by Breitkopf & Haertel. It is titled *Concerto Coda supplementaria corrispondente alla Versione in quattro tempi omettendo il coro Finale.* The score is dated 13 August 1908.

The *Coda supplementaria* makes the simple and drastic suggestion of cutting the fifth movement out altogether and supplies a link between the end of the *Cadenza* of the fourth movement and the end of the fifth movement after the choir has finished. To be absolutely precise, the link proceeds from the end of the 33-bar episode in the piano *Cadenza* in B major (both versions of the *Cadenza* have the same 33-bar episode, marked prestissimo), at the bottom of page 155 of the piano score, to the 9/4 C major bar in the last movement, at the top of page 177 (between No. 94 and No. 95) in the piano score, marked *un poco largamente*.

The actual link between these two points proved to be only 11 bars long, 4 bars of which were rests. (See Appendix.)

Artistically such a cut is inexplicable. It ruins the overall archsymmetry of the *Concerto*, ends conventionally with the fast fourth movement and destroys the sense of mystical tranquillity which Busoni claimed was the essence of the work. Although many critics of the *Concerto* would sigh with profound relief at a shortening, or more particularly a cutting out of the choral movement, I cannot accept this version seriously. The point is that Busoni did not have it published, and he was not averse to alternative versions of the same work as we well know. It seems that we can consign this alternative version back to the museum where it belongs, and explain it away as a temporary abberation, a momentary act of despair on the part of the composer. The *Concerto* should be played as it stands, with no compromises.

NOTES

1. Ferruccio Busoni, *Letters to His Wife*, trans. Rosamond Ley (London, Edward Arnold, 1938) p. 54.

2. Ibid., p. 58.

3. Guido Guerrini, *Ferruccio Busoni: La Vita, La Figura, L'Opera* (Firenze, Casa Editrice Monsalvato, 1944), pp. 243-53.

4. Busoni, *Letters to His Wife*, p. 63.

5. Ibid.

6. Ibid.

7. Translated by Edward J. Dent for a performance of the *Concerto* by Egon Petri at the Queen's Hall on 21 February 1934.

8. Written by Busoni for the periodical *Pan* (Berlin, February 1912). See Ferruccio Busoni, *The Essence of Music and Other Papers*, trans. Rosamond Ley (London, Rockliff, 1957), pp. 49-50.

9. Busoni, *Letters to His Wife*, p. 64.

10. Edward J. Dent, notes on the *Concerto* for a performance by Egon Petri at the Queen's Hall on 21 February 1934. Program pp. 11-20.

11. See Busoni's program note to the *Concerto*.

12. Busoni, *Letters to His Wife*, pp. 64-65.

13. Guerrini, *Ferruccio Busoni*, p. 250.

14. A quick comparison of the *Etude* for piano (SB 185) and the *Prima Pars*, for example, reveals: (1) the same key of D flat major; (2) almost the same chords; (3) the actual theme slightly changed; (4) theme 10 also appears in this *Etude*, proving that there was a strong connection between 10 and 12 in Busoni's mind, as indicated in the text; (5) the piano part at the top of p. 73 is almost identical with a similar passage on the last manuscript page of the *Etude*; (6) the change of key to F major immediately after the statement of 12 occurs both in the *Concerto* and the *Etude*, although the actual music is quite different. There is very little real plagiarizing from the early sources. It is interesting that figure H is grafted on to the original theme 10, as heard in the old *Etude*, to give it a Janus-like aspect, acting as a link between 9 and subsequent themes.

15. Norman Del Mar in *Richard Strauss* (vol. 2, p. 195, n.36) discussing *Die Frau Ohne Schatten*, says of a certain section of this opera: "The resemblance of this passage to the central climax of Busoni's monumental Piano Concerto is too striking to be ignored."

16. Busoni, *Letters to His Wife*, p. 58.

17. Ibid., p. 59.

18. Ibid., pp. 64-65.

19. Translated by Walter M. Clement. Published in a concert program for a performance of the *Concerto* by Egon Petri at the Queen's Hall on 21 February 1934. There is also a more modern, freer translation by Lauren Miller, but the virtue of Mr. Clement's translation is that it can be sung to Busoni's setting.

20. The subject of "Aladdin" continued to fascinate Busoni even after the *Concerto* was written; as late as October 1906 we discover him working on the libretto of the proposed opera. (See Busoni, *Letters to His Wife*, p. 105.)

21. Guerrini, *Ferruccio Busoni*, p. 253.

8

Other Works for Piano and Orchestra

Busoni . . . is the exact antithesis of these vestiges of one's past which no longer retain their living connections with our present. His personality was far too overpowering for that, and the imprint he left on anyone who had the privilege of coming into contact with him was too indelible. How vivid the memory of everything connected with him remains to this day!

Joseph Szigeti

CONCERTSTÜCK FÜR PIANOFORTE MIT ORCHESTER Op. 31a
Leipzig Breitkopf & Haertel 1892 Part. B. 1107 Composed in 1890 The two-piano reduction appeared in 1892 Leipzig Breitkopf & Haertel Klav. Bibl. 19292

This piece, dedicated to Anton Rubinstein, won the first Rubinstein prize for composition in 1890. It was widely recognized that Busoni should also have won the piano prize at the competition, but Rubinstein himself felt that, at least during the first awards, one prize should go to a Russian.

The *Concertstück* is often dismissed in writings on Busoni as an early work and therefore as too derivative and immature. Much has been made of the Brahms influence in particular. This seems to me overemphasized. True, the passage given in Figure 8.1 could well have been inspired by similar passages in the Brahms d minor *Concerto*, but it is an isolated instance, not a typical one; and even when the solo part feels and sounds like Brahms, the combination with orchestra has none of the Brahmsian opulence, but is already finely etched even at this early stage, and contrapuntally rather than harmonically conceived.

J. C. G. Waterhouse writes of a particular section of the *Concertstück*:

For 1890 this is extraordinary. The vertical combinations, it is true, are orthodox enough Wagner-Liszt; but semitonal melodic steps have virtually replaced tonal and

Figure 8.1. By kind permission, Breitkopf & Haertel, Wiesbaden.

triadic concepts as the basis of the music's logic, to an extent not matched even in *Tristan*, where chromatic scales are still usually heard as sighing suspensions or appogiaturas within a harmonically conceived framework. We see here an exceptionally early instance of what was to become a fundamental principle of Busoni's more chromatic harmony: a peculiarly individual use of the melodic step of a semitone, in both directions and at all levels of the texture, to give the music a sort of controlled instability that is strangely unsettling.[1]

This is perhaps a trifle overenthusiastic; the passage in question (the meno mosso, sostenuto section, page 16 in the solo part) is full of those sighing, chromatic, harmonically resolving suspensions that one finds in *Tristan*—however in principle the observation is perfectly sound. What I find particularly interesting in this interlude is Busoni's constant avoidance of the temptation to overscore, to richly double parts. Wagner is certainly apparent in some of the progressions, but not in their scoring; the characteristic Busonian aloofness and serenity, often interpreted as coldness, is present in a marked degree. Is this the result of studying much late Beethoven at this stage of his pianistic career? Bach is present too, in the passacaglia-like tread that introduces the solo part (see Figure 8.2), and in the contrapuntal working out of passages such as the one given in Figure 8.3. Liszt, although responsible for some of the purely pianistic figurations,

Figure 8.2. By kind permission, Breitkopf & Haertel, Wiesbaden.

Figure 8.3. By kind permission, Breitkopf & Haertel, Wiesbaden.

is markedly absent, for we find no violently virtuosic explosions; once again Busoni avoids the temptations that would seem to obviously beset the path of a young composer-virtuoso writing a concert piece for his instrument.

Therefore, instead of a thundering, exuberant display piece by the young Busoni, we are unexpectedly presented with an almost anti-romantic refinement. The positive qualities of this composition lie in its being a real precursor of much later Busoni. From this point of view, it would be legitimate to regard the great *Concerto Op. XXXIX* as an almost retrograde step.

The *Concertstück* begins with an orchestral introduction setting out the four principal themes, with some interrelationship between the themes themselves. (See Figure 8.4.) There is also a motive, common to I and III, a simple rising scale—preceded by a drop of a third in III—which is used soloistically later in the work. I have called it V, although it is not a separate theme.

Figure 8.4. By kind permission, Breitkopf & Haertel, Wiesbaden.

Adhering as the piece does to the outward trappings of sonata structure, the solo entry would serve as the expected second half of a double exposition: Busoni overcomes the problem of repetition by ostensibly giving the piano new material, which is, however, clearly derived from theme IV, in three forms, all of which assume later importance. (See Figure 8.5.) Theme IVa serves as a sort of walking bass in passacaglia style; IVb is a more diatonic, simpler version of the chromatic theme; and IVc consists of two notes of the same theme, used as a sequential dyad.

Figure 8.5. By kind permission, Breitkopf & Haertel, Wiesbaden.

Thus, the true developmental process begins with the entry of the piano, or even earlier, since the four themes can almost be said to be derived out of an organic growing process.

The piano also immediately evolves a rhythmic variant of IV, which is combined with IVc and treated in canon. (See Figure 8.6.) The double

Figure 8.6. By kind permission, Breitkopf & Haertel, Wiesbaden.

exposition then ends with a coda in which solo piano and orchestra represent the themes not already used in the solo entry, namely a massive version of II, an elaborated version of III, and V in double octaves. Themes IV and IVb are heard some more; the whole exposition ends with the passacaglia derivation IVa in the piano leading to a close in D major.

In some catalogues of Busoni's work the *Concertstück* is described as an Introduction and Allegro. Considered as a sonata, the allegro which now follows is, formally, the development section.

The tutti allegro theme (VI) has some rudimentary resemblances to both II and III, possibly incidental and just possibly the beginnings of a technique of cellular metamorphosis, soon to become completely natural to Busoni. (See Figure 8.7.) By the time of the *Concerto Op. XXXIX* and the sonatinas (see Chapters 7 and 6) such techniques were refined and used with the utmost flexibility.

Figure 8.7. By kind permission, Breitkopf & Haertel, Wiesbaden.

The cadenza that follows the allegro tutti opens with a contrapuntal passage, the subject of which is, perhaps, yet another derivative of II. (See Figure 8.8.) The countersubject in this passage is composed of falling 3rds in quavers, which give way to a diminution of motive I, which appears for the first time since the opening of the *Concertstück* in this rapid disguised form and then more openly in virtuoso alternate hand sequences. Yet another version of IV appears, which I have labelled IVd (see Figure 8.4). As IVc used the first two notes of IV, so IVd now uses the remaining three notes.[2]

Figure 8.8. By kind permission, Breitkopf & Haertel, Wiesbaden.

Theme I now appears in Brahmsian mold. (See Figure 8.9.) Throughout
the development, V has made spasmodic appearances: it is now a short,
nervous, upward-thrusting figure. Finally, at a vivace tempo, it makes a
full-blooded entry extending over a bar and a half. The allegro theme (VI) is
heard once more, and the development is at an end.

Figure 8.9. By kind permission, Breitkopf & Haertel, Wiesbaden.

Now follows a short bridge passage (meno mosso, sostenuto), leading
back to the recapitulation, concerning which Waterhouse was quoted
earlier on. The recapitulation does not confine itself to repeating material
from the exposition; some sections of the development are used as well.
Themes II and III are ignored from here on: the concentration is on various
guises of IV, I (the Brahmsian variant), and V (the vivace variant).
Although some sections reappear unchanged, the developmental process
continues. For instance, the coda (a più allegro), uses I in stretto,
rhythmically altered and inverted; logically, V is also heard in downward
double octaves. There is a very Brahmsian pedal point with languorous
suspensions resolving sequentially downward, starting with the flattened
7th, then a final D major double-octave rush. But even here, where one
would expect fireworks, the virtuoso element is held in very strict check.

The *Concertstück*, although firmly rooted in D major (the opening is in d minor), is nevertheless harmonically unstable in parts (see the first solo entry and the later cadenza), either modulating rapidly, or else using the semitone makeup of theme IV to create tonally ambiguous passages. It alters time signatures rather more frequently than would have been common at the time. Finally, the writing of long cadenza stretches for the piano, the tenuous scoring, and avoidance of piano and orchestra in combination merely to whip up a frenzy are all indicative of Busoni's next work for this combination: the *Indian Fantasy*.

INDIANISCHE FANTASIE FÜR KLAVIER MIT ORCHESTER
Op. 44   Leipzig   Breitkopf & Haertel   1915   Part. B.   2346
Composed in 1915   The two-piano reduction by Egon Petri appeared
in 1915   Leipzig   Breitkopf & Haertel   EB 4773

On 22 March 1910, during one of his American tours, Busoni wrote to his wife from Columbus:

ABOUT RED INDIANS

I spoke to a Red Indian woman. She told me how her brother (a talented violinist) came to New York to try to make his way. "But he could not associate his ideas with the question of daily bread." How much good it does one to hear of such sentiment in the United States!

Then she said that her tribe ought to have an instrument something like this: A hole should be dug in the earth and strings stretched all round the edges of it. I said (in the spirit of the Red Indians): An instrument like that ought to be called "the voice of the Earth." She was quite enthusiastic about this.

Miss Curtis was formerly my pupil in harmony. Do you remember her in New York? She has devoted the whole of this year to the study of Red Indian songs and has brought a beautiful book out. She gave it to me "In remembrance of the first performance of Turandot in New York." She is a fine, cultivated, rich girl. . . .

The Red Indians are the only cultured people who will have *nothing to do with money*, and who dress the most everyday things in beautiful words.

How different is a business man from Chicago compared with this! Roosevelt is called "Teddy" by him; and by the Red Indians "Our great white father."

We know that there exists a correspondence between Busoni and his ex-pupil the American ethnomusicologist Natalie Curtis (1875-1921), dating from these years; unfortunately, the letters are not yet in the public domain. Curtis wrote *The Indians' Book*, a standard text on Indian music. The two must have met during Busoni's American tours for Busoni mentioned her in letters to his wife, and explained how painstaking the explanations she gave him of red Indian music were. It is evident, too, that he felt some sort of obligation to his American pupil, for almost a year later he wrote (to his wife once again) about the possibility of composing something simple using the Indian motives: "I thought at first of putting one or two scenes into one act, with Red Indian ceremonies and actions (very simple) and to join them together with one of the usual 'eternal' stories; mother, son, bride, war, peace, without any subtleties. It requires the highest kind of subtlety to listen to music of that kind and to reproduce it correctly" (Kansas City, 9 March 1911).[3]

It was not until 1913, however, during summer—his customary months for composing—that Busoni finally commenced writing using Indian motives. He worked on the *Indian Fantasy* for piano and orchestra sporadically, and did not complete it until 1915. The first performance was a modest affair which took place in Zürich in January 1916 with the composer playing the solo part. The second performance, one that attracted considerable attention in the European press, took place in London in June 1920. This time Busoni conducted, and Egon Petri was the soloist. The work is dedicated to Natalie Curtis. Concurrently, he produced two other compositions as a result of his interest in the music of the red Indians: the *Indian Diary* Book I, for piano (see below) and the *Indian Diary* Book II for small orchestra, subtitled *Gesang vom Reigen der Geister* (Song of the Spirit's Dance). Both of these were composed in 1915 and published the following year.

Busoni agonized over both the title and the formal construction of the *Indian Fantasy*. Some of his working sketches have been preserved; on one page he writes grandiosely "Concerto Secondo—(Fantasia, Canzone e Finale su dei motivi delle Pelli-Rosse)—per Pianoforte con Orchestra." But a three-movement work must have seemed too ambitious: it would be difficult to title another work *Concerto* after the mammoth *Op. XXXIX*. So, on another page, he writes "Indianische Suite für Clavier mit Orchester," and below it: "I. Fantasie." A little later we find a more detailed layout, still adhering to a three-movement format. On yet another page, the title appears in English: "Indian Rhapsody: Begun April 2d, 1913." On this page, the opening of the piece, as it exists in its final form, is already apparent.

Vacillations about the title of the piece were symptoms of a deeper disturbance concerning the handling of the material at hand. Guido Guerrini is wrong when he states in his book that "it is a pity that the original themes as received by Busoni are not known, as this fact makes it impossible to discover Busoni's transformations."[4] We have, among the sketches, a full page of closely written material. The page is headed *Indianische Motivi,* and contains numerous red Indian melodies taken in their original form from Natalie Curtis's *The Indian Book*.[5] Busoni grouped and numbered these in various ways, and in the pages of sketches referred to this table of motives by adhering to his own Roman numbering. The page is dated 6 August 1913.

We know that Busoni had been hard at work during July of that year at the *Fantasy;* it seems as though, exasperated by the wealth of material at hand, he finally had to put it all down in more organized form.[6] Fourteen groups of themes (with subthemes) are listed. How does one, with such a multiplicity of melodies, make a coherent whole? After the discipline of the *Concerto Op. XXXIX*, and even the early *Concertstück*, in which large—or even enormous—structures are built up from strictly regulated, logical, economic means, the *Indian Fantasy* must have presented a formidable challenge. The implication of the title *Concerto* was therefore abandoned in favor of *Rhapsody* or *Suite* or, finally, *Fantasie*. The Lisztian usage of the term *Rhapsody* implies a one-movement piece in two sections; but Busoni was drawn to a three-movement concept from the start. The piano part, too, despite its difficulties, avoids Lisztian bravura and its extensions: Busoni had exhausted these in the *Concerto*. *Suite* must have been a temptation: it would be an obvious solution to handling the many themes. But Busoni chose *Fantasy*, originally the name of the first of the three movements.

Sketches for the formal construction include two layouts:

Introduzione; cadenza I

Introduzione cont.; cadenza II

Variazioni

Blue Bird

Finale

(*Blue Bird* is the name of one of the themes.)
    Or, more fully, on another page:

I   Introduzione
      Fantasia
      Introduzione ripresa
      Fantasia
      Variazioni
      Cadenza

II   (Lullaby)—Blue Bird

III   Finale guerresco

(Lists and numbers of themes to be used are also on this sketch.)
    Both sketches correspond closely to Busoni's final plan in which the separate movement form is abandoned, and the three main sections are linked via piano cadenzas:

I   Orchestral introduction
      Piano solo: fantasia
      Orchestra and piano together
      Piano solo: cadenza, leading into andante

II   Andante, quasi lento, again leading via rhapsodic passages into vivamente

III   Vivamente

On 23 July 1913, Busoni had written to his wife, from Berlin: "I have reached the critical moment in my piece where many ideas have to be forced into one form."[7]

But despite all of Busoni's formal attempts at organization, it was, in the long run, inevitable that the finished product would consist largely of a suite-like progression of themes, cleverly arranged into a larger format, with piano passages acting as buffers between the sections. That Busoni had realized the traps he had set himself is evident from a letter to his wife (Kansas City, 9 March 1911): "It is absurd to make a Symphony with Indian melodies, after the Leipzig model (like Dvorak), or a Meyerbeer-ish opera (like Herbert's recent one). It needs a great deal of study to get inside Indian life."[8] Thus, the possibilities before Busoni were: (1) to use the Indian themes as themes for a symphony or concerto; (2) to set the themes very simply in short, separate pieces as a suite; or (3) to absorb the Indian themes and rhythms to such an extent that, without disrupting their essential spirit, larger structures become possible and almost natural. The last possibility was out of the question for many reasons: time, inclination, a different culture. It was the sort of thing a Bartók or Kodály would do, but with their own heritage. The second possibility Busoni did consider, as we know from letters and sketches: his first thoughts were that a simple treatment was appropriate before more elaborate use of the material could be made. However, his deeply rooted sense of order must have rebelled against such an idea; perhaps the very obviousness of the solution turned him against it. Therefore, he tried approaching possibilities 1 and 2 conjointly; he presented the themes in succession, as he would have done in a suite, but at the same time wove them into a more elaborate, European mold in traditional concerto format. He had the sense, however, to preserve the melodic and/or rhythmic character of the originals to a large extent: the treatments are relatively simple. At the same time, Busoni altered some of the themes to suit himself. On 18 July 1913 he wrote to his wife from Berlin: "The Red Indian themes are not very pliable or productive. I shall have to put a good deal of my own into the Rhapsodie."[9] Actually, most of the Indian motives are presented in a form very close to their original. The *Blue Bird* melody, for example, which Guerrini finds to be "of a regular and classical form and almost Gregorian nature (God only knows as a result of what strange mental intrusion)" is quoted verbatim.[10] Of course, the piano-orchestral settings and harmonizations lend a distinctly European flavor to this melody.[11]

A predominant feature of the *Fantasy* is the solo-piano material in cadenza style: Busoni had already shown a predilection for large amounts of it in the *Concertstück*, and here he takes it to even greater length. Such writing is contrary to a real concerto concept, and indeed, in his own *Concerto*, Busoni does not indulge himself this way but treats the piano symphonically almost throughout. In the *Fantasy*, however, the cadenza is not only allowed full play, but is used as a structural device, either to link the three movements or, as in the first movement, to provide most of the musical substance. It is in the two long cadenza passages of the first movement that the truly fantastic character of the work is heard. Guerrini calls this a "dust-cloud" effect. (See Figure 8.10.) (In his sketches, Busoni asks for this to be played "nebbuloso, fuggitivo.")

Figure 8.10. By kind permission, Breitkopf & Haertel, Wiesbaden.

The wild, swirling chromatic figures, weaving round premonitions of the themes, are the earmarks of these cadenzas. Is this Busoni improvising? It is possible that we have here a more modern equivalent of the Liszt composition—first improvised, then written down. Whatever their origin, in these pages Busoni is writing in a totally new way for the piano: the difference between this and the *Concerto* of 11 years before is positively startling. These interim years were very productive ones for Busoni. Most of his prophetic and problematic pieces stem from this time—the sonatinas, the *Nocturne Symphonique*, and the *Berceuse élégiaque*. It was then that he wrote to Petri about his "aversion to scoring tutti passages," and the *Indian Fantasy* has almost none: the orchestra is used as an assembly of soloists, and the older coloristic doubling and mixing of colors are avoided more and more. Many harmonies are arrived at polyphonically. Guerrini says of this: "The *New aesthetics* pass from theory into practice."[12]

The middle section is more conventional: here the Indian melodies are given very simply at their first presentations, and the harmonies and strong tonal centres are late romantic in origin. As a contrast this is effective, and if one might object to stylistic intermixing (something which never bothered Busoni), the complications that characterize the mature Busoni are never excluded for any length of time, and the harmonic world of the first movement soon re-establishes itself in the second.

In the last movement we are plunged into the twentieth century of Bartók and Stravinsky, through relentless and often barbaric rhythms used in ostinato, with rhythmic phrases such as this one occurring:

(See theme XI in Busoni's list: this is the original rhythm.) The piano part retains its "fantastic" filigree nature: using the Lisztian technique of repeating a theme while the piano plays an elaboration of it in the high register of the instrument, coupled with a Mozartian economy of means. (See Figure 8.11). As compared to the nebbuloso of the first movement, this is forthright and insistent; and the writing for piano and orchestra is now amalgamated instead of sequentially contrasted. Nonetheless, much of the fuggitivo remains, since many of the virtuoso passages are played softly and lightly.

Figure 8.11. By kind permission, Breitkopf & Haertel, Wiesbaden.

I have it on Petri's authority that, in later years, Busoni regretted the way he had written the end of the *Fantasy*. The work should have ended right where the pianist comes rushing down, pianissimo, with semiquavers in alternate hands to the lowest C on the piano. It would have been both apt and witty, but Busoni the traditionalist won out, and nine absolutely superfluous bars are added, consisting of the reiteration of a C major chord, swelling to a rather ordinary tutti sforzando, in an attempt to complete the work by reference to the opening in C major. But the *Fantasy* does not depend on this type of key relationship, and traditional tonality is missing from much of the passage work. A plea therefore for future performers of the *Fantasy*: leave the bass drum on this last piano note, the low C, but omit the cymbal stroke: see page 59 of the full score.

The unity of the piece remains in question. By force of circumstance, Busoni had to write a major work using many motives, thus having to find other unifying principles than his usually very strict thematic ones. Did he succeed in his expedient of using the outward mold of a concerto form by apparently selecting motives so as to provide both contrast, where necessary, and cohesion, where the themes are similar in intervallic content? Is it reasonable to say that, just as one can arrive at non-tonal content by constant and quickly successive modulation, one can arrive at non-thematic content via a profusion of themes? If the latter, could it have been one of the paths that Busoni was exploring? I suggest below (see *Concertino* for piano and orchestra Op. 54) that this may have been the case, as the piano became for Busoni more and more a vehicle for pure fantasy.

The *Indian Fantasy* is an unaccountably neglected piece. It is easy to listen to and of very moderate length. Those who find the *Concerto Op. XXXIX* oppressive—and many do, for many reasons—may be interested in discovering the "new music" in this *Fantasy*, a blood brother to the early *Concertstück* and to the later *Concertino* Op. 54.

INDIANISCHES TAGEBUCH, ERSTES BUCH   VIER KLAVIERSTUDIEN ÜBER MOTIVE DER ROTHÄUTE AMERIKAS
Leipzig   Breitkopf & Haertel   1916   EB 4837   Composed in 1915

The *Indian Diary* Book I is so closely related to the *Indian Fantasy* that it is more appropriate to treat it here rather than in the chapters on solo piano works. The *Diary* consists of four separate pieces, three of which are taken directly from the *Indian Fantasy*.

A comparison of the pages of the *Diary* and *Fantasy* reveal the following: No. 1 is taken from pages 9-12 of the *Fantasy* (pages refer to the two-piano edition); this is the first solo cadenza. No. 3 is based on pages 24-28 and 39 of the *Fantasy*. No. 4: see pages 32-35, 36 and 40 of the *Fantasy*. Most of the new material in these three pieces occurs in the composition of suitable beginnings and endings; sometimes a reduction of the orchestral or piano-orchestral material is presented.

No. 2 is totally new, and is linked in spirit with the last movement of the *Fantasy*, as it presents an ostinato pattern with a melody above it built on an exotic scale. The piece is often quoted as an example of Bartók in Busoni, but it is almost all soft and fleeting. (See Figure 8.12.)

Figure 8.12. By kind permission, Breitkopf & Haertel, Wiesbaden.

The origin of the themes used in the *Diary* are as follows:

1. He-Hea Katzina Song—Hopi (p. 518)
2. Song of Victory—Cheyenne (p. 176)
3. Blue-Bird Song—Pima (p. 319)
3. Corn-Grinding Song—Lagunas (p. 466)
4. Passamquoddy Dance Song—Wabanakis (p. 25)
4. He-Hea Katzina Song—Hopi (p. 157)

(Translation of Indian title, name of tribe, and page numbers are from the second edition of Natalie Curtis's book.)

CONCERTINO FÜR PIANOFORTE UND ORCHESTER. II. ROMANZA E SCHERZOSO Op. 54 Leipzig Breitkopf & Haertel 1922 Part. B. 2639 Composed in 1921

This work is part of a trilogy of compositions, additionally comprising the clarinet *Concertino* Op. 48 and the flute *Divertimento* Op. 52; all three of these late works are distinguished by a Mozartian lightness, clarity, and conciseness, the result of Busoni's great love of the Viennese master toward the end of his life. There is some confusion over the correct title of the Op. 54. Some Breitkopf catalogues also describe the work simply as *Romanza e Scherzoso* Op. 54, and add in parentheses "Concertino II Satz."

But a note in small print in the score says that the Op. 54 can be played separately or following the *Concertstück* Op. 31a. Evidently Busoni thought of the composite work (that is, Op. 31a followed by Op. 54) as having the title *Concertino*. In some catalogues the *Concertstück* is described as "Concertino D dur für Klavier und Orchester, Op. 31. I.

Introduzione e Allegro." In fact a composite edition was issued by Breitkopf & Haertel in 1922, titled *Concertstück für Pianoforte mit Orchester, Op. 31ª. Concertino für Pianoforte und Orchester. II. Romanza e Scherzoso op. 54*, with a new catalogue number: Part. B. 2824.

The structure of the *Romanza e Scherzoso* is simple enough: an andantino sostenuto is followed without a break by an allegro molto. The allegro molto is briefly interrupted by a return of the andantino tempo.

A table of the themes shows that three main motives are used in the Romanza; these then appear in transformations in the rest of the composition. These transformations are labelled Ia, IIa, and IIIa. Theme III is curiously treated: in the *Concertino* context, this theme in its transformed version appears in the brief return of the Andantino, within the Allegro movement. In the *Perpetuum Mobile* (the solo piano piece drawn from Op. 54, see below) this transformation is heard in a fast tempo. This explains two appearances of IIIa on the table of motives. (See Figure 8.13.)

Figure 8.13. By kind permission, Breitkopf & Haertel, Wiesbaden.

As well as these strictly regulated themes, there is a motive or figure used generally in the piano part of the allegro. This semiquaver pattern often reshapes into diatonic and chromatic scale runs; quite basic arpeggio-like patterns also make their appearances in the allegro molto, so that much of the Op. 54 consists of athematic—very simple, but very fast—florid runs, arpeggios, and chromatic-diatonic weaving; most of these seem to derive from a Mozartian source but nevertheless are non-thematic. In the massive *Concerto*, as my analysis shows, all the piano patterns were directly evolved from basic sources. Here, continuing a trend already noted in the *Indian Fantasy*, much of the writing takes wing and defies any analysis. Dent talks of the Op. 54 as being like a "soap-bubble" due to its very light scoring, presto pace, and absolutely linear piano part: how is a soap bubble analyzed? Even the themes in the allegro make extremely shadowy appearances against the constant patter of semiquavers; their deliberate, four-square contours (take IIa as an example, in particular) are used mockingly, sometimes to the point of becoming grotesque (the opera *Arlecchino*, Op. 50, uses this technique, often quoting from other composers), but, before we can grasp their full import, they are gone. The *Scherzoso* itself whispers away at the end into the same insubstantiality. The parallel piano writing is made to serve this purpose: in the fast movement the left and right hand play mostly an octave apart, sometimes a 3rd or 6th. The absolutely diatonic character of the themes and runs are set off by unexpected shifts of key and juxtapositions in the allegro; the *Romanza* is more firmly rooted in f minor, though still unpredictable and refined: a true statement of the "Young Classicism."

As far as the concept of combining Op. 31a and Op. 54 goes, Busoni must have been concerned by the lack of performances given the *Concertstück* Op. 31a. Virtuosi generally like to sink their teeth into something a little longer than one-movement concert pieces which, except for those of Liszt, do not get overplayed. Busoni's scheme, therefore, was to attach a new piece to the *Concertstück*, creating a substantial composition for piano and orchestra. There was a lapse of 31 years between the two opuses, with a consequent development of style, taste, technique, and approach to keyboard writing. Most commentators categorically state that the works are too different to be ever played together successfully. Many differences do exist, starting with the dedications: one to Rubinstein, the second to Casella; that in itself implies an adherence to a new way of thinking. More significantly, the piano writing in the first is romantic, in the second neo-classic, and the harmonic fields of the two create quite differently colored worlds. The stylistic discrepancy is enormous, but Busoni was never particularly troubled by strange mixtures or by what might be called a counterpoint of styles.

One cannot help feeling that the idea of combining the two came to Busoni as an afterthought, either during the course of composing the Op. 54, or after it was done. Knowing something about Busoni's methods, my

first impulse was to compare the basic thematic cells of the two works, to try
to discover some common ground: there was none. This seems so unlike
Busoni, so illogical generally, that I ascribe the idea to pure expediency,
such as the performance of the *Op. XXXIX* without the last movement (see
Chapter 7). Possibly, Busoni was no longer troubled by such considerations, if what I have said about athematic writing is correct. In broad
general terms, there are some similarities: both consist of a slow introduction followed by an allegro, both have the allegro interrupted by a
return of tempo I, both end in a D tonality, both are roughly of the same
duration, and both have a tenuous approach to orchestration, with much
stress on polyphony. But it seems most unlikely that the Beethovian logic of
Op. 31a will often be joined with the fleeting apparitions of Op. 54.

PERPETUUM MOBILE (NACH DES CONCERTINO II   SATZE
OP. 54)   Leipzig   Breitkopf & Haertel   1922   EB 5225   part of
Klavierübung   book 5   1st ed.   Also published separately as
*Perpetuum Mobile (nach des Concertino II   Satze Op. 54) Für
Pianoforte zu zwei Händen   (Aus der Klavierübung funftem Teil)*
Leipzig   Breitkopf & Haertel   1922   EB 5231   Finally, it also
appeared in the second edition of the *Klavierübung*   book 9
Leipzig   Breitkopf & Haertel   1925

Just as the *Indian Diary* is closely related to the *Indian Fantasy*, so the
Perpetuum Mobile is very closely derived from the *Romanza e Scherzoso*,
though not through simple transferance.

The first few pages are certainly very close: *Perpetuum Mobile*, from its
beginning to page 8, is virtually identical to the Op. 54 from page 12 (the
start of the allegro molto) to the bottom of page 20 (though transfers from
piano and orchestra to piano solo involve certain changes and adjustments).
At that point in Op. 54, the music leads into the return of the andantino
tempo. But in the *Perpetuum*, Busoni obviously wanted to keep the relentlessly fast pace going after page 8, so the two, then, to some extent, part
ways.

Thus, the piano part of Op. 54, pages 21, 22, and 23, is responsible for
the next section of the *Perpetuum*: page 8, fifth system, first bar until page
9, first system, third bar. Busoni uses similar pianistic figures but, whereas
in Op. 54 they are confined to the same octaves, in the *Perpetuum* they are
distributed over the keyboard. It is in this area that a discrepancy in the use
of theme IIIa occurs: in Op. 54 (page 25) it appears in a tranquillo tempo. In
the *Perpetuum* page 8, first four lines, it continues in the presto tempo. The
two works come close again on page 9·of the *Perpetuum* and then return to
the allegro molto of Op. 54. Much of what follows, however, is again
different.

Where the Op. 54 solo part is comparatively simple to both read and play, the *Perpetuum Mobile* is extremely difficult. It requires a virtuoso pianist of the highest order to bring off the speed, clarity and lightness essential to this piece.

NOTES

1. J. C. G. Waterhouse, "Busoni: Visionary or Pasticheur?" *Proceedings of the Royal Musical Association*, 92d session, 1965-66.

2. Theme IV is very close to the B.A.C.H. theme beloved by Busoni in later years; the appearance of even a short quasi-Bachian contrapuntal passage in the *Concertstück* is significant. Busoni was of course writing fugues and double fugues at an extremely early age. (See Chapter 2.)

3. Busoni, *Letters to His Wife*, p. 186.

4. Guerrini, *Ferruccio Busoni*, p. 263.

5. Natalie Curtis, *The Indians' Book*, (New York/London, Harper & Bros., 1907; reprinted: New York, Dover, 1968). This book is considered to be a standard text in American ethnomusicology. The original themes, as received by Busoni, are easily accessible in this book. See note 6.

6. The following themes from Busoni's list are to be found in *The Indians' Book*:

    II: Blue-Bird Song—Pima (p. 319)
   III: Corn-People Gatzina Song—Acoma (p. 453)
    V: Victory Song—Winnebago (p. 289)
   VI: Warrior Song—Winnebago (p. 286)
  VII: Lullaby—Hopi (p. 498)
 VIII: Corn-Grinding Song—Laguna (p. 466)
  IX: Corn-Grinding Song—Laguna (p. 464)
    X: Passamquoddy Dance-Song—Wabanaki (p. 25)
  XI: Hand-Game Song—Cheyenne (p. 187)
  XII: (a) Corn-People Gatzina Song—Acoma (p. 451)
            (b) Korosta Katzina Song—Hopi (p. 514)
            (c) As in (b) (p. 515, with triplet variant used by Busoni in the *Fantasy*)
 XIII: He-Hea Katzina Song—Hopi (p. 517); p. 518, later in the same song, is used in the opening Cadenza, and is the basis of the first piece of the *Indian Diary*
 XIV: Two motives written on staves ruled by Busoni at the bottom of the page. Motive on right-hand side is Cradle Song—Kwakiutl (p. 307). Motive on left-hand side is Flute Song—Hopi (p. 532).

Themes I and IV are apparently not in the book, but we know from Natalie Curtis that not all the songs she collected were included in the book: for example, the Hopi Indians provided her with 60 songs of which only 9 are included in *The Indians' Book*. Perhaps these two motives (which Busoni used in the *Fantasy*) are to be found in the unpublished papers of Natalie Curtis. Miss Curtis, who discussed the material with Busoni personally, no doubt showed him some other material she had, not included in the book. We know from Busoni's treatments of the identified themes that he followed them very faithfully, in most cases not even transposing them.

7. Busoni, *Letters to His Wife*, p. 230.

8. Busoni, *Letters to His Wife*, p. 186.

9. Busoni, *Letters to His Wife*, p. 228.

10. Guerrini, *Ferruccio Busoni*, p. 266.

11. Busoni described this episode in the *Fantasy* as a lyric interlude, "an Indian maiden washing her hair at the river"; the theme immediately following the Blue Bird (see No. 27 in the score) he half seriously, half in jest, put forward as a candidate for a true American national anthem.

12. Guerrini, *Ferruccio Busoni*, p. 264.

9

The Fantasia Contrappuntistica

There can be no question that Busoni had one of the most prodigious intellects in the history of European art. In the faculty of sheer intellectual grasp he excelled other composers with the exception of Mozart. At an age when most composers are gingerly making their first tentative jottings, he had a complete and exhaustive command of traditional technique, had realized the inadequacy of such a technique for a contemporary composer, and was already formulating the ideas on which his later and characteristic work was to be based. He was perfectly conscious of his powers: he paid homage to the past by embracing it in the gigantic sweep of his intellect and he saluted the future through his consciousness of his own moral and intellectual superiority—a consciousness that was compatible with true dignity and humility.

That as a man Busoni was a colossus, one of the very greatest personalities of our time, cannot, after evidence of all the intelligent and cultivated men who knew him, be seriously questioned. By musicians and artists, by intimate friends and acquaintances, his personality has repeatedly been described as "god-like." The electric atmosphere that his mere presence on the concert platform produced was merely one manifestation of that tremendous and indefinable energy which emanated from him in all his activities. . . . He . . . hardly even realized that his destiny was "tragic." As van Dieren remarks, it was left to his biographers to discover that for him. . . .

Wilfred Mellers

The last decade of J. S. Bach's working life (c. 1739-1949) had included the assembly and composition of a number of works which represented contemporary and former techniques and applications in music. One of several projects incomplete at Bach's death, the work later published by C. P. E. Bach as *The Art of Fugue* (1752), was to have demonstrated contrasted applications of fugal techniques. The last fugue of the publication, an extended example that is thought by many to have been planned to conclude the collection, had already given rise to much speculation before Busoni's time. It is incomplete and had been published in a form that only provides certain clues regarding the substantial materials that Bach had intended to add before its composition was interrupted, never to be resumed.

In 1880, Gustav Nottebohm (1817-1882) demonstrated the contrapuntal possibilities of the unfinished fugue with the theme of *The Art of Fugue*. The subsequent controversies need not concern us here, interesting as they are, for by Busoni's youth the theory had already been postulated that, had Bach lived, he would have completed his fugue by combining the three fugue subjects with the main subject of *The Art of Fugue*, thus creating a quadruple fugue. It is hard to believe that a brain such as Bach's would have failed to see the possibilities of such combination or rather that the three subjects would have been composed at all without such counterpoint in mind. This is made all the more plausible from the trend of the fragment we have—Bach had in fact gotten as far as combining the three fugue subjects.

Donald Tovey has supplied a brilliant solution to the final fugue in strict style; there have been many other editions scored for various instruments, for no definitive scoring has come down to us from Bach, although most of the work lies well on the keyboard or on two keyboards.

Busoni's approach, like Tovey's, was prompted by the desire to solve the problem of the final fugue. Like Tovey, he was a scholar in the sense that he knew all the techniques and used them; unlike Tovey, he was not an academic. To reconstruct a Bach fugue did not interest him in the slightest. In a sense, Bach was dead: no artistic purpose was served by writing an ending as Bach may have done; but looking at it from Busoni's point of view, Bach was also very much alive. Busoni believed that the Bachian technique was not exhausted, but could serve as a beacon for the music of the future, and the notion of an extended fugal work in which the materials are first exposed then combined with increasing intensity naturally appealed to his personal philosophy., In his idea of the deliberate juxtaposition of strongly contrasting period styles to forge a single work and of the imposition of his will over the music of other composers Busoni was ahead of his time. Although such procedures had been used before him, none was as daring or as extreme as his. Subsequently, his own efforts in this field were outstripped by other, more extreme composers and tendencies.

It is from this vantage point that we must survey the vast landscape of the *Fantasia Contrappuntistica* in all its versions.

The work is written for either one or two pianos, since Busoni functioned best at the keyboard and found it a matter of convenience, for the original score is set out more or less in keyboard terms. But, like Bach's *The Art of Fugue*, Busoni's *Fantasia Contrappuntistica* is an abstract piece—the scoring is of secondary importance. This is not to say that it is a cold, mathematical essay in musical logic; it presents an intensity of emotion equal to and often surpassing the more obviously romantic works of Busoni.

It is interesting to note that the work has been arranged for organ by Wilhelm Middelschulte (Breitkopf & Haertel, EB 3612) and also by Helmut Bornefeld (Breitkopf & Haertel, EB 6342); and Frederick Stock, the Chicago conductor was allowed by Busoni to arrange one of the early versions for orchestra. There have been other arrangements. The work does not suffer by such treatment—its nature is not essentially pianistic, even in Busoni's layout. The piano setting is really a form of open score, an invitation for orchestral treatment. It amazes me that a brilliant orchestral form of the *Fantasia Contrappuntistica* has not yet appeared and taken its rightful place in the repertoire. Taking all this into consideration, attacks on Busoni for tampering with *The Art of Fugue* are misguided; the composer makes it clear that he has no pretensions to completing the Bach work—he uses a fragment of Bach and writes a work of his own around it, and even the fragment is altered. Busoni felt no obligation to maintain the Bach style. Far from any discrepancy, the integration of Bach and Busoni is, in my opinion, complete and masterful.

In dealing with Bach, Busoni sometimes takes a fragment and builds a composition upon it; sometimes he transcribes Bach for the modern piano, and sometimes transcribes freely, introducing more modern chromatic harmony, and the major-minor ambiguities that are so prevalent in his own compositions. The *Fantasia Contrappuntistica* partakes of all these approaches and takes three elements from Bach: (1) The melody of the chorale prelude *Allein Gott in Der Höh' sei Ehr'*; (2) The main theme of *Contrapunctus I* of *The Art of Fugue* (BWV 1080); and (3) Extended fugal materials from the unfinished *Contrapunctus XIX* (BWV 1080/19).

It is only (3) above that can be reasonably called a transcription, but even here, little changes designed to integrate the work more with the pure Busoni which surrounds it, are constantly introduced. The first and second are really simply thematic materials. Number (1) is used as a theme for variations, and (2) appears at the end of the work in contrapuntal combination with the other themes.

The five published Busoni works in chronological order that constitute, in whole or in part, variants of the *Fantasia Contrappuntistica* are (1) *"Meine Seele Bangt und Hofft zu Dir;"* (2) *Grosse Fuge;* (3) *Fantasia Contrappuntistica—Preludio al Corale;* (4) *Chorale-Vorspiel und Fuge;* and (5) *Fantasia Contrappuntistica—Choral-Variationen.*

The chorale used in versions (1), (3), (4), and (5) as a theme for variations is one and the same, despite varying titles. In the Bach Gessellschaft edition, the melody is identified as *Allein Gott in der Höh' sei Ehr'*, and all of Bach's settings may be located under this title. I have been unable to account for Busoni's subtitle of the *Elegy* No. 3: the words, as far as I have been able to ascertain, do not appear anywhere in the verses to these chorale melodies, and there is no other chorale melody by this name. The words may have been Busoni's own. Bach himself set the melody at least ten times for organ, as well as producing contrasted versions in vocal works both preserved and unpreserved: the melody lays claim to being Bach's most frequently treated theme.

"MEINE SEELE BANGT UND HOFFT ZU DIR"
CHORALVORSPIEL No. 3 of *Elegien   6 neue Klavierstücke*
Leipzig   Breitkopf & Haertel   1908   Klav. Bibl. 26042-26046
Also No. 3 of *Elegien 7 neue Klavierstücke* Leipzig
Breitkopf & Haertel   1908-1909 EB 5214   Composed in 1907.

This came into being as a set of variations on a Bach chorale, in Busoni's new style soon after the turn of the century. The chorale melody is first heard in a sort of skeleton form. Did Busoni get the idea for this from Bach's fughetta on the same chorale melody? (See Figure 9.1.) At any rate, there is no reference to Bach as the piece progresses, from a statement of the chorale (right hand in A major, left hand E flat pedal, plus inner part) in polytonal setting, through a wild middle section, finally to a calmer third section, with the strange diffuse organ sound and its typical attendant Busonian ambiguities. (See Figure 9.2.) The variations are unnumbered and blend into each other in fantasia style.

We know that, when the *Elegy* was written, Busoni had no idea of its eventual incorporation into the *Fantasia Contrappuntistica*. Oddly enough, most of the *Elegies* came from large works: the *Elegy* No. 3 was destined to do the same, but in chronologically inverse order.

GROSSE FUGE   KONTRAPUNKTISCHE FANTASIE ÜBER JOH.
SEB. BACH'S LETZTES UNVOLLENDETES WERK FÜR KLAVIER
AUSGEFÜHRT   New York   G. Schirmer   1910   Limited edition
Composed in 1910

The *Fantasia Contrappuntistica* in its first reasonably complete version was written during an exhausting concert tour of the United States early in 1910. That year in particular was an amazingly productive one—Busoni managed, despite concerts, to work simultaneously on a number of major projects (including *Die Brautwahl* and the *Indian Fantasy*) and contributed essays to periodicals as well.

A first inkling of a new idea stirring in Busoni's fertile imagination is a letter to his wife from Chicago dated 15 January 1910: "Middelschulte is going to bring me an essay by Bernard Ziehn today, on Bach's uncompleted fugue."[1] Bernard Ziehn[2] and his pupil, Wilhelm Middelschulte, were two German musicians who had settled in Chicago and were mostly devoted to

Figure 9.1. By kind permission, Breitkopf & Haertel, Wiesbaden.

Figure 9.2. By kind permission, Breitkopf & Haertel, Wiesbaden.

the teaching of counterpoint; the "Bach uncompleted fugue," was of course the last section of *The Art of Fugue*. Busoni must have been enormously interested, for we next read: "I am studying counterpoint again, for which Chicago has stimulated me very much" (Minneapolis, 20 January 1910).[3] It was in his nature to be the perpetual student and be quite happy to "study" counterpoint after having mastered it many years before.

By 19 February, the composition seems well under way: "I have altered the plan for the Fantasia Contrappuntistica (on Bach's last and greatest work). I shall not begin with a Fantasy, but bring into the fugue itself everything in the nature of fantasy. It will sound like something between a composition by C. Franck and the Hammerclavier sonata, with an individual nuance" (Cincinnati, 19 February 1910).[4] Three days later he wrote from Louisville: "The fugue is becoming monumental." Finally, after what was creatively a tense and tiring month: "I intended finishing this monster fugue in February, and I *have succeeded*, but I shall never undertake such a thing again!" (New Orleans, 1 March 1910).[5] Busoni did not know then that he would continue to revise this work until his death, although he was right as far as not "undertaking such a thing again": the *Fantasia*, or as it was known at this primary stage, the *Grosse Fuge*, was the culmination of his study of Bach and the last major opus of its kind that he tackled—henceforth the polyphony would become thinner, less tonal, more liberated than in the *Grosse Fuge*. In his next letter about this work, Busoni writes: "The fugue is the most important of my piano works (with the exception of the concerto). . . . You see the plan is unusual. Every note 'sits'" (Atlanta, 3 March 1910).[6] In the following letter Busoni writes: "I am still intoxicated by the 'great fugue'" (Toledo, 5 March 1910).[7] This blow-by-blow account of the battle with *The Art of Fugue* is still exciting to read in the full context of the letters. If one remembers the travelling conditions in those days, and looks at the places and dates of the various letters and the programs Busoni played, a sense of astonishment at the man's stamina and concentration must be the main reaction.

In his letter of 3 March 1910 Busoni lists the structure of the work as follows: "First Fugue, Second Fugue, Third Fugue and the working out of the three, Intermezzo, 1st Variation, 2nd Variation, 3rd Variation, Cadenza, Fourth Fugue, Coda."[8]

Fuga I—this is a transcription for two hands from Bach's score. Four introductory bars are added before the fugue commences. Bach's bars 87, 88, and 89 are omitted. Changes and deviations from Bach consist of (1) transcriptional doublings in octaves and sometimes transpositions into different octaves; (2) some stylistic trills; and (3) chromatic alteration of the parts. This last is the most serious and significant of the three. Some subtle false relations are introduced. (See Figure 9.3.) The reasons for these are to prepare the ear for the transition from Bach to Busoni, with its wild chromaticisms.

Figure 9.3. By kind permission, Breitkopf & Haertel, Wiesbaden.

Fuga II—Bach's bars 174-80 are omitted, and three bars of Busoni's inserted instead.[9] At bar 180 Busoni brings in the bass in octaves, poco forte; the compression of six bars into three was probably felt necessary due to the fairly large surge of crescendo needed as a lead up to this moment. The other procedures in this fugue are similar to those employed in Fuga I.

Fuga III—Bach wrote only 47 bars of this fugue, but since his intentions were obviously to exploit the combinations of the three subjects to the full, Busoni continues this task. That portion of Fuga III that takes us to the point where Bach left off is now two bars longer, but Busoni also makes quite significant changes toward the end of the Bach fragment. The Fuga is worked in masterly fashion and at great length—this is the most complex movement of the *Grosse Fuge*. Naturally, Busoni writes his own brand of counterpoint. (See Figure 9.4.)

Figure 9.4. By kind permission, Breitkopf & Haertel, Wiesbaden.

Intermezzo—marked *misticamente* and later *visionario*—a quiet episode after the cumulative climax of the long fugue. This is based on the B.A.C.H. motive. (See Figure 9.5.)

Figure 9.5. By kind permission, Breitkopf & Haertel, Wiesbaden.

The three variations follow. It must be made clear that Variation I does not necessarily relate to Fuga I, Variation II to Fuga II, and so forth. By now, all three themes are known to the listener, so that each variation uses all three themes in various ways. However, it would be true to say that Variation I uses predominantly theme I, and is a tranquil variation, and so does roughly correspond to Fuga I; but we hear the other two themes in this variation as well. Variation II is mostly on the B.A.C.H. theme, and Variation III mostly on the second theme. By now the language is fantastic, and as far from Bach's stability as one could imagine. (See Figure 9.6.) Wilfrid Mellers quotes this same passage and says of it: ". . . The separation of the lines on, as it were, different planes of tonality creates an effect strangely disembodied, suggesting a deliberate withdrawal from experience."[10]

Figure 9.6. By kind permission, Breitkopf & Haertel, Wiesbaden.

The third variation ends on an enormous moment of climax—the Cadenza that follows is meant to act as a foil to this, much as the Intermezzo did after the third fugue. But, unlike the Intermezzo, the Cadenza begins with a considerable display of energy and only gradually manages to sink to the *molto sommessamente* near its end—the accumulated energy had been too great. Hints of what is to follow also occur in the Cadenza: against the B.A.C.H. theme, we hear, softly, the main theme of *The Art of Fugue*.

Fuga IV—Busoni acknowledges Bernhard Ziehn in a footnote as having shown him the possibility of combining the three fugue subjects with *The Art of Fugue* theme. The fugue works up to another big climax and subsides over an ostinato B.A.C.H. bass, which leads to the Stretta.

Stretta—uses the B.A.C.H. theme in a rhythmic version found in the Bach work. (See Figure 9.7.) This rises to a final fury, and the subject of the first fugue is stated maestoso in massive chords to end the *Grosse Fuge*.[11]

Figure 9.7. By kind permission, Breitkopf & Haertel, Wiesbaden.

FANTASIA CONTRAPPUNTISTICA   PRELUDIO AL
CORALE "GLORIA AL SIGNORE NEI CIELI" E FUGA A
QUATTRO OBBLIGATI SOPRA UN FRAMMENTO DI BACH
COMPILATA PER IL PIANOFORTE   (EDIZIONE
DEFINITIVA)   Leipzig   Breitkopf & Haertel   1910
EB 5491   Composed in 1910   Also in volume 4 of the Bach-
Busoni Ausgabe   Breitkopf & Haertel   1916   wherein the
title is simply *Fantasia contrappuntistica*

Busoni did not let the *Grosse Fuge* rest very long. In another letter, only
six weeks after completing the work, we read: "I had a beautiful idea on the
train yesterday. I thought I would arrange the great fugue for orchestra.
Transcribe the choral prelude (Meine Seele bangt und hofft zu dir) as an
Introduction to it and let it occur as a reminiscence just before the Stretta in
the fugue" (Denver, 18 April 1910).[12]

By June of the same year this idea had become reality, but for solo piano,
not orchestra. This is generally known as the definitive version, although
there were two further ones to be published.

The first main section of the *Fantasia Contrappuntistica* (the first version
to actually use this name) is subtitled *Preludio corale* and consists of
variations on the chorale melody *Allein Gott.* . . . Of the 11 pages
comprising this section, 8 are taken straight from the *Elegy* No. 3 with
almost no change at all, approximately 2 pages are the same harmonically
but have been enormously improved in effectiveness. The opening is now as
given in Figure 9.8 and later as in Figure 9.9.[13] Only on one page, which in
any case forms the introduction to fuga I, is there new material.

Fuga I is substantially the same as in the *Grosse Fuge*. The additions to
Bach are more complex, and some bars are actually moving in five parts.
The extra part is, as before, designed to introduce the B.A.C.H. theme,
almost a form of subliminal suggestion before this theme is due to make its
formal appearance. (See Figure 9.10.)

Fuga II. As well as the cuts in the *Grosse Fuge*, one more cut has been
introduced. Bars 163-66 of the Bach have been deleted. Since the chorale
melody has now become part of the work, Busoni introduces it as in Figure
9.11 and continues using it thus in other comparable moments of this fugue.

Fuga III is again substantially the same. The piano writing has been
doubled in octaves in some entries; there is one memorable and unplayable
octave trill in the left hand.[14]

The Intermezzo is the same. So are the three variations and the Cadenza.

The Fuga IV (which is preceded by an extra bar in the tempo of the
fugue), Busoni does something unfortunate: he cuts 42 bars out of the main
body of the fugue, and inserts them into an addendum, to be played ad lib.
Obviously, right through the years of working on the *Fantasia
Contrappuntistica*, Busoni, demonstrably uncompromising, was concerned
by the length of the work. This is curious, since the *Hammerclavier* sonata

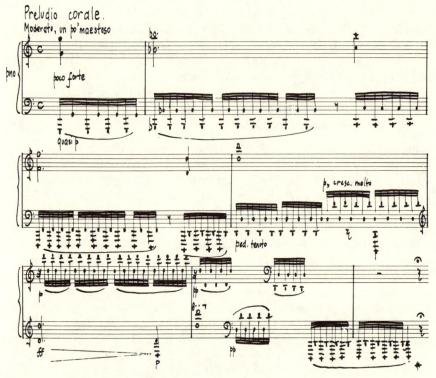

Figure 9.8. By kind permission, Breitkopf & Haertel, Wiesbaden.

and a few other things in his repertoire were longer than the *Fantasia*, which never takes over half an hour in any of the versions; on the other hand none of these works—except the *Goldberg Variations*—were exclusively polyphonic, and Busoni did suggest a cut version of the *Goldberg Variations* in his edition of the work. (See Chapter 11.) We shall see later how Fuga I is cut in a yet later version. But this abridgement of Fuga IV, to return to the 1910 version, is particularly unfortunate; tucked away at the back of the volume, it is never played. Even Egon Petri omitted it in performance and recording. Busoni must have curtailed it because of the introduction of the recapitulation of the Corale between the end of Fuga IV and the Stretta, but musically it is a mistake: the proportions of the work are upset, the quadruple fugue loses in stature by being over so quickly, and the enormous climax in the fugue also misfires. The fugue should have been published complete and the cut suggested within the main text.

After the truncated fugue, over a continuation of the ostinato B.A.C.H. bass, the Corale makes a memorable return. Sorabji says of this moment: "At the climax of the entire composition where all the chords are gathered together and intertwined, such an 'elevating excitement of the soul' is

Figure 9.9. By kind permission, Breitkopf & Haertel, Wiesbaden.

Figure 9.10. By kind permission, Breitkopf & Haertel, Wiesbaden.

Figure 9.11. By kind permission, Breitkopf & Haertel, Wiesbaden.

produced by the sheer overwhelming mastery of the thing as is equalled in but very little existing music."[15]

The Stretta is now linked to this Corale via an extra four bars acting as introduction. The end of the *Fantasia* is pianistically amplified, when compared to the *Grosse Fuge*: another interesting example of transmutation, so well known to the student of Liszt and his variants of the same piece. (See Figure 9.12.)

Figure 9.12. By kind permission, Breitkopf & Haertel, Wiesbaden.

CHORAL-VORSPIEL UND FUGE ÜBER EIN BACHSCHES FRAGMENT (DER "FANTASIA CONTRAPPUNTISTICA" KLEINE AUSGABE)   PRELUDIO AL CORALE E FUGA SOPRA UN FRAMMENTO DI BACH (EDIZIONE MINORE DELLA "FANTASIA CONTRAPPUNTISTICA")   Leipzig Breitkopf & Haertel   1912   VA 3829   Composed in 1912 Also in volume 4 of the Bach-Busoni Ausgabe   Breitkopf & Haertel   1916

In the preface to this edition Busoni writes:

The Editor has added to the uncompleted fugue a conclusion representing some combinations with the there given subject, the addition of the fourth (chief) subject, and the completion of the form. Then follows a further addition in the shape of the more ample and free treatment of the whole thematic contents. A still more extensive, and final version was published as an independent work by Messrs Breitkopf & Härtel under the title of "Fantasia Contrappuntistica." The present smaller Edition is intended more for pianoforte study than for performance at concerts.

Elsewhere, in a letter to his wife, concerning this work, we read: "I am in a pleasant mood, although the weather has become grey, for (this is the principal reason) today I have finished another small work which is good: 'Der Fantasia contrappuntistica Kleine Ausgabe' to which, as introduction, I wrote three Variations over the same choral ('Allein Gott in der Höh' sei Ehr'), which are quite new . . ." (Berlin, 20 July 1912).[16]

The form of this *kleine* version is relatively simple: three variations on the chorale; Fugues I, II, and III; and Fugue IV leading into Stretta.

The variations are the most interesting aspect of this version. They represent new material which will later be grafted on to the already existing variations in the 1910 version. In the first variation the chorale melody is heard in reasonably pure form; another, fast variation has some affinity with the Bach chorale prelude *Allein Gott . . .* in the Kirnberger Collection. (See Figure 9.13.) Busoni also provides two endings to the variations: one to

Figure 9.13. By kind permission, Breitkopf & Haertel, Wiesbaden.

be played with the fugue, one if the variations are done on their own. This is a sort of thinking out aloud, for the version, by Busoni's own statement, is hardly intended for performance. He must have known already then that he was not quite finished with the *Fantasia*.

Fugues I, II, and III are interesting from one point of view only: all cuts from Bach have been restored. (Fuga I has a *suggested* cut of 18 bars: even in this short version of the *Fantasia*, Busoni was bothered by this fugue.) All his additions have been deleted. This is a simple and straightforward transcription from Bach, faithful to the original in every detail: there is no attempt at all to make it pianistic, as it truly is a study score. Fuga III is carefully marked at the moment where Bach ends and Busoni begins. This fugue is considerably shorter than in previous versions. Fuga IV begins in d minor, in conformity with the other three fugues; two cuts are present, the whole is very thin and essential. There is no chorale re-capitulation. The stretto is a skeleton of what it was and is simple to play.

Busoni has published here his basic solutions to the fugues. There are no octave doublings, very few expression signs; the Bach originals could have been transcribed by any competent musician—at any rate they lie well for the hands. The ending of Fuga III, the whole of Fuga IV, and the Stretta are only interesting as originals of the final version. Except for the new variations on the chorale, which are most exciting, this version of the *Fantasia* is not really valuable. It should be mentioned here that one of the variations introduces into its texture the theme B.A.C.H.; this is turned to very good use in the two-piano version, as a further bond between the chorale variations and the fugues.

FANTASIA CONTRAPPUNTISTICA CHORAL-VARIATIONEN ÜBER "EHRE SEI GOTT IN DER HÖHE" GEFOLGT VON EINER QUADRUPEL-FUGE ÜBER EIN BACHSCHES FRAGMENT FÜR ZWEI KLAVIERE Leipzig Breitkopf & Haertel 1922 EB 5196

Petri often used to say that Busoni could have been a great architect. It was a subject that interested him intensely; we can easily confirm this from letters written while on tour; in his own playing and writing the approach was predominantly architectural.[17] "Sculptural" was a word often applied to his performances.

It should come as no surprise, therefore, to find an architectural sketch graphically depicting the structure of the *Fantasia Contrappuntistica*; this sketch was actually published in the two-piano version.[18]

The proportions are symmetrical for visual reasons: in actual fact, various inequalities exist—(1) is longer than (6), (7), and (8) combined; (2), (3), and (4) are each longer than (6), (7), and (8) and are unequal among themselves; and (10) is not as long as it may appear from this sketch. I stress

Plan des Werkes

A. Analytischer:

> 1. Choral - Variationen (Einleitung — Choral und Variationen — Übergang)
> 2. Fuga I. 3. Fuga II. 4. Fuga III. 5. Intermezzo. 6. Variatio I. 7. Variatio II.
> 8. Variatio III. 9. Cadenza. 10. Fuga IV. 11. Corale. 12. Stretta.

B. Architektonischer:

E. B. 5196

Reprinted by kind permission, Breitkopf & Haertel, Wiesbaden.

the obvious here, because the length of (10) will come under discussion later on, and because the sketch may give a reader unacquainted with the work the idea that the *Fantasia* is rigidly regulated in its proportions. In practice, as the work gathers momentum, the sections tend to get shorter.

The two-piano version has great advantages over the other versions but has some bad faults. Let us take the movements in turn. The chorale variations are greatly improved and completely reworked. Busoni now combines the variations from the 1910 and 1912 versions to form a whole. Some parts are completely new, some gain by the added richness and clarity of two pianos. (See Figure 9.14.)

Fuga I—After adding to the introductory movement, Busoni must have been plagued again by the resultant length of the work.[19] Therefore he decided to cut Fuga I, which, as we have seen, troubled him right from the

Figure 9.14. By kind permission, Breitkopf & Haertel, Wiesbaden.

start. This time, however, the cut is ruthless—the Bach fugue is reduced to about half its original length. It could be legitimately claimed that the cut was made because this fugue is more difficult to arrange and least successful on two pianos; but there are later cuts, just as ruthless, which cannot be explained in the same way.

Fuga II—Broadly, the same as in the 1910 version. Much of the harmony is chromaticized and modulations more assertively modernistic than Bach would have used are introduced, like the sudden slip of key in Figure 9.15.

Fuga III—About 15 bars have been cut, if compared to the *Grosse Fuge* and the 1910 version. A codetta, quoting part of the opening, rounds this off more neatly than in the other versions.

Intermezzo, Variations I, II, and III, and Cadenza—no musical changes.

Fuga IV—Cut rather savagely; my objections here are even more vociferous than to the cuts in Fuga I and to the similar cut in the 1910 version. The two-piano version is more massive—the buildup and length of Fuga IV are therefore vitally important. Busoni, once more in the interests of brevity, makes a bad judgment here. This time, there is no Addendum in the back to remedy the fault. The chorale re-capitulation and Stretta gain much in the new version; the last few bars also are more effective.

Figure 9.15. By kind permission, Breitkopf & Haertel, Wiesbaden.

To underline the obvious, polyphony can be much cleaner on two pianos than one, and therefore the fugues are heard with more clarity in this version: what a pity then, that they are so curtailed.

In overall length, the two-piano version and the 1910 version are about the same, which is what Busoni must have aimed at. The two-piano version introduces much new material and invention throughout; the sound of the two instruments clashing and blending is enormously impressive: even with its faults, the *Fantasia* in this version makes great music. It is a totally new sound for this combination, and there is nothing quite like it in the literature, until the Bartók *Sonata for Two Pianos and Percussion*, which it antedates by some 15 years.

Toward a Complete Edition of the *Fantasia Contrappuntistica*

Had Busoni lived longer, he would no doubt have explored the possibilities of the *Fantasia* still further. The two-piano version brought him closer to an orchestral version, something he had always dreamt of but never found time to do. Petri told me that after writing the two-piano version, Busoni wanted to re-write the solo version in the light of what he had in the meantime discovered and score the work for orchestra. I would go a step further and suggest that the two-piano version also needs a little re-writing; the scoring could then be made from such a two-piano version.

Solo Piano Version. The following steps should be undertaken: (a) the new variations of the 1912 version have to be added to the 1910 version. This can be done most efficiently by taking the 1912 variations and introducing them after the low tremolo on page 5, last line—the graft is unnoticeable (see Figure 9.16). The end of this segment needs a little re-

Figure 9.16. By kind permission, Breitkopf & Haertel, Wiesbaden.

writing to bring it back to the key of G major. Petri and I devised a Busoni-like modulation (see Figure 9.17); (b) the Addendum to Fuga IV must be incorporated into the main text; and (c) the ending should be adopted from the 1922 version. (See Figure 9.18.) Apart from this, the last bar on page 10 and the first line on page 11 should, in the light of later versions, be changed from G major to g sharp minor; and the side slip of key quoted earlier could be introduced into Fuga II, although this is not really essential. This would then constitute a complete and definitive version of the *Fantasia*. The variations would differ from the 1922 version in order of appearance, but would be perfectly satisfactory; other differences are inevitable because of the varying medium.

Two-Piano Version. This is the more effective version, and really needs restoration of the severely abbreviated fugues only: (a) restore Fuga I as found in the 1910 version; (b) restore cut in Fuga III; and (c) restore cut in Fuga IV. The restoration needs arranging for two pianos, and there is some guesswork involved here, but there are many Busoni two-piano models available.

Orchestral Version. In almost all versions of the *Fantasia*, Busoni suggests instruments in the performing indications to the pianist. He obviously had orchestral colors in mind. The two-piano version should be used as the basis for an orchestral version.[20]

It seems to me that critics have not been astute enough in pointing out the chief fault of the *Fantasia Contrappuntistica*—its demands on the listener. After all, we have shown that the old quibble about stylistic discrepancies is

Figure 9.17. By kind permission, Breitkopf & Haertel, Wiesbaden.

Figure 9.18. By kind permission, Breitkopf & Haertel, Wiesbaden.

	CHORALE VARIATIONS	FUGUE I	FUGUE II	FUGUE III	INTERMEZZO
ELEGY	✓	-	-	-	-
GROSSE FUGE	-	Bach bars 87-89 omitted	Bach 174-180 compressed into three bars	2 bars added to Bach fragment	✓
1910 VERSION	Slight augmentation & reworking of Elegy	As above; Some textural thickening B-A-C-H theme introduced	As above; Bach 163-166 also cut. Chorale theme introduced	As above	✓ As above
1912 VERSION	New set of variations	No cuts at all. (Suggested 18 bars cut) Original BACH	No cuts. Original BACH	Original clearly separated from BUSONI- Shorter Fugue than above	-
1922 VERSION	1910 & 1912 versions integrated	Bach fugue cut to about ½ its original length	As in 1910 version. Some chromaticisms introduced	About 15 bars cut from 1910 & grosse fuge codetta introduced	Musically substantially As above (1910)
NEW SOLO VERSION	Add 1912 variations as suggested in text. See also pages 10-11 mentioned in text	As in 1910	As in 1910	As in 1910	✓ As in (1910)
NEW 2 PIANO VERSION	As in 1922	Restore fugue as in 1910	As in 1922	Restore fugue as in 1910	✓ As in 1922
ORCHESTRAL VERSION	As in 1922	As in 1910	As in 1922	As in 1910	As in 1922

(IT IS INTERESTING TO OBSERVE THAT THE INTERMEZZO, VARS I,
ARE THE SAME IN ALL VERSIONS)

158

FANTASIA CONTRAPPUNTISTICA

VARIATION I	VARIATION II	VARIATION III	CADENZA	FUGUE IV	CHORALE	STRETTO
-	-	-	-	-	-	-
✓	✓	✓	✓	✓	-	✓
✓ As above	✓ As above	✓ As above	✓ As above	42 bars cut out - printed as addenda		Extra four bars - some pianistic amplification
-	-	-	-	2 cuts & much thinner & essential ✓	-	Simplified version
Musically substantially As above (1910)	Musically substantially As above (1910)	Musically substantially As above (1910)	Musically substantially As above (1910)	Cut rather savagely; no addenda included	Both of these much improved in effect ✓	✓
✓ As in (1910)	As in (1910)	As in (1910)	✓ As in (1910)	Restore addenda to main text	As in 1910	As in 1910. Use ending from 1922 (see text)
✓ As in 1922	✓ As in 1922	As in 1922	As in 1922	Restore cuts, including addenda	As in 1922	As in 1922
As in 1922	As in 1922	As in 1922	As in 1922	As in 1910 addenda & cuts restored 1922 used otherwise	As in 1922	As in 1922

II & III & CADENZA

159

false. Technically, the work is masterly; moreover, it does not lack contrasts, excitement, and extremes in texture: its moods are kaleidoscopic and range from sheer bravura to remote mysticism. Why then, if a work has all these positive qualities, does it not become a favorite in the concert hall? Pianists are no longer intimidated by the difficulties presented by this piece; they would play it if the demand to play it existed.

Busoni refused to compromise his artistic vision and demanded that audiences listening to the *Fantasia* recognize the Bach fugues, identify the main theme of *The Art of Fugue* when it appears near the end, keep in their minds the three fugue subjects, and thus perceive the variations when they appear, be able to hear the contrapuntal intricacies, remember the chorale tune, and place it near the end. This is, even today, simply wishful thinking—only a specialist audience would be able to do all this, and then it would need warning in amply written and musically illustrated program notes.

Busoni insists that the sound medium in which the work is played is unimportant; this may be so from his point of view.[21] In practice, even the greatest pianist cannot overcome the basic unsuitability of the instrument for playing such complex music. Dent says that the one-piano version of the *Fantasia* is unplayable—and in a certain sense, it is. Perhaps "unhearable" would have been a more apt description, if such a word exists. The two-piano version is clearer, but still suffers from similar drawbacks. I think it a great pity that Busoni did not realize his idea of scoring the *Fantasia*, and believe that an orchestral version may yet rescue this work from the encyclopedias, and make it more accessible to the concert-goer. As it stands, the *Fantasia* is known only to some musicians, is studied more often that it is heard, and discussed more often that it is played.

NOTES

1. Busoni, *Letters to His Wife*, p. 154.
2. Bernhard Ziehn (1845-1912), though German born, spent most of his professional life in the United States. He taught at the German Lutheran School in Chicago, was synagogue organist in the same city, and then established himself in private teaching as a theorist. Author of a number of books, it was his last, published posthumously as *Canonical Studies: A New Technic in Composition* (Milwaukee and Berlin, Kaun Music Co., 1912), that fascinated Busoni, and led to his essay "Die 'Gothiker' von Chicago," describing the work of Ziehn and his pupil Wilhelm Middelschulte (1863-1943). Busoni defined Ziehn as "a theoretician who points to the possibilities of undiscovered lands—a prophet through logic. As a master of harmony he stands alone. . . . Ziehn indicates the existence of undiscovered territory and trains young Columbuses." (Fedele d'Amico, ed., *Lo sguardo lieto* [Milano, Il Saggiatore, 1977] p. 387.) Busoni thus valued Ziehn's discoveries in the new realms of chromatic harmony and especially the concept of symmetrical inversion. Examples of this technique are given in the annotations

following Fugue VIII in Book 2 of the Well-Tempered Klavier, and both Ziehn and Middelschulte are quoted as well as a few bars from the Intermezzo of the *Fantasia Contrappuntistica*, a work which in its 1910 version bears the dedication "An Wilhelm Middelschulte, Meister des Kontrapunktes." It is clear that without Ziehn's and Middelschulte's inspiration, much of the *Fantasia Contrappuntistica* would have turned out differently.

3. Ferruccio Busoni, *Letters to His Wife*, trans. Rosamond Ley (London, Edward Arnold, 1938), p. 154.

4. Ibid., p. 155.

5. Ibid., p. 156.

6. Ibid., pp. 156-57.

7. Ibid., p. 158.

8. Ibid., p. 156.

9. Busoni must have become impatient with the episode here before the subject enters in the bass. Also, his chromatic change just at this point may, for dramatic effect, beg an earlier entry.

10. Wilfrid Mellers, *Romanticism and the 20th Century (from 1800) (Man and His Music)* (London, Rockliff, 1957), p. 183.

11. The climax of the fugue is given in open score in an addendum, worked out in six parts; this is virtually unplayable with two hands, at least with any contrapuntal clarity: it would probably sound most satisfactorily played by an instrumental consort.

12. Busoni, *Letters to His Wife*, pp. 174-75.

13. This "three hand" version manages to introduce the chorale in the middle register, as well as something close to the original chords and octaves; the rhythms accorded to the chorale in its earlier presentation are here modified.

14. Unplayable for ordinary mortals. Perhaps Busoni could do it. The significance of this, and other unreasonable (in the pianistic sense) demands in the *Fantasia Contrappuntistica* is that the abstract nature of the work is highlighted. Busoni knew too much about the piano to write such things in a purely pianistic context.

15. Kaikhosru Sorabji, *Around Music* (London, Unicorn Press, 1932), p. 27. Sorabji, now perhaps relatively unimportant as both writer and composer (although there has been recently a revival of interest in this strange personage), is of special interest to Busoni scholars because of his own work's relationship to Busoni's and his early—and to my mind, perceptive—appreciation of Busoni's aesthetic aims. I find, too, his often acid writings still readable and amusing.

16. Busoni, *Letters to His Wife*, p. 203.

17. Winifred Burston related that she arrived from Australia to study with Busoni at about the same time as Burley-Griffin, the American architect, had planned Canberra, the Australian capital. The scheme made worldwide news as a city that was to be totally predetermined in every detail. Busoni was very interested and questioned Burston closely about the idea: he was most chagrined to find that she was not terribly interested in city planning, having come half way around the world to study music.

18. In a letter to Hugo Leichtentritt, Busoni explained that the formal idea of the *Fantasia Contrappuntistica* was suggested by the Palace of the Popes in Avignon. (See Hugo Leichtentritt, "Ferruccio Busoni," *Musical Review*, VI, 1945, p. 206.) And indeed, upon finding some photographs of this building, I was struck by a great

likeness between the facade of the palace and the sketch included in the two-piano version. There is the same idea of larger towers flanking smaller arches. The clearest photograph that I saw to illustrate this interesting similarity is plate no. 102, titled "Facade occidentale du Palais des Papes," to be found in Francois Cali's *Provence, Land of Enchantment*, trans. Ernest and Adair Heimann (London, Allen & Unwin, 1965).

19. Stephen Daw, the noted Bach scholar, suggested that it may not have been the length of the work that troubled Busoni so much as the proportions and disposition of its internal materials. Like Bach and other composers who he admired, he presumably hoped to produce a work of economical power of expression; it would appear that his revisions were all directed toward the production of a concentrated whole of commanding authority. Pure length is (beyond a certain minimum) surely barely relevant to such an aim: it is the arrangement of the contents of the frame that is important, not its size.

20. Solo Version: the author has in fact given performances of such a definitive version of the *Fantasia*. The work's length is only extended by a few minutes, and totals something short of 35 minutes. The two-piano version has been restored and performed by the author. The orchestral version has been completed by the author, under the title *Concerto for Orchestra: Completion and Realization of Busoni's "Fantasia Contrappuntistica"* (1984).

21. "The *Fantasia Contrappuntistica* is thought of neither for pianoforte nor organ, nor orchestra. It is music. The sound-medium which imparts this music to the listener is of secondary importance." (Ferruccio Busoni, *The Essence of Music and Other Papers*, trans. Rosamond Ley (London, Rockliff, 1957), pp. 48-49. See also Edward Dent, *Ferruccio Busoni: A Biography* (London, Oxford University Press, 1933), p. 199.)

10

The Klavierübung

There was something Faustian about Ferruccio Busoni, that restless, tormented man of pianistic genius, the theorist and intellectual who was one of the founders of the modern style of piano playing, the avant-garde composer who worked out new scale systems, the titanic technician and master of pianistic effects.

Harold Schonberg

FIRST EDITION

SECHS KLAVIERÜBUNGEN UND PRÄLUDIEN (DER KLAVIERÜBUNG ERSTER TEIL) Part 1: Six exercises and preludes) Leipzig Breitkopf & Haertel 1918 EB 5066 Composed in 1917

DREI KLAVIERÜBUNGEN UND PRÄLUDIEN (DER KLAVIERÜBUNG ZWEITER TEIL) (Part 2: Three exercises and preludes) Leipzig Breitkopf & Haertel 1919 EB 5067 Composed in 1917-1918

LO STACCATO (DER KLAVIERÜBUNG DRITTER TEIL) (Part 3: Staccato) Leipzig Breitkopf & Haertel 1921 EB 5068 Composed in 1919-1921

ACHT ETÜDEN VON CRAMER (DER KLAVIERÜBUNG VIERTER TEIL) (Part 4: Eight studies after Cramer) Leipzig Breitkopf & Haertel EB 5224. Originally published as *8 Etudes de Piano par J. B. Cramer choisies des 16 nouvelles Etudes Op. 81 (No. 85-100) révues et publiées par Ferruccio B. Busoni* Berlin Schlesinger 1897 S. 8772

VARIATIONEN PERPETUUM MOBILE TONLEITERN (DER
KLAVIERÜBUNG FÜNFTER TEIL) (Part 5: Variations Perpetual
motion Scales) Leipzig Breitkopf & Haertel 1922 EB 5225
Composed in 1922

SECOND EDITION

KLAVIERÜBUNG IN ZEHN BÜCHERN VON FERRUCCIO
BUSONI ZWEITE UMGESTALTETE UND BEREICHERTE
AUSGABE (First Book: Scales Second Book: Scales in extended
forms Third Book: Broken chords Fourth Book: "For three
hands" Fifth Book: Trills Sixth Book: Staccato Seventh Book:
Eight studies after Cramer Eighth Book: Variations and variants
on Chopin Ninth Book: Seven pieces for the cultivation of
polyphonic playing Tenth Book: Studies after
Paganini-Liszt) Leipzig Breitkopf & Haertel 1925 FB
VIII Composed in 1922-1924

The *Klavierübung* was published by Breitkopf & Haertel in two different
editions: the first, in five parts, was issued between 1918 and 1922; the
second, in 10 books (one volume) was published posthumously in 1925.

In the first edition, parts 1 and 2 are subdivided, and numbered
consecutively from I to IX; the six exercises and preludes of part 1 are in
actual fact six sections of exercises and preludes dealing with various
technical problems. Part 2, therefore, begins with a subdivision numbered
VII, and proceeds to end with a subdivision numbered IX.

Since the second edition of the *Klavierübung* is by far the more comprehensive one, we shall consider its contents in the order in which they
appear; save in the one instance where the first edition includes material
missing from the second, which we will clearly mark as belonging to the
first edition only.

Comparing the two editions presents a rather confused picture:

	SECOND EDITION	FIRST EDITION
First Book: *Scales*		
(a)	Five exercises for the thumb	Part 1, I
	Three exercises without using the thumb	Part 1, I
(b)	Eleven further exercises	Part 5, in section marked "Scales," 1
(c)	Twelve polytonal scale combinations	Part 5, in section marked "Scales," 2
(d)	Eight exercises in different keys and patterns of scales played by alternating hands	Part 5, in section Marked "Scales," 3

(e) Five exercises for broken and   Part 5, in Appendix, marked "thirds"
    double thirds
    Not in 2d edition   1. Two extra exercises under (a)
                                            2. Nach Liszt
                                            3. Two short pieces, "Allegretto"
                                               and "Tempo di Valse," half-page
                                               each

Second Book: *Scales in extended forms*
(a) Extended exercise and Preludio   Part 1, II
(b) Seven exercises on various   Part 1, III
    double chromatics
(c) Preludio, followed by   Part 1, III
    exercise
(d) Another Preludio and   Part 1, III
    exercise
(e) Schema and eight variations   Part 1, IV
(f) Nach Schubert-Liszt   Part 1, IV
(g) Excerpt from *Indian Diary*   Part 1, IV
(h) Nach Auber-Liszt.   Part 1, IV

Third Book: *Broken chords*
(a) Six arpeggio exercises   Part 1, V
(b) Three extension arpeggio exercises   Part 1, V
(c) Nach Bach   Part 1, V
(d) Six further arpeggio   Printed in Part 3, as
    exercises   "Nachsatz zur V. Übung"
(e) Nach Beethoven   Part 1, V
(f) Contrary motion extension study   Part 1, V
(g) Contrary-similar motion combined   Part 1, V
(h) Extended broken octaves   Part 1, V
(i) Preludio   Part 1, V
(j) Nach Beethoven   Part 2, VIII[1]
(k) Preludio   Part 2, VIII
(l) Tempo di valse   Part 2, VIII
(m) Excerpt from *Prélude &*   Not in first edition
    Etude (en arpèges)

Fourth Book: *"For three hands"*
(a) Preludio alla Tarantella   Part 1, VI
(b) Nach Offenbach   Part 1, VI
(c) Nach Beethoven   Part 1, VI
(d) Excerpt from *An die Jugend*   Part 2, IX[2]
(e) Nach Schubert   Part 2, IX
(f) Excerpt from the *Concerto*   Part 2, IX
    Op. XXXIX

Fifth Book: *Trills*
(a) Three extended exercises   Part 2, VII
    in trills (forming one "preludio")
(b) Nach Bach   Part 2, VII

(c) Nach Beethoven	Part 2, VII
(d) Preludio (without the third finger)	Part 2, VII
(e) Nach Gounod	Part 2, VII
(f) Preludio	Part 2, VII
(g) Nach Liszt	Part 2, VII
(h) 7 Variationen nach einem Motive von Beethoven	Printed in part 3 as an Appendix
(i) Extended piece, "veloce e leggiero"	Not in first edition

Sixth Book: *Staccato*

(a) Foreword	Foreword to Part 3
(b) Vivace moderato	(b) through (j) comprise Part 3
(c) *Variations-Studie nach Mozart, 1*	
(d) *Variations-Studie nach Mozart, 2*	
(e) Motive (name of a piece)	
(f) Preludio (excerpt from *Toccata*)	
(g) Nach Mendelssohn	
(h) Nach Bizet	
(i) Nach Liszt	
(j) Allegro	

Seventh Book: *Eight studies after Cramer*

Acht Etüden nach Cramer	Part 4

Eighth Book: *Variations and variants on Chopin*

(a) *Neun Variationen über ein Präludium von Chopin*	Part 5 (published in a slightly different version as *Zehn Variationen über ein Präludium von Chopin*)
(b) Varianten zu Etüden und Präludien von Chopin	Part 5 (one page shorter than second edition)

Ninth Book: *Seven pieces for the cultivation of polyphonic playing*

(a) *Sieben kurze Stücke zur Pflege des polyphonen Spiels*	Only the first piece appears in the first edition in Part 1, I
(b) *Perpetuum Mobile*	Part 5

Tenth Book: *Studies after Paganini-Liszt*

(a) Etüden nach Paganini-Liszt	Etude No. 4 appears in part 3, as *Variations-Studie nach Paganini-Liszt, 1* Etude No. 6 appears in part 3, as *Variations-Studie nach Paganini-Liszt, 2*
(b) *Introduzione e Capriccio*	Not in first edition

We see that the Second Book is equivalent to the first edition Part 1, Nos. II, III, and IV.

The *Klavierübung* consists of a large selection of materials of various lengths: short exercises, demonstrating technical principles; extended exercises, sometimes running into a few pages, but still mostly of technical, not musical interest; short pieces, demonstrating in musical terms ideas set forth in the exercises (sometimes these pieces are called preludio, at other times they are left without titles or other means of identification, except a tempo marking; some of these pieces or preludios are quite complete, and run into numbers of pages); extended pieces of concert standard not appearing anywhere else or published separately; excerpts from the music of other composers, edited, arranged, or fingered by Busoni (these are usually from his repertoire, and are shown by a "nach" label); excerpts from Busoni's own music; and complete pieces by other composers, edited or in concert arrangements.

The First Book consists purely of exercises, both short and extended, employing unusual and unorthodox fingerings: for example, the first five exercises employ passing the thumb under the fifth finger, and crossing the fifth finger over the thumb. The next three exercises are a throwback to old keyboard technique in which the thumb was not used at all. This whole first section (a) is marked presto.

It is at this point that the first edition has some material that was later deleted, for no apparent reason: two further short exercises involving further use of the principles set forth in earlier exercises.

Then three musical examples are given of this unorthodox fingering: an excerpt from one of the cadenzas in Liszt's *Totentanz* (see chapter 12); and two short preludio-type pieces of half a page each, one labelled simply allegretto, the second, tempo da valse.

The second edition now continues (section (b)) with a series of 11 connected exercises marked allegro moderato, and passing through a cycle of keys, containing yet more variants of principles already shown. Next (section (c)), Busoni carries the modulation idea to the point of polytonality: the practice of various simultaneous key couples is suggested, namely, C major and A major and many others, both in similar and contrary motion.

Then follows a presto volante (section (d)), and here the patterns are written mostly on one stave; ingenious use of alternate hand technique is demonstrated. Finally, there is an appendix (section (e)), with fingerings for various broken and double 3rds; this appendix should be studied in conjunction with allied material from the Busoni edition of the *Well-Tempered Klavier* (see chapter 11).

The Second Book forms scale patterns into new configurations by combining them with other technical forms. For instance, (a) contains an extended exercise exploiting scale movement in which chords are incorporated into the stepwise motion; a preludio (allegro festivo) follows, beginning in D flat but ending in C major. Section (b) offers a glimpse into Busoni's favorite technique of creating a "sixth finger," by sliding from black to white key in chromatic passages; seven exercises utilizing different parallel double chromatics (including double major 2nds) are given. Preludios and exercises then follow ((c) and (d)), still based on chromatic-sliding fingerings. The slurs created by the slide fingering brings to Busoni's mind a new technical scheme: various patterns of slurs in quavers, triplets, and semiquavers; hence a schema and eight variations appear (e). Three excerpts now illustrate slur uses in context: (f) Nach Schubert-Liszt (see chapter 12); a one-page study based on the eleventh and twelfth bars of the *Indian Diary*, No. 1 now follows (g); and (h) is Nach Auber-Liszt (see Chapter 12).

The Third Book begins, like the second, with broken chords using the thumb and fifth finger passing over and under each other (a). Extended arpeggio exercises follow (b), reminiscent of the Chopin Op. 10 No. 1 *Etude*; (c) is Nach Bach (see chapter 11); chains of all types of 7th chords and their derivatives are given next (d); (e) is Nach Beethoven (see Chapter 14); in (f) similar- and contrary-motion broken chords are mixed, requiring some big stretches; (g) is marked allegro vivace and is another venture into the same problem; a number of broken-octave exercises then follow, ranging all over the keyboard, somewhat like the Rubinstein E flat *Etude* from Op. 23 (h); a rather charming allegro moderato preludio follows, in 3/2, with stretches in both hands (i); (j) is yet another Nach Beethoven (see Chapter 14). The next preludio (k), and a tempo di valse (l), are both quite complete pieces, worthy of public resurrection; and the last piece in the book is based on the *Prélude & Etude* (see Chapter 5), and presents not an excerpt, but pianistic alternatives to some of the material from it, which, since the *Etude* dates from two years before, possibly represent later thoughts.

The Fourth Book is distinguished from the preceding ones in containing no exercises at all, only illustrations of the pianistic trick of three-hands technique from various sources. Section (a) preludio, alla tarantella: this little piece in F sharp major is based on *Elegy* No. 2 (*All' Italia!*, middle section); (b) Nach Offenbach, and (c) Nach Beethoven (see chapter 14); and (d) labelled perpetuum mobile et infinitum: Studie nach Bach (Aus: "an die Jugend") (see Chapter 11); (e) Nach Schubert (see Chapter 14); and (f) simply says "aus meinem Concerto." The performing instruction is trattenuto e fantasticamente. The excerpt is from the *Concerto Op. XXXIX*, second movement, page 45 of the two-piano score.

The Fifth Book mostly comprises various pieces; even the first section (a) which consists of three extended trill exercises, is so set out that the three exercises are joined to each other, and the whole forms one "preludio" (moderato). (For identification of (b) Nach Bach and (c) Nach Beethoven, see Chapters 11 and 14). The preludio (d), moderato alla breve, is to be played without using the third finger. Nach Gounod (e) is discussed in Chapter 12 (see cadenza for Gounod/Liszt *Faust* paraphrase). Section (f) is an effective preludio (allegro) with straightforward trill decoration running through it. Two more excerpts from other composers follow: (g) Nach Liszt (see chapter 12) and (h) 7 variationen nach einem motive von Beethoven (see Chapter 14).

The book ends with a most unusual piece: it has not even been graced with a title, only the directive veloce e leggiero. A sinister five-page essay in Busoni's best spectral style, this piece is unfortunately completely unknown, inserted between various technical demonstrations.

The foreword to the Sixth Book ("staccato"), is really a foreword to the whole *Klavierübung*. It has never appeared in English, and, as it contains some interesting ideas, I offer this free translation:

TO THE MUSIC SCHOOL AND CONSERVATORIUM OF BASLE

Forced to interrupt the continuation and elaboration of this work (which will extend through the rest of my life because of the amount of material gathered and experience accumulated), I deem it appropriate to offer here a few words of explanation: words that would be more fitting as introduction, instead of thus strangely appearing in the middle of this work.

True enough, this Klavierübung is based on an all-embracing plan, but the plan is not presented in conformity with rigid pedagogic principles; it is, at any rate, not without gaps; furthermore, insofar as it is within the author's power, this Klavierübung achieves a comparative completeness only by the inclusion of his own works on Bach and Liszt.

The author's area of interest lay in avoiding discouraging the student with theoretical fantasies that could not be executed: on the other hand, of course, the student himself is not always able to judge to what extent his abilities can cope with the difficulties which confront him. Nevertheless I maintain that it is cheap and irresponsible to write technical combinations that transcend instrumental and physical possibilities, thereby presenting the student with an insurmountable task. This gives him a false notion of his own inability, and drives him to exaggeration and desperation. The examples given for transposition, are designed to do justice to the principles set out above, and are not to be carried out beyond anything that is comfortable to play.

I have also given attention to devising exercises that are stimulating, and, in part at least, entertaining: the aim of this was to make the pupil realize that the study of an Art is something to be enjoyed.

Consequently, as well as using my own well-received Bach transcriptions, my favourite Mozart, and the universally-welcome Bizet, I also included the less-celebrated Gounod and Offenbach, in part at least as a protest against a period that esteems the boring and cultivates the ugly; but mainly because they gave me the opportunity of devising certain pianistic combinations.

Unlike the first part of Klavierübung, with its "Six Exercises and Preludes," and the second part, which, although of similar length, had only three such Exercises and Preludes, this third part contains only one: i.e. the tenth "Übung," that is dedicated exclusively to the untramelled art of performance. Here too there is a mixture of the borrowed and of my own. If there is any possible reproach of irreverance towards Liszt, that Master Pianist of us all, whose Paganini Variations I have allegedly presumed to revise, I counter such criticism with the plea of studious intent, which motivated me to create an uninterrupted staccato study from this piece.

The brilliance created as a result has justified its execution: the form finally attained should merit at least the description of a truly witty miniature piece of art.

And so "Lo Staccato," as an independent portion of the complete Klavierübung, itself still a fragment, is now delivered to the public.[3]

This is one of the author's moments of truth, when he releases what he has so strongly guarded and nurtured, when he forgoes all the powers and all the rights to his creation, and then, finally, he gives of his own self.

The protection which an author imparts to his work through an accompanying preface, is dubious. Presented with due solemnity and abundant flourish between the title page and the first page of the music, it is, in most cases, not read; if it is read, not taken to heart; if taken to heart, misinterpreted. Nevertheless I have had a preface printed here: a form of tradition to which I have to bow. [Reprinted by kind permission, Breitkopf & Haertel, Wiesbaden.]

The music begins with a rather hectic and difficult study in staccato chords, vivace moderato, con precisione (a); and another preludio piece (b). For discussion of (c) and (d), Variations-Studie nach Mozart, 1 and 2, see Chapter 13. Section (e) is a three-page alternating-hand staccato study, titled *Motive*, allegro risoluto; a sequential study employing various intervals, including bars of consecutive seconds. Section (f), although not identified as such, is a note-for-note excerpt from the Prelude in Busoni's *Toccata* (see Chapter 5). Three "nach" pieces now follow (g, h, and i): Nach Mendelssohn (see Chapter 12), Nach Bizet (see Chapter 6), and Nach Liszt (see Chapter 12). The Nach Bizet consists of the opening three pages of the *Sonatina super Carmen* copied exactly, with a few bars of flourish to provide it with an ending—the *Sonatina*, of course, goes on to other things. Since both the *Sonatina* and this book of the *Klavierübung* were written about 1920, it is impossible to tell whether the *Sonatina* grew from this excerpt or whether the excerpt came from the *Sonatina*. The Sixth Book finishes with another fierce-looking study in staccato chords, marked allegro.

The Seventh Book contains *Eight Studies after Cramer* (see Chapter 14).

The Eighth Book has two sections, both based on Chopin: (a) *Variations on a Prelude of Chopin*. (Nine variations in the second edition, ten variations in the first. The Variations are, of course, a reworked version of the *Variations and Fugue on a Prelude of Chopin*, Op. 22; see Chapter 5 and (b) variants of Etudes and Preludes (see chapter 14).

The Ninth Book consists of two major parts: *Sieben Kurze Stücke* and the *Perpetuum Mobile*. (See chapter 8 for a discussion of the latter.)

SIEBEN KURZE STÜCKE ZUR PFLEGE DES POLYPHONEN
SPIELS   Originally published as *Fünf kurze Stücke zur Pflege des polyphonen Spiels auf dem Pianoforte*   Leipzig   Breitkopf & Haertel
EB 5240   Also *Sechs kurze Stücke zur Pflege des polyphonen Spiels*   Wiesbaden   Breitkopf & Haertel   1954   EB 6205[4]

The seven pieces follow a cycle of keys of ascending fourths: Nos. 1 and 2 are in E major and e minor, respectively; No. 3 in a minor; No. 4 in d minor, ending in D major; No. 5 in G major; No. 6 in c minor; and No. 7 in F major.

No. 1 (titled *Preludietto*) made its initial appearance in the first edition of the *Klavierübung*, where it served as a demonstration piece of unorthodox crossover fingering; its appearance here is unaltered. It also acts as a prelude to No. 2, a much lengthier piece. Whereas No. 1 had a Bachian ring to it, No. 2 immediately enters a different world. (See Figure 10.1.) Nos. 2, 3, 4,

Figure 10.1. By kind permission, Breitkopf & Haertel, Wiesbaden.

and 5 have the same basic sound and problem: they bring out a melodic line through a chromatic, wandering sort of counterpoint-accompaniment; for example, in No. 3, where the counterpoint is in slow double notes, and in No. 2, where the one hand has to cope with two lines, one to be heard clearly, the other subdued. In No. 4 the hands play separately at first, providing two strands each: this marvellous piece combines a chorale melody with a tarantella-like counterpoint, somewhat in the manner of Bach's *Wachet auf!* chorale prelude. The music develops into an accompanied canon and then, as the tension mounts, into a double canon, the second canon accompanying the first. No. 5 has a richly ornate, baroque-style counterpoint, with the foreshadowing of the theme of No. 6 woven into it. Throughout, although the sound often has an almost Schönbergian atonality (I use the word deliberately, despite Schönberg's abhorrence of it, as the best description of the "free" period between the end of tonal chromaticism and the start of organized dodecaphonic technique), the point of departure is always Bach. Even No. 6, nach Mozart, falls into this category (see chapter 13). The last piece is an interesting attempt to provide a way of notating the use of the third pedal on a Steinway grand; the sounds to be held by the middle pedal are notated on a third staff. (See Figure 10.2.) Musically, the possibility of holding a pedal chord down while unrelated harmonies move above it without any blurring, is briefly but effectively probed. Like many of the other preludios in the *Klavierübung*, these seven pieces deserve more attention than they receive.

The Tenth Book consists of material discussed in other chapters: the *Etudes after Paganini-Liszt* (see Chapter 12) and *Introduzione e Capriccio* (*Paganinesco*) (see Chapter 14).

7.

Figure 10.2. By kind permission, Breitkopf & Haertel, Wiesbaden.

It is appropriate here to mention three short essays by Busoni concerning piano playing: "The Requirements Necessary for a Pianist" (written in Minneapolis, 1910, for the *Signale der Musikalischen Welt*, Berlin); "Rules for Practising the Piano" (from a letter to his wife, 20 July 1898); and "Playing from Memory" (answer to a questionnaire for *Die Musik*, Berlin, May 1907). All three are to be found in the English edition of the *Essence of Music*, in a section titled "Piano Playing and Piano Music," pages 80, 81, and 84 respectively. The essays are valuable more for their expression of Busoni's methods of practice and playing than as purely pedagogical aids.

The reader is also referred to the following technical writings to be found in Busoni's edition of the Bach *48 Preludes and Fugues* (see Chapter 11); in the notes to Prelude IX, Book 1: suggestions for new fingerings for thirds, diatonic and chromatic; as an appendix to Fugue X, Book 1: an essay on octave playing; as an appendix to Prelude XI: an essay on trill playing; after Fugue XVI, Book 1: further observations on fingering of thirds; and as a supplement to Book 1, another essay on fingering, giving (1) fingerings for simple chromatic scale (seven different ones given), (2) fingering for double chromatic scale, and (3) fingering for various alternating hand chromatic scales. See also various etudes and studies for piano in other chapters.

Busoni was not, by nature, a teacher; his master classes and composition classes were group sessions and special ones at that, held only at certain limited times. Their effect upon the pupils was undeniable, but if by teaching we mean individual, painstaking tuition, with much probing and elucidation of technique and its problems—the sort of thing that Petri was so famous for—then Busoni was not a teacher. Asked about this in a radio interview, Petri admitted as much and added: "He was really more interested in the effect his playing had on us, rather than in our own playing." Petri then went on to say that, naturally, Busoni's powerful intellect and pianism left indelible marks on all who came in contact with him, but that this very power had also negative side effects on people: they would give up in despair at their own inadequacy. "Busoni had this effect on people, simply by being such a giant."[5] The master classes, at any rate, ceased very early in the century. Busoni became far more interested in teaching composition. Why then, in 1920, should he have gone into the trouble of producing the *Klavierübung*, and why did he work on a second massive edition until the end of his life?

Busoni was not really interested in piano pedagogy. The *Klavierübung* is not, even by his own admission in the preface to *Lo Staccato*, a systematic or complete exposition of technique and its problems. Moreover, it is far too difficult for anyone but the brilliant student; many of the examples are for the accomplished pianist, for the interested professional. The technical problems and solutions are all, without fail, individual, arresting, and unorthodox. They represent, deliberately, one point of view only, and a point of view often hard to emulate. The obvious—and sometimes easier— solutions never make their appearance in the pages of the *Klavierübung*; Busoni assumed that the player had already known them from other sources. At the end of many of the exercises and pieces, Busoni gives a list of works for further study, containing similar problems: the works are invariably from his own amazing repertoire. What we have in the *Klavierübung* is not so much a method as a record by Busoni of his approach to the keyboard: his fingerings, tricks, shortcuts, improvisations. No wonder he says, in that same preface to *Lo Staccato* that he had released "what he has so strongly guarded and nurtured." No wonder that, despite the pressure of so many activities, Busoni felt the compulsion to go on working at this opus. He was literally giving "of his own self."

It is a great pity that the preludio pieces, which appear throughout the first six books of the *Klavierübung*, have not been published separately. They present an aspect of Busoni not known even to the specialist pianist—the miniaturist: sometimes slight, in a witty romantic-salon genre, sometimes whimsical; often insubstantial and ghostly in that night-music idiom which is so much part of Busoni. Some of these preludios are written in a very advanced language, and far from being merely technical illustrations, deserve, in collection, consideration with other of his pieces like the *Elegies, Indian Diary*, and the sonatinas.

Nevertheless, we must not underestimate the real value of the *Klavierübung*: although it cannot be actually used as a method or a course of study in technique, it is beyond the reach of most students, and it often stresses the unorthodox at the cost of the obvious, used in the right way, the *Klavierübung* can be stimulating and most useful in opening up new technical horizons. It contains a rich source of concert material, sadly neglected; and finally, it is a good introduction to the study of Busoni's music and its keyboard problems.

NOTES

1. The three works labelled part 2, VIII constitute the complete VIII section of part 2, first edition.

2. The three works labelled part 2, IX constitute the complete IX section of part 2, first edition.

3. Busoni has a footnote here about a further volume of the *Klavierübung*, to be titled "Chromaticon," being in preparation. A volume with such a title, however, did not eventuate.

4. There were originally only three pieces in the set, composed on three successive days (21, 22, and 23 March 1923) while Busoni was confined to his bed. Two more pieces were written later that same year. In the final edition of *Seven Pieces . . . ,* Nos. 1 and 7 were new; in the 1954 edition of *Six Pieces . . . ,* No. 7 is omitted.

5. See also Bibliography: Marga Weigert, "Busoni at Weimar," *The Music Review,* and Ursula Creighton, "Reminiscences of Busoni," *Recorded Sound.*

Busoni and Other Composers

11

Busoni and Bach

> The Bach transcriptions of Busoni are entities in which both Bach and Busoni live at the same level of interest and emotion. Busoni finds his goal in the personality of Bach, as a poet finds his goal in nature. It is a past world, but one still alive and pulsating, which Busoni carries within himself; a world which he develops and transforms as if by magic.
>
> "Magic": the very word was dear to Busoni. With an aesthetic sense derived from intuition rather than justified by philosophy, he saw in art the essential power of transformation of reality.
>
> Guido Pannain

Petri told his pupils many anecdotes relating to Busoni's first American tour; Bach and Busoni had become so ingrained in the public's mind as being almost synonymous that, at least on one occasion, Gerda, Busoni's wife, was introduced by a society matron as "Mrs. Bach-Busoni."[1]

Busoni issued his Bach editions in two separate collections: the 25-volume complete keyboard works known as the *Klavierwerke*, and the 7-volume Bach-Busoni edition. The full contents are given below.

JOH. SEB. BACH   KLAVIERWERKE UNTER MITWIRKUNG VON EGON PETRI UND BRUNO MUGELLINI HERAUSGEGEBEN VON FERRUCCIO BUSONI   Leipzig   Breitkopf & Haertel 1894-1923   EB 4301-25   This 25-volume edition was also issued later as *Joh. Seb. Bach   Klavierwerke   Neue Ausgabe von Ferruccio Busoni, Egon Petri und Bruno Mugellini*

Although Busoni's name appears on the cover of all 25 volumes, he had little or nothing to do with the actual editing of some of these. The idea of the scheme was his, and with his usual thoroughness he edited the following volumes: 1, 2, 3, 4, 5, 14, 15, 16, 18 (see complete listing of works below).

Most of these were also reprinted in the 7-volume Bach-Busoni edition, now very rare. Then, according to Petri, "Busoni either got bored or was taken up with some new idea; in any case, he had already taken the prize plums out of the Bach pudding—the works he really *wanted* to edit himself. He then passed the project on to me. I proceeded to edit the works *I* was interested in, and so poor Mugellini was landed with the cast-offs."

Petri had expected that Busoni would supervise his and Mugellini's editorial efforts and so took great care and endless trouble to emulate the master; much to his surprise however, Busoni did not seem to be particularly interested in reading Petri's and Mugellini's proofs. The title *Busoni-Ausgabe* is really misleading. What we have is an edition of Bach by three different persons, with both Petri and Mugellini adopting very similar principles to those of Busoni.[2]

The complete layout of the 25-volume edition is as follows:

I.   *Das Wohltemperierte Klavier I Teil* (heft 1-4) (Busoni), 1894, EB 4301.

II.   *Das Wohltemperierte Klavier II Teil* (heft 1-4) (Busoni), 1916, EB 4302.

III.   *18 Kleine Präludien, Fughetta, 4 Duette* (Busoni), 1916, EB 4303.

IV.   *15 Zweistimmige Inventionen* (Busoni), 1914, EB 4304.

V.   *15 Dreistimmige Inventionen* (Busoni), 1914, EB 4305.

VI.   *Französische Suiten 1-6* (Petri), 1918, EB 4306.

VII.   *Englische Suiten 1-3* (Petri), 1916, EB 4307.

VIII.   *Englische Suiten 4-6* (Petri), 1917, EB 4308.

IX.   *Partiten 1-3* (Petri), 1918, EB 4309.

X.   *Partiten 4-6* (Petri), 1923, EB 4310.

XI.   *Konzerte nach Marcello, Telemann, etc. Nr. 1-8* (Mugellini), 1915, EB 4311.

XII.   *Konzerte Nr. 9-16* (Mugellini), 1915, EB 4312.

XIII.   *Italienische Konzert, Partita h moll* (Petri), 1918, EB 4313.

XIV.   *Chromatische Fantasie und Fuge; Capriccio über die Abreise des vielgeliebten Brudes; Fantasia Adagio und Fuge; Präludium Fuge und Allegro* (Busoni), 1915, EB 4314.

XV.   *Aria mit 30 Veränderungen* (Busoni), 1915, EB 4315.

XVI.   *Fantasie und Fuge, Andante, Scherzo; Sarabanda con partite; Aria variata alla maniera italiana* (Busoni), 1921, EB 4316.

XVII.   *Tokkaten* (Petri), 1922, EB 4317.

XVIII. *Tokkaten, Fantasie und Fuge a moll* (Busoni), 1920 and 1918, EB 4318.

XIX.   *Präludien und Fugen* (Mugellini), 1917, EB 4319.

XX.   *Präludien, Fughetten und Fugen* (Mugellini), 1917, EB 4320.

XXI.   *Fugen* (Mugellini), 1917, EB 4321.

XXII.   *Fantasien (Präludien) und Fugen* (Petri), 1922, EB 4322.

XXIII.   *Suiten* (Petri), 1923, EB 4323.

XXIV.   *Suiten und 2 Sonaten* (Mugellini), 1921, EB 4324.

XXV.   *Sonaten, Konzert und Fuge c moll, Capriccio E dur, 3 Menuette* (Petri), 1923, EB 4325.

This Bach-Busoni edition was issued in a six-volume format in 1916 and a seven-volume format in 1920.

BACH-BUSONI GESAMMELTE AUSGABE BEARBEITUNGEN, ÜBERTRAGUNGEN, STUDIEN UND KOMPOSITIONEN FÜR PIANOFORTE NACH JOHANN SEBASTIAN BACH VON FER-RUCCIO BUSONI VOLLSTÄNDIGE UND VERVOLLKOMMNETE AUSGABE Leipzig Breitkopf & Haertel 1916

BEARBEITUNGEN, ÜBERTRAGUNGEN, STUDIEN UND KOMPO-SITIONEN FÜR DAS PIANOFORTE NACH JOHANN SEBASTIAN BACH VON FERRUCCIO BUSONI VOLLSTÄNDIGE UND VERVOLLKOMMNETE AUSGABE Leipzig Breitkopf & Haertel 1920

The first six volumes of the 1920 edition are identical to the 1916 edition, the seventh volume contains new material.

The breakdown of the contents is as follows:

1. *Bearbeitungen, I. Lehrstücke: Widmung; 18 kleine Präludien und eine Fughetta; 15 zweistimmige Inventionen; 15 dreistimmige Inventionen; vier Duette; Präludium, Fuge und Allegro Es dur* (*Widmung* is a complete miniature combining the notes B.A.C.H. with the Fugue in C major from the first book of the *Well-Tempered Klavier.*)

2. *Bearbeitungen, II. Meisterstücke: Chromatische Fantasie und Fuge; Klavier-Konzert, D Moll; Aria mit 30 Veranderungen.*

3. *Übertragungen: Präludium und Fuge für die Orgel, D Dur; Präludium und Fuge für die Orgel, Es Dur; Orgel-Toccata, D Moll; Orgel-Toccata, C Dur; zehn Orgel-Choral-Vorspiele; Chaconne für Violine.*

4. *Kompositionen und Nachdichtungen: Fantasia; Preludio, Fuga e Fuga figurata; Capriccio, B Dur, über die Abreise; Fantasie, Adagio und Fuge, C Moll; Choral-Vorspiel nebst Fuge über ein Bachsches Fragment; Fantasia contrappuntistica.*

5. *Das Wohltemperierte Klavier, I.*

6. *Das Wohltemperierte Klavier, II.*

7. *Bearbeitungen, Übertragungen, Studien und Kompositionen. Bearbeitungen: Drei Tokkaten in e-Moll, g-Moll und G-Dur; Fantasie und Fuge in a-Moll; Fantasie, Fuge, Andante und Scherzo. Übertragungen: Chromatische Fantasie und Fuge für Violoncell und Klavier übertragen. Kompositionen und Nachdichtungen: Improvisation über das Bachsche Chorallied "Wie wohl ist mir, o Freund*

der Seele" für zwei Klaviere; Kanonische Variationen und Fuge (über das Thema Friedrichs des Grossen) aus J. S. Bach's "Musikalisches Opfer" gezogen und für Klavier dargestellt; Sonatina brevis. In Signo Joannis Sebastiani Magni. In freier Nachdichtung von Bachs Kleiner Fantasie und Fuge d-Moll. Anhang: Versuch einer organischen Klavier-Notenschrift.

Writing the epilogue to the Bach seven-volume edition, Busoni recollected:

I have my father to thank for my good fortune, because during my childhood he insisted on my studying Bach at a time and in a country that did not rank the master much higher than a Carl Czerny. My father was a simple virtuoso clarinettist who loved to play fantasies on Il Trovatore and the Carnival of Venice; his musical training had been incomplete, he was an Italian and an admirer of the bel canto. How did such a man, ambitious on behalf of his son, happen to hit upon exactly the right thing? The only way I can explain it is as a mysterious revelation. Moreover, by this means he trained me to be a "German" musician and showed me a path that I have never entirely abandoned even though I always retained the Latin characteristics that were inherent in my nature.[3]

An association of his father, Ferdinando Busoni, with Bach can be seen in the *Fantasia nach Bach*, written in his memory. His father's insistence on Bach and other polyphonic composers resulted in having a great deal of the Leipzig master in the repertoire of the young pianist. Even before the advent of the Bach-Busoni organ transcriptions in 1888, there was a representative selection from Bach and Handel in his repertoire. And, of course, the very act of transcription, its techniques, and aesthetics were at least partly due to a study of Bach's own transcriptions.

Busoni was fortunate, too, in that his composition teacher, Dr. Wilhelm Mayer (also known by his compositional pseudonym of W. A. Rémy) taught a great deal of Bach, analyzing the *48 Preludes and Fugues*, and set his pupils contrapuntal exercises. Thus, many of Busoni's earliest compositions (see Chapter 2) are in this style, and some of his first compositions that he performed were various gigues, gavottes, preludes, and fugues. This early polyphonic mastery was already noted by Hanslick in a review in the *Neue Freie Presse* on 13 February 1876; he wrote about a bracket of original works that the 10-year-old had performed: "These reveal the same musical awareness which we enjoyed so much in his playing; not a sign of precocious sentimentality or contrived effect, just sheer pleasure in the play of notes, in lively figuration and little combinatorial techniques. Nothing operatic, not a trace of dance rhythm, on the contrary a remarkable seriousness and maturity which suggests a devoted study of Bach." At this early age Busoni had already also developed the ability to improvise polyphonically. Hanslick again: ". . . I gave the boy several motifs on the piano which he immediately worked out imaginatively in the same serious manner, mostly in imitative and contrapuntal style."

Bach was the favorite composer of Busoni's youth; a love that endured right through his life, whereas attachments to various other composers were not so constant. Because contrapuntal thinking was completely native and natural to Busoni from his earliest years, he kept returning to Bach and rediscovering in him a rich source of ideas. Revelation of compositional techniques in Bach had immediate and serious repercussions on his own works, not to speak of compositions inspired by fragments of Bach; witness some of the works described in this chapter, also in the chapters on transcriptions, and the *Fantasia Contrappuntistica.*

At least four of the six sonatinas, which include in their number some of his most serious and intimate utterances, could not have been written without his love and study of Bach, and the discovery of Bach's use of what Busoni termed the *Ur-Motiv*: what I have called the "cellular" technique in Chapter 6.

Busoni, it was said, performed everything in a prophetic manner: a composer who belongs exclusively to the past held no interest for him. The future of music lay in a "cultivated, final polyphony."

Busoni's works that have some relationship with Bach can be classified into four broad types:

1. Transcriptions that are generally faithful to the original, changes being governed by the sonorities and techniques of the medium; nevertheless, small musical alterations occur from time to time.

2. Editions intended as a record of Busoni's own interpretations, and/or a pedagogical guide. Although these are the most faithful of the Bach-Busoni output, it does not necessarily follow that Busoni did not introduce elements of (1) into them. Various pianistic adaptations are constantly employed. Sometimes alternate versions, cuts, and additions are also provided; Busoni usually admits liability for these.

3. Original compositions based on a piece or a fragment of Bach. These depart from the original to an extent governed only by Busoni's own imagination; Bach is used as a thematic foundation or departure point; sometimes the original is viewed from an unfamiliar standpoint.

4. There is one major opus by Busoni that incorporates all three of the above elements: the *Fantasia Contrappuntistica* (see Chapter 9).

DAS WOHLTEMPERIERTE KLAVIER   ERSTER TEIL   BEAR-
BEITET UND ERLÄUTERT, MIT DARAN ANKNÜPFENDEN
BEISPIELEN UND ANMERKUNGEN FÜR DAS STUDIUM DER
MODERNEN KLAVIERSPIELTECHNIK VON FERRUCCIO
BUSONI in Vol. I of the *Klavierwerke*   Leipzig   Breitkopf &
Haertel   EB 4301 a-d   Copyright G. Schirmer 1894-1897   Ed. 198
Also issued as Vol. 5 of the Bach-Busoni edition titled *"Das
wohltemperierte Clavier" von Johann Sebastian Bach   Bearbeitet,*

erläutert und mit daran anknüpfenden Beispielen und Anweisungen
für das Studium der modernen Clavierspieltechnik herausgegeben
von Ferruccio B. Busoni Leipzig Breitkopf & Haertel 1916
BWV 846-69

DAS WOHLTEMPERIERTE KLAVIER ZWEITER TEIL MIT
ANMERKUNGEN UND STUDIEN VERSEHEN VON FERRUCCIO
BUSONI in Vol. II. of the *Klavierwerke* Leipzig Breitkopf &
Haertel 1916 EB 4302 a-d Also issued as Vol. 6 of the Bach-
Busoni edition titled *Das wohltemperierte Klavier von Johann Sebas-*
tian Bach Zweiter Teil mit Anmerkungen und Studien von Ferruccio
Busoni Leipzig Breitkopf & Haertel 1916 BWV 870-893

These two books are now listed by Breitkopf & Haertel in Wiesbaden, in
their 1982/3 catalogue under altered nos: Book I (EB 6860/63) and Book II
(EB 8276/79).

The Bach editions, and especially the *Well-Tempered Klavier*, hereafter
referred to as WK, together with the Liszt editions, were to be Busoni's
principal editorial gift to posterity.

The first book of WK emphasizes the pianistic aspects of Bach's art. In his
preface, Busoni says: "To the foundations of the edifice of music, J. S. Bach
contributed huge blocks, firmly and unshakably laid one upon the other.
And in this same foundation of our present style of composition is to be
sought the inception of modern pianoforte playing. . . ." There follows a
brief but accurate survey of piano literature, with some comments on
transcriptions and editions. Busoni then goes on to say that "the present
edition . . . also aims in a certain sense at refounding, as it were, this
inexhaustible material into an advanced method, on broad lines, of piano
playing; this aim will, however, be carried out principally in Part I, that
being preponderant in the variety of its technical motives."

Other works are suggested for further study of Bach, including arrangements by Liszt, Tausig, and d'Albert; and Busoni concludes with an
injunction against amateurism: "If . . . truth were stated in plain terms by
every conscientious teacher to zealous beginners, the standard wherewith
people are now-a-days content to compare the artistic and moral capacities
of students would speedily be raised to a height inconveniently beyond the
reach of the generality. By such means a barrier might gradually be built up
against dilettantism and mediocrity, and thus against the degeneration of
art."

One is reminded of Busoni's remark reported by van Dieren: "We must
make the texture of our music such that no amateur can lay hands on it," he
once said, embittered by some dreadful assault and battery on a Mozart
sonata.[4]

The Schirmer edition of the WK Book I includes below the title the
following: "Revised, annotated, and provided with parallel exercises and

accompanying direction for the study of modern pianoforte technique." Thus, in the footnotes to the very first prelude, Busoni proposed four individual and clever technical derivations, but this is not the only indulgence Busoni permitted himself. His highly fertile imagination and incredible pianism naturally suggested all sorts of digital acrobatics; at the same time, right through the edition of the WK there is constant and irrefutable evidence of a highly critical and analytic brain, coolly dissecting the most complex of Bach's structures with great clarity of vision.

The edition is a valuable aid to teachers and performers alike, besides being a record of Busoni's own rendition of these pieces. The suggestions, pianistic and interpretative, are invariably sound—the layout of the actual printing clear and bold to the eye. I find the whole endeavor a model of its kind. The criticisms levelled at Busoni's editions of Bach are similar to the ones invariably brought up in connection with his transcriptions (see Chapter 15); but a quick reference back to the subtitle quoted above will serve to establish what Busoni was trying to do. He did not suggest that his Bach editions were authentic, although they are scholarly. He was concerned with a vital interpretation on the modern pianoforte, and it is toward this ultimate goal that every indication in the music is directed. Modern scholarship has discovered some errors in the text, usually in the question of ornamentation, but this in no way changes the overall value of the edition or its inherent musical vision.

Perhaps one day some enterprising publisher will bring out in full a book of studies based on Busoni's suggestions in the footnotes of the WK. Such a volume would provide rich material for technical study without recourse to the usual anti-musical "daily exercises," in spite of which music still flourishes. Busoni rarely wrote out such studies in full; students are faced with a fragment, followed by "etc." If the ideas were realized in full, however, they would possibly achieve a permanent place in the technical repertoire. To most timids minds, the transformation of Bach into studies is a horrifying idea. To Busoni there was no such contradiction. Rather such studies than Czerny! He loved Bach's music with every fiber of his being and loved it in every form. And he always stressed that he had not destroyed the original.

A list of studies forming an imaginary volume based on Busoni's edition of the *Well-Tempered Klavier* follows.

FROM BOOK I

Prelude 1   1.   Legato study
            2.   Legato, alternating hands study
            2a. Legato, hands together[5]
            3.   Staccato alternating hands
            4.   Spiccato, left-hand crossing (see Liszt-Paganini E major study)

Prelude 2	5.	Trill study
	6.	Holding fifth fingers legato study
	7.	Alternating double notes
	8.	Parallel double notes
Prelude 3	9.	Alternating double and single notes (fully written out)
Prelude 5	10.	Left hand playing semiquavers and the original bass
	11.	Another version of 10
	12.	Combination of Prelude and Fugue (see *An die Jugend*)
Prelude 6	13.	Study without using the thumb
	14.	Extension study
Prelude 10	15.	Octave study
Prelude 15	16.	Staccato chord study
	17.	Passage study
	18.	Variant of 17
	19.	Another variant
Fugue 15	20.	Staccato study for two pianos (written in full)
Prelude 17	21.	Fuller setting, legato left-hand octaves
Prelude 21	22.	Left hand crossing over
	23.	Left hand wider crossing over
	24.	Right hand crossing over
	25.	Right hand wider crossing over
	26.	Extension study (written in full, with double note runs)

FROM BOOK II

| *Prelude 15* | 27. | Legato, holding note study |

Note that only one study appears from Book II.[6] Busoni makes his attitude to this book clear in the introduction:

Bach allowed 20 years to elapse between the publication of the first and second part of the Well-Tempered Clavier, and it is about 20 years since I began to make notes of my reflections about the work. An intelligent reader, therefore, will expect to find that the treatment of the second part will show a different physiognomy from that of the earlier one. . . . Here I purposely avoid repetitions of earlier arguments and turn aside from what is purely pianistic. . . .[7]

Such a change of attitude was not deliberate.

In the intervening years he had changed from a mere virtuoso to a philosopher; and, as he said to Petri on many occasions, had he the time, he would have gone back and re-done some of his earlier Bach editions. The leisure was never afforded him. And so we find further in this introduction a short synopsis of the significance of fugue form, some of the fugues in particular, and finally the admission that "as editor, I have devoted some diligence to establishing a definite connection between prelude and fugue, occasionally showing this by means of examples. In the later examples I believe I have overstepped Bach's intentions. All changes and additions, however, follow the educational intention of giving the learner an insight into the mechanism of the composition. . . ."

Just as Book I was full of technical studies, Book II is now devoted to what Busoni calls "composition studies," illustrating in various ingenious ways Bach's techniques and skills, discovering connections between various fugues, establishing links between preludes and their corresponding fugues.

This last relationship seemed a very important thing to Busoni. It is true as a result, he often seems to "overstep Bach's intentions." An example of this thematic probing can be found in the D major Prelude and Fugue from Book I, which are to be played simultaneously.[8] Now, in his constant search for musical unity, Busoni interchanged the E flat major fugue from Book II and Book I and also the G major fugues. However, the aesthetic and thematic reasoning behind this is convincing enough. Both pianistically and musically, though seemingly audacious, it succeeds.

Apart from such forthright procedures, Book II of the WK is full of far more subtle discoveries, probings into the cellular and generative shapes that occur over and over in Bach's music, clarification of decorations superimposed on primary contrapuntal shapes, earlier versions of some of the pieces quoted in full, and suggested performance alternatives by Busoni himself.

Although purely pianistic suggestions still abound (Busoni was too much the performer for this to be ignored), they are sparser than in Book I; in a sense simpler and less drastic. The performing and editing instructions, also, are thinner, less specific. Some of the pieces look like an *Urtext* publication. Once more we are faced with the simplicity that marked Busoni's performances of Bach in his later life; a simplicity that at the same time was full of that sort of subtlety that is impossible to indicate editorially.

JOH. SEB. BACH   VIER DUETTE FÜR PIANOFORTE   BEARBEI-TUNG VON FERRUCCIO BUSONI   Leipzig   Breitkopf & Haertel 1915   EB 4765   Also issued as *Vier Duette* in Vol. III of the *Klavier-werke*   1916   EB 4303   and as *Vier Duette   Joh. Seb. Bach   Kon-zertbearbeitung von Ferruccio Busoni* in vol. 1 of the Bach-Busoni edition   1916   BWV 802-5 (E)

Displaying an affinity with these works remarkable for the time, Busoni writes: "As regards their significance, these Four Duets might suitably find their place at the end of Bach's Pianoforte works. They represent perfect maturity and finality in art, and are astounding even in Bach. They compare with his 2-part Inventions much as Beethoven's last Bagatelles with his youthful compositions. And this is an all sufficient explanation of their unpopularity hitherto."

Busoni's editing at times assumes dimensions of an arrangement for the concert platform, as well as strict and thorough attention to the compositional aspects of these pieces. Duet No. 1 is unaltered, except for a suggested "modern" chromatic setting of the theme, obviously not meant to be treated as a performance idea but symptomatic of Busoni's belief that Bach was a prophet. In Duet No. 2, alternatives are given in the canonic sections, and a concert ending is suggested. A few minor alterations are suggested in Duet No. 3. Some alterations in Duet No. 4 are designed to highlight a certain number of Bach's melodic contours on the pianoforte. There is a footnote by Busoni at the end of this fourth Duet: "The 'Duettos' have been published in a Concert Arrangement by the same Editor." There is very little difference between this edition and the concert edition—the suggestions have now been incorporated into the main text, and a few minor ornamental touches have been added. The only significant difference is that Busoni alters the order of the Duets: the e minor first, the G major, a minor, and finally the F major with the concert ending.

ZWÖLF KLEINE PRÄLUDIEN   SECHS KLEINE PRÄLUDIEN
FUGHETTA   In Vol. III of the *Klavierwerke*   Leipzig   Breitkopf
& Haertel   1916   EB 4304   Also in Vol. 1 of the Bach-Busoni
edition   1916   BWV 924, 939, 999, 925, 926, 940, 941, 927, 928, 929,
930, 942   BWV 933-38   BWV 961

Regarding this edition of the Preludes (*12 Small Preludes* and *6 Small Preludes*), Busoni says:

. . . I have tried to draw the attention of the student to the structure and meaning, by various additions in brackets (or in small type). They are not to be regarded as would be corrections of the text, any more than, for example, the double bar-lines, which I have added. I consider this form of explanation clearer than a profusion of footnotes, which I formerly employed so largely. It was my especial endeavour to indicate the "thematic idea," which forms, as it were, the framework of Bach's construction—whereby it may be seen that my little didactic work deals as much with the compositions themselves, as with their pianistic interpretations.

Busoni also gives fanciful titles to some of the preludes, "invented by the editor with a view to stimulating the interest of the student."

Thus, No. 4 of the *6 Small Preludes*, in D major, is subtitled *Duettino sopra un basso continuo*. To support this view, the piece is followed by Busoni's arrangement of it for four hands.

The *12 Small Preludes* are suggested as a cycle of pieces, to begin with No. 2 and end with No. 1.

The little *Fughetta* in c minor is supplied with an extension to the coda, and the suggestion that No. 3 of the *12 Small Preludes* (also in c minor) might be used as a prelude to this *Fughetta* at a "pupil's performance."

ZWEI- UND DREISTIMMIGE INVENTIONEN FÜR DAS
PIANOFORTE VON JOHANN SEBASTIAN BACH   MIT BEZUG
AUF DEN VORTRAG UND DIE COMPOSITION BEARBEITET
UND ERLÄUTERT VON FERRUCCIO B. BUSONI   Leipzig
Breitkopf & Haertel   1892   Also issued as *15 zweistimmige
Inventionen   Joh. Seb. Bach, Bearbeitung von F. B. Busoni* in vol. IV
of the *Klavierwerke*   1914   EB 4305   and as *15 dreistimmige
Inventionen   Joh. Seb. Bach   Bearbeitung von F. B. Busoni* in Vol. V
of the *Klavierwerke*   1914   EB 4305   Also issued as *Inventionen* in
Vol 1 of the Bach-Busoni edition   1916   Breitkopf & Haertel also
published foreign language editions: Spanish EB 2307a/b   English EB
3127-3128   Italian EB 3345 and EB 3389   French EB 4428-29
American, G. Schirmer Ed. 1498, 1512, 1574   BWV 772-86   BWV
787-801

As with all of Busoni's editions of Bach, an introduction indicates the
particular aspect of the music that is to be stressed, while at the same time
the music is edited with his typical thoroughness. In the case of the
inventions, Busoni indicates in his preface that "a commentary, which,
besides the technical hints, and remarks upon execution—is intended to be a
contribution towards the study of Form." And so, the copious notes either
deal with analysis or with style and its related technical problems: there is
no pianistic adaptation to be found in the Inventions.[9] Busoni apparently
saw in these pieces not as much concert as pedagogical material; more
purity of line and not so much the gothic architecture he so loved in some of
the bigger pieces from the "48" and other Bach fugues he edited. He
probably did not know that Bach stated in a preface to the fair copy of the
Sinfoniae that these pieces, originally appearing in a little instructional
album for W. F. Bach, were intended to demonstrate techniques of both
performance and composition.

An interesting feature of Busoni's pianism is his use of crossover
fingerings with the thumb stationary; the edition is generally full of very
useful and ingenious suggestions.

Characteristic of the change of heart that overcame Busoni as his distaste
for the purely exhibitionistic aspect of the virtuoso career gained ground is
the interpretation of the two-part Invention No. 15 in b minor. The
published indications are "Non legato, not too moderate in movement." In
later years, as Busoni indicated in the preface to the second edition, he
preferred to play this Invention slowly, slurred as shown in Figure 11.1, and

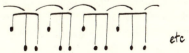

Figure 11.1

rather reflective in character, thus again anticipating a more recent style of Bach performance.[10]

JOHANN SEBASTIAN BACH   CHROMATISCHE FANTASIE
INTERPRETIERT VON FERRUCCIO BUSONI   Berlin   N. Simrock
1902   Also issued as *Chromatische Fantasie und Fuge   Joh. Seb.*
Bach   Herausgegeben von Ferruccio Busoni in Vol. XIV of the
Klavierwerke   Leipzig   Breitkopf & Haertel   1915   EB 4314   and
as *Chromatische Fantasie, Johann Sebastian Bach   Interpretiert*
von Ferruccio Busoni in Vol. 2 of the Bach-Busoni edition
1916   BWV 903

Busoni was frequently castigated for his version of this great work. Petri tells of his own playing of it at a concert, and being criticized by some musicians next day for departing from Bülow's edition. Evidently, for many years Bülow's romantic excesses were considered authentic even by well-educated European musicians; Busoni's edition was an attempt to discard these editorial frills and reinstate the Bach to its original grandeur, at the same time keeping in mind the modern concert pianoforte. In his preface to the Breitkopf edition, Busoni writes:

In this piece, the important point was to reconstruct its original meaning, to cleanse it of those "Manners and Mannerisms" which time, the manifold transcripts, the accustomed routine of "Piano-classes," and the vanity indigenous to the concert-room had accumulated for it. In his interpretation, the editor has endeavoured to restore a greater unity of conception, to reduce the many small sections to a few large ones, and thus to allow the broad, tragic line of the Fantasy to take effect. The four divisions resulting from this conception of the work might be superscribed: Toccata, Chorale (Arpeggio), Recitative and Coda. The Recitative is entirely one-voiced, that is to say, assigned to one and the same voice throughout, even where it turns into passage-playing, and leaves the more restricted position of a vocal part to spread over the whole range of the keyboard. Tone and execution must be rendered accordingly, preserving unity as far as possible, and standing out in bold relief against the intervening "Orchestra" or "Cembalo." The misrepresentations of all former texts have been rectified; the amendments introduced endeavour to obtain everywhere convenience for the player, and here and there, a greater volume of sound.[11] [See Figure 11.13.]

After his version, Busoni includes the original Bach *Fantasia* for comparison: no editor could be more honest; very few are as honest.

It is interesting to note that the *Fuge* did not, in Busoni's opinion, measure up to the *Fantasia*. He often omitted it in his own concerts. The editing here is rather routine, except for the last two pages, which have some interesting ideas.[12]

There is a little-known arrangement by Busoni of this work for cello and piano (EB 4838), and though the worth of this 1917 transcription may be questionable, his reasons for doing it vindicate Busoni's remarks quoted above. According to Petri, the cello arrangement was done principally for two reasons: (1) to introduce an ensemble problem, to force the players to play the piece more in strict time, and less with the sort of romantic rubato found in Bülow's edition; and (2) in the Recitative, to separate the melodic line (given to the cello) from the accompaniment, to underline the essentially vocal nature of this section; a fact, Busoni strongly felt, too often ignored by pianists, and one that must have offended the Latin love of melody in him.

JOH. SEB. BACH   CAPRICCIO ÜBER DIE ABREISE DES VIEL-GELIEBTEN BRUDERS—SOPRA LA LONTANANZA DEL SUO FRATELLO DILETTISSIMO   KONZERTBEARBEITUNG VON FERRUCCIO BUSONI   Leipzig   Breitkopf & Haertel   1915   EB 4764   Also issued as *Capriccio über die Abreise des vielgeliebten Bruders   Capriccio sopra la lontananza del suo fratello dilettissimo* in Vol. XIV of the *Klavierwerke*   Leipzig   Breitkopf & Haertel 1915   EB 4314   and as *Capriccio über die Abreise des vielgeliebten Bruders—sopra la lontananza del suo fratello dilettissimo   Joh. Seb. Bach   Konzertbearbeitung von Ferruccio Busoni* in Vol. 4 of the Bach-Busoni edition   1916   BWV 992

This is interesting for its realization of the adagissimo movement, both in harmonic and pianistic terms. (See Figure 11.2.) The fugue is also made more effective by some suggestions and the omission of one bar; however, the original is printed with the edited text.[13] Some ornaments are not quite correct.

JOHANN SEBASTIAN BACH   FANTASIA, ADAGIO E FUGA FÜR DAS PIANOFORTE   FÜR DEN KONZERT-VORTRAG ZUSAMMENGESTELLT UND ERGÄNZT VON FERRUCCIO BUSONI   Leipzig   Breitkopf & Haertel   1915   EB 4766   Also issued as *Fantasia, Adagio e Fuga   Joh. Seb. Bach   Für den Konzertvortrag zusammengestellt und ergänzt von Ferruccio Busoni* in Vol. XIV of the *Klavierwerke*   Leipzig   Breitkopf & Haertel   1915 EB 4314   and also in Vol. 4 of the Bach-Busoni edition   1916   BWV 906 and 968

Bach did not compose such a work. Busoni found three separate pieces and was attracted by the idea of presenting them as one, thus rescuing them from undeserved oblivion. The first movement is the now quite well known *Fantasia in c minor* (BWV 906). The second is the *Adagio* (BWV 968), Bach's own transcription of the first movement of the third sonata for solo violin. The last movement is the unfinished *Fugue in c minor* (BWV 906-2);

Figure 11.2. By kind permission, Breitkopf & Haertel, Wiesbaden.

the catalogue number indicates that it was meant by Bach as a companion piece for the above *Fantasia*. Busoni took upon himself to complete this fugue, which was brilliantly accomplished, with a reference in the coda to the second movement, thus creating a link between the second and third movements, admittedly a link not intended by Bach. It should be made clear here that Busoni was totally unaware that the *Fantasia* and incomplete *Fugue* were originally a compound work by Bach, and identified as such by more recent research. He says in his introduction: "The pieces which we have here combined into one group, were originally independent one from the other, and can remain separate." Given the choice of a number of fantasias in c minor among Bach's miscellaneous works, Busoni, by a stroke of musical intuition, joined the *Fugue* with the correct one.

JOH. SEB. BACH PRÄLUDIUM, FUGE UND ALLEGRO IN ES DUR FÜR PIANOFORTE ZU ZWEI HÄNDEN   BEARBEITUNG VON FERRUCCIO BUSONI   Leipzig   Breitkopf & Haertel   1915 EB 4778   Also issued *as Präludium, Fuge und Allegro in Es-dur Joh. Seb. Bach   Bearbeitung von Ferruccio Busoni* in Vol. XIV of the *Klavierwerke* Leipzig Breitkopf & Haertel 1915   EB 4314   and also in Vol. 1 of the Bach-Busoni edition   1916   BWV 998

Busoni once again indulges in his penchant for thematic and structural order and makes a very interesting performance suggestion aimed at making the work more unified.

Instead of playing as Bach had written—*Präludium, Fuge* (first part, quick middle section, reprise of first part), *Allegro*—Busoni suggests *Praludium, Fuge*, first part, quick middle section, *Allegro*, fuge first part reprised, in more grandiose style. Although the music is printed as Bach wrote it, Busoni's suggestions are included in the notes and analyses.

FANTASIE, FUGE, ANDANTE UND SCHERZO   JOH. SEB. BACH HERAUSGEGEBEN VON F. BUSONI   In Vol. 7 of the Bach-Busoni edition Leipzig Breitkopf & Haertel 1920   Also in Vol. XVI of the *Klavierwerke*   1921   EB 4316   BWV 905, 969, 844

This composite "work" is the basis of the *Sonatina brevis* (see Chapter 6).

SARABANDA CON PARTITE   ARIA VARIATA ALLA MANIERA ITALIANA   Both in Vol. XVI of the *Klavierwerke* Leipzig Breitkopf & Haertel 1921   EB 4316   BWV 990 and 989

There is nothing specially interesting about Busoni's work on these two sets of variations. There are some admirable fingerings and interesting ideas on interpretation but one expects this in a Busoni edition.

It is doubtful whether Busoni was terribly involved in these variations. He says in his preface: "This volume contains as appendix an echo of the Aria with variations, the remaining smaller works[14] with variations . . . [that] . . . will fulfil their purpose more definitely rather as material for practice."[15]

TOKKATA E MOLL   TOKKATA G MOLL   TOKKATA
G DUR JOH. SEB. BACH HERAUSGEGEBEN VON F. BUSONI
In Vol. XVIII of the *Klavierwerke* Leipzig Breitkopf & Haertel
1920 EB 4318 Also in Vol. 7 of the Bach-Busoni edition
1920 BWV 914, 915, 916

In a preface dated Zürich, August 1916, Busoni establishes the fact that "toccata" used to signify a free improvisatory piece; his editing and general approach to the three toccatas in this volume bear this out. The e minor *Toccata* even begins with the indication "Alla breve, improvvisando."

The G major *Toccata* is set out as a concerto in the Italian manner, and the first movement is divided into solo and tutti entries.

ARIA MIT 30 VERÄNDERUNGEN (GOLDBERGSCHE VARIA-
TIONEN) DIESE AUSGABE SCHLIESST IN SICH EINE KONZERT-
FASSUNG (ARIA, 20 VARIATIONEN UND FINALE DIE VOM
HAUPTTEXTE TRENNBAR IST) In Vol. XV of the *Klavierwerke*
Leipzig Breitkopf & Haertel 1915 EB 4315 Also as *Aria mit 30
Veränderungen für das Klavier Joh. Seb. Bach Herausgegeben
von F. Busoni* in Vol. 2 of the Bach-Busoni edition 1916 BWV 988

The text is not to be regarded as accurate: the *Aria*, especially, has many errors.[16] The value of the edition lies in its solution of the many keyboard problems involved in playing a work designed for a two-manual instrument on the modern piano. (See Figure 11.3.) The interpretative and technical solutions, while strongly individualistic, are interesting and instructive.

Figure 11.3. By kind permission, Breitkopf & Haertel, Wiesbaden.

Busoni had a novel idea of the form of the variations, and divided the gigantic work into three main sections: "The division into groups signifies, not only a breathing pause, an arrangmement of the sections, a synopsis: it personifies also three distinct conditions of creative production; interplay within the circle; inward penetration; outward exaltation."[17] The first group ends with variation 13, the second with variation 25. Also, there is a suggested concert version of the Variations, which disregards the repeats and suppresses some of the variations entirely, reducing their number to 20. The order of this version is: Aria, Variations 1, 2, 4, 5, 6, 7, 8, 10, 11, 13. Second group: 14 (or 17), 15, 19, 20, 22, 23, 25. Third group: 26, 28, 29, Quodlibet, Aria. Busoni gives detailed and explicit reasons for his choice of omissions.

This may not be as unauthentic as it sounds. It is debatable in the first instance whether the *Goldberg Variations* were meant to be played right through as one piece, as recitals of that type were very unusual in Bach's time; the extreme length of the work frequently prevents its programming even today. Busoni's solution would at least mean more performance of this masterpiece on the platform, and, of course, when the suggestion of curtailment was made, there were no LP recordings. Furthermore, Busoni's visionary interpretation of the Variations—cuts aside—should, in my opinion, be of value to today's performers.

Regarding the Aria da capo at the end of the piece, "the editor considered it desirable to restore the theme to its original melodic outline, simplified and freed from the elaborate network of ornamentations;—thus giving the conclusion something hymn-like in effect, and increasing the volume of tone, by transferring it to the lower octave—the first appearance of the same theme at the beginning may be considered as its own first Variation." (See Figure 11.4.)[18] This, clearly, is inspired by the modern pianoforte,

Figure 11.4. By kind permission, Breitkopf & Haertel, Wiesbaden.

rather than having any particular relevance to the harpsichord where use of 16′ pitch would have been implausible and probably considered undesirable by the composer.

ZWEI KONTRAPUNKT-STUDIEN FÜR KLAVIER NACH JOHANN SEBASTIAN BACH   NR. 1   FANTASIE UND FUGE   A MOLL J. S. BACH = (F. BUSONI) Leipzig Breitkopf & Haertel 1917 EB 4940 Also issued as *Fantasie und Fuge   A-moll   Joh. Seb. Bach   Herausgegeben von F. Busoni* in Vol. XVIII of the *Klavierwerke* 1917   EB   4318   Also   in   Vol.   7   of   the   Bach-Busoni edition   1920   BWV 904

In this edition it is at once evident that Busoni's Bach studies have led him into discoveries which, as he admits in the preface, he knew little or nothing of in 1894, when Book I of the WK appeared. If we turn to Busoni's footnotes on the E flat Prelude and Fugue from Book I however, we find an interesting idea. It will be recalled that Busoni actually printed the Prelude from Book I with the Fugue from Book II; as part of his justification for so doing, he quoted a comparison of the themes (see Figure 11.5) and further

A comparison of the themes in question is calculated to support the editor's opinion.

It will also be of interest to note that the subject of the great E flat major (triple) fugue for the organ must likewise be considered as belonging to this same family of themes. This subject reads:

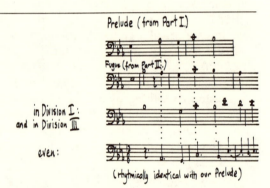

An obbligato countersubject in sixteenth notes, developed in Division III of the organ fugue, completes the resemblance of the latter with the prelude now under consideration.

We are, therefore, fully justified in the conception that these 3 E flat major fugues form (intellectually) one work, or at least three workings—out of one and the same idea—as three branches from one parent stem, a conception wherein Bach's inexhaustibility is presented to our renewed astonishment.

Figure 11.5. By kind permission, Breitkopf & Haertel, Wiesbaden.

established a similarity with the theme of the great organ triple fugue, also in E flat major. But, as Busoni admitted in the preface to the *Two Contrapuntal Studies*, he cited this as an example, whereas he later discovered it to be an abstract rule. He then introduced the term *ur-motiv* as a sort of basic cell, and proceeded to show how the *Fantasie and Fugue* are built up from it. Busoni even constructed a few bars of the *Fantasie* and the

Fugue combined to underline his thesis that the basic cell of the two movements is the same. (Schenker, in Vienna, had already become absorbed by this idea prior to 1917). The *Fugue* is printed with the ur-motiv constantly quoted in its basic form above and below the music in small type. Busoni says of this work that "it is a wonderful structure not often met with in the WK."[19]

To us, the interesting things are that a cellular type of analysis is being applied to Bach and applied successfully. At this date it opened up the possibility of looking at much of Bach in this different way. Busoni suggests by constant cross references that Bach had certain pet ur-motives which he used again and again. This, too, is an area of research, which in no way lowers our estimate of Bach's inventive genius, but on the contrary, is "a conception wherein Bach's inexhaustibility is presented to our renewed astonishment."[20] As Busoni learned from Bach, so he applied his discoveries to his own compositions; some of the sonatinas, for example, contain striking uses of the ur-motiv technique.

ZWEI KONTRAPUNKT-STUDIEN FÜR KLAVIER NACH JOHANN SEBASTIAN BACH   NR. 2   KANONISCHE VARIA- TIONEN UND FUGE (ÜBER DAS THEMA KÖNIG FRIEDRICHS DES GROSSEN) AUS J. S. BACH'S "MUSIKALISCHES OPFER" GEZOGEN UND FÜR DAS KLAVIER DARGESTELLT   Leipzig Breitkopf & Haertel   1917   EB 4940   Also issued as *Kanonische Variationen und Fuge (über das Thema Konig Friedrichs des Grossen) aus J. S. Bach's "Musikalisches Opfer" gezogen und für Klavier dargestellt von Ferruccio Busoni* in Vol. 7 of the Bach-Busoni edition 1920   BWV 1079)

Busoni begins his preface (dated 1916) with a quotation from Schweitzer:

The *Musical Offering* contains in all ten canons, including the *fuga canonica* at the end of the first part. They are not canons in the ordinary sense of the word, aiming at a definite musical effect, but clever musical charades, of the kind that the musicians of that time were fond of propounding to each other. The solutions of the first six canons are given by Kirnberger in his *Kunst des reinen Satzes*. In two of them—the fourth and the fifth—Bach aims at a certain musical symbolism. Over the fourth, in which the theme is treated in augmentation in contrary motion, he writes: "Notulis crescentibus crescat Fortuna Regis," ("may the good fortune of the King increase like that of the note-values"). The fifth, a circle canon ascending through the scale, is inscribed: "Ascendenteque Modulatione ascendat Gloria Regis, ("and as the modulation ascends, so may it be with the glory of the King").[21]

Busoni then goes on to say that the quotation "seek and ye shall find," written by Bach at the head of the second canon, gave him the impetus for issuing such an edition of the *Musical Offering*. The original Bach is fully quoted, and then is followed by Busoni's realization and solution of the canonic puzzles, all adapted to the keyboard, although he warns us that the

Offering is not a keyboard work but rather an abstract work to be studied. (In the 1960s it was discovered that the *Offering* was originally produced in a highly practical form, implying special instrumentation.) Nonetheless, Busoni's solution, set out as a series of variations with the Royal Theme quoted at the beginning of the piece, is eminently playable on the piano and is an accurate and original representation of Bach's canonic solutions. The tenth canon is omitted since Bach expressly scored it for violin, flute, and keyboard.

Considering the popularity of so much Bach-Busoni, it is rather odd that this work has been neglected by pianists; especially since it is probably the most "authentic" of all the Busoni keyboard transcriptions.

KONZERT D-MOLL FÜR KLAVIER UND STREICHORCHESTER
VON JOHANN SEBASTIAN BACH   FREIE BEARBEITUNG VON
FERRUCCIO B. BUSONI   Leipzig   Breitkopf & Haertel
1900   Klav. Bibl. 22675   Also issued as *Joh. Seb.*
Bach   Klavier-Konzert, D-moll   Freie Bearbeitung von
F. B. Busoni   Solostimme mit hinzugefügter 2.
Klavierstimme an Stelle des Orchesters   1900   EB 2956   Also as
Konzert für Klavier in D moll   Joh. Seb. Bach   Freie Bearbeitung von
F. B. Busoni in Vol. 2 of the Bach-Busoni edition   1916
BWV 1052

Lest the reader may receive the impression that Busoni re-scored the work or altered the scoring in any way, I hasten with reassurances. The reasons for the publication of an orchestral score were as follows:

1. Right through the concerto, the piano is given moments and bars of rest instead of playing continuously as in the Bach score; with a modern piano and a full string orchestra, many tuttis do not need the piano reinforcement. This makes the keyboard stand out when it functions as a soloist, unlike the situation in Bach's day, when it was a totally different matter for a harpsichordist playing with a small group of strings. The conductor, therefore (another modern addition), has a score that would vary from the original.

2. Busoni introduces some cuts in the concerto—notably the double re-capitulation in the first movement—and some episodes in the last.

3. In the last movement's perpetuum-mobile-like cadenza, Busoni gives the sequentially re-iterated quaver chords to the strings, while the piano continues with a barrage of semiquavers. This is the only re-orchestrated moment in the whole work (bars 251-63).

Such things carry their own admirable audacity—but Busoni was never fainthearted. In actual performance, the cuts, the solo and tutti highlighting, and the one moment of re-distribution, all combine to produce a heightened direction to this wonderful concerto. The cuts are suggested by some other editors as well, though it is true that they publish the complete work. In later years Busoni would have included the original Bach with his own version.

Naturally, it is the keyboard part of the concerto that comes under extensive revision. We have already noted the fact that the pianist rests during the tutti; other devices that Busoni introduces into the solo part are (1) doubling the bass in octaves; (2) doubling the treble part, either an octave below or above; (3) using a wider span of keyboard by transposing some passages into a higher octave; and (4) omitting the Bachian basso continuo, and writing in a more florid left-hand part.

Unfortunately, there are undoubted lapses in Busoni's approach where there is confusion in his mind between Bach and Liszt, between musical effect and romantic exuberance. Some of these lapses are printed as ossias but some are not as, for example, the Lisztian flourish at the end of the third movement. (See Figure 11.6.) The chords at the end of the second

Figure 11.6. By kind permission, Breitkopf & Haertel, Wiesbaden.

movement are also in rather questionable style. (See Figure 11.7.) On the other hand, many suggestions and amendments, while still upsetting the purists, are stylistically and pianistically most effective and, it seems to me, not really contrary to the spirit of the concerto and of baroque embellishment generally. (See Figures 11.8 and 11.9.) Passages as in Figure 11.10, although effective, will find objection among some players.

As it stands, Busoni's edition of the Bach *Concerto*, apart from being a permanent record of the man's playing, is also a musical hotchpotch of inequality. If it is to be rescued from complete obscurity, into which it has

Figure 11.7. By kind permission, Breitkopf & Haertel, Wiesbaden.

now descended (there was only one extant recording anyway, by Alexander Borovsky), some compromise may be necessary, not because of the contemporary taste for authenticity but because there are definite stylistic discrepancies in the Busoni version.

Some years ago, convinced of the excellence of some of Busoni's ideas and equally unimpressed by others, I gave a performance of this concerto in which I utilized the main directions taken by Busoni, namely, the cuts, the tutti-solo idea, some of the keyboard re-distributions. I restored Bach in the too-Lisztian flourishes, avoided the re-scored section due to the practical problem of altering orchestral parts, and played the slow movement exactly as Busoni had set it out, except for the disastrous last chords. This is in a way the most successful of the three movements, and, despite a few over-thick left-hand chords, Busoni manages to create a florid and melodically enriched cantabile in the right hand.

Figure 11.8. By kind permission, Breitkopf & Haertel, Wiesbaden.

The result, I believed, was a justification of Busoni's vision of this work, eminently suitable to be played as a modern concerto on the pianoforte with a complete string section, giving full reign to the dynamics available on the instrument but always in style, stressing the interplay of solo-tutti to dramatic effect, utilizing the glorious cantabile qualities of a modern pianoforte in the slow movement. It may not be authentic Bach, but it is certainly vital and noble Bach.

Figure 11.9. By kind permission, Breitkopf & Haertel, Wiesbaden.

Figure 11.10. By kind permission, Breitkopf & Haertel, Wiesbaden.

Bach in the "Klavierübung"   (Pages given as in the second edition, see Chapter 10)

1. Page 30, Book 3, "Chords."[22] Suggested exercise based on Prelude No. 1, Book I, W K .

2. Page 57, Book 4, "Three Hands." An extract from the combination of the D major Prelude and Fugue found in *Au die Jugend.*

3. Page 66, Book 5, "Trills." One of the *Goldberg Variations* (var. 28), exact.

"In der Art eines Choralvorspiels" No. 3 of the DREI ALBUMBLÄTTER
EB   5193   (see Chapter 5)

There is no acknowledgement by Busoni of the origin of this piece. It is based on the chorale *Christ lag in Todesbanden*, No. 371[23] in the Breitkopf edition of Bach Chorales (*371 Vierstimme Choralgesänge Für Klavier oder Orgel oder Harmonium. EB 10*).[24]

In miniature form this little piece again re-demonstrates Busoni's free and visionary treatment of Bach. It is instructive to compare even the simple opening bars in the two versions. (See Figure 11.11.) The Busoni, transcribed an octave lower in doubled values, is typical of his Bach sound on a modern grand piano; the slight chromatic alterations and added ambiguous major-minor tonalities are but another example of Busoni looking upon Bach not only as a past composer but also one containing seeds for future explorations.[25]

There follows an interesting idea of using the tenor line from the opening phrase of the chorale for a variation; and then, again, the extraordinary sound, as in Figure 11.12. The fanfare is used as a tonal prism a number of times, and finally this motive ends the piece in the same somber register of the piano from which it came.

FANTASIA NACH JOHANN SEBASTIAN BACH FÜR DAS
KLAVIER Leipzig   Breitkopf & Haertel   1909   EB 3054   Also issued as *Fantasia   Ferruccio Busoni   Alla Memoria di mio Padre Ferdinando Busoni † il 12 Maggio 1909 †* in Vol. 4 of the Bach-Busoni edition   1916

Among the choral variations for organ of J. S. Bach, we find one on "Christ, der du bist der helle Tag" (BWV 766). Busoni used it for his *Fantasia nach Bach.* The chorale appears in the same key as in the original and, as well, two variations are utilized: Partita II (a 2 Clav.), exactly as in the original, and Partita VII, with modifications.

Unusually, other chorales associated with Bach enter into this work—we shall try to establish later the reasons for using seemingly unrelated chorales.

As in the case of the *Albumblatt* No. 3, Busoni does not acknowledge his

Figure 11.11. By kind permission, Breitkopf & Haertel, Wiesbaden.

sources, although the work is titled "nach Bach," and the cover proclaims, in bold letters, "Bach-Busoni Fantasia."

1. The *Fantasia* opens with a darkly colored, Bach-like improvisation, low on the keyboard; gradually, through the semiquaver patterns a chant-like melody emerges, thematically associated with a chorale as yet unheard: "Christ, der du bist der helle Tag." The section ends in a tranquil fashion with A flat major arpeggios.

2. A dolente episode follows, using subsidiary material from the first section, and a mournful drooping chromatic figure:

Figure 11.12. By kind permission, Breitkopf & Haertel, Wiesbaden.

This leads into a full statement of the Bach chorale—"Christ, der du bist der helle Tag" (Bach: Partita I).

3. The chorale is heard with Bachian harmonies in a typical Busoni setting with massive sonorous chords. An effect of organ echoes in a cathedral is added after each line of the chorale.

4. The Bach original Partita II.

5. An F major section largely based on Bach's fughetta on "Gottes Sohn ist Kommen" (BWV 600). Why did Busoni introduce another chorale when he was always so obsessed with unity in his compositions? Perhaps because the phrase introduced is thematically related to the other chorale. The F major key acts as a foil to the somberness of the preceding episodes, and further cohesion is obtained by Bach's own similar style in both 4 and 5.

6. Through an abrupt and unexpected transition we find ourselves in f minor again. Substantially, this is the Bach partita VII, but instead of following Bach to the end of this variation, Busoni now moves into 7.

7. A grandiose statement of "Lob sei dem allmachtigen Gott," again largely based on Bach (BWV 602), with a complex counterpoint continuing in both hands. This chorale melody has some thematic similarities to the other two used. We pass through the key of A flat major, met in section 1, into F major, and, as the exaltation dies down, into a soft reminiscence of the third phrase of the chorale "Christ, der du bist der helle Tag."

8. An altered, abbreviated re-capitulation of 2.

9. A coda, consisting of a re-capitulation, this time in F major, of the arpeggios from 1. This section is marked riconciliato, and "Pax Ej!" Our suspicions of a bell-like sound in 1 are now confirmed ("quasi campana"), but although Busoni writes "tranquillissimo," the work still ends darkly on three low f minor chords. The riconciliato was not to be achieved so easily.

This poetic and deeply felt work is therefore now seen to be in the favored arch form. The movements are coupled: 1 and 9, 2 and 8, 3 and 7 (maestoso settings), 4 and 6—the two original Bachian sections, which leaves 5—"Gottes Sohn . . ." as the keystone of the arch.

Whether the chorale melodies had extra-musical connotations for Busoni we shall never know; it could well be that these chorales were heard by the composer in his youth.

Preludio, Fuga e Fuga figurata, Studie nach J. S. Bach's wohltemperier-tem Klavier in AN DIE JUGEND   (see Chapter 5)   Also in vol. 4 of the Bach-Busoni edition

The work consists of three parts: (a) the D major Prelude from the first book of the "48," substantially as it appeared in Busoni's edition, with Bach's last three bars written out as five bars "without changing the tempo," without moving into an adagio; (b) the D major Fugue, written out in double values (twice the number of bars), so that both pieces are given in semiquavers. The Fugue is again taken from the Bach-Busoni edition and is broken off three bars before its conclusion; and (c) a contrapuntal combination of the Prelude and Fugue. The last three bars of the Fugue are then played to complete the whole work.

Already in the edition of the "48," Busoni had written: "The thematic relations between the Prelude and Fugue are closer than may generally be assumed; their common harmonic basis would render it possible to super-impose the one piece on the other, of course with some modifications." This is the realization of that germinal idea. It is more than a stunt, because it demonstrates Busoni's belief that this sort of unity lies behind much or most of J. S. Bach's output; it also was of value to Busoni's own growing interest in polyphony as the true music of the future.

See also in other chapters: the organ transcriptions, the Chorale Preludes, the violin Chaconne (see Chapter 16); the *Fantasia Contrappuntistica* (see Chapter 9); the Improvisation on a Bach Chorale for two pianos (see Chapter 5); Sonatina nach Bach (see Chapter 6).

NOTES

1. Another story is of Busoni being cornered at a society function by a fashionable, bejewelled, befurred lady, who insisted on asking him what he was going to play. "Opus 111 of Beethoven, and Opus 13 of Schumann, Opus 35 of Chopin, and Opus 24 of Brahms," replied Busoni offhandedly. "O, how nice," gushed the lady, "I so love Opuses."

2. Often without achieving the same clarity of result or beauty of sound.

3. In "Zeitgemässe Nachwort zu der Bach-Ausgabe von Ferruccio Busoni," *Der Bär* Yearbook (Leipzig, Breitkopf & Haertel, 1923), trans. Edward Dent in *Ferruccio Busoni: A Biography* (London, Oxford University Press, 1933), pp. 17-18.

4. van Dieren, *Down among the Dead Men*, p. 36n.

5. *Klavierübung*: lst ed., parts I, V; 2nd ed., Book 3.

6. It is interesting to note that, to the best of our knowledge, Bach himself did not use the term *Well-Tempered Klavier* with regard to Book II, but simply headed the work "Twenty-four Preludes & Fugues." It is therefore plausible that he intended the two sets of preludes and fugues to represent somewhat separate treatments of similar ideas.

7. Ferruccio Busoni, *The Essence of Music and Other Papers*, trans. Rosamond Ley (London, Rocklift, 1957), pp. 96-97.

8. See Bach in *An die Jugend*.

9. Bach did not title these compositions "Three-part Inventions." He first referred to them as *Fantasias*, and later settled on the title *Sinfoniae*.

10. As Busoni moved toward his fortieth birthday and beyond, he was more and more attracted by the gentler and lyrically expansive aspects of Bach, rather than the more rhetorical. This was reflected in his playing, his editing, and, most significantly, in the trend of his own compositions. The preface to the second edition of the Inventions specifically points to a gentler way of playing, as well as urging students not to take his directions too literally but to be individual. Finally, an interesting technical comment is made: "These days I rarely, if ever, change fingers on repeated notes (also pralltrills and mordents) and tend more and more to avoid putting the thumb under." A variant of the first Invention is also presented.

11. As an example, one of the more contentious moments, from the chorale. (See Figure 11.13.)

Figure 11.13. By kind permission, Breitkopf & Haertel, Wiesbaden.

12. In the earlier Simrock edition, Busoni had written: "The 'Fugue' remains untouched. The editor is of the opinion that it is not only of less value, but that it actually disturbs the mood created by the Fantasia; for the rest, the Fugue needs no revising hand. Finally, the Fantasia appears as a work ethically and musically complete in itself."

13. But not in the separate publication of the *Capriccio*. (Preface is dated July 1914.)

14. There is only one other work—the *Sarabande con Partite*.

15. It is further to Busoni's credit that his relative disinterest in these works is supported by the findings of contemporary scholars, who now think it entirely possible that neither of these sets of variations is by Bach.

16. Or deliberate alterations.

17. Busoni's preface, dated August 1914.

18. Vol. 15, p. 4 of accompanying notes booklet.

19. Vol. 18, p. 32.

20. Once again, Busoni anticipates current thought. The detailed structure of Bach's music in motives is becoming prominent not only in musicological circles but also in performing ones, where it is giving rise to fresh treatments of Bach's music, especially on keyboard instruments.

21. Albert Schweitzer, *J. S. Bach*, trans. Ernest Newman (London, Adam & Charles Black, 1911), p. 422.

22. As in WK, hands combined, instead of alternating.

23. Charles S. Terry in his *Bach's Four-Part Chorals* (London, Oxford University Press, 1926), quotes six different settings by Bach of this hymn by Martin Luther; two of the settings are in d minor, one of these being a figured bass setting; the other four are in e minor, the key of Busoni's *Albumblatt*. There are no real significant differences in the six versions, however.

24. Busoni also uses part of the *Albumblatt* in *Doktor Faust*: see p. 176 of the vocal score.

25. See Chapter 6 and comments on the *Sonatina brevis*.

12

Busoni and Liszt

> Busoni was one of the most important musical figures of the century.
> Just as Liszt started a movement which led to the great music of Wagner
> and Strauss, so Busoni started a movement which, we think, will lead to
> the great music of our time.
>
> Kurt Weill

> Bach is the foundation of piano playing. Liszt the summit. The two make
> Beethoven possible.
>
> Busoni

> Truly Bach is the Alpha of pianoforte composition and Liszt the Omega.
>
> Busoni

If Bach taught Busoni the art of counterpoint and structure, if Mozart
taught him clarity and conciseness of form, then Liszt taught him to write
specifically for the pianoforte. It is interesting to compare Busoni's editions
and arrangements of the three composers destined to affect him more than
any others. The influences overlap, of course, but often Busoni "improves"
in the very areas in which he has learned most from the composer in
question. Thus, he does not hesitate to add contrapuntal elaborations and
combinations to Bach, to complete unfinished works, and offer new
thematic interlacings. With Mozart, his main preoccupation seems to be
editing out everything superfluous or repetitive. With Liszt, he concentrates
on the purely pianistic.

There used to be a popular myth—and the misconception still exists—
that Busoni was a pupil of Liszt, indeed, the greatest pupil of Liszt. In actual
fact, Busoni's personal connections with Liszt were tenuous. Anna Weiss-
Busoni had played once for the old Abbé Liszt; young Ferruccio had played
for him too, although Liszt had refused to supply a testimonial to Busoni's
father. On the other hand, Busoni had heard Liszt play and was sadly

disappointed; Liszt was in his declining years and was no doubt out of practice. Busoni found the playing cold and uninspiring.

It was not Liszt who stood in Busoni's mind as the epitome of what piano playing should be, it was Anton Rubinstein. The contact was more prolonged and more personal. Rubinstein was at the height of his powers as a pianist. It was from him that Busoni inherited the monumental concept of performance that, intermingled with his own intellectual inclinations, was to last him for the rest of his life. Rubinstein, too, because of a closer association, took a personal interest in Busoni's welfare. His testimonial is, as Dent observes, more in the nature of advice to Ferdinando Busoni rather than a recommendation. Rubinstein was no doubt aware of Ferdinando's tendency to exploit the child prodigy Ferruccio for all he was worth: his advice was to let the young pianist study seriously, "and not be forced to play in public to earn a living," so that one day he would "do honour to his country as a distinguished musician."[1] Busoni, inspired as he was by Rubinstein's leonine approach to the keyboard, included some of the Russian's music in his own repertoire: two of the concerti (op. 70 in d minor and Op. 94 in E flat major), some etudes and the Op. 88 *Variations*; however, these works figured in his earlier programs only.

We are more concerned, however, with Liszt's influence as a composer rather than as a pianist, although the two must have been related, at least in Busoni's youth; after his disappointment with Liszt the pianist, he felt little affinity for Liszt the composer until he was well into his twenties. For someone as precocious as Busoni, this was late. It was only in the 1890s that Busoni gradually and cautiously acquired a knowledge and understanding of Liszt, began to collect Liszt editions, and include him with ever-increasing frequency in his concert programs.[2]

By the turn of the century, Busoni had become famous as an interpreter of Liszt, acclaimed even by Liszt's pupils as a true exponent. Busoni reported to Gerda from London, 9 December 1899: "I have seldom played so well, and the impression which I saw I had made was a great triumph for *me*, a comfort and a pleasure. After the Adagio nobody could speak a word. After the Norma Fantasy (during which Dayas'[3] eyes nearly started out of his head) he sprang up and said, "What a pity that the 'Old Man' did not hear it, he would have given you his sword and died in peace. . . ."[4] This was by no means an isolated incident. Busoni's reputation as a Liszt exponent and scholar had grown to such an extent by 1907 that he was asked to join the editorial panel appointed to supervise the publication of the Liszt collected works for Breitkopf & Haertel.

Perhaps the climax of Busoni's public appearances in the Lisztian cause (a cause that met with frequent and vitriolic opposition, particularly in Germany and England) was his contribution to the celebrations of the centenary of Liszt's birth: a series of piano recitals given in the Beethoven-Saal in 1911. I give the full program of these recitals not only to show the extent of Busoni's knowledge of Liszt and his endurance as a pianist but also as fairly typical of the programs played by virtuosi of the day:

1. (31 October)   a. *Grandes Etudes d'exécution transcendante*
                    b. *Fantasie über 2 motive aus Mozart's "Die Hochzeit des Figaro"*

2. (7 November)   a. *Années de Pélerinage, Première Année, La Suisse*
                    b. *Légendes*
                    c. *Adelaide von Beethoven*
                    d. *Réminiscences de Don Juan*

3. (14 November)   a. *Années de Pélerinage, Deuxième Année, Italie*
                    b. *Gondoliera*
                    c. *Tarantella*
                    d. *Sérenade de Rossini*
                    e. *Il Trovatore* (Verdi)
                    f. *Valse e capriccio sur Lucia e Parisina* (Donizetti)
                    g. *Fantasie über Norma* (Bellini)

4. (21 November)   a. *Années de Pélerinage, Troisième Année*
                    b. *Deuxième Ballade*
                    c. *Bénédiction de Dieu dans la solitude*
                    d. *Valse oubliée*
                    e. *Die Zelle in Nonnenwerth*
                    f. *Polonaise C-moll*
                    g. *Galop chromatique*

5. (28 November)   a. *Variationen über "Weinen, Klagen, Sorgen, Zagen" und das "Crucifixus" aus Bach's H-moll—Messe*
                    b. *Sonate H-moll in einem Satz*
                    c. *Transcriptionen nach Schubert: Erlkönig, Die Forelle, Ungarischer Marsch*
                    d. *Ungarische Rhapsodien: V, XIII, XII*

6. (12 December)   a. *Grandes Études d'Après les Caprices de Paganini*
                    b. *Bearbeitungen von F. Busoni: Fantasie und Fuge über den Choral "Ad nos ad salutarem undam," Mephisto-Walzer, Polonaise E-dur*

Busoni summed up his varying but growing responses to Liszt the composer in a letter to his wife from Norderney dated 2 August 1907: "Liszt I misunderstood at first, then I adored him, and then quietly admired him."[5]

Apart from Busoni's work on Liszt as an editor and transcriber, there also exist the following essays on Liszt, all published in *The Essence of Music and Other Papers*:

1. Mozart's *Don Giovanni* and Liszt's *Don Juan* Fantasy (also found in the preface to Busoni's edition of this work)

2. Biographical and critical study drawn up as a foundation to the proposed collected edition of Liszt's pianoforte works

3. Foreword to the studies by Liszt

4. Program note from Zürich

5. Program note from 1911 series

6. Open letter about Liszt to Kastner

7. Various references to Liszt in other writings

The first three articles are of considerable importance, and it is by reading the second one especially that we realize the extent to which Busoni had broadened his knowledge of Liszt, from an initial lack of interest to becoming a specialist collector and authority on various Liszt versions and editions. What really concerns us here, however, is not so much Busoni's knowledge of Liszt, as the effects that such knowledge must have had on his own creative development.

Liszt's lasting influence on Busoni occurs in at least seven spheres of creative activity:

1. It was the Italian trait of Liszt that Busoni admired above all: the clear melodic line, with the fine lace of ornament around it. Almost all of Busoni's mature piano works (with the exception of the polyphonic pieces) are based on this Lisztian principle of glittering or veiled embroidery. (See Figure 12.1.)

Figure 12.1. By kind permission, Breitkopf & Haertel, Wiesbaden.

2. Further, the actual pianistic figurations of Busoni are derived from Liszt, and represent extensions of the Lisztian sequences. (See Figure 12.2.)

Figure 12.2. By kind permission, Breitkopf & Haertel, Wiesbaden.

3. Busoni's discovery of late Liszt was a great revelation. Bartók, too, a few years later, must have been thrilled to read through some of these enigmatic and prognostic pieces.[6] Thus, beginning with Busoni's *Elegies*, there are traces of Liszt's late style. (See Figure 12.3.)

Figure 12.3. By kind permission, Breitkopf & Haertel, Wiesbaden.

4. One of the aspects that fascinate us about Liszt is his dualism, the presence in his music of the divine and the satanic, side by side. Busoni's dualism is of the same basic kind, although extended and rarified. Liszt's more obvious religioso moods, sometimes verging on ecstasy, have been replaced by a more elusive, more personal mysticism. (See Figure 12.4.) Liszt's devil is the fully fledged romantic variety, breathing sulphur and swishing his tail—we meet him in the *Dante* sonata, in the *Mephisto-Waltz*, and in many other pieces. Busoni's dark forces are more subtle, more fleeting, more grotesque, often more frightening by their very insubstantiality. (See Figure 12.5.)

Figure 12.4. By kind permission, Breitkopf & Haertel, Wiesbaden.

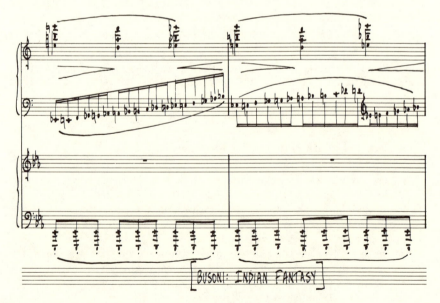

Figure 12.5. By kind permission, Breitkopf & Haertel, Wiesbaden.

5. This almost necromantic quality in both Liszt and Busoni appears in yet another aspect of their work: as transcribers. Both loved the art of transcription and cultivated it assiduously; both possessed the power of taking another composer's work (often a simple or even banal melody) and imbuing it with their own personality. On the other hand, both transcribed Bach with a reverence and faithfulness not always reserved for other composers. (See Chapters 15 and 16.) Liszt's love of Bach and his transcriptions of the organ works were matched in the first instance and surpassed in the second by Busoni. There seems little doubt too, that consciously or subconsciously, Liszt's example of condensing works for better pianistic effect, gave Busoni a valuable precedent. We read in his *Open letter about Liszt*[7] a defense of Liszt's editions of Schubert's *Wandererfantasie*. Busoni's own contributions to concert arrangements range from Mozart to Schönberg. Finally, even though Busoni tried his hand at operatic fantasias at an early age (see Chapter 4), his *tour de force* in this field, the *Sonatina super Carmen,* has undoubted Lisztian traits (see Chapter 6).

6. Liszt issued many works in various editions, sometimes over the span of years, as for instance the famous three versions of the *Transcendental Studies*. Busoni, in a different way, is frequently fascinated with an idea, so that it appears in a number of works, often quite unrelated ones; usually a major opus is surrounded by a constellation of smaller works, utilizing similar materials, but never in quite the same manner. Liszt's habit of suggesting a pianistic ossia for a passage can be found in Busoni's own work, although to a much lesser extent, and also in Busoni's editions of Liszt. Busoni's intimate study of various versions of the Liszt *Etudes* provided the impetus for his own edition of the *Paganini Etudes,* often combining Lisztian ideas from several editions. (See below.)

7. Busoni's approach to the roles of the piano solo and orchestra is derived from Liszt. The soloist sits apart from the orchestra and comments, improvises, embellishes, and dreams upon themes provided by the orchestra. The piano part is a romantic memory of the orchestral, but it is difficult in Busoni's case to make such a simple generalization, for his concerto writing also comes from many other sources, Bach and Mozart prominent among them.

FRANZ LISZT MUSIKALISCHE WERKE   HERAUSGEGEBEN VON FRANZ LISZT-STIFTUNG   II   PIANOFORTEWERKE   ETÜDEN FÜR PIANOFORTE ZU ZWEI HÄNDEN   Leipzig   Breitkopf & Haertel   The three volumes of Liszt's etudes edited by Busoni were numbered II.1, II.2, and II.3, with catalogue numbers FL 32-34, FL 35-36, and FL 37-43, respectively.

Between 1901 and 1936, 34 volumes of the works of Liszt were published under the direct supervision of the Franz Liszt-Stiftung; the editors, who contributed prefaces to their respective volumes, included pupils of Liszt (José Vianna da Motta, Bernhard Stavenhagen, August Stradal), composer-pianists with affinities and interests in Liszt (Béla Bartók and Ferruccio Busoni), and various other experts.

The three volumes edited by Busoni, prefaced with a long introduction, are reprinted and translated by Rosamond Ley in *The Essence of Music* (pages 154-66), although two pages—numbered VI and VII in the Leipzig edition—containing comparative examples from early and definitive versions of the *Transcendental Studies*, are not reproduced. This essay-introduction is followed by a table of variants in contemporary editions of Liszt.

The *Etudes* edited by Busoni comprise:

II.1: Study in 12 exercises (first version of *Transcendental Studies*) Op. 1; 12 great Studies (second version, *Transcendental Studies*); Mazeppa (first version).

II.2: Bravour-Studies (*Transcendental Studies*, final version); Great Fantasia di Bravura on Paganini's Campanella, Op. 2.

II.3: Bravour-Studies after Paganini's Caprices (*Paganini Etudes* first versions); Grand Etudes after Paganini (final versions); Morceau de Salon, Etude of Perfection from the Method of Methods (*Ab Irato*, early version); Ab Irato, Great Etude of Perfection (final version); Three Concert Studies; Gnome-Dance, In the Woods.

(The English titles are given here as they appear in the Liszt-Stiftung edition. The clarifications in brackets are my own.)

Only in Volume II.1 does Busoni offer a mere handful of ossias, marked "F.B." in small print. The other volumes do not do even this, and, except for the signed preface to each volume, Busoni's name does not appear anywhere else. The whole tone of the Stiftung edition was, indeed, completely scholarly: Busoni's virulent critics were often conveniently apt to overlook his inclusion in such a project and continued to accuse him of "disrespect for the original."

SECHS PAGANINI-ETÜDEN FÜR KLAVIER   REVIDIERTE AUSGABE VON FERRUCCIO BUSONI   Leipzig   Breitkopf & Haertel   1912   EB 484   Liszt's definitive version of these studies is here reprinted exactly as it appeared in the Liszt-Stiftung   The etudes were also issued separately as EB 2551-56

Pianists and the concert-going public were very familiar with Busoni's transcription of *La Campanella*, which was possibly performed as often as the Liszt original. Very few pianists, and certainly none of the public, are aware that Busoni edited and transcribed the other Paganini etudes as well.

With a few changes, Busoni's final thoughts on the following etudes appear in the second edition of the *Klavierübung* (1925) under the title *Etüden nach Paganini-Liszt*.

PAGANINI-LISZT TREMOLO ETÜDE NR. 1 EINE TRANS-SKRIPTIONSSTUDIE VON FERRUCCIO BUSONI, BEARB. AUSGABE FÜR STUDIUM UND KONZERT   Leipzig   Breitkopf & Haertel   EB 5238

Speaking of the first version, Busoni says in his preface to the Stiftung edition: ". . . as a kind of homage to Clara's husband (worldly-wise or a Mephistophelian whim?) over the first of these studies is printed Liszt's predecessor's treatment of it: 'Cette seconde version est celle de Mr. Robert Schumann.'"

Why Liszt singled out Schumann's rather tame and ineffective transcription for inclusion is a mystery. I mention this only because the Lisztian note quoted above appears in tiny print in the Stiftung and can easily be missed; thus the Schumann version may be taken for an early Liszt transcription. Busoni had at his disposal only the one early Liszt version.

In the Busoni edition, the Preludio is given both in the Liszt notation and in Busoni's with suggestions for breaking up the passages between hands. The etude itself departs at times from Liszt's obvious intention of playing as much of it as possible with the left hand alone and suggests various clarifications of the line by using the right hand. Some wide leaps in a latter part of the etude are made simpler by redistribution between the hands.

To the purists who still throw up their hands in horror at such cavalier treatment, one must politely but firmly point out that Liszt himself reworked his compositions with this end always in mind: to preserve the effect, using simpler means. The study of Liszt versions is the study of differentiation by Liszt himself between musical effect and virtuosity for its own sake.

The Busoni edition is notable not only for its ingenious pianistic solutions to problems, whether by redistribution, crossing of hands, or fingering. This alone would not have satisfied Busoni; he also provides ossias, much as Liszt himself has always done. (See Figure 12.6.)

Figure 12.6. By kind permission, Breitkopf & Haertel, Wiesbaden.

LISZT-BUSONI   ANDANTINO CAPRICCIOSO   ETÜDE NR. 2
NACH PAGANINIS CAPRICEN   PIANO SOLO   BEARB.
AUSGABE FÜR STUDIUM UND KONZERT   Leipzig   Breitkopf
& Haertel   1917   EB 4958   Transcribed in 1916

The original Liszt is printed here above the Busoni version, and we can thus compare at firsthand the heightened effectiveness of Busoni's pianistic suggestion. Even on the second page, in such a simple effect as the distribution of the quick downward scale flourish, Busoni leaves an unmistakable touch. (See Figure 12.7.) One of the Busoni alterations to an

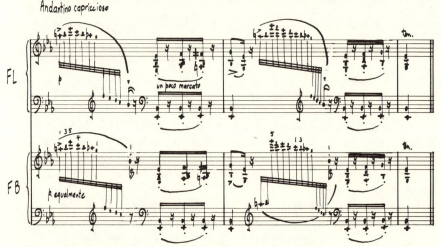

Figure 12.7. By kind permission, Breitkopf & Haertel, Wiesbaden.

arpeggio passage is really taken from Liszt's own earlier version. (See Figure 12.8.) Just before the octave section, Busoni gives the last run to both hands, with the right hand playing pianissimo minor thirds presto, one of the things that he excelled in. The octave section is substantially the same; at its very end, Busoni thins out the left hand a little. The reprise is the same; Busoni adds a coda at the very end of his own composition. This is shorter than Liszt's coda by five bars. In the study published separately, both the Liszt and Busoni codas are included. In the *Klavierübung*, however, only the Busoni coda is given.

FRANZ LISZT   LA CAMPANELLA   ETÜDE NACH PAGANINIS
RONDO FÜR PIANOFORTE   BEARBEITETE AUSGABE FÜR
STUDIUM UND KONZERT   Leipzig   Breitkopf &
Haertel   1916   EB 4839

This famous study has two ancestors: *Fantasie de Bravoura sur la Clochette de Paganini* Op. 2 and *Grande Etude d'execution transcendante*

Figure 12.8. By kind permission, Breitkopf & Haertel, Wiesbaden.

d'après le Caprice de Paganini. The latter description is of course an error on Liszt's part. *La Campanella* does not belong to the caprices, but is the theme of a rondo by Paganini.

Busoni thus had three sources to draw on for his famous concert version; the two pieces mentioned above and the final version of *La Campanella*. We know that he admired the Op. 2 fantasy tremendously, for he says in the preface:

It is composed of a free, slow introduction, a capricious fleeting anticipation of thematic material, leading up to a connecting sentence which is brought to a climax by the most daring bravura; the theme, a *Variation à la Paganini* and a *Finale de Bravura.* The care, choice and minuteness of detail given to the directions for performance in these most youthful pieces by Liszt (like *Apparitions, Harmonies poétiques, Fantasie Romantique Suisse,* etc.) leave almost no doubt regarding the pianist-composer's intentions. The method for their execution is marked out step by step and suggestions are even made for the purely pianistic performance (as for example: "Marquez les 6 temps de la mesure en jetant la main avec souplesse"). For this reason they are worth the closest attention and are instructive for the Liszt style.[8]

The very opening departure by Busoni—the playing of the theme first simply, then with leaps—is taken from Op. 2, at least in essence, or from the early version of *La Campanella*.

As with all the etudes, many of Busoni's changes are purely pianistic, with hardly a note altered; but on the other hand he does not hesitate to introduce his own ideas. *La Campanella* is too readily accessible and too well known to quote from, but a study of the three Liszt versions compared with Busoni's would be of great interest to all pianists. Such a study is aided by the Busoni edition, which consists of the Liszt definitive version printed above it, as with etude No. 2.

PAGANINI-LISZT ARPEGGIO ETÜDE NR. 4 EINE TRAN-SKRIPTION-STUDIE VON FERRUCCIO BUSONI Leipzig Breitkopf & Haertel 1923 EB 5206

This, like *La Campanella*, exists in three versions by Liszt; in this case, all three are musically alike, and Liszt is concerned only with problems of pianism. The first and second versions suffer from an overabundance of notes, with a consequent inhibition of speed; the tempo is given as andante quasi allegretto. It is not until the third version that Liszt thins out the texture sufficiently to be able to put vivo on the front of the study.

The only difference between the Busoni versions published separately and those incorporated within the *Klavierübung* is that in the latter the Liszt version is missing, while in the former it is printed above the Busoni; otherwise the two are completely identical, even to the spacing of the lines. Removing the single line of the Liszt version has, incidentally, given rise to an oversight at the very start of the study: the tempo indication vivo has been omitted together with the Liszt line.

Busoni concentrates on Liszt's third version, and is mostly concerned with redistribution and, sometimes, octave displacement.

PAGANINI-LISZT LA CHASSE ETÜDE NR. 5 EINE TRAN-SKRIPTION-STUDIE VON FERRUCCIO BUSONI Leipzig Breitkopf & Haertel EB 5239

Two versions of this exist, although the early one has almost enough ossias to make up yet a third.

Busoni uses two concepts from this early version: octaves broken inward, written by Busoni as an ossia (see Figure 12.9) and, more significantly, a

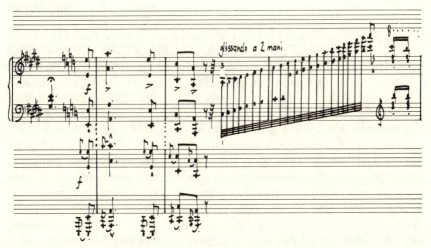

Figure 12.9. By kind permission, Breitkopf & Haertel, Wiesbaden.

whole added section just before the final E major section. (See Figure 12.10.)
This idea is taken wholly from the early Liszt version.

There is an ingenious fingering for the glissandi in 6ths, executed by
playing the right-hand glissando with the third finger and left-hand
glissando with the thumb and keeping the interval the same by wedging the
right-hand thumb into the "V" formed by the left-hand thumb and second
finger. At the very end, Busoni adds an inimitable touch of his own by a
reminiscence of the glissando. (See Figure 12.11.)

Figure 12.10. By kind permission, Breitkopf & Haertel, Wiesbaden.

Figure 12.11. By kind permission, Breitkopf & Haertel, Wiesbaden.

PAGANINI-LISZT THEMA MIT VARIATIONEN   ETÜDE
NO. 6 EINE TRANSKRIPTION-STUDIE VON FERRUCCIO
BUSONI BEARB. AUSGABE FÜR STUDIUM UND KONZERT
Leipzig   Breitkopf & Haertel   1914   EB 4360   Transcribed in 1913

This etude in Busoni's edition departs further from the two Liszt versions than any of the other etudes; it is specifically marked as a free arrangement but in the *Klavierübung* only.[9]

The theme consists of arpeggiated chords, narrower in range; performance indication is given as vivace moderato tutto staccato and the second half of theme is not repeated. Variation I is generally cleaner, with less broken chords. It is closer to the original violin writing. Variation II is omitted. Variation III is as for I. The Liszt opening is now transformed, as in Figure 12.12. In Variation IV the opening bar rhythm is altered, as in Figure 12.13. Variation V is an ossia-like transcription. (In *Klavierübung* only, it is omitted in the separate edition.) (See Figure 12.14.) In Variation VI the left hand is altered. (See Figure 12.15.) Busoni adds a variation (Variation VIa) here closer to the notes and spirit of the Liszt original Variation VI. (In *Klavierübung* only, it is omitted in the separate edition.) Variation VII is omitted. Variation VIII becomes as in Figure 12.16. Variation IX is reasonably faithful to the original. (In *Klavierübung* only, it is omitted in the separate edition.) Variation X is omitted. Variation XI becomes a Coda of Busoni's own composition; it starts with the four against three rhythm and ends with brilliant octave passages, played leggierissimo. (In *Klavierübung* only. The separate edition presents an ossia to the Liszt versions.)

Throughout this etude, Busoni scales down the dynamics from the Lisztian thunder to leggiero, staccato, and senza pedale. He thus stresses the fantastic character of the piece rather than the virtuosic; in this version we enter Busoni's favorite world of half light, E. T. A. Hoffmann stories, and sinister apparitions. The Coda and the editing are brilliant solutions to the

Figure 12.12. By kind permission, Breitkopf & Haertel, Wiesbaden.

Figure 12.13. By kind permission, Breitkopf & Haertel, Wiesbaden.

Figure 12.14. By kind permission, Breitkopf & Haertel, Wiesbaden.

Figure 12.15. By kind permission, Breitkopf & Haertel, Wiesbaden.

interpretative problems of this etude, in some ways the most obvious of all
the six. Thus, this theme and variations, in Busoni's hands, is the most
individual, the one furthest removed from the Liszt original; it deserves to
be as popular as the Busoni-Liszt *La Campanella*, but at present writing it is
hardly known outside a small circle of pianists. The Coda has harmonic
sequences that Liszt would not have used, certainly not at the time of

Figure 12.16. By kind permission, Breitkopf & Haertel, Wiesbaden.

writing these etudes and probably not even at the end of his life. But as we have found before, such considerations did not concern Busoni, who saw in Liszt (as in Mozart and Bach) foreboding as well as achievement. Such a Coda was simply his own vision of what may have been implied in the original.

The etudes, especially in Busoni's 1925 edition, owe surprisingly little to the earlier Liszt versions; the cases of borrowing from these consist of isolated passages only and have had no overall effect on Busoni's interpretation. It is precisely in this field of interpretation, whether musical or purely pianistic, that Busoni comes into his own. The Liszt etudes are, therefore, no different in outlook from other Busoni editions—they set out to clarify, simplify, individualize, and look forward; the backward glance is only in aid of such goals.

Breitkopf & Haertel, in catalogues of the day and in lists of works printed on covers of their various publications, give this information:

Franz Liszt Ausgewählte Klavierwerke Revidiert von F. Busoni und J. V. da Motta Aus Franz Liszts Musikalischen Werken herausgegeben von der Franz Liszt-Stiftung. Abendklänge-Harmonies du soir; An der Quelle-Au Bord d'une source: La Campanella; Consolations-Tröstungen Nr. 2 in E dur, Nr. 3 in Des dur, Nr. 5 in E dur; Gnomenreigen; Gondoliera aus "Venezia e Napoli"; Konzert-Etude Nr. 3 in Des dur; Sonett 123 des Petrarca; Tarantella aus "Venezia e Napoli"; Waldesrauschen.

As with the Bach editions, a possible misconception that Busoni and da Motta collaborated on these works of Liszt must be clarified. Nothing of the sort happened; they exchanged some letters and aired some general ideas about methods of editing, but there was no actual collaboration. Therefore, these pieces published separately by Breitkopf & Haertel are an exact replica of the Liszt-Stiftung edition; the editing is really a restoration of the original authentic text and must be understood in that sense rather than our usual connotation of the word in reference to Busoni editions. Since in the complete Liszt edition Busoni only looked after the etudes and da Motta after other pieces, including ones mentioned above, since such work was done independently, and finally, since publication of the separate pieces is totally identical with the complete edition, any listing of Busoni and da Motta as co-editors is erroneous. (Some re-publications have even given the editors as "Busoni-da Motta.")

TOTENTANZ   PHANTASIE FÜR PIANOFORTE UND OR-
CHESTER (BEENDET AM 21 OKTOBER 1849) VON FRANZ LISZT
ERSTE FASSUNG NACH UNZWEIFELHAFTEN HANDSCHRIFTEN
ZUM ERSTEN MALE HERAUSGEGEBEN VON FERRUCCIO
BUSONI   Leipzig   Breitkopf & Haertel   1919   Part. B.   2483
Transcribed in 1918

There is a foreword by Busoni, dated Zürich, 20 November 1918:[10]

I am indebted to the Marquis Casanova the owner of the original manuscript of this work, for his great kindness that has made it possible for me to make a clean copy of the original.
   This interesting (70 years old by now) ms consists of two parts:

1. a (bound) copy of the oldest version of "Totentanz," presumably copied by Pruckner in Stuttgart, from whose estate the entire ms comes.

2. 28 full pages in Liszt's own hand, on 7 loose sheets.

The bound copy contains additions and alterations, made by Liszt in his own hand, which, judging by the appearance, were undertaken three times at different intervals: they are made sometimes in pale, sometimes in red ink, and with red pencil, and can be clearly distinguished from one another.
   From the third variation on, however, the whole copy is crisscrossed and Liszt refers to the loose sheets, which we may be certain, completes the version that the composer regarded as definitive at that time.
   The last few pages of the bound copy contain a subsequently added (first) sketch of the piano part of the fugato-variations; the first pages of the same bound copy the orchestral part of the fugato-variation; both the piano part and the orchestral are in Liszt's hand. Both in the bound copy and in the loose sheets there are added Cadenzas, which, in the circumstances, were often put down where there was any space left in the fully written-up pages; the result of it is that these additions present a fantastic and confusing picture of the sketch; yet they can be fully decoded as a result of the errors and directions accompanying them. Consequently the achievement of a pure copy demanded great care and no small amount of ingenuity which Mr. Philipp Jarnach (to whom I am indebted for the practical execution of the work) has displayed to a most praiseworthy degree.

The two older versions of the TOTENTANZ differ from the latest version principally by the insertion of the liturgical "De Profundis"[11] which imparts to the piece a propitiating sanctification, a soothing contrast. The continually unfolding ornamental passages for the piano, are of the most exciting kind. In the oldest (crossed out) version there are some alternative versions of those: Liszt rejected them as inadequate, yet to us they are quite amazing, because of their seemingly endless variety.[12]

The editor thus regards this work as complete, and which can take its place beside its younger brother—in fact, it even exceeded it in parts. [Reprinted by kind permission, Breitkopf & Haertel, Wiesbaden.]

Since it was Busoni's intention to provide an interesting pianistic-musical alternative version of this familiar work, our investigation of this edition will be compared with the standard performing edition.

In the opening Andante the deep bell-like tolling is omitted from the piano part and given to the orchestra instead (tam-tam, bassoons, trombones, timpani). The piano's first entry is with the cadenza, which is identical in both versions; the chord introducing and punctuating the cadenza is just a quaver in the Busoni edition and two quavers in the Liszt. Also, see Figure 12.17 for another example of change. The blind octaves at

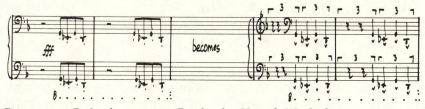

Figure 12.17. By kind permission, Breitkopf & Haertel, Wiesbaden.

the end of the cadenza become runs in double thirds. Alternating chords now appear in the allegro as tremolos in both hands. The Allegro moderato is substantially the same. One trill missing is in the right hand on E. Variations I and II are identical. Variation III is marked Allegro animato instead of molto vivace.

One extra bar is added near the end; the piano part is otherwise identical. Variation IV (canonique) is completely omitted. Busoni proceeds to the fugato. The orchestral part of Variation V (fugato) is varied and generally simpler throughout, consisting of the *Dies Irae* theme stated in its bare version rather than varied as in the later Liszt edition. The piano part is identical until the d minor episode leading into the cadenza, after which it is quite different. In Busoni, this episode is interrupted by a new short cadenza and then resumed, ending with the high trill in the piano part on A-B flat. The Sempre allegro ma non troppo is omitted.

The short variation Allegretto scherzando is marked as an alternativo. The pianistic figure is reversed from the familiar. (See Figure 12.18.) This

Figure 12.18. By kind permission, Breitkopf & Haertel, Wiesbaden.

short 16-bar variation is followed by two 16-bar variations as in the Liszt
with some orchestral variants. The variation with left-hand octaves is
identical and an ossia is offered. The following solo variation is omitted.
Busoni moves straight to the next variation with leaps in both hands, and
blind octaves. The piano part here is the same, but not the orchestral; the
cadenza, however, is shorter and different.

From here on, the Busoni edition differs greatly. A long extended section
marked *De Profundis*, and first introduced by soft brass and woodwind,
interrupts the inexorable flow of the music. This section, marked adagio ma
non troppo is in two sections: (1) Brass and woodwind, choir-like, with soft
strummed piano chords and (2) *De Profundis* theme again, piano in
widespread soft arpeggios. A savage allegro appears next, commencing
with soft timpani strokes and building up; it is, in fact, the *De Profundis*
theme compressed. A cadenza follows, with similarities to the one near the
end of the Liszt version. Next is a scherzando variation, still using the *De
Profundis* theme. Another cadenza, mostly in octaves, parallel or wide
leaping. This leads into an alla breve. The alla breve restates in octaves the
Dies Irae, supported by full orchestra; there is some slight similarity with
the Liszt ending in that glissandi, though only a few, make an appearance.
An addendum includes a variant of the variation immediately preceding the
De Profundis; so ends this fascinating edition of the *Totentanz*.

It is a great pity that the Busoni and Liszt versions cannot be compared
aurally side by side; no recording of the Busoni exists, but upon scanning
the comparative description of the Liszt and Busoni versions, a number of
points may be stressed. Pianistically, the Busoni offers some interesting
alternatives and performing suggestions. In some of the variants it may be
legitimately pointed out that the later Liszt versions achieve comparable
results with less effort; however, such moments are few. Orchestrally, the
Busoni is starker. Some of the variants are simply a matter of taste, there is
little to choose between them. Often, the theme is presented simply, rather
than in the more elaborate Liszt version.

Liszt is remarkable in that the "demonic" is pursued relentlessly throughout the piece, except for Variation IV (canonique), which is marked "religioso." This is short and is soon transformed into a rather sentimental section (dolce and, later, andante dolcissimo). It occurs rather too early in the work to offer real contrast and serves simply as an interruption to the mood of the opening. It is based on the *Dies Irae* and despite the "religioso" indication hardly succeeds in establishing the "catholic" mood evidently desired by Liszt. Busoni omits this variation. The effect is to allow the demonic to continue and build up to almost unendurable tension. The *De Profundis* is then introduced. Dramatically, it is far more effective; musically, the scoring is more evocative, and the mood unmistakable, as of a distant choir.

RÉMINISCENCES DE "DON JUAN"   KONZERT-FANTASIE
ÜBER MOTIVE AUS MOZARTS "DON GIOVANNI" FÜR
DAS PIANOFORTE   GROSSE KRITISCH-INSTRUKTIVE
AUSGABE VON FERRUCCIO BUSONI   Leipzig   Breitkopf &
Haertel   1918   EB 4960

This edition is prefaced by an essay titled "Mozarts 'Don Giovanni' und Liszts 'Don Juan-Fantasie.' "[13] At the outset Busoni roughly traces the genesis of the Don Juan legend and makes some comments about the Mozart score; this is of general interest. What is more pertinent is Busoni's attitude toward the question of characterization; he finds fault with some of da Ponte's situations and characters, and then goes on to say: "By paraphrasing the three most important moments in the opera, Liszt, guided by his excellent instincts, has attempted to underline the 'demoniacal' (which lies nearer the 1830 epoch than Mozart's time). The choice of these three moments from the whole opera is significant of his unerring perception of what is important to it. In this kind of thing Liszt never failed. . . ."

More remarks follow about the structure of Liszt's fantasias, the psychology of picking the right themes for treatment, and of Liszt's ornamentation. Finally, Busoni appeals to pianists to duplicate the transparency of the Mozart score in this Liszt *Fantasia* and, further, not just to surmount the difficulties, but surmount them "with grace." And then, two personal observations:

During the lifelong course of his pianistic studies the editor has always endeavoured to simplify the mechanism of piano playing and to reduce it to what is absolutely indispensable in movement and expenditure of strength. His mature opinion is that the acquirement of a technique is nothing else than fitting a given difficulty to one's own capacities.

. . . Thus the editor has placed the version of the fantasy which suits him, under Liszt's unchanged original text, not as a conclusive model, but merely as a result of his own experiences which are for him decisive. By doing this he wished to give an instance of how one can and should arrange a setting for oneself without distorting the sense, content and effect.

This essay is particularly interesting for its remarks on Liszt, not necessarily because they are correct as far as Liszt is concerned, but because they throw light on Busoni's attitude to the performance of this *Fantasia*. For Busoni the operatic paraphrase was not the vulgar exhibitionistic virtuoso piece that many of us have come to believe, and which, in truth, it often is, but a psychological compression of the opera and its drama into the medium of the pianoforte. The pianist's responsibility, then, as seen by Busoni, is to know the opera, the characters depicted, the excerpts used in the paraphrase in correct context, the texture of the original, and the style both of the opera and of the transcriber; only after such prior knowledge can the pianist play the piece successfully. This edition is intended, therefore, to highlight precisely such considerations as listed above. The suggestion for pianists to "arrange a setting for oneself" is closely allied with Busoni's whole philosophy in regard to notation. (See Chapter 15.)

The attitudes and remarks are all amply born out in the edition under discussion; it presents a fascinating record of a Busoni interpretation, and is one of the most thorough editions of its kind by Busoni, with illumination thrown upon all manner of problems inherent in the performance of this difficult *Fantasia*. Many of Busoni's deviations from the Liszt text are based on Liszt's own version of the same work for two pianos, which Busoni considered superior. For some idea of Busoni's elegant reading of the *Réminiscences de Don Juan*, his performance of this work on a Welte piano roll should be heard. (See Chapter 19.)

RHAPSODIE ESPAGNOLE (FOLIES D'ESPAGNE ET JOTA ARAGONESE)   VON FRANZ LISZT   ALS KONZERTSTÜCK FÜR PIANOFORTE UND ORCHESTER BEARBEITET VON FER-RUCCIO B. BUSONI   Leipzig   C. F. W. Siegel   No. 11 595, The same publisher also issued the two-piano reduction No. 11 596   Also New York   G. Schirmer   1894   Vol. 1252

Busoni had Liszt's own example to follow in arranging the *Spanish Rhapsody*. He acknowledges as much in his article "Value of the Transcription" in a program note for the third of the Nikisch concerts, Berlin, November 1910:

Rather more than seventeen years ago when my impulse of enthusiasm for Liszt, which was kindled early, was fresh and imitative, I transcribed the Spanish Rhapsody symphonically after Liszt's model of Schubert's Piano Fantasy (*The Wanderer*) and Weber's Polonaise arranged for piano and orchestra. . . . The Spanish Rhapsody in its original form, for pianoforte alone, puts the greatest demand on the player without affording him the possibility—even with the best success—of moving to the climaxes in a sufficiently brilliant light. These obstacles lie in the composition, the shortcomings of the instrument and the limited endurance of the pianist. Moreover, the national character of the piece requires shades of colour such as only the orchestra can give. The remodelling of this piece gives greater opportunity to the pianist for bringing out his individual style.[14]

The reasons for the arrangement are clear enough from the above. These different procedures are pursued:

1. A passage left as in the original piano part, with no orchestra.
2. A passage fully scored, with no piano.
3. The piano and orchestra often alternate.

A surprising portion of the arrangement falls under these simple headings. The piano part reproduced from Liszt is more often than not completely identical. Frequently, Busoni avoids adding new material by doubling the piano in octaves, or doubling the left hand with the orchestral bass. At other times fairly simple passages are extended to occupy both hands, while the melodic emphasis is carried by the orchestra. There is thus much less new material than one would expect (see item 4).

4. Something is added—usually a florid piano part or an orchestral melodic counterline only suggested in the original setting. A good example of this occurs on page 48 (see description below).
5. Completely new material is introduced: this occurs in the following places (pages refer to the Schirmer edition):
    (a) Page 3—the piano flourishes are extended by a bar (bars 3 and 6).
    (b) Page 4—lines 3 and 5—an extra group of sextuplets is added, probably for reasons of symmetry.
    (c) Pages 26-27—the cadenza is totally new, in extemporizatory style.
    (d) Page 31—first line, the run is added.
    (e) Page 45, line 3, bar 3 till page 47, line 1, bar 6—cadenza-like addition, in strict time, punctuated by orchestral chords.
    (f) Page 47—lines 2 and 3—not new material, but the non troppo begun twice; the Liszt version starts as at the top of page 48.
    (g) One bar added just before the un poco maestoso, page 50.
    (h) Last bars extended, through octave flourishes.

Items (a), (b), (d), (g), and even (h) are very minor additions, all falling into the class of spontaneous flourishes; they require no comment. Of the remainder, it is salient that both (c) and (e) are cadenzas, one free, one measured; both also fall into that class of piano writing that can be described as either decorative or bridge-like.

Item (f) only occurs because Busoni makes a false start at the non troppo allegro section; the first time, the piano accompanies the orchestra in maestoso chords while the second time the orchestra goes its own way, following the Liszt original, while the piano has the *Jota Aragonese* theme against it.

This is the only structural alteration in the *Spanish Rhapsody*; the whole arrangement is faithful to Liszt, and contains a minimum of new material. A measure of Busoni's success in this case is that the *Spanish Rhapsody* is heard more often in his arrangement than in the original.

Unlike other Busoni editions and transcriptions, which may have been undertaken to re-interpret, throw new light on, or explore new combinations of themes,[15] Busoni arranged the *Spanish Rhapsody* primarily to provide a new piece for the piano-orchestra repertoire and realize various limitations inherent in Liszt's solo setting.

EPISODE AUS LENAU'S FAUST   DER TANZ IN DER DOR-FSCHENKE (MEPHISTO WALZER) VON FRANZ LISZT   MIT ANLEHNUNG AN DIE ORCHESTERPARTITUR FÜR DAS PIANO-FORTE NEU BEARBEITET UND DEM GRAFEN A. ROZWADOW-SKI GEWIDMET VON FERRUCCIO BUSONI   New York G. Schirmer   1904   No. 17   311   Also issued as *Mephisto-Walzer   Episode ("Der Tanz in der Dorfschenke") aus Lenau's "Faust" von Franz Liszt*   Leipzig   J. Schuberth   1904 (copyright G. Schirmer)   No. 7543   Also re-issued by G. Schirmer as *Franz Liszt   Mephisto Waltz   Episode from Lenau's "Faust": Dance in the Village Inn   Based on the Orchestra Score and Newly Arranged for the Piano by Ferruccio Busoni*   Vol. 1649

Busoni's edition of the *Mephisto Waltz* must be compared with the original Liszt to be of any significance to a potential listener or performer. Busoni, with his knowledge of variants by Liszt of the same work, was always on the lookout for pieces that would show up in a novel and interesting way. This accounted for his editions of the *Totentanz* (from an older manuscript copy), the *Don Juan Fantasie* (partly from studying the two-piano version), as well as many other editions and free adaptations.

Liszt's piano version of the *Mephisto Waltz* was also linked with, if not transcribed from, the orchestral, so that Busoni's set problem was to use the same basic material but with different and justifiable results. With a master work like the *Mephisto Waltz*, it was no longer a question of improving it or making it more effective; even Busoni could not presume to that. All he could hope to do was to offer an alternative transcription with pianistic merits of its own. There is no doubt that in this he was wonderfully successful. So different are many pages of the two versions that the most instructive point I can make is to present five short excerpts in the Liszt and Busoni transcriptions. (See Figure 12.19.) *The Mephisto Waltz* provides a

Figure 12.19. By kind permission, Breitkopf & Haertel, Wiesbaden.

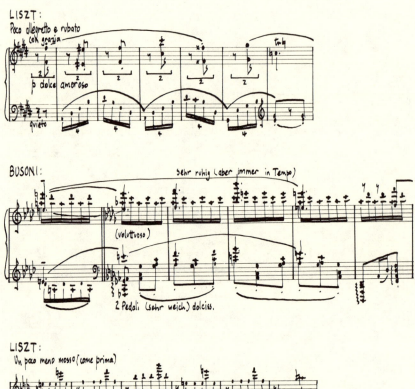

Figure 12.19 *continued*

Figure 12.19 *continued*

rare opportunity to compare the same work transcribed by two undoubted masters of the art.

FRANZ LISZT POLONAISE NO. 2 E DUR   NOUVELLE ÉDITION, AUGMENTÉE D'UNE CADENCE FINALE, PAR FERRUCCIO BUSONI Berlin Simrock 1909 No. 12 604

This so-called new edition is in reality exactly the same as any other standard edition of this *Polonaise*—Busoni's hand does not make its appearance until the very end of the piece, where, deleting the last 26 bars by Liszt, he writes his own cadenza-finale: 39 bars long, bristling with difficulties but enormously effective and exciting, as anyone who has heard the piano roll played by Busoni can testify. (See Figure 12.20.) There is no harmonic audacity in Busoni's cadenza; he remains within the stylistic language of the *Polonaise*, but the lightning leggiero runs, the brio staccato octaves in the left hand and the direction brilliantissimo are devices characteristic of Busoni's own piano writing, as well as blending with the Liszt romantic gesture.

Figure 12.20

The cadenza is built upon the combination of the polonaise rhythm and motive, with a chromatic staccato idea introduced by Liszt earlier in the piece but unexploited.

FRANZ LISZT FANTASIE ÜBER ZWEI MOTIVE AUS W. A. MOZARTS DIE HOCHZEIT DES FIGARO NACH DEM FAST VOLLENDETEN ORIGINALMANUSKRIPT ERGÄNZT UND MORIZ ROSENTHAL ZUGEEIGNET VON FERRUCCIO BUSONI Leipzig Breitkopf & Haertel 1912 EB 3830 Composed in 1912

The original Liszt manuscript from which Busoni created this work may now be found in the Nationale Forschungs- und Gedenkstätten der klassischen deutschen Literatur in Weimar (Ms I 45). It contains no tempo indications, dynamics, or interpretative directions. Liszt must have had some doubts about various bars, since question marks are evident in the score, which has all the appearance of a rough copy quickly written out. Nevertheless, the music, compared with Busoni's printed realization, is substantially complete, and Busoni really did not have to compose much to organize the work into its final form. Apart from the very small compositional elaborations, he contributed the music of 5, 10, 1, 4, and 16 bars duration. The two most important insertions into Liszt's text are on page 28 (10 bars by Busoni) and the ending—the last 16 bars—which are also by Busoni, taking up the Liszt manuscript where it abruptly ends.

Surprisingly, the Liszt manuscript also contains 15 pages of music devoted largely to the Minuet from *Don Giovanni*, and occurs where Busoni composed his own 10 bars on page 28. It is possible that Liszt intended to combine motives from the two Mozart operas later in the piece. The Liszt manuscript pages are unnumbered, so another possibility is that two separate works have been misplaced in the Weimar library holdings. Since the transition to and from the *Don Giovanni* music is in C major, the 15 pages of manuscript can be played or omitted without any damage to the harmonic scheme. The *Don Giovanni* paraphrase begins on a fresh page and at no time are motives from both operas seen on the same page of Liszt's manuscript. To the best of my knowledge, it would be highly unlikely that Liszt would combine motives from separate operas in one paraphrase; I know of no such instance in his published output.

Since the material from *Figaro* had already created a by no means insubstantial composition, Busoni ignored the *Don Giovanni* music altogether, though it contained some interesting ideas, including one in which the right hand plays in 3/4 against the left hand in 2/4, the bars of the two hands not coinciding. As is to be expected, Busoni's text contains many ossias and pianistic clarifications; some large stretches are simplified, although in one particular spot he marks a succession of 10ths specifically as "non arpegg." But it is in the area of interpretation that his edition elicits the most admiration. His colorful and imaginative performing suggestions (in

Italian), as well as the more routine addition of articulation, dynamics, and tempo, all contribute toward the clarification and, indeed, strengthening of this *Fantasie*. Busoni's aim here was to rescue an unknown and incomplete Liszt work from undeserved oblivion. His edition stays within Liszt's language; and although Busoni's part in the endeavor was considerable, he successfully concealed it.

Liszt began the *Fantasie* in 1842, and he performed it at least once in Berlin in the following year. Notwithstanding, the manuscript copy as we now have it is unfinished. The magnificent *Fantasie* is based on Figaro's "non più andrai" and Cherubino's "voi che sapete."

FRANZ LISZT   UNGARISCHE RHAPSODIE NR. 19 FÜR PIANO-FORTE ZU ZWEI HÄNDEN   ZUM KONZERTGEBRAUCH FREI BEARBEITET VON FERRUCCIO BUSONI   Leipzig   Breitkopf & Haertel   1920   EB 4959

Comparing the original Liszt with the Busoni, I found up to 19 variants, some small, some major. This does not mean a cavalier and arbitrary treatment of the text of which little is changed. Busoni's editing falls into the categories of:

1.   Adding performance instructions or dynamics.

2.   Altering some figures to achieve a more characteristic Hungarian parlando effect; for example, see Figure 12.21.

Figure 12.21

3.   Additions of decorative figures, either by extension of existing figures or creation of new ones for purposes of connection or improvisatory effect. We know that Busoni did this sort of thing quite spontaneously (Chapter 19, vide Chopin *Prelude* and *Study*) and here we have a record of such extemporization.

4.   Altering figurations to achieve a desired effect. (See Figure 12.22.) Such a change was brought about to accomplish the volante that Busoni sought. In another section, Liszt leaves patterns unchanged for 20 bars; Busoni finds this dull, and introduces some variations into the accompaniment—but nothing too drastic.

5.   As well as adding, Busoni is not averse to cutting. There are two cuts in this *Rhapsody*: one of approximately 20 bars and one of over 100. In both cases they consist of material mechanically repeated by Liszt. The first cut is in the Lassan, the second and larger in the Friska. The cuts are designed to tighten up the structure of the Rhapsody.

Figure 12.22. By kind permission, Breitkopf & Haertel, Wiesbaden.

HEROISCHER MARSCH IN UNGARISCHEM STYL FÜR DAS PIANO-FORTE VON F. LISZT   NEU HERAUSGEGEBEN UND EGON PETRI GEWIDMET VON FERRUCCIO BUSONI   Berlin Schlesinger   1905 S 2977A

This is not one of the more interesting of the Busoni editions of Liszt: we do not find in this *March* the new insight that is so often a hallmark of Busoni. The variants from the original Liszt (not included in this edition) are mostly of a fairly ordinary pianistic nature; there are not many of them, and the ones that are present are not always logically carried out.

Hanspeter Krellmann, in his thorough fashion, gives a comparative list of variants from the original.[16]

BUSONI CADENZA TO LISZT-GOUNOD "VALSE DE L'OPÉRA FAUST"

There is no published work of Busoni under such a title, yet Petri in his recording of the Liszt *Faust Waltz* plays a "Busoni cadenza," of great charm and effectiveness. Fortunately, this cadenza has been published, but with no title other than *Nach Gounod*. This is hidden among the countless technical experiments making up the gigantic *Klavierübung*. If we look up Part 2, VII, of the first edition of the *Klavierübung*, or the Fifth Book of the second edition, we shall find this piece among others written for trill exercises.

The placing of it into the *Faust Waltz* now becomes a simple matter. The Busoni cadenza begins just like the Liszt cadenza, soon after the andantino section. The join at the beginning is given in Figure 12.23. The end of the

Figure 12.23. By kind permission, Breitkopf & Haertel, Wiesbaden.

cadenza and its return to the *Faust Waltz* was essayed by Busoni, as in
Figure 12.24. This little section was never published, being a simple variant
of the Liszt cadenza ending, but passed on aurally through pupils and
friends such as Petri; it can be heard in Petri's recording.

HUNGARIAN RHAPSODY NO. 20

The Staatsbibliothek Preussischer Kulturbesitz Musikabteilung has a
manuscript (N. Mus. Nachl. 4, 87) in Busoni's hand headed: *20.
Ungedruckte Ungar. Rhapsodie von Franz Liszt.* It is a copy of the twentieth
of the *Magyar Rhapsodiak, Rhapsodies hongroises* (Raabe 105 No. 20
Grove 242 No. 20). The manuscript that Busoni used to make his copy from
in 1900 was in the Liszt Museum in Weimar and was not in Liszt's hand but
Raff's; the original Liszt is in the Archiv der Gesellschaft der Musikfreunde
in Vienna. Raff's manuscript is now in the Nationale Forschungs- und
Gedenkstätten der klassischen deutschen Literatur in Weimar (Ms I 10, 12).

Unlike the *Figaro Fantasy*, the manuscript of the twentieth Rhapsody that
Busoni uncovered in the Liszt Museum was neatly written out and complete
with performance indications, including fingering. Busoni's copy is an exact
duplicate of the original, including Liszt's fingering, and preserves for most
of the time the same line spacing as in Raff's manuscript. Busoni must have
intended editing the work for publication. He even designed a florid-
looking title page which reads: *Rhapsodie hongroise, (vingtième, inédite)*

Figure 12.24. By kind permission, Breitkopf & Haertel, Wiesbaden.

après d'une copie dans le Liszt-Museum de Weimar. F. Liszt. (Ferruccio Busoni.)

There is precious little actual editing—a few ideas, two suggested cuts; Busoni possibly became disenchanted with the notion and abandoned it.

The work, unpublished in Busoni's time—hence his interest in it—was finally published in November 1936 (Universal Edition, edited by Dr. Octavian Beu) under the title *Rumänische Rhapsodie*; a misnomer, since music other than Rumanian appears in it. Pianists exploring the work will discover material later used in the sixth and twelfth Hungarian Rhapsodies.

SCHERZO VON FRANZ LISZT NACH DER ORIGINALEN HAND-SCHRIFT, ZUM ERSTEN MALE HERAUSGEGEBEN VON F. BUSONI Berlin Bard 1922 Supplement to *Faust, eine Rundschau* Vol. 1, No. 1

The supplement consisted of two pages of Liszt's manuscript followed by two pages in Busoni's hand, which is a straightout realization of Liszt's rather messy scrawl. The Liszt is dated 27 May 1827; the Busoni 5 April 1909 (London).

If one consults the Liszt-Stiftung edition part II, Vol. IX (Pianoforte-werke), this *Scherzo* will be found. In a preface written by José Vianna da Motta, and dated Lisbon, summer 1927, we read:

The ms [of this Scherzo] was in the possession of Ferruccio Busoni, and was given to him, as a gift, by the London pianist Fritz Hartvigson.

Otto Lessmann had already reported (in "Allgemeinen Musikzeitung" 1896, S. 288) that Hartvigson had located this ms in an old edition of Liszt's piano works. A facsimile had appeared in the "Allgemeinen Musikzeitung" in 1896, as well as, partially, in a supplement in Vol. 1 of the periodical "Faust. Eine Rundschau."

Busoni did not know that it had already been published . . . and published it again in 1922 as "for the first time" in "Faust," in facsimile and in the facsimile of his own copy.

It only remains to mention a few snippets of Liszt that appear as demonstrations of various techniques in the *Klavierübung*:

Totentanz excerpt (first edition only, Part 1).

Schubert-Liszt: excerpt from *Auf dem Wasser zu singen* (first edition, Part 1; second edition, Book 2).

Auber-Liszt: excerpt from the *Tarantella*, from the *La Muette de Portici* (first edition, Part 1; second edition, Book 2).[17]

Bellini-Liszt: excerpt from the *Norma Fantasie* (first edition, Part 1; second edition, Book 4).

Nach Liszt: three variations on a theme from *Venezia e Napoli*—the *Gondoliera*. This could stand occasional hearing as an encore or fill-in piece. Its four pages are of sufficient duration for such a purpose (first edition, Part 2; second edition, Book 5).

Excerpt from the *Mephisto-Waltz*, marked "quasi-galopp" (first edition, Part 3; second edition, Book 6).

Mendelssohn-Liszt: from the *Wedding March & Elfin Chorus* (first edition, Part 3; second edition, book 6).

Légendes. (1) *St. Francois d'Assise. La Prédication aux oiseaux.* It seems that in March 1910 Busoni had prepared a revised and annotated edition of this work. It was not published in his lifetime and appears in the Busoni-Nachlass catalogue as No. 279. Unfortunately, it disappeared during World War II. Despite extensive searching, I have been unable to trace this manuscript.

Fantasie und Fuge über den Choral "Ad nos, ad salutarem undam" (see Chapter 16).

NOTES

1. Edward J. Dent, *Ferruccio Busoni: A Biography* (London, Oxford University Press, 1933), p. 27n.

2. In the course of his life, Busoni, through constant alertness and unsparing effort, had acquired a unique and valuable library of Liszt first and rare editions. It was but another posthumous tragedy of his life that the library was auctioned off and thus dispersed forever.

3. A pupil of Liszt.

4. Busoni, *Letters to His Wife*, p. 34.

5. Busoni, *Letters to His Wife*, p. 116.

6. Whereas the *Concerto Op. XXXIX* represented the culmination of Busoni's studies of the heroic-romantic Liszt, so subsequent Busoni must represent delving into preimpressionistic-prophetic Liszt.

7. Ferruccio Busoni, *The Essence of Music and Other Papers*, trans. Rosamond Ley (London, Rockliff, 1957), p. 138.

8. Ibid., p. 163.

9. The separate edition presents a luxuriousness to the eye; no less than four parallel versions are given: the original Paganini, Busoni's version, Liszt's first version, and Liszt's second version.

10. Published here in English for the first time.

11. The episode later separated from the work was further used by Liszt for a passage in his "Harmonies poétiques et religieuses." (Busoni's footnote.)

12. The supplement contains one such specimen. (Busoni's footnote.)

13. Busoni, *The Essence of Music*, p. 89.

14. Ibid., pp. 85-86. The Liszt arrangement of his *Rhapsody No. 14* as the *Hungarian Fantasy* for piano and orchestra is a closer analogy to Busoni's transcription.

15. Although there is the one instance already described, of the *Jota* and allegretto piacevole theme combined.

16. Hanspeter Krellmann, *Studien zu den Bearbeitungen Ferruccio Busonis* (Regensburg, Gustav Bosse Verlag, 1966), p. 149.

17. It may be of interest to note that there exists in the Staatsbibliothek Preussischer Kulturbesitz (N. Mus. Nachl. 4, 88) a copy of Liszt's *Tarantelle (di Bravura) d'après la Tarantelle de la Muette de Portici d'Auber* in a standard edition with Busoni's interpretative markings, possibly in preparation for a new concert version.

13

Busoni and Mozart

> Mozart, you have to know, was Busoni's god. They both had the same basic attitude towards music—a sort of intellectual objectivity without dryness. Busoni studied Mozart all his life.
>
> Dimitri Mitropoulos

We take our Mozart festivals, concerts, and recordings very much for granted these days; it is hard to imagine a musical world in which the great Austrian composer was just being discovered and revived. This was the very situation when Busoni was in his heyday. Mozart, long treated as a composer of fairly light and pretty music, was finally being awarded his place among the great dramatic and profound masters, and the efforts of men like Köchel, Richard Strauss, Donald Tovey, and Edward Dent paved the way for our broader understanding and acceptance of Mozart today.[1]

Busoni, in his own inimitable way, shared in the great excitement of the day, in this unearthing of a new Mozart, but his attitude was different from that of the academic or the musicologist. He was primarily interested in Mozart as a composer of music that was valid and meaningful for the twentieth century. In this, his attitude toward Mozart was similar to his attitude toward Bach: he felt no slavish worship for the *Urtext*, but allowed himself the liberty to ornament, alter, augment, or compress according to his own interpretative instincts. This attitude, however, created quite different results in Busoni's Bach and Mozart editions.

Mozart, after all, wrote for a pianoforte—even though not a modern pianoforte; Bach had written for a different instrument. Busoni, therefore, was more reluctant to alter the textures of Mozart, where with Bach he had felt justified. Apropos of this, it is valid to note that Beethoven is hardly touched by Busoni, except for the little *Ecossaisen* and the cadenzas to the concerti; the larger works were never edited. Busoni rightly sensed that Beethoven wrote for the modern pianoforte, so that corrective treatment was unnecessary. Yet Beethoven figured most prominently in Busoni's repertoire.

Liszt was another matter (see Chapter 12). Here Busoni not so much changed as suggested pianistic variants and alternative effects. There was no question of adapting Liszt; but to return to Mozart.

Among the fairly extensive list of works that may be credited to Mozart-Busoni, we find that the overwhelming number are fairly straightforward transcriptions: there is no work based on a fragment or idea of Mozart, a favored procedure in connection with Bach. There exists one study on Mozart in *An die Jugend*; as well, a number of pieces "after" Mozart. Generally, the deviations are much slighter than those of Busoni's Bach works.

Mozart attracted Busoni for reasons different from Bach. There was Busoni's love of melody, clarity, economy, and perfection of form, all so obvious in Mozart. Not that these were missing in Busoni's estimation of Bach—he was attracted to Bach for other qualities.

That he felt deeply about Mozart we can confirm by reading his essays and aphorisms, by studying his concert programs, and finally learning something about his editorial schemes concerning Mozart.

Busoni was just as individual in his approach to the playing of Mozart as to other composers. This is shown by the story of his two Berlin concerts at which he was scheduled to play six Mozart concerti under Gustav Brecher. Busoni antagonized Brecher from the start by insisting on certain tempi; Brecher felt it was not the prerogative of a mere pianist to do so. Rehearsals were made more painful by Busoni's personal approach to rhythm which Brecher found difficult to follow. He finally stormed off the platform at the last rehearsal announcing that "it is impossible to accompany such playing!" The concertmaster took over the baton, and conducted the first concert—perfectly satisfactorily—without a rehearsal.

Of Busoni's writings about Mozart, perhaps the most important, and certainly the most poetic and perceptive are the *Aphorisms*, written to commemorate the one hundred-fiftieth anniversary of Mozart's birth, which appeared in the *Lokal Anzeiger*, Berlin, 1906. There is one aphorism for every year of Mozart's short life and, as the productivity in these short years was incredible, so were Busoni's sayings brief but meaningful. Hugo Leichtentritt has said that each of these sayings could be expanded into a whole chapter.[2] A sampling: "His art is like a sculptor's masterpiece—presenting from every side a finished picture. . . . He can say very much, but never says too much . . . He gives the solution with the riddle. . . . Even in the most tragic situations he still has a witticism ready, in the most cheerful he is able to draw a thoughtful furrow in his brow. . . . His spirit is not pure out of ignorance."[3]

Apart from these aphorisms, there are also: "For the *Don Giovanni* Jubilee"—written for the *Neue Zeitschrift Für Musik*, Leipzig, 16 October

1887. A very substantial article, a study in depth not only of the opera and some of its associated problems (translations, authenticity of scoring) but also of Mozart himself; "Mozart's libretti"—written in 1920, published in *Von Der Einheit Der Musik* and "Mozart's Don Giovanni and Liszt's Don Juan Fantasy," written in 1917 as a preface to Busoni's edition of the Liszt *Don Juan Fantasy*. There are various other cross-references to Mozart in many other articles and letters by Busoni.

Some striking parallels exist in the careers of Mozart and Busoni, parallels that Busoni must have been aware of, and that would have troubled him all his early life. His parents, certainly his father, expected achievements of little Ferruccio equal to those of the great master Mozart himself. After all, both were child prodigies; both toured as such, with other members of the family; both were admitted at a very early age as diplomees of the Accademia Filarmonica in Bologna, for composition and piano playing; both were ardent and amusing letter writers with a gift for often penetrating satire; both were pianist-composers, attaining their pinnacle writing opera and for the piano; both were influenced by German and Italian outlooks on music; both were brilliant extemporizors; and both publicly improvised on given themes as part of their child prodigy concerts.

Whether such parallels had any real effect on Busoni as a composer we can only surmise. For in the most important aspects of their personalities, the two were quite different; Mozart did not appear to have had Busoni's doubts, agonies, and searches.

Naturally, Busoni's study of Mozart brought forth fruit not only in transcriptions and editions, but also in influence upon his own original music. *Arlecchino* is Mozartian, so is the *Rondo Arlecchinesco* and the *Sonatina ad usum infantis*; the early *Lustspiel Overture* was even written at one sitting in true Mozart tradition. The purity of the Mozart line can be traced in works such as *Doktor Faust* and the *Romanza and Scherzoso* Op. 51, but possibly the works most akin to Mozart are the two wind concerti, the *Concertino for Clarinet and Small Orchestra* Op. 48 and *Divertimento for Flute and Orchestra* Op. 52. Busoni's interest in these instruments at this particular time must have been inspired by writing cadenzas for the clarinet and flute concerti of Mozart.

But although Busoni was eclectic in his tastes, he did not write "neo-classic" music in the more accepted sense of the word—in the "Stravinskian" manner of Mozart with "wrong" notes, or Bach with "wrong" notes (if I may be permitted to make a great simplification). The model was transmuted and blended into his own style. The very word *neo-classicism* was coined by Busoni, but he meant something quite different from what it actually became, as evidenced in his essays.

Through all his upheavals, he did not waver in his love of some Mozart works. *The Marriage of Figaro* was to Busoni, for many years, "a lighthouse in a stormy sea." Petri tells of Busoni arriving one day, despairing, after studying this opera, and announcing that "if I cannot be as good a composer as Mozart, I shall shoot myself!" But not many years later, Busoni discovered that there were "signs of human weakness in it . . . and I rejoiced at the discovery that I do not stand so far beneath it as I did—although on the other hand this discovery means not only a positive loss, but also points to the transitoriness of all human achievement. And how much more transitory must be my own!"[4] On this occasion he appeared, also with the *Figaro* score, with the "signs of human weakness" underscored in pencil.

At the end of his life, already ill from nephritis and heart disease that finally killed him, Busoni found time to consider two Mozart projects: first, the writing of recitatives for the *Magic Flute* for a La Scala production, from which Busoni had to withdraw due to illness; and second, a more interesting and valuable scheme—an edition of all the Mozart piano concerti.

Neither of these plans saw the light of day, but Busoni must have valued them highly to have even considered these at a time when he was so ill and knew that every spare minute should be devoted to the completion of *Doktor Faust*.

Busoni wrote cadenzas and fermatas for 10 Mozart concerti, mostly toward the end of his life. If we discount the earlier version of the cadenza for K. 466 and accept the later version as more desirable (see below), we can then say that all the cadenzas appear within eight years of Busoni's death. As with Mozart himself, the Busoni cadenzas were written primarily for his own performance of these works, and so there was no attempt to equate their technical difficulty with that of the concerto for which they were written; in some cases the cadenza is much more difficult than the concerto it serves—at least for most pianists.

More serious and problematical, however, is the inequality of style; critics of these cadenzas invariably underline the fact that a pianist playing a Mozart concerto should either play a Mozart cadenza if available, or else endeavor to find or write one that is in the style of the rest of the concerto. Such an outlook, though aesthetically justifiable, may not be strictly accurate historically. The existing Mozart cadenzas are in any case obviously sketches for performance; in the concert hall, Mozart would embellish and amplify, in the same way as he would embellish and amplify the piano part of the concerti themselves. It was not until Beethoven included the cadenza as an integral part of a concerto (in the *Emperor*) that the composer's attitude toward this conventional insertion into the concerto design underwent a change. In Mozart's day, the pianist or other instrumentalist was expected to improvise and also take the opportunity to display his technique. The abuse of this privilege eventually led composers to write out and publish their cadenzas in full.

The question is centered basically around the role of the performer. A paradox exists here today. We expect our modern virtuosi to be self-effacing and not to come between us and the composer yet deliver the music with all the fire, power, and virtuosity necessary; in fact, to establish the solo instrument as a personality in conflict with the orchestra. Further underlining this individuality, the soloist is given a cadenza to play—how is he to fulfil both self-effacing and aggressive functions simultaneously? It could be that when style is considered in such a context, a second element must be added to the purist mixture: the style of the performer, which consciously or not, intentionally or not, is presented to the audience, although in a lesser proportion, with the style of the composition. In the cadenza, the style of the performer has an opportunity to come to the fore more prominently than elsewhere in the concerto; and so our aesthetic senses were offended to hear heavy romantic pedalled extravaganzas within the framework of Mozart, Haydn, Beethoven, and others composed by virtuosi of the last century and early part of this century. The problem is not as simple as some would have us believe; the role of the performer keeps undergoing change and has varied from the extreme of romantic sovereignty to the more recent submissive role as a mere instrument of the composer; some postwar developments in composition seem to be aimed at a partial restoration of the performer's dignity and responsibility by demanding of him the onus for some decisions regarding the structure, sequence, and sometimes the actual notes to be played, with many cadenza-like possibilities at his disposal. Thus the circle turns.

In the light of the above remarks, it may be easier to understand Busoni's attitudes in the matter. He was no self-effacing virtuoso—this much is obvious from his whole attitude toward piano playing and transcription. He took upon himself the responsibility of presenting a work from his point of view and regarded such a responsibility as inherent to the performer. His composition of the cadenzas for the Mozart concerti was a reflection of such a stand. We are now in a position to examine the stylistic components making up these cadenzas, to make a general evaluation, and then to examine each cadenza briefly on its own.

1. *Orchestral Style*—there is often an attempt to write in a Mozartian orchestral style. (See Figure 13.1.) Such episodes, although they may look "Lisztian," are in fact meant to be played lightly and incisively, as though by woodwind choir. The spread out chords, seemingly incongruous, may also be regarded as a "score" chord compressed into two staves; Mozart often wrote such chords but not for piano.

2. *"Modernistic" Style*—the most controversial aspect of the Busoni cadenza. (See Figure 13.2.) The major-minor ambiguity is of course a trademark of the Busoni style; the sequences, moving by strictly logical means through unexpected keys, are an extension of Mozart's sequential technique. Such passages are, therefore, a result of Busoni's consideration of Mozart as a composer of the future as well as the past and his own self-imposed responsibilities as a performer of a Mozart concerto.

Figure 13.1. By kind permission, Breitkopf & Haertel, Wiesbaden.

Figure 13.2. By kind permission, Breitkopf & Haertel, Wiesbaden.

3. *Lisztian Style*—the more regrettable feature of these compositions.[5] Fortunately,
the excursion into Lisztian pianism is rare. A typical thickening of a cadential trill
appears in Figure 13.3. Such trills can be easily simplified; other passages may
only look Lisztian; the temptation for the pianist to thunder his way through such
passages must be resisted: more often than not, they are really from category (1).

Figure 13.3. By kind permission, Breitkopf & Haertel, Wiesbaden.

4. *Integrated Style*—usually, Mozart's cadenzas consist of flourishes and
conventional passage work, with some reference to subject matter. As pointed
out above, these cadenzas were really sketches for Mozart to elaborate on
further; however, even in this form, it is obvious that Mozart did not regard the
cadenza as an essential factor in the unfolding process of his music but more as a
gesture on the part of the soloist. Busoni attempted to combine Mozart's point of
view with Beethoven's. His cadenzas, while preserving the dramatic gesture, are
also carefully integrated with the rest of the movement and constitute a careful
and further working out of the basic thematic materials, often throwing into relief
aspects of the themes not specifically underlined or explored by Mozart.

5. *Monumental Style*—in view of the above, Busoni's cadenza often underlines the
monumental aspect of the themes being developed: another lesson learned from
Beethoven.

Basically, these five factors sum up Busoni's attitude toward the problem
of writing a cadenza to a Mozart concerto. In his last few years, he often
expressed the desire to go over these compositions, to eliminate the
thickened trills, and to thin out some of the more "growly" chords in the
lower register of the piano, but such refinements are necessary only in
isolated bars and can be easily carried out by the performer. As a model of
such a process we have Busoni's own revision of the cadenza to K. 466. (See
Figure 13.4.)

As is to be expected, Busoni's standpoint contains paradoxes. On the one
hand, he asserts his right as a performer to play his own cadenza, even
when there is a Mozart one available; on the other hand, he invokes a later
compositional development (Beethoven) by departing from an improvisatory type of cadenza to an elaborate, tightly integrated, and carefully
worked out style. In texture, Busoni is very faithful to the original, but in
counterpoint and sequential harmony he feels free to write chromatically, a
derivation of his personal style.

Figure 13.4. By kind permission, Breitkopf & Haertel, Wiesbaden.

In performance, the result is that, although startling, the Busoni cadenza fits in surprisingly well; the harmonic excursions do not sound as "modern" as they used to and the inexorable intellect controlling the music and the textures, the sudden flashes of insight, the imaginative pianism, all make for an exciting experience. Thus, Busoni achieves what he set out to do: preserve his individuality and outlook yet weld the cadenza and concerto into a logical unity.

In the brief identification of each separate cadenza that follows, mention is made if a Mozart cadenza also exists for the particular concerto in question.

KADENZEN ZU W. A. MOZARTS KLAVIERKONZERT NR. 20
D MOLL KV 466   Leipzig   Breitkopf & Haertel   1907   Klav.
Bibl. 25 517

Busoni wrote quite extensive cadenzas to both the first and last movements. What is significant is that these exist in two versions—the published version and another handed down to Petri, which offers some alterations. The dating of this second version is uncertain; Petri indicated to me that it was composed circa 1920.

In essence, the two versions are the same, but the later version deletes some overloaded chording and contains generally a purer, thinner line. It is illuminating to compare the two versions as evidence, on a small scale, of Busoni's changes of outlook. (See Appendix.)

I have been unable to trace an actual copy of this second version in Busoni's own hand. The changes were indicated to Petri verbally; he sketched them into his printed copy, and passed it on to his pupils in this form. I made a complete copy of this second version, with its few ossias, and went over it with Petri. As far as we could tell, it is an accurate representation of Busoni's alterations as it now stands in this book. It could well be that Busoni never made a fine copy of this cadenza at all. Like the cadenza to Liszt's *Faust* paraphrase and the alternate ending to *All' Italia!*, this "new" cadenza was, in all possibility, sketched out roughly, memorized for performance, passed on to close friends like Petri, and then forgotten.[6]

ZWEI KADENZEN ZU W. A. MOZARTS KLAVIERKONZERT NR. 9
Es DUR, KV 271   Leipzig   Breitkopf & Haertel   1916   Klav. Bibl.
27 893

Busoni wrote cadenzas for the first and second movements of this youthful concerto. (See also *Andantino* below.) The cadenza to the slow movement is particularly successful.

Mozart cadenzas exist for this concerto.

KADENZ UND CODA ZU W. A. MOZARTS KLAVIERKONZERT NR. 23 A-DUR, KV 488 Leipzig Breitkopf & Haertel 1919 Klav. Bibl. 28 475a

There is a cadenza to the first movement and a suggestion for the piano to play in the last four bars a simple imitative figure against the orchestra.

A Mozart cadenza exists, but it has no similarity to Busoni's.

KADENZEN ZU W. A. MOZARTS KLAVIERKONZERT NR. 24 C-MOLL, KV 491 Leipzig Breitkopf & Haertel 1919 Klav. Bibl. 28 475b

Apart from a cadenza for the first movement, Busoni wrote two fermatas for the slow movement and one for the last (inserted just before the change to 6/8). Those to the slow movement are curious little canonic episodes, a little reminiscent of the slow canons in the *Sonatina seconda*. (See Figure 13.5.) One can imagine the indignation they caused—and would cause even today—in performance.

Figure 13.5. By kind permission, Breitkopf & Haertel, Wiesbaden.

KADENZEN ZU W. A. MOZARTS KLAVIERKONZERT NR. 21
C-DUR, KV 467   Leipzig   Breitkopf & Haertel   1922   Klav. Bibl.
28 669

We have for this concerto: a short fermata at the solo entry; an extensive elaborate cadenza in a self-contained ternary form; two short fermatas for the last movement; and a fairly long cadenza for the last movement, noted for Mozart-like sequences that constantly move into unexpected keys.

KADENZEN ZU W. A. MOZARTS KLAVIERKONZERT NR. 22
Es-DUR, KV 482   Leipzig   Breitkopf & Haertel   1922   Klav. Bibl.
28 670   Composed in 1919

Here Busoni provided a cadenza to the first movement; and in the third movement the three fermatas are fully realized. (See also *Rondo Concertante*, in which the third fermata—or more correctly because of its length, cadenza—is slightly amplified, for reasons explained under that heading; the second fermata is slightly altered, the first is the same.)

KADENZEN ZU W. A. MOZARTS KLAVIERKONZERT NR. 19
F-DUR, KV 459   Leipzig   Breitkopf & Haertel   1922   Klav. Bibl.
28 671   Composed in 1920

Busoni wrote two cadenzas for this concerto: first movement cadenza and a short cadenza for the third movement, which appears in fuller form for two pianos in another work. (See *Duettino Concertante*.) Mozart supplied cadenzas for both these movements.

FERRUCCIO BUSONI   KADENZ ZU W. A. MOZARTS
KLAVIERKONZERT NR. 25   C-DUR, KV 503   Leipzig   Breitkopf
& Haertel   1923   Klav. Bibl. 25 289   Composed in 1922

This is by far the most ambitious and extensive of the cadenzas. It runs into 10 full pages and bristles with technical difficulty. Two events of special interest occur:

1. The combination of a theme from the concerto with a motive from the *Jupiter Symphony*; this may be viewed with amusement or dismay, but is indicative of Busoni's alert turn of mind, always alive to all manner of contrapuntal combination, and to his outlook on this great piano concerto. In his mind there was a strong kinship between the two works, and such alliance of themes was excusable. At any rate, the *Jupiter* motive works into the cadenza quite naturally (see Figure 13.6), and most musicians will agree with Busoni that there is indeed much common spirit between the works in question.
2. The cadenza continues over the orchestral tutti, and the piano, unable to stop by virtue of its tremendous momentum, prolongs its glittering passages right to the end of the movement.

Figure 13.6. By kind permission, Breitkopf & Haertel, Wiesbaden.

KADENZEN ZU W. A. MOZARTS KLAVIERKONZERT NR. 17 IN G-DUR, KV 453 Leipzig Breitkopf & Haertel 1922 Klav. Bibl. 28 717 Composed in 1921 Also Wiesbaden Breitkopf & Haertel EB 6803

Busoni composed a cadenza to the first movement of this concerto, realized the four fermatas in the slow movement, and also provided a cadenza for this slow movement. Mozart had written cadenzas for both the first and second movements, but Busoni chose to ignore these; his cadenzas have no common ground with Mozart's.

This concerto was one of Busoni's favorites; he chose it as the first to be edited in conjunction with Egon Petri as part of his complete series of Mozart concerti. It is also the last cadenza that he composed for a Mozart concerto.

W. A. MOZART FANTASIE FÜR EINE ORGELWALZE, WERK 608 FÜR ZWEI KLAVIERE BEARBEITET VON FERRUCCIO BUSONI Leipzig Breitkopf & Haertel EB 5220 Transcribed in 1922

Mozart wrote his great f minor *Fantasy* for mechanical organ in 1782 (according to *Grove's Dictionary*; W. J. Turner's *Mozart* gives 1791); in 1791 he transcribed it for piano four hands. I have used this version as a basis for comparison with Busoni's two-piano arrangement.

The *Fantasy* K. 608 was written together with K. 594 (*Adagio and Allegro in F Minor* for mechanical organ) and K. 616 (*Andante in F Major* for mechanical organ). All three works are set out on four staves, even when there was no contrapuntal necessity to notate in this manner; presumably Mozart had in mind four separate planes of operation for the mechanical organ. In any event, he overestimated the possibilities of the mechanical or clock organ in this regard. However, in the arrangement for piano four hands, we have a faithful reproduction of the original four staves; most other transcribers of this work have limited themselves to organ or piano settings, although there are also some orchestral arrangements.

By all rights discussion of this work should be found in the chapter on organ transcriptions. It differs, however, from Busoni's other organ transcriptions in that the sound is linear and lucid; Busoni avoids the thick chords and massive sonorities prevalent in these. Even the climaxes are built up rather less through density than by octave doubling and consequent intensification of lines.

The *Fantasy* is also one of the most faithful of Busoni's Mozart transcriptions; up to the end of the Andante, there are no changes at all. At this point, the florid cadenza passage leading back to Tempo I is elaborated and extended by a few bars.

The second change occurs at this Tempo I; Mozart's 12 bars are extended to 14 in Busoni's version, before the double fugue begins. The double fugue is now shortened by 2 bars.

Busoni omits Mozart's last reference to the opening theme and allows the double fugue to sweep on to the very end. This necessitates a further cut of 11 bars.

This last is the most drastic of the alterations Busoni makes. It came about for two reasons. First, Busoni interpreted the opening section as being slightly slower than the fugue; therefore, the appearance of this section toward the end would mean a slowing down of the pulse. Second, Busoni believed that the reappearance of this section was redundant and preferred the accumulated tension of the double fugue to complete the piece. In performance, this view is justified.

Despite my assertion that this is basically a faithful transcription, we must not expect a note-for-note transfer to the two-piano idiom, even allowing for necessary adjustments such as octave displacements and doubling; such a procedure, possible to anyone, would have bored Busoni to distraction. Little chromatic changes appear here and there. Mozart's figure is changed from what appears in Figure 13.7 to Figure 13.8 (a diminution of one of the themes) in some of the double fugue episodes to achieve greater formal cohesion; some trill-like semiquavers are added in the first fugue and the pianos are used in a range exceeding Mozart's own piano range. Busoni's suggestion regarding a difference in tempo between introductory theme and fugues works remarkably well and sets off the fugues in clear contrast to the rest of the *Fantasy*.

Figure 13.7

Figure 13.8. By kind permission, Breitkopf & Haertel, Wiesbaden.

Busoni's foreword to this arrangement, dated June 1922, reads, in rough translation:

This piece was written to create a programme of my own works for two pianos. With the Duettino concertante, which it precedes, it forms a greater sonata. The Fantasie for mechanical organ consists of (in the style of an Italian Overture) an Allegro (Fuge), an Andante, and a final Allegro (Double Fugue): f-Minor, Ab Major, f-Minor. To these faster and slower parts the Duettino concertante gives a F-Major-Finale, suitably attached to the Fantasie as a "rounding-off" piece. The programme for two pianos would then consist of:

1. Improvisation über Bach'sches Chorallied.
2. (a) Fantasie für eine Orgelwalze.
   (b) Duettino Concertante.
3. Fantasia Contrappuntistica.[7]

W. A. MOZART   OUVERTÜRE ZUR OPER DIE ZAUBERFLÖTE ÜBERTRAGUNG FÜR ZWEI KLAVIERE VON FERRUCCIO BUSONI
Leipzig   Breitkopf & Haertel   EB 5241   Transcribed in 1923

In the foreword to my arrangement of Mozart's Fantasie for mechanical organ I have given a concert programme of my own works that could provide an evening of 2-piano music. But in public performance this programme proved too short, and this arbitrary circumstance gave me the opportunity of paying tribute to Mozart's genius by transcribing his Magic Flute Overture for 2 pianos: this being the only manner in which, to my mind, the otherwise insurmountable task of transcribing this work for piano could be solved. This setting, a true transcription, and a very small rearrangement, should be placed at the opening of the programme.[7]

F.B.
June 1923

As with the other transcription from the *Magic Flute* (see below), this is absolutely faithful, bar by bar, to the original. In this case, the whole overture is transcribed from beginning to end; there are no cuts, no harmonic changes, and only pianistic adaptations of orchestral effects. Alternating hands provide a witty and effective idea. (See Figure 13.9.) Arpeggios broken downward compare with orchestral piling up at tutti endings. (See Figure 13.10.) The piece is great fun to play without being

Figure 13.9. By kind permission, Breitkopf & Haertel, Wiesbaden.

Figure 13.10. By kind permission, Breitkopf & Haertel, Wiesbaden.

excessively difficult, and the interaction between the two pianos is most
diverting for the audience as well.

   The *Magic Flute* held a special interest for Busoni: his plans for
Oehlenschläger's *Aladdin* were that it would be "something like the Magic
Flute"; when searching for an opera, he considered Goethe's sequel to the
Magic Flute. Finally, when *Doktor Faust* came to be written, the *Magic
Flute* was a constant reference point. Thus it was Mozart and the *Magic
Flute* that showed him the way to the serenity and nobility of the *Piano
Concerto* and *Doktor Faust*.

W. A. MOZART ANDANTINO AUS DEM 9 KLAVIER-
KONZERT WERK 271 FÜR KLAVIER ALLEIN FREI ÜBERTRAGEN
UND MIT EINER KADENZ VERSEHEN VON FERRUCCIO BUSONI
Leipzig Breitkopf & Haertel 1914 EB 3987

This is one of Busoni's most successful transcriptions, the solo-tutti effects are beautifully calculated and sound quite unmistakable, yet the piece stands in its own right as a solo piano work.

The *Andantino* also embodies in summary almost all of Busoni's attitudes toward Mozart. At the very opening, and also in later appearances, the contrapuntal possibilities of the c minor theme are immediately seized upon and exploited as a canon at the octave, a crotchet apart. Various ornamental figures are slightly altered, some appoggiaturas are changed to triplets, and some melodic lines embellished—but all these changes are aimed at a constantly unfolding line, and the accompanying and contrapuntal additions all enhance it.

In common with other Mozart arrangements, Busoni makes two cuts: one of 5 bars and the other of 18 bars' duration. It is notable that such a procedure is not adopted in Busoni's Bach arrangements. Busoni genuinely felt that Mozart, more often than not out of a sense of convention, repeated sections of his works unnecessarily; his cuts are aimed at increasing the tension of the overall work, maintaining its flow from beginning to end without any feeling of slackening. It is of course debatable whether Mozart's aims in this slow movement coincided with Busoni's; however, it is undoubtedly true that Busoni's cuts do make for more conciseness and directness without any loss of other qualities. In this particular case, the cuts represent exact repetitions of materials already heard.

Another mannerism of Busoni's editing of Mozart is his habit of increasing a melodic leap by an octave, then introducing a florid run to come back to the right pitch, or extending the run past the right pitch by yet another octave. (See Figure 13.11.) The Mozart fermata just before the cadenza is amplified by Busoni.

Figure 13.11. By kind permission, Breitkopf & Haertel, Wiesbaden.

The actual cadenza is the same as the one published separately (see above).

MOZART   RONDO CONCERTANTE FÜR PIANOFORTE UND ORCHESTER KV. 482   NEU BEARBEITET VON FERRUCCIO BUSONI   Leipzig   Breitkopf & Haertel   1922   Part. B.   2604 Transcribed in 1919

A number of points arise out of this edition:

1. Mozart's left-hand line is often simply a continuo part. Busoni takes this oppor-
    tunity to ignore the doubling of the bass line, and gives the left hand other
    material to play. Sometimes he divides the line between the hands, allowing him
    to emphasize more easily some rhythm or accent; at other times, the left hand
    doubles the right hand in runs, usually a third or sixth below; finally (as in the
    very opening of the *Rondo*, when it is too early to introduce elaborations),
    Busoni occasionally leaves out the original bass, filling it in with chords instead.

2. The *Rondo* is given fully realized fermatas and a cadenza. These have also been
    published separately (see above). The cadenza given here is an amplified version
    of the one published separately.

3. The main theme of the *Rondo* is given a variety of guises in its manifold
    appearances. (See Figure 13.12.) Such practice is typical of Busoni and, as it
    happens, is now proven to be historically correct. In the published version of the
    concerto, Mozart gives the main theme in its bare form every time; yet we know
    that contemporary practice demanded variants improvised or devised by the
    performer. (Pianists who play only "what's in the music" in Mozart are being far
    less faithful than they presume.) Busoni may have known this or sensed it
    intuitively; his variants are always interesting yet not too far divorced from the
    original.

Figure 13.12. By kind permission, Breitkopf & Haertel, Wiesbaden.

4. The usual small changes in figures, typical of Busoni's Mozart editing, appear here as well.

5. At times Mozart leaves unadorned dotted minims, indicating the extremes of passage work and the bare harmony in the left hand; the player was expected to make up runs and passages following such an outline. Busoni provides solutions.

6. The *Andantino* is given a slightly fuller setting; Busoni assumed that Mozart provided the bass note, and expected the pianist to play the full harmony. Sometimes such harmony is played as a broken chord; just before the pizzicato section in the *Andantino* the piano left hand foreshadows and imitates the strings.

7. Some obvious and expected cadential trills in Mozart are omitted by Busoni in favor of unexpected runs or dominant arpeggios.

8. Since the cadenza ends with a statement of the main theme, Busoni cuts it from the Mozart score in the tutti immediately following. On the other hand, Busoni adds some extra bars soon after, containing a whimsical reference to the main theme.

9. The piano has some scalar flourishes right to the end of the movement.

The whole of the *Rondo* is a valuable record of how Busoni played Mozart, and an intelligent guide to imaginative and creative pianism.

DUETTINO CONCERTANTE NACH MOZART FÜR ZWEI
PIANOFORTE   Leipzig   Breitkopf & Haertel
1921   EB 5190   Transcribed in 1919

Busoni's treatment of the florid passages is very similar to that already described in the *Rondo Concertante*; as is his abolition of a static continuo bass. Some passages in triplets are changed into semiquavers. The two-piano treatment, in general effect, reminds us of the *Magic Flute* overture; there is a constant and witty interplay between the two pianos, dazzling concertante passages, and an infectious chatter. The spirit and substance of the original Mozart could not have been better captured, whatever we may feel about all the changes wrought. (I admit that my acquaintance with the original Mozart came *after* playing the Busoni version, and the Busoni has, since then, always seemed the more successful of the two.) Busoni is free here of all piano-orchestra considerations and has the opportunity to distribute material between two solo pianos; there is no feeling of a first and second piano in the sense that one is more important than another. The solo and orchestral parts have been evenly redistributed.

Apart from textural changes necessary due to the choice of medium, other alterations are:

1. Cut from bar 106/second crotchet to bar 114/first crotchet, inclusive.

2. Mozart's first fermata omitted altogether and a running passage substituted leading directly into the re-statement of the rondo theme.

3. Second fugato is shortened by 15 bars.

4. The stop at the cadential 6/4 chord is eliminated, and once more Busoni devises a passage that leads directly into a quasi cadenza using fugato material.

5. The quasi cadenza takes up all of page 17 and the first three lines of page 18 in the Busoni two-piano score up to the final statement of the rondo theme in F major.

6. The concert ending is Busoni's own, and is a form of perpetual motion, disappearing pianissimo in an upward chromatic swirl of notes.

It is clear even from such a short description that Busoni's aim in editing the work was a type of telescoping; an attempt to gain maximum movement through elimination of two fermatas and devising of a new ending, as well as by some cuts. The fact that the edition is for two pianos is, in Busoni's particular case, merely incidental. Believing as he did in the Unity of Music (the independence of music from its performing medium), the same cuts and rewriting would have applied to an edition of the movement for piano and orchestra. There is no doubt about this. Therefore, it would be both correct (from Busoni's point of view) and possible to take Busoni's edition and re-apply it, if we so wished, to the piano and orchestra; it would, in fact, take very little effort on our part. The cadenza published separately for this concerto could be used, or, better still, an accompanied cadenza could be devised from the *Duettino Concertante*. The concert ending would easily separate into piano and orchestral parts.

Characteristically, Busoni does not acknowledge his source.[8] The title simply says *After Mozart*.

Variations-Studie nach Mozart, 1 in KLAVIERÜBUNG 1st ed.
Part 3   2d ed. Book 6

This little diadem is a transcription of the Serenade from *Don Giovanni*. Taking only two pages, this piece used to be a favorite encore of Egon Petri and embodies an original and striking use of blind octaves in one hand, with melody and accompaniment in another: a different slant on the trick of "piano three hands" type of writing.

Giga, Bolero e Variazione   Studie nach Mozart   In AN DIE JUGEND
(see Chapter 5)   Also in KLAVIERÜBUNG 1st ed. Part 3   2d ed.
Book 6   titled *Variations-Studie nach Mozart, 2*

The piece begins with an edited version of the well-known Mozart chromatic *Gigue* in G, K. 574. Section A is mostly an octave lower than written, otherwise it is unchanged. Section A is then repeated at correct pitch, with some left-hand octaves added. Section B is mostly an octave higher than written, with some added accacciaturas. The coda is omitted.

Section B is then repeated at correct pitch, with some left-hand octaves added and a coda inserted in full. (Obviously, it was cut from the first playing of Section B to avoid anti-climax on repeat.)

This, as it stands, could be printed separately as an edited version of the Mozart *Gigue*. It is curious how even a miniature piece like this is molded and left with the unmistakable Busoni imprint. There is more than a grain of truth in a remark made jocularly to Petri: "I never play a piece unless I can change something in it!"

The *Bolero*, which immediately follows, is taken from the finale of act 3 of the *Marriage of Figaro*; the 44 bars of andante, described by Mozart as a fandango, are given here by Busoni as a *Bolero*. The music is virtually unchanged: the first part is transposed from a minor to e minor; half way through Busoni abruptly modulates to g minor to allow a smoother transition to the *Variation*, which is in G major. The Mozart remains in a minor throughout; an attempt—only partially convincing—to link up the *Gigue* and the *Bolero* is made by presenting the 'tema della giga' in the left hand in staccato octaves.

In accordance with his general practice, Busoni does not acknowledge the source of his borrowings; even as learned a commentator as Leichtentritt refers to the *Giga, Bolero e Variazione* as being based on "two brilliant piano pieces of Mozart."[9] (See Figure 13.13.) The *Variation* that follows

Figure 13.13.

consists of the *Gigue* now played in semiquavers, in 2/4 time. Busoni adds a multitude of passing notes; the texture becomes much more complex and chromatic, reaching a peak (six bars before the end) in Busoni's extraordinary elaboration of Mozart's already chromatic writing. (See Figure 13.14.) Some of the rhythmic groupings move away from 4 + 4 and

Figure 13.14. By kind permission, Breitkopf & Haertel, Wiesbaden.

become 3 + 2 + 3 and 2 + 3 + 3, and sections A and B are played without repeats, unlike the original *Gigue*. In the *Klavierübung* version of this work, the *Gigue* is left unchanged; there is one very little alteration in a left-hand part. For the *Bolero*, during 1920 Busoni must have looked very critically at his effort of 1909; he wished to incorporate the Mozart into *Lo Staccato* as a technical demonstration, as well as a piano piece worth playing in its own right. Perhaps he felt that the *Bolero* did not really contribute much, so he cut it out completely, allowing the 6/8 *Gigue* to move directly into its 2/4 variant without interruption. The last page of the *Variation* is somewhat altered, and the extraordinary chromaticisms referred to above, constituting the coda, are stressed even more by repetition an octave higher.

Nach Mozart No. 5 of the FÜNF KURZE STÜCKE ZUR PFLEGE DES POLYPHONEN SPIELS AUF DEM PIANOFORTE Also No. 6 of SECHS KURZE STÜCKE ZUR PFLEGE DES POLYPHONEN SPIELS and SIEBEN KURZE STÜCKE ZUR PFLEGE DES POLY-PHONEN SPIELS (see Chapter 10)

The sly ambiguity of the title is yet again a characteristic jest on Busoni's part. Three of the four pages are an exact transcription from the *Magic Flute*, act 2, scene 8. This is the famous adagio in quasi-Bachian style. The melody sung by the Two Armored Men (tenor and bass, an octave apart) is treated by Busoni as a "corale" and set in the style of his Bach chorale-prelude transcriptions. The fourth and final page of this piece is a variation of the first page but even here the strange looking triplet "quasi appoggiature" figures are also taken from the opera and may be found in the Terzetto scene from the Three Genii in act 2.

This last page was devised to round off the piece; in the opera, the adagio is of course interrupted by Tamino's entry, and an allegretto follows. Since Busoni's prime concern was a transcription of the adagio section for purposes of polyphonic playing, he had to compose an ending, and the variation of the first introductory section achieves just that.

This is not the first time that we have had occasion to catch Busoni at being evasive about the source of some of his "nach" pieces. In this case, he identifies the corale tune but leaves the impression that the setting of it is his own. (See Chapter 11.)

THE G MAJOR CONCERTO, K. 453

One of the many unpublished Busoni manuscripts has this inscription on it: "W. A. Mozart, Klavier Konzert G dur (KV 453). Bearbeitung der Solostimme von Ferruccio Busoni. Übertragung des Orchesters von Egon Petri. Ausgabe für zwei Klaviere."[10]

This was the first step—and an incomplete one at that—toward Busoni's dream of publishing the complete series of Mozart concerti. The original Mozart solo part would have appeared as the top line, below it Busoni would have placed his amendments to the solo part and the third line would contain Petri's reduction of the orchestral part. Such was the grandiose dream, cut short by Busoni's early death. We have only this incomplete manuscript to show the extent of the loss to future generations of pianists.

The manuscript contains the full text of the Mozart original. The orchestral reduction, except for some scribbled pencil sketches, is missing, although the bars are neatly ruled for it to be inserted. But what interests us is the Busoni "line." It contains, first of all, the cadenzas to the first and second movement, already described above. The only new material is in the form of detailed editing of a reasonable portion of the solo part; enough, at any rate, to give us some idea of what comparable sections of this movement would be like. Other clues to Busoni's treatment of Mozart figurations can also be gleaned from the cadenza to the first movement. Thus, without much guesswork, a reasonably complete edition of this first movement would be possible. This, coupled with the cadenza to the first movement and the fermatas and cadenza to the second, gives us two out of three movements in a substantially complete Busoni edition.

There are three other Mozart concerti that could and should be published in full with Busoni's editing:

1. K. 271—we have cadenzas to both first and second movements; the arrangement of the slow movement for solo piano could be easily adapted into the concerto format to include various cuts and pianistic alterations and suggestions.
2. K. 482—last movement fully arranged and edited. A cadenza exists to the first movement. Fermatas for the third movement fully realized.
3. K. 459—cadenzas to the first and third movements. The *Duettino Concertante* could easily be re-cast into concerto form.

A published "Busoni" version of these four concerti, combined with a study of his other cadenzas, would give us a valuable picture of his Mozart methods; suggestions for one particular movement could also apply to similar bars in another movement; thus, these four concerti at least could be given performances that, in some good proportion, would approximate Busoni's wishes.

OVERTURE TO THE MAGIC FLUTE ARRANGED FOR PIANOLA

This work should really come under the scope of the present study. It is impossible to know, however, what Busoni did in this arrangement. It was not published, and the manuscript used to be in the possession of Egon

Petri; unfortunately, it was left behind in Poland when Petri fled from the Nazi invasion. All Petri could remember about it was its similarity to the two-piano version, except that at the end, "it was marvellous—he had the whole keyboard going with the tonic dominant figure." Petri of course referred to the last five bars (shown in Figure 13.15) in the two-piano version. The manuscript may well still be safe and sound in Poland. Recently, the letters from Busoni to Petri (unfortunately only one side of this correspondence) came to light and they too had been left behind in Petri's old house in Zakopane.[11]

Figure 13.15. By kind permission, Breitkopf & Haertel, Wiesbaden.

The arrangement for pianola cannot be of great value; it is symptomatic of Busoni, however, that he was interested enough, with all his myriad activities, actually to sit down and work out an arrangement for a mechanical piano. Jürgen Kindermann[12] suggests 1908 as a possible date for this arrangement.[13]

SYMPHONIE NO. 30 VON W. A. MOZART (KV 202) BEARB. VON F. B. BUSONI   ARRANGEMENT FÜR PIANOFORTE ZU 2 HÄNDEN Leipzig   Breitkopf & Haertel   VA 823

SYMPHONIE NO. 32 VON W. A. MOZART   (KV 318) BEARB. VON F. B. BUSONI   ARRANGEMENT FÜR PIANOFORTE ZU 2 HÄNDEN Leipzig   Breitkopf & Haertel   VA 824

SYMPHONIEN VON W. A. MOZART. BEARBEITUNG FÜR DAS PIANOFORTE ZU ZWEI HÄNDEN   SYMPHONIE NO. 37 (KV 444) VON W. A. MOZART   BEARB. VON F. B. BUSONI   Leipzig Breitkopf & Haertel   VA 825

Hanspeter Krellmann notes bar by bar any small deviations from the originals.[14] These arrangements are really rather ordinary—they could have been done by any clever young composer-pianist. There is no imprint of Busoni's personality, and his prime aim in these arrangements (one cannot even class them as transcriptions), was to transfer the notes from the score onto two staves in playable fashion. The aesthetics of transcription are missing in these efforts. It seems that the three symphonies were done for Breitkopf in 1888 purely for income. This sort of arrangement was used by students and amateurs to get to know the music. Various duet versions of the symphonies that survive until this day are manifestations of the same need. Despite the efficient, and at times clever, arranging, therefore, this was basically hackwork for Busoni, which he had to carry out during his early career as was common with many other composers.

C MINOR FUGUE FROM THE STRING QUARTET K. 546 ARRANGED FOR PIANO

The Busoni-Nachlass No. 259 in the Deutsche Staatsbibliothek consists of two pages of fairly neat copy in Busoni's hand, constituting an arrangement for piano two hands of the first 57 bars of Mozart's Fugue in c minor from the *Adagio and Fugue* in c minor for string quartet, K. 546. The *Fugue* also exists as K. 426, for two pianos. Together with Busoni's two pages, the Nachlass contains an old cover from the Breitkopf & Haertel edition of this particular quartet.

The two pages of manuscript have the appearance not of a fragment, but rather of a finished product, the rest of which has been unfortunately lost. Since Busoni's habit was to date his manuscripts after the last bar, we have no certainty as to the time of writing of this arrangement. Taking into account factors such as paper used, ink, style of manuscript, and style of arrangement, I would say the work dates from approximately 1888.

The original fugue is 119 bars long, so that here we have about half of the piece in Busoni's own hand, certainly enough to use as a model for completion; the half that exists lies well for two hands and, although containing no particular surprises, is a successful pianistic arrangement. To help us further in the task of completion, we have Mozart's own version of the same piece for two pianos; I doubt whether Busoni knew of the two-piano version at the time of writing his arrangement.

SONATA IN D MAJOR FOR TWO PIANOS (K. 448) ARRANGED WITH A CADENZA   Completed in 1921

This work is mentioned in a number of authoritative sources.[15] The opening bars of the cadenza may be found in the Appendix; the complete text is part of SB 335. No editing or arranging of the D major sonata, however, has come to light. Busoni's copy of the Breitkopf standard edition of this work (Breitkopf no. 2425, containing the *Sonata* and the c minor *Fugue* for two pianos K. 426) exists; that he had a new edition and arrangement of this work in mind is beyond doubt but, like many of his projects, this one never eventuated.[16] The printed copy contains some scribbled ideas and general directions, mostly in the piano I part of the first movement; the changes indicated are characteristic and interesting, but there are simply not enough of them to warrant the term *arrangement* or to even consider publication of a Busoni "edition."

What Busoni would have done we can only guess, and must consult his other Mozart editions for clues. As for the cadenza itself, we have a rough, but complete copy in Busoni's own hand, headed *Cadenza per la Sonata Mozart's*, and dated 16 November 1921.

For Mozart/Liszt/Busoni, *Don Juan Fantasie* and *Figaro Fantasie*, see Chapter 12.

NOTES

1. Egon Petri could remember those days at the turn of the century and just after. He told me that the playing of Mozart, especially by pianists, was a novelty: up to then, the inclusion of a Mozart sonata in a recital was a candied offering to the audience. Pianists who treated Mozart in more masculine fashion were suspect. I asked him about Haydn. "Haydn was then yet not discovered. Busoni, despite his enormous repertoire, never played Haydn." We can now understand how it was possible for the first performance (in Berlin) of the great G major concerto (K. 453) to be given by Busoni as late as 1922.

2. Hugo Leichtentritt, *Ferruccio Busoni* (Leipzig, Breitkopf & Haertel, 1916), p. 37.

3. Ferruccio Busoni, *The Essence of Music and Other Papers*, trans. Rosamond Ley (London, Rockliff, 1957), p. 104.

4. Edward Dent, *Ferruccio Busoni: A Biography* (London, Oxford University Press, 1933), p. 168.

5. The adjective is used here not in a sense derogatory to Liszt, whose music Busoni loved. In later years Busoni himself decried this aspect of the cadenzas, and Petri passed on to me one such cadenza shorn of its Lisztian attributes (see Appendix).

6. The much vaunted Beethoven cadenza to the first movement, violates, in my opinion, a principle of this concerto. Mozart avoided at all times giving the syncopated opening theme to the piano, creating a dramatic tug-of-war based on this thematic independence of soloist and orchestra. Beethoven immediately throws this syncopated rhythm (which would have appealed to him enormously) to the pianist at the very start of his cadenza, thus destroying the thematic division effected by Mozart.

7. Busoni's forewords to the f minor *Fantasie* and the *Magic Flute* overture are omitted in more recent reprints.

8. There are a number of such instances in his arrangements-transcriptions.

9. Hugo Leichtentritt, "Ferruccio Busoni as a Composer," *Musical Quarterly* (January 1917), p. 81.

10. *Busoni-Nachlass* SB 341.

11. I have not seen these letters personally, but Ulla Klesper, Petri's daughter, wrote to me that the letters were unfortunately a little difficult to understand, since we only had one half of the correspondence; also the matters dealt with were inclined to be personal—of a "nagging" nature, as she put it—rather than musical, and therefore not of general interest. It may still prove of some value to have these published before they disappear again.

12. Jürgen Kindermann, *Thematisch-chronologisches Verzeichnis der Musikalischen Werke von Ferruccio B. Busoni*. p. 447.

13. Ronald Stevenson, "Busoni and Mozart," *The Score* 13 (Sept. 1955), pp. 25-38, gives 1905, followed by a question mark.

14. Hanspeter Krellmann, *Studien zu den Bearbeitungen Ferruccio Busonis*, pp. 161-63.

15. See Dent, *Ferruccio Busoni*, and Kindermann, *Thematisch-chronologisches Verzeichnis der musikalischen Werke von Ferruccio B. Busoni*.

16. *Busoni-Nachlass* SB 335.

14

Busoni and Other Composers

Busoni was unique and his way with Beethoven completely his own, and nothing for others to build on. His range and power of performance were tremendous, but he remade the works in his own image. I particularly recall his hair-raising "Hammerclavier" in the early 1920's. It was not pure Beethoven . . . but it did have me sitting on the edge of my seat.

. . . He had the most remarkable sense of rhythm—alive, elastic, marked by wondrous imagination and freedom. His reading of Liszt's E major Polonaise, available from an old piano roll, makes this abundantly clear. Everyone should hear it.

Claudio Arrau

We have now dealt with the three composers who figure most prominently in Busoni's transcriptions and editions. These composers also exerted an influence on Busoni the composer and were represented very extensively in his concert repertoire.

Fascinated as Busoni was with the blending of his own ideas with those of established composers via all the means at his disposal, the actual list of other composers whose names appear in conjunction with that of Busoni in his complete catalogue of works is rather long—too long, say many critics of Busoni, pointing out that such constant reliance on ideas of other composers is a betrayal of a lack of invention on Busoni's own part.

Some of these works unfortunately fall into a class of writing which can only be described as bread-and-butter work. These belong to Busoni's early days and were executed neither with great diligence nor conviction but simply to earn money quickly. In the chapter on Mozart, we have already come across such labors in the form of Busoni's arrangements for piano of some Mozart symphonies.

Interesting works such as cadenzas to the Beethoven and Brahms violin concerti and the Weber *Clarinet Concerto* are not within the scope of this book.

In what follows, composers are dealt with in alphabetical order.

BEETHOVEN

Busoni was not attracted to Beethoven from an early age as he was to Bach and Mozart. Beethoven, as Liszt, came to Busoni gradually, and for a concert repertoire as wide as Busoni's there are many seemingly strange gaps in the Beethoven works performed, gaps that can be easily explained, however, if we understand that Busoni played much early Beethoven in his ascending years as a virtuoso not so much out of personal conviction as of conventional necessity. When Busoni had attained his stature as a concert artist, however, he retained only the Beethoven that interested him: the late works, notably the *Hammerklavier* sonata, which was said to be electric under his fingers, some of the late *Bagatelles*, and some middle-period works and concerti. Although Edward Dent speaks of Beethoven's "serenity" as a positive influence on Busoni, particularly in works such as the *Piano Concerto Op. XXXIX* and the *Second Violin Sonata*—and this is probably so, for Busoni was mostly attracted to Beethoven's last period, the Beethoven of inner vision, cut off from the world—it seems that, taken in a broader view, there were many aspects of Beethoven toward which Busoni felt little or no sympathy.[1]

If we turn to Dent's book on Busoni, we find on page 230 this quotation from a letter written to Egon Petri: "The Latin attitude to art with its cool serenity and its insistence on outward form, is what refreshes me. It was only through Beethoven that music acquired that growling and frowning expression which was natural enough to him, but which perhaps ought to have remained his lonely path alone. Why are you in such a bad temper, one would often like to ask, especially in the second period."[2] It is not surprising, therefore, that works of the second period feature very little in Busoni's concert programs.

In the *Essence of Music* in corroboration of the above, we find the following essays on *Beethoven*: "What Did Beethoven Give Us?" (Berlin, 1920); "Beethoven" (from the Zürich programs, 1915); and "Beethoven and Musical Humour" (posthumous).

As can be seen by the dates, these are all writings of full maturity. Busoni's only other thoughts on Beethoven occur in sporadic references in various letters, and in his analysis of the fugue from Op. 106 (see below).

In the first essay, Busoni points out that "throughout two generations it was the aim of ambitious composers to write their nine symphonies. . . . 'One follows a great example most faithfully by turning away from it' I said once, and by that I meant that an example is great because it creates a *new* type. . . . Since Beethoven, everything must be 'powerful' . . . now one sits down to listen with closed eyes and hopeless earnestness."[3]

This is, of course, not a criticism of Beethoven the composer, but a declaration of varied temperament; also a pointed barb at the post-Beethoven symphonies. Busoni freely admits, and admires, Beethoven's "sincerity" and "subservience of virtuosity to the Idea."[4] In a letter to his wife (Moscow, 13 November 1912), he says: "When Beethoven feels with humanity, his feeling is so strong that he needs very few technical means to express it." In the same letter, of *Fidelio*: "There is little music that is more beautiful."[5]

In the second essay, he refers to the *Hammerklavier* sonata, as "the most powerful composition for the pianoforte of all time." But in the third and final essay, he accuses Beethoven of lack of humor.

We must come to the conclusion that Busoni missed in Beethoven the Latin qualities he found in Bach, Mozart, and Liszt; and just as in these three he found augury and the possibility to edit and present original works in a new way, so in Beethoven he discovered complete self-sufficiency and hence his condemnation of composers "filled with monomania to write their nine symphonies."

I asked Petri whether Busoni's playing of Beethoven was marked by the sorts of changes that occurred in his performances of other music; the reply was that Busoni rarely changed a note in Beethoven; the playing underlined the monumental aspect of Beethoven's music and moreover was marked by great flexibility and rhythmic freedom, with far more stress on the melodic element in Beethoven than is usually given by most pianists.

All this is borne out by the fact that in Busoni's huge output there are only three works relating to Beethoven.

ECOSSAISEN FÜR PIANOFORTE VON LUDWIG VAN BEETHOVEN   FÜR DER KONZERTVORTRAG BEARBEITET UND FRÄULEIN GERDA SJÖSTRAND ZUGEEIGNET VON FERRUCCIO B. BUSONI   Leipzig   Breitkopf & Haertel   EB 2550

This little *coup de maître* of Beethoven's, which has graced so many encores, is justifiably popular and is usually heard in the Busoni arrangement of 1888-1889 which has been published all over the world, not only separately, but also in collections of "favorite" pieces.

Structurally, Busoni cut out a few bars of conventional introduction by Beethoven; then, more importantly, he wrote a coda that brings back the first *Ecossaise* and by this means tied the piece together very successfully and provided an effective and brilliant conclusion.

The Beethoven text is left untouched, but Busoni supplied ingenious editing that tried to give a different character to each episode and a varied turn to each refrain.

Although a simple illustration, the Beethoven *Ecossaisen* are a true example of Busoni editing on its most successful level.

BEETHOVEN'S CADENZEN ZU DESSEN CLAVIER-CONCERTEN AUSGEWÄHLT UND HERAUSGEGEBEN VON FERRUCCIO BUSONI Magdeburg Heinrichshofen 1901 No. 4281 and later No. 798

The following cadenzas appear in this volume: cadenza for the first movement of the C major concerto, cadenza for the first movement of the c minor concerto, cadenza for the first movement of the G major concerto, and cadenza for the last movement of the G major concerto.

Busoni's introduction explains the purpose of his editing, and incidentally also betrays his attitude to cadenzas by the performer:

The question as to which cadenzas should be played in Beethoven's Concerto is answered by this volume.

The improvisations contained therein and written by Beethoven himself correspond most clearly to the spirit and the style of his "Piano-Symphonies." Pianists, therefore, who do not play their own cadenzas, should give preference to those composed by the Master.

Cadenzas written by the performer are doubtless admissible as they are in unity, and keeping with the performer's individuality; and this is evidently the composer's object in ceding his place to the performer. Whereas cadenzas emanating from third persons should be discarded, as introducing into the performance a third element still more alien to the whole.

The alterations and workings out of the passages which the editor has published in the present edition, render the pieces more suitable for the modern concerthall, without altering the original idea of the composition. Bearing this in mind, but a limited number has been selected, preference having been given to those practically best suited for concert-playing.

Weimer 1900

A typical example of the heightened effect of the Busoni edition is from the very first cadenza. (See Figure 14.1.)

ZWEI CADENZEN ZU L. VAN BEETHOVEN'S CLAVIER-CONCERT NO. 4, G. DUR I) CADENZ ZUM ERSTEN SATZE II) CADENZ ZUM RONDO Hamburg D. Rahter No. 3000

It is interesting to compare Busoni's own cadenzas to the Beethoven Piano Concerto No. 4 with his editing of, and selection from, Beethoven's original texts. Though youthful, the cadenzas have many good qualities, and in later life, after having renounced many of his earlier compositions, Busoni apparently retained some affection for this particular opus, which was

Figure 14.1

awarded the Rubinstein Prize for composition in 1890 and was published
the following year.

Even at this early stage of his career, he was clear in his mind as to the
function a performer's cadenza had to fulfill. The style of writing is true
both to Beethoven (in its fluctuations between compound and simple time,
in the episodic layout, in some of the recitative-like passages) and to Busoni
(in the wide pianistic style, some of the abrupt modulations, the divisions
between hands), but, whereas Beethoven's cadenzas are written out
improvisations, Busoni's have more of the flavor of composition, both in
the careful technical indications and in the combination of themes. (See
Figure 14.2.)

THIRD APPENDIX TO VOLUME I   ANALYTICAL EXPOSITION
OF THE FUGUE IN BEETHOVEN'S SONATA, OP. 106   In Busoni's
edition of *The First Twenty-Four Preludes and Fugues of The Well-
Tempered Clavichord*   (see Chapter 11)

Figure 14.2

This is a bar-by-bar analysis of this fugue, written out in full on three staves, and subjected to the most minute dissection, which throws a great deal of light not only on Beethoven's but also on Busoni's technique.[6]

In a footnote to the analysis, Busoni writes:

We should not regard the study of piano-fugue (which is, in fact, the chief aim of the Well-Tempered Clavichord) as completely concluded, without a mention of the climax of all piano-fugue composition, the last movement of Beethoven's opus 106—a work of elementary power.

By the illumination of its formal structure, light is also thrown on its conception; nothing in this fugue is so obscure and turbid as to explain its undeniable unpopularity.[7] (We should rather ascribe it to the immanent feeling of unrest—the lack of pleasurable ease.)

Only frequent and finished performance, and the provision of a complete view of Beethoven's intellectual procedure, can make head against, and possibly overcome, this unpopularity. The editor has tried both ways, in order to lift this piece, decried as "ugly and unpianistic" but really masterful and full of genius, to its rightful place before the public. In this he has merely followed Hans von Bülow, whose model edition of this Fugue is supplemented here in one direction.[8]

Beethoven in *Klavierübung* (page references are to the second edition):

1. Page 33 (Book 3—akkordisches). An excerpt from the *Waldstein* sonata used as a basis for a technical exercise.

2. Page 41—same section—from the *Sonata* Op. 26, with six suggested variants.

3. Page 55 (Book 4—"a trois mains"). Part of the c sharp minor *Quartet* Op. 131 transcribed for piano.

4. Page 69 (Book 5—triller). Based on part of the fugue from Op. 106, valuable in that Busoni writes out the trills in full and demonstrates how it is fitted against the other parts. Petri always reminded his pupils that trills depend not on speed, but on evenness and control; they have to be worked out in their rhythmic groupings. Busoni does this very thing here.

5. Page 83—same section. Seven variations on a motive from the *Emperor* concerto.

BIZET

Kammer-Fantasie über Carmen für Pianoforte   (see Chapter 6)

The first three pages of this work appear in *Klavierübung*: second edition, page 110, Book 6—*Lo Staccato*.

BRAHMS

Sechs Choral-Vorspiele für die Orgel von Johannes Brahms Op. 122
Für das Pianoforte ausgewählt und übertragen von Ferruccio Busoni
(see Chapter 16)

As a very young man Busoni knew Brahms personally and had been encouraged by him.[9] Although his opinion of Brahms as a pianist was not high, Busoni was attracted to the personality of the man. As a composer, Brahms exerted only an early influence, noticeable in such works as the *Variationen und Fuge* Op. 22, *Etude en forme de Variations*, and the *Concertstück*. Hence, Busoni's repertoire of Brahms was rather small and included only the big works, most of which he played less and less in his later years; his interest in arranging Brahms was also minimal and included only the above work for piano. There is a cadenza for the Violin Concerto.

A story relating to Busoni's performance of the concerto in B flat is worth re-telling here.[10] It was during Busoni's residence at Helsingfors. He had not played this work before, and his pupils were most curious how a pianist of Busoni's stature would attack such a problem. However, the date scheduled for performance loomed closer and closer, and still no sound came from Busoni's room, despite many clandestine listenings at the door. Finally, in desperation, some of the pupils peeped into the practice room, whether through the keyhole or the window or some other way, it is not known exactly. There was Busoni at the piano, with the concerto before him, going through the motions of the work, without actually playing. A day or so before the performance, he asked someone to come in and check his memory. He knew the keyboard so well that it must have diverted him to try this experiment—learn a Brahms concerto without playing a note of it.

CHOPIN

FRÉDÉRIC CHOPIN   POLONAISE EN LA BÉMOL. OEUVRE 53 INTERPRETÉE PAR FERRUCCIO BUSONI   Trieste   C. Schmidl 1909   C. Sch. 4171

Busoni altered nothing in the structure of this great *Polonaise*, hackneyed though it was even then. His editorial comments in this particular instance are directed toward the finer shadings of phrasing, accents, chord layout, and dynamics, but this is unmistakable Busoni,[11] from little details like extending the b flat minor scale just before the left-hand octave section (see Figure 14.3) to the combination of the octaves and the "strumming" effect.

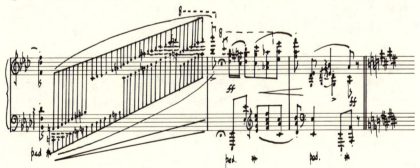

Figure 14.3

(See Figure 14.4.) This is typical of the master editor. Other memorable details are the indications to play the strummed chord (Figure 14.5), and the simple but effective rewriting of the chord of Figure 14.6 to that of Figure 14.7, to bring out the melodic F; the whole *Polonaise* is full of these telling

Figure 14.4

Figure 14.5

Figure 14.6

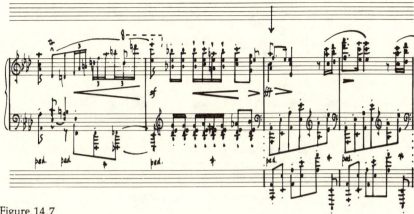

Figure 14.7

individual touches: we have here a valuable record of Busoni's performance of this piece: it is a great pity that the music is so hard to come by, for otherwise this interesting version would no doubt attract more performances.

Busoni had planned to put out an edition of the Chopin *Preludes*, but, like so many other projects, it came to naught for various reasons, chiefly lack of time. He regarded the *Preludes* as the most forward thinking of all Chopin's writings, and threw his listeners into confusion by treating them in massive sculptural style; generally, it may be said that Busoni's Chopin was the hardest of all his interpretations to accept, refusing as he did even to leave a vestige of the salon in his treatment of this composer. He had a preference for the bigger works like the *Ballades*, *Scherzos*, and *Etudes*, and toward the end of his life felt more and more doubt about Chopin as a composer. The reader is referred to Dent and Bernard van Dieren[12] for more on this interesting topic.

Chopin in *Klavierübung* (page reference is to the second edition): pages 151-77 (Book 8—Variationen und Varianten zu Chopin).

This consists of:

1. *Variations on Chopin's c minor Prelude*. See Chapter 5. One of the variations is a little waltz titled "Homage to Chopin."

2. The variants, which are illustrations of technical problems and solutions, taken from the *Etudes* and *Preludes*.
   (a) Variant of Op. 10, No. 1—broken chords in both hands.
   (b) Variant of Op. 10, No. 2—chromatic figure played by thumb and second finger.
   (c) Five other suggestions for variants, plus a scheme to modulate through all keys for practice of these variants (this is missing in the *Klavierübung* first edition).
   (d) Op. 10, No. 9—broken figures in the right hand.

(e) Op. 10, No. 7—starting more simply, finishing with both hands playing semiquaver chords.

(f) Op. 10, No. 8—passage work extended.

(g) *Prelude* Op. 28, No. 3—passage work in the right hand. The full *Prelude* is transcribed and thus can be performed.

Some of these were germinal ideas for future editions of the *Etudes* that never came to fruition; some were Busoni jokes (like the upside-down *Prelude* Op. 28 No. 3) which came about during lighthearted pianistic banter with other musicians such as Petri, who told many stories of such witticisms contrived on the spot, often consisting of combinations of themes by various composers or transformations of melodies by one composer into those of another by some adroit melodic or harmonic twist.

CORNELIUS

FANTASIE ÜBER MOTIVE AUS "DER BARBIER VON BAGDAD," KOMISCHE OPER VON PETER CORNELIUS, FÜR PIANOFORTE COMPONIRT VON FERRUCCIO B. BUSONI   Leipzig   C. F. Kahnt Nr. 2880

In 1886, the youthful Busoni, in financial straits, was offered 150 marks by the publishing firm of Kahnt to write a fantasia on Peter Cornelius's comic opera: the next morning he arrived to collect his fee. He had composed it overnight, without access to a piano and without previous knowledge of the opera, thus fulfilling the publisher's request to write a fairly short and easy piece.

This fantasy falls into six easily identifiable sections:

1. The first 25 bars using the descending motive C sharp-G sharp and chromatic semiquavers from the overture.

2. Quotations from the orchestral opening of act 2, and from the opening of act 2, scene 1 (material already heard in the overture and in act 1, scenes 5 and 7).

3. A further development of the opening of act 2, scene 1, Margiana's aria "Er Kommt!" Marked "schneller" (page 6, at the double bar), this section ends with a short quote from the introduction to act 2.

4. Material from act 1, scene 1—the opening characteristic figure, from the introduction to the servants' choir, beginning at the top of page 8 the cadenza that follows uses this figure again with material from Abul's vocal cadenza from act 1, scene 7, and this fourth section concludes with material from Nurredin's aria "Margiana!" from act 1, scene 1.

5. Material again taken from the end of act 1, scene 1, the G major section with Nurredin and the choir singing "Komm, deine Blumen . . ." beginning at the top of page 10. This is very short.

6. A fast 6/8, based on the overture; from the double bar on page 10.[13]

I have detailed the sources of this *Fantasia* to enable an easy comparison of the work with a vocal score. While the feat of assimilation of this vocal score and the composition of the *Fantasia* in one sitting is to be admired, the resultant work must be judged an artistic failure, in common with Busoni's other early excursion into opera fantasy based on Goldmark's *Merlin*. It was not until the *Sonatina super Carmen* many years later that Busoni returned, with eminent brilliance, to this genre. By then he had no doubt thoroughly studied the Liszt fantasias and realized that it was not merely a question of using the memorable melodies, loosely strung together with a few artful modulations and interspersed cadenzas; one had to capture the essence of the drama enacted on stage, as well as re-set the chosen melodies in an individual and meaningful way. The virtuoso glitter, divorced from such considerations, was meaningless.

CRAMER

8 ETUDES DE PIANO PAR J. B. CRAMER CHOISIES DES 16 NOUVELLES ETUDES OP. 81 (NO. 85-100) RÉVUES ET PUBLIÉES PAR FERRUCCIO B. BUSONI I Partie: Ecole du Legato (No. 1-4) II Partie: Ecole du Staccato (No. 5-8) Berlin Schlesinger 1897 S. 8772 Also as *Acht Etüden von Cramer* in *Klavierübung* 1st ed. part 4 Leipzig Breitkopf & Haertel EB 5224 and in *Klavierübung* 2d ed. Book 7 Leipzig Breitkopf & Haertel 1925

Busoni, characteristically ignoring the well-known Cramer etudes nos. 1-84, selected 8 of the 16 late and relatively unknown etudes and edited them for publication.

The 1897 Schlesinger edition is very faithful to the original Cramer, and any changes are indicated as ossias. The first three etudes contain no ossias at all, and Busoni contented himself with merely providing fingering. The fifth etude omits Cramer's slow introduction. The first edition of the *Klavierübung* (part 4) is identical to the 1897 Schlesinger. However, the final version of the *Klavierübung* incorporates the ossias into the text without reference or mention of the original, and contains musical and pianistic changes as well, with the exception of the first three etudes, which remain untouched.

GADE

NOVELLETTEN FÜR PIANOFORTE, VIOLINE UND VIOLON-CELL COMPONIRT UND HERRN FERDINAND HILLER GEWIDMET VON NIELS W. GADE OP. 29 BEARBEITUNG FÜR ZWEI PIANOFORTE ZU VIER HÄNDEN VON F. B. BUSONI (UNTER BEIBEHALTUNG DER ORIGINAL-PIANOFORTES-TIMME) Leipzig Breitkopf & Haertel No. 17 721 (original Gade score) No. 18 144 (Busoni's arrangement)

As in the Schumann below there is very little arrangement involved. Breitkopf issued the work in two parts, piano I and piano II. Piano I is simply the full score of the trio, completely unaltered; Busoni's name does not appear under the title or with that of Niels Gade. Piano II consists of the string parts arranged for piano, very simply and directly, with many parallel octaves and double octaves. Busoni's name as arranger is printed here.

The work itself is a pleasant, undistinguished salon trio in five short movements somewhat reminiscent of Mendelssohn. This Busoni arrangement of 1889 is of passing interest only, and is purely routine.

GOLDMARK

C. GOLDMARK MERLIN KLAVIER-AUSZUG ZU ZWEI HÄNDEN F. BUSONI Leipzig J. Schuberth & Co. No. 3272

C. GOLDMARK MERLINO TRASCRIZIONE DI CONCERTO PER PIANOFORTE DI FERRUCCIO B. BUSONI SOPRA MOTIVI DELL' OPERA MERLINO DEL MAESTRO C. GOLDMARK Milano F. Lucca No. 46 819 Transcribed in 1887

The opera fantasy on Goldmark's *Merlin* was written a year after Busoni's efforts in this direction with Cornelius's *Barber of Bagdad*. It is much longer, more elaborate, and of considerable technical difficulty.

It is curious, but perfectly legitimate, to find that the fantasy is based on material from the overture and act 1 only. Like the *Bagdad Fantasy*, this one is divided into clear-cut sections:

1. The opening motive of the overture, and the 6/8 figure featuring prominently in the orchestral accompaniment to the Daemon's song in scene 2, are the raw materials of this opening section. A motive prominent at the end of act 1, of a rising sixth, is also heard.

2. Page 6—music of Lancelot's appearance in scene 4. Same key as in opera.

3. Page 10—orchestral intermezzo from the same scene, immediately following the above. Original key preserved.

4. Page 14—combination of themes from the preceding two sections.

5. Page 19—return to the opening motive, with the rather lovely main theme of the overture transposed from D flat to E flat major. A short cadenza is inserted between these two themes. The motive with the rising sixth is reiterated.

6. Page 26—the harp melody accompanying Glendower's song in scene 1 is given extensive treatment, with sinister staccato semiquavers reminiscent of the Daemon's appearance in scene 2 acting as background.

7. Page 30—the finale is taken, in the same key of F major from scene 5, and occupies six full pages of bravura.[14]

This fantasy could only have been written by a man with an extraordinary command of the keyboard; it ties in with our accounts of Busoni as a young virtuoso, who, in his early days, tended to sacrifice musical considerations for technical ones, no doubt spurred on by his father and given his father's examples of opera fantasies (the full account of which is to be found in Dent, with its humorous and pathetic overtones). The quite natural motivation of wanting to earn some money, to please his publishers, his exposure to the salon-virtuoso music of the day, and his own extraordinary technique, all account for a piece such as *Merlin*. It too, like its simpler predecessor—the fantasy on *Barber of Bagdad*—must be classed a failure but at least a far more interesting failure. One must doubt, of course, whether a successful fantasy could have been written at all, given such poor material as makes up most of this opera. Busoni does not help by piling sequence upon sequence and involving himself in endless repetitions of the same melody with different embellishment; the piece is simply too long, given its raw thematic constituents. Pianistically, it already shows the amazing fecundity of Busoni's inventiveness and resourcefulness with some obvious debts to Liszt (see Figure 14.8), but dramatically it is uninteresting

Figure 14.8

and does not present a coherent whole. One is often reminded of fantasias by the lesser romantic virtuosi, coupled with attempts to build tension by writing hothouse sequences, successful examples of which are to be found in the Wagner-Liszt *Isolde's Love-Death*, and the Liszt *Rhapsody No. 5*.

As well as writing a fantasia on Goldmark's *Merlin*, Busoni also prepared a piano reduction but not a vocal score, which exists as well, with no arranger given and dated September 1886 (J. Schuberth & Co. No. 6181). The whole opera is reduced to two pianistic staves, with the first words of arias printed above or below the music; the vocal lines, as was the fashion at that time, are incorporated into the reduction and not printed above the orchestral reduction as in a true vocal score. There is nothing very distinguished about the reduction. It is yet another case of Busoni "drudgery," as Dent puts it, from this period.

GOUNOD

Cadenza for *Faust-Waltz*. In *Klavierübung*, second edition, page 73, Book 5—triller. See Chapter 12.

MENDELSSOHN

Busoni's attitude toward this composer altered somewhat during the course of years. As a young virtuoso he played most of the standard Mendelssohn items like the *Rondo Capriccioso*, the g minor *Concerto*, the *Variations Sérieuses*, and other smaller works. By 1907, he could write in this vein to his wife, from Norderney: "During the summer I examined my development and found that progress has been great. As you know, I got beyond Schumann and Mendelssohn first of all. . . ."[15] The letter proceeds with further terrifying judgments of other composers. And yet, toward the end of his life, Busoni, searching for a new simplicity, discovering the chasteness of John Field, wrote: "If one wished to speak of a Mozart school there would not be many names to mention but those few are very important. At the head of the list are those three masters of undisputed importance: Rossini, Cherubini, and Mendelssohn."[16] It was at this time that he rediscovered the *Songs without Words* and admired them for their classical purity. Nevertheless, as a composer, Busoni only coupled his name with Mendelssohn's on two fairly unimportant occasions.

F. MENDELSSOHN BARTHOLDY   SYMPHONIE NR. 1 IN
C. MOLL OP. 11   FÜR 2 PIANOFORTE ZU 8 HÄNDEN BEAR-
BEITET VON F. B. BUSONI   Leipzig   Breitkopf & Haertel
VA 1253

This is purely routine work, stemming from 1890, done for a quick fee, and absolutely typical of the hundreds of similar arrangements of the era.

Mendelssohn also makes a brief appearance in the *Klavierübung* second edition, book 6, page 108. It is an excerpt from the Liszt transcription of the *Wedding March and Elfin Chorus* from *Midsummer Night's Dream*; as such, it really has more connection with Liszt than with Mendelssohn.

NOVÁČEK

SCHERZO AUS DEM STREICHQUARTETT IN E MOLL VON
OTTOKAR NOVÁČEK ZUM CONCERTVORTRAGE FÜR
PIANOFORTE BEARBEITET UND FRÄULEIN RAGNHILD LUND
ZUGEEIGNET VON FERRUCCIO B. BUSONI   Leipzig   E. W.
Fritzsch   1892   EWF 523

Ottokar Nováček was Busoni's personal friend. His tragic early death put
an end to a brief and unfulfilled career as a composer, cutting short the
possibility of development shown in his early work. These days known
only by his *Perpetuum Mobile* for violin and orchestra, Nováček also wrote
some more ambitious works, including a concerto for piano and orchestra
(*Concerto Eroico*), once quite highly thought of and which Busoni
performed.

We know that Busoni was generally very helpful to Nováček, and
possibly this arrangement was a gesture on his part as much as anything
else. It is also certain that this transcription, although only partially successful, is one of Busoni's first steps toward the great transcriptions of his later
years. For the first time he is no longer satisfied merely to transfer the notes
from one medium to another, is far more conscious in the course of
transcribing of the final pianistic sound, and is not afraid to make necessary
adjustments at the cost of infidelity to the original. For the first time, too,
we find him bold enough to tamper with the structure of the piece he is
transcribing, to cut out bars if he feels it tightens up the musical argument
and alter figures to accommodate figurations more pianistically. It could be
that transcribing the music of a friend gave him such courage but I believe
that we are here witnessing the beginnings of Busoni's awareness of what
true transcription means, an awareness and conviction that finally gave him
the courage and/or foolhardiness, depending on one's point of view, to
alter proportions in the music of the master Mozart himself.

Krellmann gives a detailed bar-by-bar comparison of this Busoni transcription and the Nováček original, with some illustrations.[17]

The transcription is quite effective, and partakes of that night-music
grotesqueness so dear to Busoni's heart and found so often in his own
music; from such considerations it is interesting to look at this *Scherzo* side
by side with Busoni's own *Perpetuum Mobile*.

OFFENBACH

Barcarole from the *Tales of Hoffman*. In *Klavierübung*, second edition,
page 53, Book 4—"a trois mains." This two-page delightful little piece can
be—and has been—used as an encore, a quiet parting joke.

PAGANINI

Introduzione, Capriccio (Paganinesco)   In AN DIE JUGEND   (see Chapter 5)   Also in KLAVIERÜBUNG 2d ed. only Book 10— *Etuden nach Paganini-Liszt*, titled *Introduzione e Capriccio*

The *Introduzione* is a transcription for left hand alone of the opening of the C major *Caprice* No. 11 from Paganini's *24 Capricci per violino solo* Op. 1; this returns in grandiose style at the end (after the *Capriccio* had run its course) in E major, with duplets transformed into triplets. The middle section, the *Capriccio*, is a transcription of the *Caprice* No. 15.

It is evident that Busoni was using Liszt as a model transcriber of Paganini, in particular the Lisztian technique of using sections of various caprices and combining them into one piano work. The transcribing is exuberant to say the least and reminiscent of the earlier versions of Liszt's own Paganini transcriptions. Busoni was interested in Liszt's treatment of Paganini, not in Paganini per se. (See Chapter 12.)

SCHÖNBERG

KLAVIERSTÜCK OP. 11   NR. 2 VON ARNOLD SCHÖNBERG KONZERTMASSIGE INTERPRETATION VON FERRUCCIO B. BUSONI   Wien   Universal Edition   UE 2992   Transcribed in 1909

In 1903, as a young man, Schönberg was sent to Busoni by Schenker. They kept in touch until Busoni's death and professed mutual admiration, although toward the end of his life Busoni spoke out sharply against some of Schönberg's practices: "Anarchy, the arbitrary placing of intervals, next and over one another."[18] A manifesto published by Busoni in the periodical *Melos* stated: "Anarchy is not liberty. . . ."[19] We know that Schönberg was influenced by Busoni's ideas, beginning with the *New Esthetic of Music* at the turn of the century and going on to Busoni's later ideas about a new polyphony; broadly, these tied in with what Schönberg himself was doing. One should also read Busoni's account of a "Schönberg Matinée" in the *Essence of Music*.[20] After Busoni died, there was some consideration given to the idea of Schönberg completing *Doktor Faust*.

But in 1910 Schönberg was only at the start of his career: Busoni's sanction of the Op. 11 piano pieces by his transcription and all that that implied must have meant a great deal to Schönberg, especially in Berlin where Busoni was an acknowledged figure; privately he may have quavered at the liberties Busoni took with his music.

This is surely one of the most extraordinary concert interpretations that Busoni published. In his preface he says: "This composition demands of the player the most refined touch and pedal; an intimate, improvised, 'floating,' deeply felt presentation; the performer's loving abandonment in its content, whose interpreter—merely a piano arranger—deems it an artistic honour, to be allowed to be present." It is obvious from his editing that he feels in sympathy with Schönberg; indeed, there is at times a striking similarity in approach between this piece and some passages from Busoni's own sonatinas, although these have a more disciplined approach in their control over basic materials. Schönberg tends to improvise here, as Busoni had already noted; this quality of free extemporization allowed Busoni to treat the text flexibly and, one is tempted to add, imaginatively.

It is impossible to discuss this transcription without comparing both scores.[21] Krellmann provides an excellent bar-by-bar analysis.[22] He regards Busoni's interpretation as a criticism of Schönberg's piece, a comment by a composer on his contemporary, both striving for a new style. In this I feel he is correct: Busoni's "criticism" may be tactful and respectful (some of his suggestions are in small print), but it is also ruthless. Another of Busoni's aims was to make this new idiom more palatable to the listener by making some of the processes involved clearer and more logical. The Busoni version of this piece may be more effective and atmospheric than the original. Now that these Op. 11 pieces are reasonably well known, it would be simple to have this tested in the concert hall; until then, I can only urge the reader to discover this example of the strange compelling power of Busoni's art of transformation.

Busoni also conducted, in the Beethoven-Saal, Berlin, on 5 November 1903, an orchestration by Schönberg of the 4 Syrische Tänze by Heinrich Schenker. The original dances were for piano duet, in which form they were published by Weinberger, Leipzig, in 1899. Schönberg returned the compliment circa 1920, when he arranged the Berceuse Élégiaque for flute, clarinet, harmonium, piano, and string quintet.[23] This was intended for the Verein für musikalisches Privataufführungen in Wien (Society for Private Musical Performances in Vienna). Josef Rufer writes:

The instrumental combination was the usual one for the salon orchestras of those days; Schoenberg chose it on purpose to show that one could easily avoid the thick, vulgar sound with which that combination was all too often afflicted. The performers were: Eduard Steuermann, piano; Alban Berg, harmonium; Rudolf Kolisch or Arnold Schoenberg, first violin; Karl Rankl, second violin; Othmar Steinbauer, viola; Anton Webern, cello.[24]

Schönberg also included the titles and examples of music by Busoni in his incomplete Instrumentationslehre. As well, a copy of Busoni's New Esthetic of Music, with written commentaries, was found among Schönberg's papers.[25]

The Busoni-Schönberg correspondence has now also been published (see Bibliography); the letters deal with general aesthetic problems as well as with specific topics such as Busoni's reworking of the Op. 11 piano piece and Schönberg's reluctance to allow the original and the transcription to be published together.

It is clear from this correspondence that although Busoni and Schönberg shared some common ideals, they also had irreconcilable differences. Busoni's ability to comment on Schönberg's music, however, new as it was then, in a clearsighted and consistent manner, was truly remarkable.

SCHUBERT

Busoni's arrangements of some of Schubert's orchestral pieces were published under the general heading OUVERTÜREN UND ANDERE ORCHESTERWERKE VON FRANZ SCHUBERT. BEARBEITUNG FÜR DAS PIANOFORTE ZU ZWEI HÄNDEN VON F. B. BUSONI.

Details of specific works appearing under this general title follow.

OUVERTURE ZUM LUSTSPIEL MIT GESANG: "DER TEUFEL ALS HYDRAULICUS" FRANZ SCHUBERT BEARB. VON FER-RUCCIO B. BUSONI Leipzig Breitkopf & Haertel No. 17 970

OUVERTURE (D DUR) FRANZ SCHUBERT BEARB. VON F. B. BUSONI Leipzig Breitkopf & Haertel No. 17 974

OUVERTURE (B DUR) FRANZ SCHUBERT COMPONIRT IM JAHRE 1816 BEARB. VON F. B. BUSONI Leipzig Breitkopf & Haertel No. 18 013

FÜNF MENUETTE MIT SECHS TRIOS UND MENUETT FÜR 2 VIOLINEN, VIOLA UND VIOLONCELL FRANZ SCHUBERT (COMPONIRT IM JAHRE 1813) BEARBEITET VON F. B. BUSONI[26] Leipzig Breitkopf & Haertel No. 18 023/24

FÜNF DEUTSCHE MIT CODA UND SIEBEN TRIOS FÜR 2 VIO-LINEN, VIOLA UND VIOLONCELL FRANZ SCHUBERT (COMPONIRT IM JAHRE 1813) BEARBEITET VON F. B. BUSONI Leipzig Breitkopf & Haertel No. 18 068

OUVERTURE (D DUR) FRANZ SCHUBERT (COMPONIRT IM JAHRE 1817) BEARB. VON F. B. BUSONI Leipzig Breitkopf & Haertel No. 18 135

OUVERTURE (E MOLL) FRANZ SCHUBERT (COMPONIRT IM JAHRE 1819) BEARB. VON F. B. BUSONI Leipzig Breitkopf & Haertel No. 18 145

OUVERTURE IM ITALIENISCHEN STILE   (D DUR)   FRANZ
SCHUBERT   BEARB. VON F. B. BUSONI   Leipzig   Breitkopf
& Haertel   No. 18 150

OUVERTURE IM ITALIENISCHEN STILE   (C DUR)   FRANZ
SCHUBERT   (COMPONIRT IM JAHRE 1817)   BEARB. VON F. B.
BUSONI   Leipzig   Breitkopf & Haertel   No. 18 162

There is not much of interest in these 1888-1889 arrangements. Schubert
generally did not figure in Busoni's repertoire; he played more Schubert-
Liszt than original Schubert and, even so, mostly before 1900.

The only other references to Schubert in Busoni's piano works are first on
page 59 of the fourth Book of the *Klavierübung* (second edition), the section
titled "three hands," where Busoni presents a two-page snippet from the *Erl-
King*, and, second, on page 23 a Schubert-Liszt excerpt from *Auf dem
Wasser*.[27] (See Chapter 12.)

SCHUMANN

KONZERT-ALLEGRO MIT INTRODUKTION   (OP. 134)
BEARBEITUNG FÜR ZWEI PIANOFORTE ZU VIER HÄNDEN
R. SCHUMANN, OP. 134   BEARB. VON F. B. BUSONI   Leipzig
Breitkopf & Haertel   VA 832

The title of this arrangement from 1888 may lead us to expect a Busoni
edition of this late and rather feeble Schumann work; actually, the solo part
is completely untouched by Busoni and is identical with the solo part as
found in the Breitkopf & Haertel edition of the complete piano works of
Schumann edited by his wife Clara. Busoni was asked to arrange the
orchestral part for a second piano. The work was published in two sections:
the solo part with orchestral cues in one and the orchestral reduction with
solo cues in the other. This was done before the more modern practice of
printing the solo and orchestral reduction in parallel staves. Busoni's name
does not even appear in the solo part, so that the attribute "arranged for
two pianos" is most misleading; there is no arrangement or even editing of
any kind involved—only the most direct and routine reduction for a second
piano. And since Schumann gave very little interesting or important
material to the orchestra in this work, Busoni's task was perfectly straightforward and was probably done in one sitting to collect his fee quickly from
the publishers for a task he could not have relished too much.

WAGNER

Wagner ultimately stood for little in Busoni's musical development; there
was a strong early influence, which was quite natural toward the closing

years of the nineteenth century. No young composer could have ignored Wagner entirely, but Busoni gradually and irrevocably moved away from the Wagner-Brahms circle of influence toward his own Italian view of Bach, Liszt, and Mozart. When he came to write his own operas, his models were Mozart and Verdi, not Wagner. Dent says that Busoni's "devotion to dogs was one of the few characteristics . . . shared with Richard Wagner."[28]

Yet it would be untrue to claim that no traces of Wagner exist in mature Busoni: there are moments in the slow movement of the *Piano Concerto* and parts of *Die Brautwahl* and *Doktor Faust* that remind us of Wagner. We know that Busoni confounded his many followers by declaring his admiration for the score of *Parsifal*, and indeed there are similarities in the orchestral texture of *Parsifal* and some of Busoni's late works. But *Parsifal* is hardly representative of Wagner, and Busoni's admiration was for the transparent scoring rather than the story or the approach to opera writing.

Only two works of Wagner feature in Busoni's piano arrangements, both executed early in his life. Their descriptions follow.

MARCIA FUNEBRE IN MORTE DI SIGFRIDO NEL DRAMMA MUSICALE IL CREPUSCOLO DEGLI DEI DI R. WAGNER TRASCRIZIONE PER PIANOFORTE DI FERRUCCIO B. BUSONI
Milano   F. Lucca   No. 39 923   Also Milano   G. Ricordi   1926
ER 655   With a preface by Gino Tagliapietra

The piece begins at the moment in the opera when Siegfried dies (the C sharp in the timpani). The March is a literal transcription from the score, with the exception of the last six bars that Busoni added to complete the piece with a reference back to the opening timpani strokes and bass chromatic rumbles so effective in the opera.

This arrangement of 1883 is a valuable demonstration that fidelity to the text does not guarantee anything. Busoni alters nothing here; he has not yet found his later freedom and individuality, his convictions, sense of structure, and control of the keyboard which allowed him to alter, revise, cut, and add to a piece by an established master. Yet this transcription, accurate and well laid out as it is, does not contain the richness and depth of the orchestral original. Krellmann quite rightly points out that it would have been interesting to have seen this same work transcribed by Busoni 15 years later. No doubt the result, while far more effective, would have also been less faithful to the original.

POLONAISE

As far as I can ascertain the Polonaise belongs to a group of arrangements carried out by Busoni in 1888-1889 for Breitkopf & Haertel. There is mention of it in Breitkopf & Haertel listings printed on the back covers of music of this vintage. It is described under "Bearbeitungen von F. B.

Busoni" as *Wagner, Richard, Polonaise. Bearbeitung für Pianoforte zu zwei Händen.* (Perlis Musicales 118).

I have been unable to trace a copy of this piece with Busoni's name as arranger. However, there is a Breitkopf & Haertel publication of a Wagner *Polonaise* in D major, originally for piano four hands, arranged for piano two hands. The date is approximately correct, but the catalogue number on this is VA 2571, not as quoted above. Breitkopf & Haertel have very kindly searched their archives but were unable to come up with a solution to the problem, largely due to the destruction of many valuable records during World War II. It seems unlikely that a publisher would commission two arrangers to work on the same piece, especially a piece as undistinguished as this Wagner *Polonaise*. If Busoni did arrange it, the VA 2571 could well be the edition; there is the confirming evidence of the publishers having advertised the arrangement. As an example, I find Busoni's arrangement listed on the back of my copy of the *Concertstück* Op. 31a, with 1892 given as the copyright date. The Perlis Musicales series was later abandoned, and my guess is that the arrangement was transferred to the Volksausgabe series. It could be that Busoni's name appeared on the original Perlis Musicales edition.

WEILL

FRAUENTANZ   SIEBEN GEDICHTE DES MITTELALTERS FÜR
SOPRAN MIT FLÖTE, BRATSCHE, KLARINETTE, HORN UND
FAGOTT VON KURT WEILL OP. 10   KLAVIERAUSZUG MIT
TEXT   Wien   Universal Edition   1925   UE 7748

Song No. 3 only reduced by Busoni. The following is printed at the head of the third song: *Die Klavierbearbeitung dieser Nummer ist die letzte Arbeit von Ferruccio Busoni* ("the piano arrangement of this number is Ferruccio Busoni's last work"). The reduction as a whole does not name any arranger on the title page, most probably it was Weill himself. Since Weill was a pupil of Busoni, he may have brought this song to him asking for help; Busoni, as was his wont, probably arranged it on the spot. As this song is the most complex of the cycle, Weill's request for assistance seems most likely. As for his assertion that this was Busoni's last work, it may well be true; Weill was very close to Busoni at the end.

It may be of interest that the fingering appearing in the piano score is Busoni's and can be clearly seen in the surviving manuscript.

NOTES

1. Even the mighty fugue from Op. 106 must be taken in these terms—as a vision, rather than a feat of virtuosity; there must be little doubt that this vision coupled with contrapuntal technique was at least a partial model for Busoni's own *Fantasia Contrappuntistica*.

2. Dent, *Ferruccio Busoni*, p. 230.

3. Much abridged.

4. See analysis of Op. 106 fugue in WK appendix.

5. Busoni, *Letters to His Wife*, p. 213.

6. Beethoven's use of cells as a method of musical development and structure was undoubtedly admitted and admired by Busoni, as shown in this analysis. I have tried in Chapter 6 to show Busoni's own use of a similar compositional method.

7. The analysis was done in 1894.

8. The quotation is from the G. Schirmer edition with text in English.

9. Brahms once declared: "What Schumann did for me I will do for Busoni." (Ferruccio Busoni, *Letters to His Wife*, trans. Rosamond Ley (London, Edward Arnold, 1938), p. 310.)

10. The story came from Egon Petri. I notice that Dent's list of Busoni's repertoire does not include the Brahms B flat concerto, although Dent does admit that the list is incomplete. Petri had an astounding memory for personal facts like this and was never in doubt about them. But even if the work in question was another one, the story must be true.

11. There is even an unplayable low A flat. (Also present in one of his transcriptions of the Brahms *Chorale Preludes*.) As early as 1907 Bösendorfer had promised to build a piano with an extended range of eight octaves for Busoni. (See Busoni, *Letters to His Wife*, p. 118.)

12. Bernard van Dieren, *Down among the Dead Men (and Other Essays)* (London, Oxford University Press, 1935).

13. Unaccountably, Hanspeter Krellmann in his *Studien* says that he could not find the material on which this last section is based and concludes that Busoni introduced music extraneous to the opera.

14. Krellmann makes the extraordinary assertion that this finale, like the one to the *Bagdad Fantasy*, has no thematic connection with the opera. Not only is the connection clear and in the same key but it would also have been impossible for Busoni as a composer to have done this, no matter what other multitude of faults those two fantasias possess.

15. Busoni, *Letters to His Wife*, p. 116.

16. Ferruccio Busoni, *The Essence of Music and Other Papers*, trans. Rosamond Ley (London, Rockliff, 1957), p. 170.

17. Krellmann, *Studien*, pp. 176-79.

18. Busoni, *The Essence of Music*, p. 24.

19. "Offener Musikbrief an Fritz Windisch," *Melos*, III/2 (17 Jan. 1922), pp. 59-61.

20. A close friend of Gerda Busoni, a Mrs. Gundolf (who also studied with Petri and then taught the piano to Petri's children and who now lives in Melbourne, Australia), relates that after Busoni heard *Pierrot Lunaire* for the first time, she overheard him say to Schönberg: "I missed the Italian influence in the music,

especially since you spoke to me of the old Italian pantomime." To which Schönberg replied: "For me, Austria is Italia."

21. Someone once asked me at a lecture on Busoni: "How does one transcribe a piano piece into a piano piece?" But in this "concert interpretation" such freedoms are taken that "transcription" seems the correct word to use.

22. Krellmann, *Studien*, pp. 179-86.

23. Now published by Breitkopf & Haertel (Partitur-Bibliothek No. 3894).

24. Josef Rufer, *The Works of Arnold Schoenberg*, trans. Dika Newlin (London, Faber and Faber, 1962), p. 125.

25. Now published as *Entwurf einer neuen Aesthetik der Tonkunst. Faksimile einer Ausgabe von 1916 mit den handschriftlichen Anmerkungen von Arnold Schoenberg. Im Anhang: Transkriptionen der Anmerkungen u. Nachwort von H. H. Stuckenschmidt* (Frankfurt am Main, Suhrkamp, 1974).

26. I have been unable to locate a copy of this publication.

27. It is also to be found in the first edition of the same work, in section IX. In both editions the excerpt is unidentified.

28. Dent, *Ferruccio Busoni*, p. 14.

Busoni and Aesthetics

15

Busoni's Theories of and Attitudes toward the Art of Transcription

His insights and ideas are just as valid today as they were when he formulated them, even though today they might be expressed differently, perhaps even in the language of science. From what Busoni thought, wrote, and created in his art, there can be elicited an unmistakable ethical attitude toward music. His unshakable ethic, which holds aloof from every trend, avoiding all that is mundane and time-bound. . . .

Vladimir Vogel

It is amazing how musical fashions change. There was a time earlier in this century when the only works of Busoni known to the public were his organ (and other) transcriptions; now, in the second half of the century, "transcription" is a dirty word, we regard such efforts with distaste, demand the original in authentic interpretation—whatever that means— and leave the performance of Bach-Busoni organ transcriptions to the few remaining virtuosi of the older generation, allowing them this privilege in view of their advanced age and consequent inability to see the error of their ways.

Busoni's arrangements, like all his artistic endeavors, embody a curious and interesting synthesis of his past and the future as he intuitively believed it to be. Fortunately, he left us some clues in his writings concerning his attitude toward transcriptions: they are tied to his notion of notation generally and his philosophy of the "Unity of Music" in particular. In *Sketch of a New Esthetic of Music* he summarizes the problem touching first upon "notation, the writing out of compositions . . . an ingenious expedient for catching an inspiration, with the purpose of exploiting it later. But notation is to improvisation as the portrait is to the living model. It is for the interpreter to *resolve the rigidity of the signs* into the primitive emotion."[1] Busoni then goes on to establish the artistic rights and duties of the performer; he accuses the "law givers" of mistaking the notational signs for the music itself, and attacks the erroneous idea of a single, "correct" interpretation. Finally, he cites the case of the performer-composer who plays his own works differently, depending on the inspiration of the moment; of this we have living proof in various recordings by composers who contradict their own scores.

Having touched upon the practical side of notation—the problem of the performer—Busoni next propounds the philosophical side: "My final conclusion . . . is this: Every notation is, in itself, the transcription of an abstract idea."[2] That is to say, that a musical work exists in absolute, pure form in the mind of the composer: his act of writing it down is already a major act of transcription; a further transcription, to a different instrumental medium, is insignificant when compared with the initial act. Performance then also can be regarded as yet a further act of transcription, "and still, whatever liberties it may take, it can never annihilate the original."[3] The obvious conclusion drawn from this second aspect of notation is a philosophical justification of transcription.

An aside occurs at this point:

Strangely enough, the Variation-Form is highly esteemed by the Worshippers of the Letter. That is singular; for the variation-form—when built up on a borrowed theme— produces a *whole series of 'arrangements'* which, besides, are least respectful when most ingenious.

So the arrangement is *not* good, because it *varies* the original; and the variation *is* good, although it *'arranges'* the original.[4]

Other implications arise from Busoni's assertion that prior to the act of notating a composition, the composition exists in an abstract state; it exists *"complete and intact . . .* both within and outside of time . . .";[5] and here we have the origin of Busoni's famous idea of the Unity of Music.

This theme appears quite frequently in Busoni's essays and, indeed, almost dominates the whole of the *Essence of Music*, whether as a poetic vision, a philosophic argument, or a practical necessity. It involves a variety of contentious problems and takes us far from the realm of transcription, which is the subject of this chapter. But briefly, it proves by various examples how even composers of Beethoven's and Bach's stature could use the same piece for completely contrary purposes; how many of our traditional associations with regard to "sacred" and "operatic" music can be proved wrong. And how, indeed, music, outside of any such associations and understood in the pure meaning of the word can have a unity within itself, indestructible by performance adaptation or varying media. In the end so much ground has been covered and so many important questions raised that "transcription" becomes a minor issue, and one wonders why there is a fuss about it at all.

Most of these questions are touched upon in two essays, both of considerable length and concentration: "The Oneness of Music and the Possibilities of the Opera"[6] and "The Essence of Music: A Paving of the Way to an Understanding of the Everlasting Calendar."[7] There are two further essays that touch directly on the problem of transcription: "Value of the Transcription" (written in Berlin, November 1910, for the program of the third of the Nikisch Concerts)[8] and "The Transcription" (from a letter to his wife, 22 July 1913).[9]

Busoni further develops the ideas already presented elsewhere, and scrutinizes the case of the *Spanish Rhapsody* of Liszt and his own transcription of this piece for piano and orchestra in particular (see Chapter 12); we find to our surprise that the motivic material of the *Rhapsody* involves the names of Mozart, Gluck, Corelli, Glinka, Mahler, Liszt, and Busoni. The question is asked: What is transcribed and what is original?

The final potent points are made: first, almost all the great masters cultivated the art of transcription, "seriously and lovingly," and second, the low esteem in which transcription is generally held is due to the undisputed number of cheap, superficial works in this branch of art, which have brought the whole idea of transcription to a state of disrepute.

Busoni regarded transcribing (and even editing, I am tempted to add) as an independent art in the highest sense of the word; it involved far more than the mere ability to transfer from one medium to another. In this field he made discoveries and created new sounds on the piano, undreamed of by the virtuosi who preceded him. Busoni attempted to imbue the art of the transcriber (and performer, often the same person) with a new freedom and dignity and with added responsibility to cope with such freedoms. He demanded from the transcriber not only the attitude of the performer and the craft of the composer but also the creativity of the composer and the independence and bravery necessary to allow oneself to reshape the work under transcription.

We know from our study of Busoni's transcriptions (see Chapters 11-14 and 16) that he lived up to his own standards. The transcription had to have a life of its own, had to live or die on its own merits. Meanwhile, his invariable answer to criticism was simply: "But I have not destroyed the original!" Put more positively one could quote Ernest Newman, who defined a good transcription as "the work of great commentators, like Scartazzini upon the *Divina Commedia*, like Conington upon Virgil, like Montague Summers upon the Restoration Dramatists."[10]

It is perfectly obvious from all this that Busoni's sphere of interest extended much further than mere pianistic writing; it just happened that the piano was his instrument. And that is why (unlike the case of Liszt) it is so difficult to even classify Busoni's transcriptions into various groups and various stages of development, to separate transcription from composition. One of the peculiarities of Busoni's transcription is that an individual technique, often changing fundamentally, is found for every piece to be transcribed. His choice of works is motivated by an interest in the solution of a new problem, and, although the art of transcription is a traditional one, Busoni takes little from the conventional armory of techniques.

Put in simpler terms, there are four basic aspects of a work that Busoni subjects to transcription:

1. Form: often a type of condensing occurs here; sometimes sequences of sections are altered and segments omitted altogether, especially outright repetitions.

2. Texture: apart from obvious textural changes that would happen in the course of transcription, Busoni often introduces deliberate darkening or lightening of color. This is tied to his interpretative ideas as well as the three other aspects listed.

3. Structure: allied to (1); Busoni views the total architecture of a piece, and, if the symmetry displeases him, he alters or adjusts it; if necessary, he adds a section.

4. Free Composition: the interpolation of music composed by Busoni into a transcription. This could be mild or decorative but it could also be quite ruthless.

The resultant Busoni transcription is hard to justify, therefore, if judged in terms of the original, for, in a way, Busoni reveals a lack of respect toward it, stylistically as well as technically; it can only be viewed in its own light, its own effectiveness and suitability. The Busoni transcription is, in most cases, unshakable on such grounds, the idea of the inherent Unity of Music is proven, and Busoni is added to the already imposing list of great creative transcribers: Bach, Beethoven, Haydn, Liszt, Brahms, Schönberg, Webern, Stravinsky, and Bartók.

It is difficult to label these composers as "public jesters," which is how Paul Hindemith refers to the transcriber in his book *The Composer's World*, in which he puts the anti-transcription case as clearly as anyone.[11]

In the long run Busoni was right, not only because the art of transcription continued after him but, more significantly, because his battle for the artistic freedom to do this and to reinstate the performer as a dignified lesser partner of the composer has justified itself in recent times with the aleatoric composers who demand such responsibilities. Busoni, although certainly not aleatoric in his own works, nevertheless played with great freedom; in his own scores he tended to give poetic rather than explicit indications, promoting flexibility of performance. The boldness of his fantasy once prompted Paul Bekker (much to Busoni's irritation) to speak of a "Jules Verne" touch.

NOTES

1. Busoni, *Sketch of a New Esthetic of Music*, p. 15.
2. Ibid., p. 17.
3. Ibid., p. 18.
4. Ibid., p. 19.

5. Ibid., p. 19.

6. In the first edition of *Von der Einheit der Musik* this essay appears as "Entwurf eines Vorwortes zur Partitur des Doktor Faust, enhaltend einige Betrachtungen über die Möglichkeit der Oper," and was written in Berlin in August 1921; the "Preface to the Score of *Doktor Faust*" was first published at the end of this essay and was written in July 1922. Both works appeared together in a little book titled *Über die Möglichkeiten der Oper und über die Partitur des "Doktor Faust"* ("Concerning the Possibilities of the Opera and concerning the Score of 'Doktor Faust'"); published by Breitkopf & Haertel, 1926; 2d ed., 1967.

7. Ferruccio Busoni, *The Essence of Music and Other Papers*, trans. Rosamond Ley (London, Rockliff, 1957), p. 193.

8. Ibid., pp. 85-89.

9. Ibid, p. 228.

10. Quoted by Kaikhosru Sorabji in "Mi Contra Fa," p. 62.

11. Larry Sitsky, "Transcriptions and the Eunuch," *Quadrant*, No. 43, X/5, (Sept.-Oct. 1966), p. 30.

16

The Organ Transcriptions

> When he played the piano his eyes took on a dreamy brightness. Below, his hands, effortless, made music, unique perfection; but above, the handsome soulful head, thrown back a little, listened and drank in the music which he created. Then something like transfiguration seemed to claim him.
>
> Stefan Zweig

As well as his theoretical writings, Busoni left one outstanding practical contribution on the art of transcription from the organ to the pianoforte: the first appendix to volume 1 of the *Well-Tempered Klavier* is a 36-page essay "On the Transcription of Bach's Organ-Works for the Pianoforte." Copiously illustrated with examples from Liszt, Tausig, and, mainly, Busoni himself, some idea of the scope of this essay may be gleaned from the headings of the topics covered:

1. Doublings
    I. Simple doubling of Pedal-part (five types are given).
    II. Simple doubling of Manual-parts (three types are given).
    III. Doubling in the Octave of all Pedal- and Manual-parts (four types).
    IV. Tripling in Octaves (nine types).
    V. Doubling of one Manual-part, the rest unchanged (four types).
2. Registration.
3. Additions, Omissions, Liberties.
4. Use of the Piano-pedals
    (a) The Damper-pedal.
    (b) The Soft-pedal.
    (c) The Sustaining-pedal.
5. Interpretation.

6. Supplementary
   (a) Two-piano settings.
   (b) "Free" adaptations.

In his preface, Busoni once more reviews ground already covered in other essays but applies the argument specifically to Bach; further, he maintains that no pianist's knowledge of Bach can be complete without playing some of his organ pieces on the pianoforte, and, since Bach's music is motivated by a basic Unity, there can "be no question as to aesthetic propriety."

Liszt is invoked as the father of contemporary pianism, but Busoni also makes it clear that he intends to "reinforce and perfect" the Liszt-Tausig methods of organ transcription. A typical Busoni aside in the form of a footnote occurs here: "Musical commoners still delight in decrying modern virtuosi as spoilers of the classics: and yet Liszt and his pupils (Bülow, Tausig) have done things for spreading a general understanding for Bach and Beethoven beside which all theoretico-practical pedantry seems bungling. . . ."[1]

Most of what follows is of a purely practical and technical nature; brilliantly set out, the essay is a model of its kind and does succeed in showing very distinctly the advances Busoni made by comparison with the Liszt school of transcription. The massive sound of the Bach-Busoni transcriptions is taken back here to its logical origins, and it becomes amply clear how Busoni arrived at his effects and also why certain liberties were taken.

The chapters on interpretation and pedal use are a faithful description of Busoni's own playing, not only of these particular transcriptions, but of much of Bach generally. No musician who knows the Busoni and the Liszt-Tausig transcriptions and who has seriously studied this essay can fail to be impressed.

PRAELUDIUM UND FUGE D DUR FÜR DIE ORGEL VON JOHANN SEBASTIAN BACH   ZUM CONCERTVORTRAGE FREI BEAR-BEITET FÜR PIANOFORTE UND FRAU KATHI PETRI ZUGEEIGNET VON F. B. BUSONI   Leipzig   Breitkopf & Haertel   No. 18 146   Also as *Joh. Seb. Bach   Präludium und Fuge D Dur für die Orgel zum Konzertvortrage für Pianoforte zu zwei Händen bearbeitet von F. B. Busoni*   Leipzig   Breitkopf & Haertel   1902 EB 3355   Also as *Praeludium und Fuge für die Orgel   Zum Konzert-vortrage für Pianoforte bearbeitet von F. B. Busoni* in *Joh. Seb. Bach Sechs Tonstücke   Klavier-Übertragung von Ferruccio Busoni Neue durchgesehene Ausgabe*   Leipzig   Breitkopf & Haertel   1902 VA 1916   Also as *Praeludium und Fuge für die Orgel   Joh. Seb.*

*Bach   Zum Konzertvortrage für Pianoforte bearbeitet von F. B.
Busoni* in Vol. 3 of the Bach-Busoni edition   1916   Also as *Preludio e
Fuga in re magg*   Milano Edizione Curci 1963   E 4720 C   BWV 532

It was Egon Petri's mother, Frau Kathi Petri, who first suggested to
Busoni that he transcribe some Bach organ music. Busoni and Kathi Petri
attended an organ recital in the Thomaskirche—one of Bach's churches—in
Leipzig, during which the *Prelude and Fugue* in D major was played. Frau
Petri turned to Busoni and made a passing remark about transcribing the
piece for piano. A week later, before he even had had time to write it down,
Busoni played it for her. It was the first of his series of great transcriptions,
and the initial step in one of his many re-appraisals of his own piano
playing. This was in 1888. Between this date and 1900 all of the Bach-
Busoni organ transcriptions appeared.

The D major *Prelude and Fugue* comes from a set of *Six Preludes and
Fugues* for organ, and is second in the Bach-Gesellschaft edition. Eugene
d'Albert transcribed it in a version less taxing to play and more faithful at
least visually to the original (published by Bote & Bock). I say visually
because the d'Albert fails to recognize the spirit of the original although the
letter is accurately reproduced. So that already in his first attempt Busoni
had understood that to do justice to the organ sound one needs reinforcing
and doubling.[2]

Comparison of the Bach original and the Busoni transcription reveals,
except for such textural freedoms, no other alterations.[3] Busoni in his essay
on organ transcription does say that there is "in the D major Fugue, an
added 'Coda,' faithfully imitated from an Episode in the Prelude."[4] I have
not been able to ascertain what this means; the fugue ends exactly as in the
Bach original.

PRAELUDIUM UND FUGE (Es DUR) FÜR ORGEL VON JOHANN
SEBASTIAN BACH   ZUM CONCERTGEBRUACHE FÜR PIANO-
FORTE FREI BEARBEITET UND SEINEM FREUNDE W. H. DAYAS
ZUGEEIGNET VON FERRUCCIO B. BUSONI   Hamburg   D. Rahter
No. 3003   Also reissued under the same title   Leipzig   D. Rahter
1914   No. 1394   Also as *Praeludium und Fuge für die Orgel   Joh.
Seb. Bach   Zum Konzertgebrauche für Pianoforte frei bearbeitet
von Ferruccio B. Busoni* in Vol. 3 of the Bach-Busoni edition 1916
BWV 552

This *Prelude and Fugue*, known as the *St. Anne*, is the second of the four
big organ transcriptions: it dates from 1890, and was first introduced by
Busoni during his stay in Helsingfors, Finland, where he was teaching at the
Conservatoire.

The material for this mighty *Prelude and Fugue* comes from the Bach *Clavier-übung* part 3 (*Organ Mass*), in which this prelude and fugue, respectively, open and close the publication; in between we find various chorale preludes set in versions for manuals only and manuals with pedals; also the four *Duets* (see Chapter 11) make their appearance here, for, of course, in Bach's day the word *clavier* was not restricted to any one keyboard instrument and included harpsichord, clavichord, and organ.

In transcribing this work from Bach's mature years, Busoni first of all devised "an harmonic suspension (instead of a full close) at the end of the . . . Prelude, followed by a cadence-like transition to the Fugue." (See Figure 16.1.) The prelude contains "a skip of 18 measures previously

Figure 16.1. By kind permission, Breitkopf & Haertel, Wiesbaden.

heard." Finally, referring to his title, Busoni states in the same essay "free arrangements, are, in view of some irreconcilable diversities in the two instruments, not inadmissible."[5]

The *Triple Fugue* (as Petri used to call it) is undoubtedly one of the most successful works of its type.

ZWEI ORGELTOCCATEN VON JOH. SEBASTIAN BACH   AUF DAS PIANOFORTE ÜBERTRAGEN VON FERRUCCIO BUSONI NO. 1 TOCCATA IN C-DUR   NO. 2 TOCCATA IN D-MOLL (issued separately) Leipzig Breitkopf & Haertel 1900 EB 1371 and EB 1372 Also as *Orgel-Tokkaten* in Vol. 3 of the Bach-Busoni edition 1916 Also as *Johann Sebastian Bach   Orgel-Toccaten auf*

das Pianoforte übertragen von Ferruccio Busoni   Wiesbaden
Breitkopf & Haertel   1967 and 1948   Also as *Due Toccate per
Organo   Trascritte per Pianoforte da F. B. Busoni   I   Toccata
in do magg   II   Toccata in re min*   Milano   Edizioni Curci   1948
E 4736 C and E 4737 C   Also issued New York   G. Schirmer   Nos.
1628, 1629 BWV 564 and 565

A particularly effective transcription and next in order of composition, the *Toccata* in C major (*Preludio, Adagio e Fuga*) No. 1 of *Three Toccatas for Organ* by Bach, was first performed in 1899 in Manchester, England, during one of Busoni's concert tours.

The preface is worth quoting in full, embodying the young composer-pianist's attitudes (he was then 34 years old):

TO ROBERT FREUND

With the publication of these "Toccatas," I, for the present, bring a number of similar and related works to a conclusion. Those presented herewith I regard as my ripest labors in this respect and therefore, I trust, as worthy to bear on the first page thereof the name of the esteemed colleague who honoured and caused me to rejoice at the most unmistakable proofs of an artist's confidence.

Originally dealt with singly as the result of fortuitous incitement, according to the degree in which the works occupied me at the time, the arrangement of these studies gradually eventuated in a systematic grouping thereof. The order thus taking form, aroused in me the thought of a regulated course and it is according to such that each of the said arrangements is now placed in the grade corresponding with its position in the progression upward of the collective work. They constitute a CONTRIBUTION TO THE HIGH SCHOOL OF PIANOFORTE-PLAYING. In their entirety they are similar to an educational building which—preferably with Bach-Music as its basis—seems capable of eventually bearing further and younger superstructures, like unto an old, sturdy oak-tree, which, although ever growing older itself, still continues to put forth the greenest and freshest of shoots.

As works which belong to this scheme of study are to be named the following works edited by me, namely:

1. Cramer, Eight Studies, in 2 parts ("The Legato-School" & "The Staccato-School")
2. Bach, 15 two-part-Inventions, edited & expounded with respect to the execution and the composition thereof
3. Bach, 15 three-part-Inventions, edited & expounded with respect to the execution and the composition thereof
4. Bach, The Well-tempered Clavier (Part I) Edited, explained and furnished with appropriate examples and directions for the study of modern pianoforte-technics.
5. Bach, Concerto in D Minor, Score-arrangement.
6. Bach, 10 Organ-chorale-Preludes, arranged for the pianoforte in Chamber-music-style.
7. Bach, Prelude and Fugue in D-Major for the Organ. Arranged as a concert-work for the pianoforte.[6]
8. Bach, Prelude & Fugue in E-flat-major for the organ. Freely arranged as a concert-piece for the pianoforte.

9. Bach, Chaconne from the IVth Violin-Sonate. Arranged as a concert-piece for the pianoforte.
10. Bach, Two Organ Toccatas. Arranged for the pianoforte.
11. Liszt, Fantasia & Fugue on the Chorale "Ad nos, ad salutarem Undam." Freely transcribed from the organ-notation for the pianoforte.
12. Liszt, Mephisto-Valse, partially according to the orchestral score re-arranged for the piano.

But, according to my personal conviction, hereto should be added a critical and instructive edition of the most important pianoforte-works of Franz Liszt (which still continue to be misunderstood, even by competent pianists), to serve as the tower in completion of the educational building. In view, however, of the fact that complicated negotiations would have to be concluded with the individual Original publishers of Liszt-editions, which are widely distributed, such a task presents considerable difficulties.

Berlin, 1900

[Reprinted by kind permission, Breitkopf & Haertel, Wiesbaden.]

It is a curious list, to say the least, both in the items of inclusion and omission and in the heavy percentage of organ transcriptions. But the date was 1900: Busoni had yet to crown his romantic period with the *Piano Concerto*, and only then would he change his style, both of composition and transcription. I stress the obvious here, since these transcriptions, whatever one may think of them, represent the young Busoni. If one admires them, the admiration may be increased with the realization that they were written at so early a stage. If one abhors them, it seems unfair to judge a man's work by efforts dating prior to his thirty-fifth year.

The transcription of the *Toccata* in question is faithful to Bach except for the insertion of three extra bars of flourish at the very end of the fugue. (The three bars are inserted between Bach's bars 140 and 141.) Naturally, as well as the physical transcription, Busoni also provides tempi and interpretative ideas since Bach's manuscript had none.

The *Toccata* in d minor (*Toccata e Fuga*) No. 2 of *Three Toccatas for Organ* by Bach, a spectacular display piece by the young Bach in virtuoso mood, is a natural candidate for piano transcription and the last of Busoni's Bach organ series. Busoni gave the premier performance in Berlin in 1901. Like the C major *Toccata*, it is an accurate pianistic representation of Bach's score; the first three bars of Bach are subbarred for clarity, but from the prestissimo immediately after the opening adagio nothing like this happens again.

The Tausig transcription of this *Toccata* is quite well known, still occasionally performed, and at one time was in competition with the Busoni version. But five minutes at the piano would convince anyone of the superiority of Busoni. First, in the matter of interpretation, Busoni's "building of the climaxes, is more monumental, in simple lines, more thoughtful and much more effective than Tausig's somewhat arbitrary rise and fall, running thus":[7]

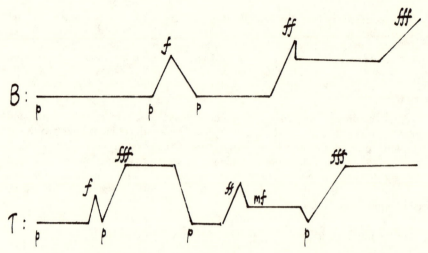

As well as this, Busoni's actual sonorities are more organ-like and massive: he assiduously avoids arpeggiated chords—a sound characteristic of the piano, but not the organ; his whole method of doubling, registration (octave placement on the keyboard), pedal, and pianistic distribution is superior to Tausig's. Some particular defects of the Tausig technique are demonstrated in the essay on transcription (see above). Incidentally, example 64 of this essay gives a worthwhile variant to the coda of this *Toccata*.

PRAELUDIUM ET FUGA   In *Zweiter Anhang des Wohltemperierten Klaviers, 1. Teil* in vol. 1 of the *Klavierwerke*   Also in Vol. 5 of the Bach-Busoni edition   BWV 533   (see Chapter 11)

The second appendix to volume 1 of the *Well-Tempered Klavier* is subtitled "Example of transcription from the organ for the pianoforte" and consists of both the Bach original and the Busoni transcription printed underneath; it is the e minor prelude and fugue, (No. 3 of *Six Preludes and Fugues*), known by its designation of the "Little" *Prelude and Fugue*, to distinguish it from the big "Wedge" *Prelude and Fugue*, also in e minor. This shortest and easiest of Busoni transcriptions has not been published separately and is, consequently, almost unknown. Yet, it is a good pianistic and musical introduction to the series; with the Bach text printed above it, an immediate reference to the effect intended is clearly shown.

CHACONNE FÜR VIOLINE ALLEIN VON JOH. SEB. BACH   ZUM CONCERTVORTRAGE FÜR PIANOFORTE BEARBEITET VON F. B. BUSONI   Leipzig   Breitkopf & Haertel   Klav. Bibl. 19 792 Also as *Chaconne für Violine allein   Zum Konzertvortrage für*

Pianoforte bearbeitet von F. B. Busoni in *Joh. Seb. Bach Sechs Tonstücke Klavier-Übertragung von Ferruccio Busoni Neue durchgesehene Ausgabe* Leipzig Breitkopf & Haertel 1902 VA 1916 Also as *Chaconne D moll mit Variationen aus der 4 Violin-Sonate Zum Konzertvortrage für Pianoforte zu 2 Händen bearbeitet von F. B. Busoni* Leipzig Breitkopf & Haertel VA 2334 Also as *Chaconne für Violine allein Joh. Seb. Bach Zum Konzertvortrage für Pianoforte bearbeitet von F. B. Busoni* in Vol. 3 of the Bach-Busoni edition 1916 Also as *Chaconne in re min* Milano Curci SRI E 4721 C Also as *Chaconne in D minor* New York G. Schirmer No. 1597 BWV 1004

There seems to be some doubt about the precise date of publication of the first edition. Dent gives 1897, which places the *Chaconne* in the middle of the period of the organ transcriptions. Busoni appears to have performed it as early as 1893, in Boston.

I have included this transcription, based on the last movement of Bach's *Partita No. II* in d minor for solo violin, in this chapter because of Busoni's organ-like treatment. In lieu of a proper preface to this transcription, we can quote a footnote from the essay discussed earlier in this chapter, which also supports this view:

The editor, in his transcriptions of the Preludes and Fugues in D, Eb, and E minor, has devoted much care to the registration, and begs to call attention to them as a series of examples in point. His piano-transcription of Bach's chaconne for violin may also be added to this series, inasmuch as the editor has, in both cases, treated the tonal effects from the standpoint of the organ-tone. This procedure, which has been variously attacked, was justified, firstly, by the breadth of conception, which is not fully displayed by the violin; and, secondly, by the example set by Bach himself in the transcription for organ of his own violin-fugue in G minor. Of this point Grieupenkerl remarks: "It is important to observe, that the Fugue by J. S. Bach was, in all probability, originally written for violin. In this form it is found among the well-known six sonatas for solo violin, and in the key of G minor; whereas it had to be transposed for organ into D minor, for the sake of the effect and of ease in execution. The Prelude is an entirely different one, and in the Fugue all passages peculiar to violin technic have been altered to suit the organ-keyboard; aside from these deviations, however, the resemblance is extremely great."[8]

It is clear, therefore, that the *Chaconne* is a type of double transcription. Busoni first mentally imagined it as an organ piece and then transcribed it for the piano in his particular style. There was never any intention to imitate the violin, so that, although faithful to the original, it maintains its own pianistic integrity as well.

The same cannot be said of the ineffectual Raff transcription for the piano or the staid Brahms version for left hand alone or, for that matter, the Schumann and Mendelssohn settings of 1854 and 1845, respectively, which simply add a piano accompaniment, leaving the original violin part untouched. The piano parts in both cases are completely subsidiary. There is also a Siloti arrangement that tries to reconcile the original Bach with the Busoni, a timid and pointless task, both from Bach's and Busoni's points of view. And of course there have been countless other versions for organ, orchestra, and various instrumental combinations; the *Chaconne* seems living proof of Busoni's dictum of Unity, at least within Bach.

A work about the interpretation of this piece. Busoni of course provided copious performing instructions and suggested many tempi changes; however, according to Petri, later in life Busoni used to play the *Chaconne* with a much more uniform overall tempo, minimizing the rather sudden shifts of speed indicated in this early publication.

Throughout the *Chaconne*, Busoni follows Bach bar by bar; there are two minor exceptions only. Once, a diminished 7th cadenza-like arpeggio is extended by one bar, allowing it to sweep over the entire keyboard; another time a four-bar sequence is repeated by Busoni (where it is not in Bach), the repetition involving a re-distribution of the material differently for the hands.

But the deviations from Bach in terms of fullness, elaboration, and added voices and chords are very extensive and not for the timid at heart; comparison with the original is a fascinating study in this, the most popular of the Bach-Busoni set of pieces, and, since this particular transcription is readily available, I see no point in offering any examples here.

FANTASIE UND FUGE ÜBER DEN CHORAL "AD NOS, AD SALUTAREM UNDAM" VON FRANZ LISZT   VON DER ORGEL AUF DAS PIANOFORTE FREI ÜBERTRAGEN UND HERRN JOSEPH SATTLER ZUGEEIGNET VON FERRUCCIO B. BUSONI
Leipzig   Breitkopf & Haertel   1897   EB 3863

Like the *Chaconne*, the Liszt *Fantasy and Fugue* lacks a preface; and, as in the case of the *Chaconne*, we can supply a preface by quoting from the essay on organ transcription once again:

Our problem is presented in a wholly different aspect when we have to metamorphose an organ-piece, by transcription for piano, wholly into the style and character of a piano-piece—actually to translate it into the language of the piano. Just as in the case of "orchestration," our success will now be the greater, the less the nature of the pianoforte is disowned, and the closer the musical thoughts are made to conform to it: they should not be simply translated, but re-poetized.

All the resources of the instrument are to be utilized where they can enhance the effect; the freedom of transcription gains wider limits, becoming wellnigh unlimited when—as in the following model examples— [Busoni gives here two excerpts from Liszt: the B.A.C.H. fugue and the *Weinen Klagen* variations, in both organ and piano versions] the transcriber works with his own compositions.

From this standpoint the editor has attempted a transcription of Liszt's Fantasia and Fugue on the chorale in Meyebeer's *Prophet*.

No statement of aim could be clearer.

As with the *Spanish Rhapsody*, Busoni had ample precedent from Liszt for arranging organ works for the piano. Apart from transcribing Bach organ works, Liszt also reworked some of his own organ compositions for the piano. Busoni, therefore, had much to study in the way of procedures by the composer himself, but, one wonders, did he know of Liszt's own setting of the *Ad nos . . .* for pedal piano and piano four hands? If he did, there is no mention of it in his transcription. It seems, rather, that the organ version was his starting point. So here we find an isolated instance of yet another type of Busoni transcription, where the starting point is the organ, as before, but the end product is a complete transformation for the piano with no imitation of the organ intended. The writing is pure Liszt in style and effect and the transformations as free and as appropriate as those wrought by Liszt himself in his own similar efforts. Understanding Busoni's purpose, the transcription is a resounding success.

ORGELCHORALVORSPIELE VON JOHANN SEBASTIAN BACH AUF DAS PIANOFORTE IM KAMMERSTYL ÜBERTRAGEN UND HERRN JOSÉ VIANNA DA MOTTA ZUGEEIGNET VON FERRUC-CIO BUSONI   Leipzig   Breitkopf & Haertel   1898   Klav. Bibl. 21 839 I and II   Also as *Vier Orgelchoralvorspiele* in *Joh. Seb. Bach   Sechs Tonstücke   Klavier-Übertragung von Ferruccio Busoni   Neue durchgesehene Ausgabe*   Leipzig   Breitkopf & Haertel   1902 VA 1916   This edition contains Nos. 2, 8, 5 and 4 only and in this order (see below)   Also as *Johann Sebastian Bach   Orgel-Choralvorspiele   Auf das Klavier im Kammerstil übertragen von Ferruccio Busoni*   Leipzig   Breitkopf & Haertel   EB 2459/60 Also as *Orgelchoralvorspiele von Johann Sebastian Bach   Auf das Pianoforte im Kammerstyl übertragen und Herrn José Vianna da Motta zugeeignet von Ferruccio Benvenuto Busoni* in Vol. 3 of the Bach-Busoni edition   1916   Also as *Preludi per Corali D'Organo trascritti per pianoforte in stile da camera*   Milano   E. Curci 1957   E 4723 C and E 4724 C

The following is a list of the *Chorale Preludes*, with Busoni's numbering, and the original sources:

BOOK I

1. *Komm, Gott, Schöpfer!* (Come, God, Creator!) No. 17 of *Eighteen Chorales* (BWV 667)

2. *Wachet auf, ruft und die Stimme* (Awake, the Voice Commands) No. 1 of *The Six Schübler Chorales*; tenor air from the cantata of the same name (BWV 645)

3. *Nun Komm' der Heiden Heiland* (Now Comes the Gentiles' Saviour)
   No. 9 of *Eighteen Chorales* (BWV 659)

4. *Nun freut euch, lieben Christen* (Rejoice, Beloved Christians) No. 22 of
   the *Miscellaneous Chorale Preludes* (BWV 734)

5. *Ich ruf' zu dir, Herr* (I Call on Thee, Lord) No. 41 from the
   Orgelbüchlein (BWV 639)

BOOK II

6. *Herr Gott, nun schleuss' den Himmel auf!* (Lord God, Heaven's Gate
   Unlock!) No. 19 from the *Orgelbüchlein* (BWV 617)

7a. *Durch Adam's Fall ist ganz verderbt* (Through Adam Came Our Fall) No. 39
    from the *Orgelbüchlein* (BWV 637)

7b. Title as in 7a; No. 16 of *Kirnberger's Collection of Chorale Preludes*
    (BWV 705)

8. *In dir ist Freude* (In Thee Is Joy) No. 17 from the Orgelbüchlein (BWV
   615)

9. *Jesus Christus, unser Heiland, der von uns den Zorn Gottes wandt*
   (Jesus Christ, Our Lord and Saviour, Who Turn'dst from Us the Wrath
   of God) No. 15 of *Eighteen Chorales* (BWV 665)

In his preface, Busoni once again refers to his 'high school of pianoforte
playing' (see above, preface to *Toccata* in C major) and to the placement
therein of the *Chorale Preludes*. We also read:

That which induced the editor to arrange a selection of Bach's Chorale-Preludes for
the pianoforte was not so much to furnish a sample of his capabilities as an arranger
as the desire to interest a larger section of the public in these compositions which are
so rich in art, feeling and fantasy. . . .

This style of arrangement which we take leave to describe as "IN CHAMBER-
MUSIC—STYLE" as in contradistinction to "CONCERT-ARRANGEMENTS"
rarely requires the highest skill of the player, with the exception of the art of
pianoforte-touch which must certainly be at the player's command. . . .[9]

But what is simple to Busoni is not so simple to another player: The
Chorales are shorter and more intimate (hence "chamber-music-style") but in
many respects are as difficult as the larger transcriptions demanding good
octaves, double notes, and the ability to bring out the chorale melody from
the surrounding web of counterpoint, sometimes very fast and light. The
arrangements, however, are enormously evocative, with some gorgeous
sonorities achieved in the slower *Chorales*. (See Figure 16.2.) Some of the
ornaments are not quite correctly realized, but such minor discrepancies are
easily corrected by the performer if offensive to the ear.

Both here and in the longer organ works, pianists often find difficulty in
stretching chords that Busoni, with his enormous hand, managed quite
comfortably. The rule in such cases is to avoid breaking the chord by

Figure 16.2. By kind permission, Breitkopf & Haertel, Wiesbaden.

rolling. Often the chord can be split into two by playing the bottom note on a previous beat or half beat; if this is musically impossible, compress the chord, transfer the unstretchable note into the span of your hand, moving it up or down an octave; the texture may vary somewhat, but the simultaneous sounding of the chord is still preferable to a roll. The bass or highest treble line should not be displaced. All this seems obvious, and yet one often hears pianists kneading the larger chords like dough. Busoni treated other composers' music very freely and would have been surprised if his own works were not subjected to similar procedures.

Busoni must have considered transcribing at least one other Bach organ *Choral Prelude*. The *Busoni-Nachlass* SB 210 consists of two closely written pages. It is the *Chorale Prelude* "Aus tiefer Noth schrei' ich zu dir" (BWV 666) copied out in full on three staves and titled *Choralvorspiel. Übertragungs-Versuch eines sechsstimmigen Orgelsatzes auf das Clavier.* The manuscript is not just a copy of the Bach original. Busoni had gone to the trouble of writing out the main lines in bold notes and the subsidiary lines in smaller size. Moreover, the *Chorale Prelude* is painstakingly fingered throughout, in the interests of bringing out the main melodic line, as an obvious experiment to see whether the piece fitted under the pianist's 10 fingers in a satisfactory manner. No interpretative suggestions appear on the music other than a few remarks written in the margins. The next step would have been to transfer the music onto two staves for the piano, but Busoni, for whatever reasons, abandoned the project.

SECHS CHORAL-VORSPIELE FÜR DIE ORGEL VON JOHANNES BRAHMS OP. 122 (EINZIGES NACHGELASSENES WERK) COMPONIRT IN ISCHL IM MAI UND JUNI 1896 FÜR DAS PIANOFORTE AUSGEWÄHLT UND ÜBERTRAGEN VON FER- RUCCIO BUSONI Berlin N. Simrock 1902 No. 11 779 English edition, London N. Simrock-Richard Schauer 1902 No. 916(S)

1. *Herzlich tut mich erfreuen* (My Inmost Heart Rejoiced) Op. 122, No. 4

2. *Schmücke dich, o liebe Seele* (Deck Thyself Out, O My Soul) Op. 122, No. 5

3. *Es ist ein' Ros' entsprungen* (A Rose Breaks into Bloom) Op. 122, No. 8

4. *Herzlich tut mich verlangen* (My Inmost Heart Doth Yearn) Op. 122, No. 9

5. *Herzlich tut mich verlangen* (My Inmost Heart Doth Yearn) Op. 122, No. 10

6. *O Welt, ich muss dich lassen* (O World, I E'en Must Leave Thee) Op. 122, No. 11

The quaint translation is from the original edition.

These, generally, are the simplest of all the Busoni organ transcriptions. None is fast, nor do they have the joyful exaltation of the Bach *Chorales*, rather, that autumnal, resigned farewell to the world, which we encounter more and more in Brahms's late works. The *Chorales* were in fact Brahms's last work; Busoni's arrangements, completed soon after Brahms's death, must have been a kind of homage to an early ideal. (See Chapter 14.) The dedication in translation reads: "As requested by the heirs of Johannes Brahms, this work is published in accordance with wishes stated in his last will." (See Figure 16.3.)

W. A. Mozart   Fantasie für eine Orgelwalze, Werk 608

This work is deliberately not included in this chapter (see Chapter 13). Although an organ transcription, it was realized in Busoni's last years after his style had undergone a total reconsideration; as such, the old massive approach with its thick piano sonorities was gone, and a new linear, transparent keyboard writing was now the norm.

Such a change of compositional style was naturally reflected in Busoni's various transcriptions; we notice the gradual shift to Mozart, as Busoni's own style of writing and performance acquired its characteristic late lucidity. This bears out my statement earlier in the chapter about the Bach transcriptions being typical of one period of Busoni's creativity only, which need not surprise us at all. After all, composition, arrangement, performance, repertoire, and theoretical reflection were all facets of the one impulse right throughout his life.

Figure 16.3

NOTES

1. English edition of the WK, Vol. I (New York, G. Schirmer, 1894).

2. There is also a brilliantly scored orchestral version by Respighi, which misfired due to opulence.

3. Hanspeter Krellmann in *Studien . . .* gives bar-by-bar analyses of all the major organ transcriptions, the *Chorale Preludes*, and the Brahms *Chorale Preludes*; such analyses only corroborate Busoni's methods, already described in his own essay. Readers are referred to Krellmann's painstaking task if they are so inclined. Our main interest here is in the general view.

4. English edition of the WK, p. 174.

5. Appendix to WK, Book 1 (p. 174 in the G. Schirmer edition, in English).

6. The preface mistakenly says "in D Minor."

7. Hugo Leichtentritt, "Ferruccio Busoni as a Composer," *Musical Quarterly*, 3 (1917), pp. 69-97.

8. English edition of the WK, Book 1, p. 167.

9. Preface to Orgelchoralvorspiele von Johann Sebastian Bach.

17

Busoni's Compositional Growth

I did not know Busoni, and I regret this whenever I hear others speak of him, for I have never heard such total unanimity of judgment about a musician. It makes me think that, in some hereafter, many who encounter him would say to him:

You taught me how man becomes immortal (Inferno, XV:85)

Luigi Dallapiccola

In retrospect, Busoni's mature output may be seen as a synthesis of tendencies evidenced extremely early; his development as a composer is marked by logical progression from one period to the next. The speed of development was both very slow and very fast: very slow in that his personal style had not arrived until his forties and extremely fast in the purely technical aspects of mastery.

Thus, the first unpublished works are heavily inclined toward counterpoint, and the conquest of Bachian fugue was the young composer's first achievement. These works were quickly followed by various essays in classical style, initially the shorter dance forms and then the first attempts at sonatas. Simultaneously with the series of full-blown sonatas came the studies in romantic expression and long-spun melodic construction, as opposed to the clipped classical melodies and cellular baroque fugal subjects. The romantic forms—etudes and variations particularly—were modelled first on Brahms, then on Schumann, and then possibly Reger; the composer went on to discover Liszt in all his multitudinous facets and finally arrived at the late Liszt pieces. Combined with all these early studies, encompassing roughly the first 30 years of his life, came the extension of transcription technique and Busoni's first original contributions in that area.

The synthesis of some aspects of these early studies were achieved fairly quickly: romantic "character" pieces with fugal episodes, complete fugues within some of the bigger works.

Precocious technical facility may have delayed the emergence of the truly original, personal vision; whatever the cause, it was not until the *Elegies*, in 1908, that it came. Scholars find the forties a late age for a composer to make his first original statements, but Bartók, for one, did not produce his truly personal works until almost the same age. These first original works constitute a short period of impressionist style—though differing in aim and essence from Debussy's impressionism—before the final creations of maturity. Thus, a rough division of Busoni's output would look something like this:

1. Works from childhood; mastery of counterpoint and classical forms (1873-1880)
2. Early large-scale works showing formal mastery, including the last manuscript sonatas (the f minor, dedicated to Anton Rubinstein, 1883; the *Variations on a Theme of Chopin*, 1884)
3. Early romantic mastery, including the first published works of miniatures and "character pieces" (*Una Festa di Villaggio*, 1882; *Marcia di paesani e contadine*, 1883)
4. Full romantic mastery, culminating in the *Piano Concerto Op. XXXIX* (1903)
5. The impressionist works (*Elegies, Nuit de Noël*, 1909)
6. A full synthesis of formal, expressive, and polyphonic styles (the *Sonatinas, Toccata, Doktor Faust*, 1910-1924)

Busoni's problem as a composer was that his fame as a pianist and transcriber overtook his merits as an original creator; he did not have the inclination of a Prokofiev to play his own music on tour, thus he was not an ardent self-advocate. His attitude toward music as an aristocratic art meant that *a priori* popular acclaim was impossible; even as a pianist he made his audiences feel inferior. Enough time has now lapsed since his death, at least for musicians to discover the truth about Busoni and debunk some of the popular legends:

1. That he was totally lacking in originality, and having played so much of the standard repertoire could do no more than regurgitate it. Anyone familiar with the piano works from the *Elegies* onward could not possibly make such a claim.
2. That he was a "simple kleptomaniac," and constantly had to use other people's music to write his own.[1] I would first refute the word *simple*; Busoni was anything but that. Kleptomania was, in some senses, part of his makeup, but not for the reasons popularly given (see the quotation from Sorabji in the comments relating to the *Sonatina super Carmen*). We are dealing here with a phenomenon of re-absorption and often total transformation of other music. It was part of Busoni's philosophy of composition, the belief that many solutions are possible to any given problem, or, in musical terms, that there are many ways of hearing basic musical materials. Incidentally, other prominent "kleptomaniacs" include Bach and Stravinsky.

3. That he was poverty ridden as a composer and therefore had to spend enormous energies in re-setting and re-using other composers' music. The sheer volume of original work from Busoni denies that allegation, such as the consistent outpouring of page after page of inventive writing in a massive score like *Die Brautwahl*.

4. It should be made clear, too, once and for all, that Busoni's attitude toward transcription, and indeed toward performance, was highly creative. This did not in any sense mean lack of reverence toward the original. On the contrary, he was that rarity among virtuosi: a true scholar. His edition of Bach was based on the *Urtext*, and he was one of the first nineteenth-century performers to use this source.

Part of Busoni's kleptomania was motivated by his belief in the past and the future as being strongly related in the cause of tradition. He tried to show, using the music of various composers as well as his own, how a work of art could be seen differently with the passage of time. A good illustration of this is his re-doing, after a number of years, some of his own compositions (see Chapter 5). Thus, the future could not suddenly spring into being, in a state of anarchy, and Busoni had harsh words to say about some of the "isms" of music in the first quarter of the twentieth century.

The re-working of his own pieces invariably took these directions:

1. The introduction of semitonal instability—the shifting of melodic lines by half-steps to create unexpected effects. An arresting case of this is in the "pure Bach" section of the *Fantasia Contrappuntistica*, where just such semitone changes are written into the "Bach" sections to soften the blow when the "Busoni" sections come along.

2. Moving the harmony bodily away from its original setting, up or down a semitone. The aim is the same as the melodic displacement: the creation of an out of focus or a bitonal effect. An early example of this appears in the *Concertstück*, and even the childhood pieces have moments involving major-minor vacillation.

3. The lightening of texture; this is normally a reaction away from the Germanic influences of Brahms in favor of a more Italian sound. Busoni was very fond of Verdi and constantly told his pupils to study Monteverdi.

4. The introduction of more staccato in line with Busoni's own style of playing in his later years.

5. The freeing of the form from conventional shackles and making it more organic. Two good examples of this are the re-workings of the *Variations* based on a Chopin prelude and the *Improvisation* for two pianos based on a Bach chorale (see Chapter 5). The second example, particularly, introduces the concept of form as a plastic, malleable thing.

The various versions of the *Fantasia Contrappuntistica* confirm Busoni's opinion that a work of art is constantly in progress and does not necessarily have to have a definitive form. The *Fantasia* is not just a work that grew

with each version; various alterations—melodic, harmonic, and formal—
appear in each version, cuts present in one are reinstated in another, and
thus the proportions of the piece within its general framework are always
altered. Each version is complete in itself, and yet also each version
complements the others (see Chapter 9).

These attempts to re-work early pieces all tend toward the introduction of
free-flowing polyphony; this, too, confirms the directions taken in the final
works where polyphony assumes ascendancy over harmony and free polyphony is preferred to strict imitative counterpoint, although Busoni never
relinquished the reins of a tightly controlled thematicism. In fact, prior to
Schönberg, Busoni was already postulating the future of melody as the
controller of all aspects of a work, including harmony. It is true that his
theoretical writings outstripped his compositions, but Busoni was by nature
both a prophet and a traditionalist; he would not embrace any innovation,
no matter how fascinating or how sound its theoretical basis. The writings,
even if not wholeheartedly adopted in practice, nevertheless do point to
certain directions in his work:

1. Polytonality: never strict (Busoni refused to adopt any theory strictly) but often
   appears in the later works;
2. New notations (See Chapter 18);
3. Exotic scales (*Turandot, Indian Diary*);
4. Freedom from bar lines (*Sonatina seconda*);
5. Modern use of accidentals—the obliteration of the use of naturals (also the
   Sonatina seconda);
6. In some of the *Elegies, Sonatinas,* and the *Toccata,* Busoni was working in areas
   very similar to those being explored in the second decade by Schönberg and his
   followers;
7. Interest in microtones and "electronic" music in the first decade of the century. As
   early as 1906, Busoni was most interested to read about a Dr. Thaddeus Cahill's
   Dynamophone, which was an electrical invention allowing the octave to be
   subdivided into any number of steps.[2] Since it was the tripartite tone that
   especially interested Busoni, he had a special harmonium constructed that
   produced such tones.[3] This particular instrument is mentioned by Harry Partch,[4]
   and Laurence Davies,[5] and was kept in the Berlin Hochschule für Musik. Petri
   mentioned having seen it there. A recent book on the history of electronic music
   devotes considerable space to Busoni as the sort of guru responsible for much of
   its history.[6]

Conjectures apart, Busoni's use of free polyphony, thematically controlled by constantly permutating cells together constituting a form of serial
"row," was ahead of the strict 12-tone development (the beginnings of
which he condemned); in that sense it is premonitory of a much more recent
phenomenon and more acceptable to the avant-garde of today as compared

to the progressive composers between the two World Wars.

It should also be said that Busoni finally rose above the normal criteria of what constitutes good taste, and a polyphony of styles is apparent in his music at times; such hybrid compositions run contrary to theory, yet they seem successful, particularly the ones involving transformations of Bach.[7]

In this way, the "normal," even the banal, the folktunes or quasi folktunes, all make their appearances in Busoni and are transfigured; as in Mahler, snatches of such "common" material appear in Busoni's pieces and are used in a nostalgic way (the *Piano Concerto, Nuit de Noël*).

Obviously, Busoni is a complex phenomenon, both as a composer and personality. Roman Vlad comes close to a precise definition of Busoni's aims when he says:

The music in which he fulfilled this aspiration, therefore, was intended to rise above purely emotional expression, not in order to arrive at a sterile "objectivity," but so as to acquire "that spiritual content which can regenerate music by excluding from it every trace of sentimentality" (to use a phrase of Hanslick's). In this connection there is a great significance in the term "represso," which, together with "visionario," "mistico" and "occulto," occurs so frequently in Busoni's music; since it is only in the silence created by the repression of emotion that one can hope to hear echoes from the deeper and more remote regions of the human spirit.[8]

John C. G. Waterhouse in an article titled "Busoni: Visionary or Pasticheur?" discusses this question at some length and comes to the conclusion that the visionary never completely ousted the pasticheur.[9] He quotes Wilfrid Mellers, who, in turn, had written ". . . he achieved spiritual integrity and grandeur only by some extent denying his physical being."[10] Waterhouse then makes the comment that "when Busoni wished to go beyond the boundaries of this limited expressive territory, he could only do so by making some kind of compromise with other composers' style."[11] And yet one of the most spiritual of all Busoni's works is the *Fantasia Contrappuntistica*, where the "compromise" with another composer's style is in truth a very deep commitment.

It seems to me that the explanation of the phenomenon may be relatively simple. If we regard Busoni's life as a mystical journey into the remoter regions of the human spirit, as a quest toward mystical serenity, the supposed dichotomy vanishes; the reason is that mystical states are only rarely achieved and are very difficult to sustain, so that the visionary, against his supremest will, is finally dragged back to earth, to his physical being, no matter with what vehemence and to what extent he denies this physical being. This makes the transitory mystical or occult state all the more poignant. There is no doubt that Busoni was interested in such topics: even the bare evidence of his music attests to it, from the earliest piano pieces that contain a sort of fascination with the supernatural, to the profound philosophy culminating in *Doktor Faust*. It should be obvious that such excursions into more distant dimensions are easier to sustain in a sonatina than in a full-length opera.[12] I would seriously question too, that Busoni would be disconcerted in any way by "compromises," "denials," or suggestions that contrary styles rubbed shoulders within his larger works; his criteria were different, and to follow him, we can only do so on his own terms.

NOTES

1. J. C. G. Waterhouse, "Busoni: Visionary or Pasticheur?" *Proceedings of the Royal Musical Association*, 92d session, 1965-1966.

2. Ferruccio Busoni, *Sketch of a New Esthetic of Music*, trans. Th. Baker (New York, G. Schirmer, 1911), p. 33.

3. Ferruccio Busoni, *The Essence of Music and Other Papers*, trans. Rosamond Ley (London, Rockliff, 1957), p. 29.

4. Harry Partch, *Genesis of a Music* (New York, Da Capo Press, 1974), pp. 429-31.

5. Laurence Davies, *Paths to Modern Music* (New York, Charles Scribner's Sons, 1971), p. 173.

6. Herbert Russcol, *The Liberation of Sound—An Introduction to Electronic Music* (Englewood Cliffs, N.J., Prentice-Hall, 1972).

7. Busoni's writings on various questions concerning the future of music, theoretical speculations, and assessments of other composers are invariably considered in general poetical-philosophical terms. He took for granted details of technique and regarded it as trivia not worth committing to print. "Isms" of any kind, particularly ones obsessed with a single method of composition, irked him anyway.

8. "Busoni's Destiny," *The Score* (December 1952), pp. 3-10.

9. Waterhouse, "Busoni: Visionary or Pasticheur?"

10. "The Problem of Busoni," *Music & Letters*, XVIII (1937), pp. 240-47.

11. Waterhouse, "Busoni: Visionary or Pasticheur?"

12. The idea of an opera being totally spiritual does not seem dramatically feasible at any rate.

18

Busoni's Theory of Notation for the Piano

> Busoni was the greatest figure—there is nobody like him.
>
> Artur Schnabel

As early as 1907, Busoni had already concerned himself with what he called the "tripartite" tone, and with the subsequent problems of notation which, admittedly, he called "subordinate." Nevertheless, after establishing the theoretical desirability of setting up "the usual semitonic series *thrice repeated* at the interval of one-third of a tone," Busoni suggests:

Merely for the sake of distinction, let us call the first tone C, and the next third-tones C sharp, and D flat; the first semitone (small) c, and its following thirds c sharp and d flat; the result is fully explained by the table below, (in Figure 18.1).

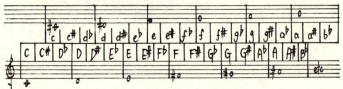

Figure 18.1

A preliminary expedient for notation might be, to draw six lines for the staff, using the lines for the whole tones and its space for the semitones, [see Figure 18.2] then indicating the third-tones by sharps and flats. . . .[1] [See Figure 18.3].

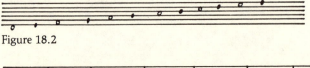

Figure 18.2

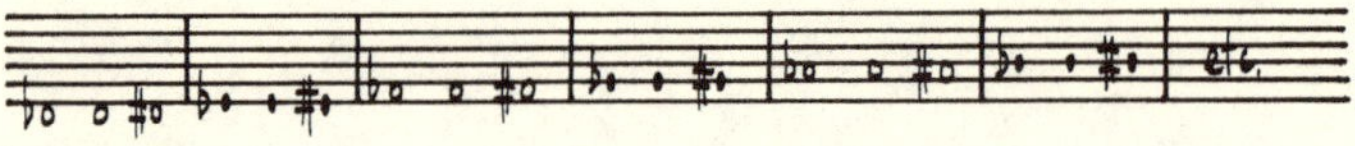

Figure 18.3

What is important here is the idea of notating the octave so that every other octave from C to C, anywhere in our musical range, would look alike. This is the probable germ of Busoni's full-length essay that followed two years later.

VERSUCH EINER ORGANISCHEN KLAVIER-NOTEN-SCHRIFT PRAKTISCH ERPROBT AN JOH. SEB. BACHS CHROMATISCHER PHANTASIE IN D MOLL VON FERRUCCIO BUSONI. Leipzig Breitkopf & Haertel 1909 No. 26 449 Also as *Versuch einer organischen Klavier-Noten-Schrift* in Vol. 7 of the Bach-Busoni edition 1920

Perhaps the single largest obstacle to the performance of much modern piano music is the difficulty of the initial reading and the subsequent necessary hours of familiarization before any semblance to the finished article shows itself. This difficulty was already apparent to Busoni in music of Schönberg and Strauss; it has since been aggravated further. The actual difficulty of reading is due to two factors: first, the profusion of sharps, flats, and naturals and second, the fact that our system of notation is not "symmetrical."[2]

The further problem of rhythm had not yet manifested itself in Busoni's day.

To return to the problem of symmetry, Busoni gives a graphic illustration of the problem. (See Figure 18.4.)[3] Bass C stands on the second ledger line;

Figure 18.4. By kind permission, Breitkopf & Haertel, Wiesbaden.

the next C on the second space and the following two Cs are one and the same note; then follows another C in the third space, and finally the last C on the second ledger line above. And yet the keyboard of the piano is a symmetrical arrangement, whereby each octave is an exact repetition of the others, consisting of 12 clearly defined intervals. Therefore, if a system of notation was developed that was truly symmetrical and followed the contours of the keyboard, we might arrive at something like Figure 18.5.[4]

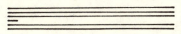

Figure 18.5. By kind permission, Breitkopf & Haertel, Wiesbaden.

The five lines represent the five black notes of each octave. The gap between the second and third lines represent the "missing" black note between E and F. Now, the spaces between the lines would represent the seven white keys. E would rest on the second line, F under the third line. For extra clarity, the white notes would be left "empty," the black notes "filled in." A chromatic

scale would then appear as in Figure 18.6 (C to C in any octave).[5] The
identification of the octaves could be easily accomplished. (See Figure
18.7.)[6] And so an arpeggio figure, which is in fact symmetrical but in our

Figure 18.6. By kind permission, Breitkopf & Haertel, Wiesbaden.

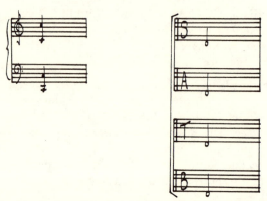

Figure 18.7. By kind permission, Breitkopf & Haertel, Wiesbaden.

traditional notation does not appear to be so, assumes in the new notation
an exact graphic representation. (See Figure 18.8.)[7] A complex chromatic
figure is illustrated in Figure 18.9.[8] Whole tone runs are particularly clear.
(See Figure 18.10.)[9]

Figure 18.8. By kind permission, Breitkopf & Haertel, Wiesbaden.

Figure 18.9. By kind permission, Breitkopf & Haertel, Wiesbaden.

Figure 18.10. By kind permission, Breitkopf & Haertel, Wiesbaden.

There remains a slight complication: in the new notation

⌀ and ⌁   are both crotchets

♪ and ♭   are both quavers

Busoni had to devise new notations, therefore, for minims and semibreves. This was very simply done by recourse to the old square notes:

⊡ and ▪   are now minims

⊓ and ▪   are now semibreves.

The new system does not preclude the use of ledgerlines. (See Figure 18.11.)[10] Also, the old notation of 8va and 16va may still be used. Finally, it is not necessary to reproduce the full SATB signature for every line, only the registers in use.

Figure 18.11. By kind permission, Breitkopf & Haertel, Wiesbaden.

After this exposition of the new system, Busoni wrote out, most appropriately, the *Chromatic Fantasia* of J. S. Bach.[11] The beginning and ending are quoted in Figures 18.12[12] and 18.13.[13]

Figure 18.12. By kind permission, Breitkopf & Haertel, Wiesbaden.

Figure 18.13. By kind permission, Breitkopf & Haertel, Wiesbaden.

Ingenious as the new system may be, it is probably no more ingenious than many other new methods of notation suggested over the years. None of them has been adopted because it is not a commercial proposition for publishers to do so, and the unanimous use of one new system all over the world is probably an impossibility in any case. Furthermore, there is the problem of reprinting all old music.

The value of Busoni's notation is that, with compromise, it can be adopted into our conventional system. I have explored this possibility in "Ferruccio Busoni's 'Attempt at an Organic Notation for the Pianoforte,' and a Practical Adaptation of It" (*Music Review*, vol. 29, no. 1, February 1968).

NOTES

1. Ferruccio Busoni, *Sketch of a New Esthetic of Music*, trans. Th. Baker (New York, G. Schirmer, 1911), p. 32.

2. Of the two factors, there have been several attempts to simplify the first: (1) abolishing key signatures, which in heavily chromatic music were more of a hindrance than a help, often resulting in unnecessary use of naturals, double sharps, and double flats and (2) abolishing naturals, the accidental applying only to the note which follows it, and never again. (Busoni does this himself in the *Sonatina seconda*.)

3. *Versuch einer organischen Klavier-Noten-Schrift*, p. 1.

4. Ibid., p. 2.

5. Ibid., p. 3.

6. Ibid., p. 4.

7. Ibid.

8. Ibid.

9. Ibid., p. 5.

10. Ibid., p. 6.

11. The *Busoni-Nachlass* SB 245 also contains examples of the new notation from other works: J. S. Bach Inventions in C major and c minor; Chopin Etudes Op. 10 No. 2, Op. 10 No. 5, Op. 25 No. 1, and Op. 25 No. 2.

12. *Versuch einer organischen Klavier-Noten-Schrift*, p. 9.

13. Ibid., p. 15.

19

Busoni's Recorded Legacy

> Busoni commanded a wider range of tone than any living pianist, although his preference for cold, unemotional shades might have caused some to doubt it. . . . It led him to a quality of tone which can only be called "white," a quality that was cold and almost inanimate. From this perfectly even basis he would start and build up a climax that reached the extreme limit of what was possible to a pianist, an avalanche of sound giving the impression of a red flame rising out of marble. His intellectual control was remorseless.
>
> Ferruccio Bonavia

It is our misfortune that Busoni lived before the days of the modern recording. Of his playing there is now only a legend, and it is on his reputation as a composer that he will have to survive or perish. The situation is analogous with that of Liszt, who was for years not taken seriously as a composer simply because he was such a magnificent pianist. Bernard Shaw, upon meeting Busoni, suggested to him that he should change his name because the public would never accept a man who could do two things well. Shaw's cynicism must have been based on hard fact, since this public suspicion of ambidexterity recurs in the case of pianist-composers over and over again.

Nevertheless, although the image of Busoni the pianist is now more and more a dim memory, there is a small recorded heritage left to us, on the early acoustic Columbias:

RECORDINGS FOR COLUMBIA MADE BY BUSONI IN ENGLAND

Prelude & Fugue No. 1 (Bach) L 1445
Etude Op. 25 No. 5 (Chopin)

* * *

Chorale Prelude (Nun freut euch liebe Christen) (Bach/Busoni) L 1470
Ecossaisen (Beethoven)
Prelude Op. 28 No. 7 & Etude Op. 10 No. 5 (connected by an improvisatory-modulatory passage)

* * *

Etude Op. 10 No. 5 (Chopin) L 1432
Nocturne Op. 15 No. 2 (Chopin)

* * *

Hungarian Rhapsody No. 13 (Liszt) L 1456 (this has cuts in it)

Kaikhosru Sorabji estimated these records to be the best piano recordings ever made and predicted that they would be a model for years to come but then this was before the days of our modern LP with its super-refined techniques of recording and editing. It is true that compared to many other piano records of the time, the Busoni renditions are startlingly clear, free of the typical woofy, overpedalled sound of the acoustically (and early electrically) recorded piano.

Busoni had offered Columbia the rights to record the complete *48 Preludes and Fugues*, but this was rejected; in those days it would have been a commercial risk; unfortunately, therefore, his individualistic approach to Bach is not preserved. The Liszt *Rhapsody* has some cuts in it due to the problem of fitting the piece on two sides of a 78. The solution to the fingering of the repeated notes is a typical exercise of Busonian pianism (given to me by Petri). (See Figure 19.1.) There is an interesting improvised

Figure 19.1

bridge passage between the Chopin *Prelude* and the *Etude*, a relic of the more liberal approach to pianism of the nineteenth century as compared with our stricter adherence to the printed page. Even in the Beethoven *Ecossaisen*, Busoni does not follow his own edition but adds a few cadential chords at the very end.

As far as I have been able to ascertain, the original matrices of these recordings are now lost, destroyed in a fire that swept through the English Columbia factory in the 1920s; it is possible, however, that using some existing set or sets of these recordings, a transfer could be made to LP, with crackles and scratches carefully edited out, leaving a reasonably static-free and surface-noise-free rendition.[1]

There is among collectors of early recordings speculation about a recording of the Liszt *Faust Waltz*. In a letter to his wife, dated 20 November 1919, Busoni writes:

. . . my suffering over the toil of making gramophone records came to an end yesterday, after playing for 3½ hours! I feel rather battered to-day, but it is over. Since the first day, I have been as depressed as if I were expecting to have an operation. To do it is stupid and a strain. Here is an example of what happens. They wanted the Faust waltz (which lasts a good ten minutes) *but it was only to take four minutes!* That meant quickly cutting, patching and improvising, so that there should still be some sense left in it; watching the pedal (because it sounds bad); thinking of certain notes which had to be stronger or weaker in order to please this devillish machine: not letting oneself go for fear of inaccuracies and being conscious the whole time that every note was going to be there for eternity; how can there be any question of inspiration, freedom, swing, or poetry? Enough that yesterday for 9 pieces of 4 minutes each (half an hour in all) I worked for three and a half hours! Two of these pieces I played four or five times. Having to think so quickly at the same time was a severe effort. In the end, I felt the effects in my arms; after that, I had to sit for a photograph, and sign the discs.—At last it was finished![2]

It would have been fascinating to hear what Busoni did with his "instant" editing: Did he include his own cadenza at the expense of some Liszt passages?[3]

Collectors have even speculated that this performance now lies safely in the library of the Maharajah of Mysore, together with many other items recorded by Busoni unknown to the outside world. But this is wishful thinking and sensationalism rolled into one. My research in this direction has so far proved entirely fruitless.

So much for the actual gramophone records. There remains the controversial question of the piano rolls. Present day pianists are often disappointed and skeptical about roll performances they hear. Many professional pianists stubbornly maintain that the standard of piano playing in those days was not as high as today, and I cannot really blame them for such an opinion, based on the majority of player piano performances one hears, either on old reproducing mechanisms or cheaply produced commercial recordings. Too often the range of dynamics is limited, there is a rather clumsy effect in phrasing and legato passages, and bad balance between melodic and accompanying elements. The reproducing mechanism frequently wheezes and grinds away and this too adds to the illusion of a "mechanical" reproduction.[4]

It is a little puzzling to compare this prevalent attitude among the present day generation of pianists with the testimonials of the recording artists early in this century.

Debussy, Paderewski, de Pachmann, Gabrilowitsch, and many, many others all wrote testimonials in glowing terms. Rachmaninoff preferred this method of recording to the gramophone for many years. Busoni wrote rather more coolly (10 June 1905): 'The Welte, so to say a cinematograph of piano playing, is an invention of quite equal importance, as surprising for mere amateurs, as it is wonderful for the skilled musicians. It will be of great use for artists, and through them, let us hope, afford great pleasure to the general public!"[5] And again, in a letter to his wife on 31 May 1908:

When I got out at the so-called *Berlin* station at Leipzig, I went straight to the Phonola. . . . Then, by the time I had played the programme for the settled fee, played an encore, written out a testimonial, signed two photographs, listened to Godowsky and myself in the machine, and also sat for a photograph "at the Phonola" it was 4.30, round about six hours since I had left the Anhalter Bahnhof.

This, combined with the "oppressive" weather, produced headache. The testimonial that I was asked to sign was already typed and read as follows: "I regard the 'DEA' as the crown of creation." I said nobody would believe it, and, of course, wrote one of my own. . . .[6]

However, this is not typical of the pianists' reactions. Concerts were held at which live playing and rolls were combined and intermixed by pianists like Cortot and Moiseiwitsch—both pianos hidden behind a screen—and responsible critics such as Ernest Newman confessed themselves unable to establish where the man stopped and the machine took over.

In the early days of the Welte rolls, one could understand a slightly overenthusiastic tendency among listeners—after all, this was really the first method to preserve performances. The pianists themselves must have been nonplussed to hear even a rough semblance of their own playing. It is no wonder that during the era of the early gramophone the rolls were preferred to the tinny scratchy sound of the acoustic and early electric recording. The doom of the reproducing piano was spelled out by the advent of a more modern recording technique.

When some of the earlier transfers of rolls onto LP appeared, I brought these to Petri to listen to; he was horrified and said that it was a travesty of Busoni's playing. One of the first things that always struck Petri, hearing Busoni, was the absolute clarity with which the melody stood out from the surrounding web of accompaniment and filigree. This characteristic is not always obvious even in more recent LP roll recordings. Is one to assume that the reproducing machine was wrongly adjusted or that the original recording was not capable of subtleties of balance? There is on the one hand the story that Gerda, Busoni's widow, hearing a piano roll of his playing after his death, was moved to tears and rushed from the room crying, "Ferruccio, Ferruccio!" On the other hand, even roll collectors and enthusiasts have repeatedly warned me in my search for Busoni rolls that what I will hear will not be Busoni but simply someone's idea of what Busoni should sound like.[7] The variable factors of the reproducing machines are subject to a wide variety of adjustments that may affect the final performance.

My ultimate view of this whole question is that:

1. Rolls are valuable at least as a guide to the way these giants of the past played. If the roll moves without slipping, then at least we have a record of the speed and rubato of the playing.

2. At best, the other more subtle factors are partially or almost wholly reproduced.

3. There is no doubt that different adjustments by different people create different resultant performances; therefore, the claim that these rolls are fully comparable to the modern recording must be taken with a large grain of salt.

4. With infinite care, with resources of first-class grand pianos and unlimited time to work on the machines and perfect the replay, startling results may be, but very rarely are, obtained.

LIST OF ROLL RECORDINGS MADE BY BUSONI

WELTE-MIGNON

La Campanella (Paganini-Liszt) 444

Prelude Op. 28 No. 15 (Chopin) 1319

Fantasy on Ruins of Athens (Liszt-Beethoven) 1322

Valse Caprice No. 3, A Major (Liszt) (from Donizetti's Lucia et Paresina) 442

Rigoletto Paraphrase (Verdi-Liszt) 445

Polonaise in E Major (Liszt) 1320

Don Juan Fantasie (Mozart-Liszt) 1323

Nocturne Op. 15 No. 2, F Sharp Major (Chopin) 441

Polonaise Op. 53 (Chopin) 440

Choral Prelude "Non freut . . ." (Bach-Busoni) 439

Adelaide (Beethoven-Liszt) 443

Hungarian March (Schubert-Liszt) 446

Fantasie on Norma (Liszt) 1321

DUO-ART

La Campanella (Paganini-Liszt) 5698

Feux-Follets (Liszt) 5686

Polonaise in E Major (Liszt) 5675 (different version from Welte, as is also *La Campanella*)

Chaconne (Bach-Busoni) 6928

Etude: La Chasse (Paganini-Liszt) 5671

Preludes Nos. 1, 2 (Chopin) 6669 English No. 024

Subsequent preludes only on English rolls:
Nos. 4, 5, 6 014
Nos. 9, 10, 11 017
No. 3 023
Nos. 7, 8 027
Nos. 12, 13 031

Nos. 14, 15   033
No. 16   035
Nos. 17, 18   036
Nos. 19, 20   037
Nos. 21, 22   038
No. 23   039
No. 24   040
Nos. 23, 24   0249
Nos. 23, 24   (combined on Scandinavian Duo-Art, W 506)

AMPICO

These are taken or adapted from rolls made originally for Ludwig Hupfeld in Leipzig.

Soirées Musicales No. 10, La Serenata   (Rossini-Liszt)   62633-H
Rigoletto Paraphrase   (Verdi-Liszt)   50676-H[8]
Ballade in g minor   (Chopin)   50047-H
Gnomenreigen   (Liszt)   51364-H

HUPFELD

TRIPHONOLA

Ballade No. 1   (Chopin)   50081
Adelaide   (Beethoven-Liszt)   51214
Etude Op. 25 No. 3   (Chopin)   51352
Hungarian March   (Schubert-Liszt)   51413
St. Francis Walking on the Waves   (Liszt)   51885
Etudes   (Paganini-Liszt)   No. 1   52174   No. 3   53797   No. 6   52175
Prelude No. 24   (Chopin)   55790
Preludes   (Chopin)   4, 5, 6, 7, 8, 9,   51591   11, 12, 14, 17, 18, 21,   51592
Rigoletto Paraphrase   (Liszt)   50265
Soirées No. 10   (Rossini-Liszt)   50608
Toccata Intermezzo & Fugue in C Major   (Bach-Busoni)   52379
Variations on a Theme of Paganini, 1-14   (Brahms)   53502

PHONOLA

Etude Op. 25 No. 5   (Chopin)   12357

ARTISTS' ROLLS

Nocturne Op. 62   (Chopin)   unnumbered
Soirées No. 6   (Rossini/Liszt)   unnumbered

ARTECHO

Nocturne Op. 15, No. 2 (Chopin) R-2021
La Campanella (Paganini-Liszt)   R-3103
Polonaise Op. 53 (Chopin)   R-3045

DUCA[9]

Orgel-Toccata   C Major   Adagio   (Bach)   1149
Chromatische Fantasie   Part I   (Bach)   1151
Chromatische Fantasie   Part II   (Bach)   1152
Choral-Vorspiel: "Nun freut euch, lieben Christen"   (Bach)   1150
Ecossaisen   (Beethoven)   1148
Sonate Op. 111   Part I   (Beethoven)   1145
Sonate Op. 111   Part II   (Beethoven)   1146
32 Variationen   (Beethoven)   1147
Ballade Op. 52   (Chopin)   1144
Abendmusik Op. 59 No. 1, 3, 61   (Jensen)   1158
Hochzeitsmusik Op. 45 No. 1: Festzug No. 2: Brautgesang   (Jensen)   1156
Hochzeitsmusik Op. 45 No. 32 Reigen   (Jensen)   1157
Années de Pelerinage 2me Année No. 1: Sposalizio   (Liszt)   1142
Paganini-Etude No. 2   (Liszt)   1137
Paganini-Etude No. 3   (La Campanella)   (Liszt)   1138
Paganini-Etude No. 5 (Liszt)   1139
Paganini-Etude No. 6   (Liszt)   1140
Rhapsodie hongroise No. 13   (Liszt)   1141
La Serenata Op. 8 No. 1   (Rossini)   1143
Divertissement à la hongroise Op. 54   Marcia und Allegretto   (Schubert)
    1159
Marche caractéristique, Op. 121   (Schubert)   1160
Bilder aus Osten Op. 66 No. 1   (Schumann)   1153
Bilder aus Osten Op. 66 No. 4   (Schumann)   1154
Bilder aus Osten Op. 66 No. 5   (Schumann)   1155

NOTES

1. This has already been done with many old recordings: the original disc is first recorded onto a very fast moving tape. The tape is then played very slowly, and the clicks and static are edited out without aurally affecting the musical sound since the interruptions are so small to the continuity as to be inaudible at normal playing speed. More sophisticated computerized processes are now also available.

2. Busoni, *Letters to His Wife*, p. 287.

3. We now know that Busoni recorded a number of unreleased items for Columbia on 18-19 November 1919. They were: Mozart, Andantino from the Concerto K. 271; Gounod-Liszt, Valse de l'opera Faust; Liszt, Sonnetto 123 del Petrarca; Liszt, Valse oubliée; Liszt, La Chasse, from the Paganini Etudes; and Weber, Finale from the Sonata No. 1, Op. 24. (Christopher Dyment, "Ferruccio Busoni, His Phonograph Recordings," *Association for Recorded Sound Collections Journal*, 10, nos. 2-3 (1979), pp. 185-87. All relevant matrix numbers are included in

---

*All these pieces are for four hands. Busoni performed them with Michael von Zadora.

this article. The matrices of all Busoni records, published and unpublished, were destroyed in the 1920s.)

4. LPs released by Argo in collaboration with the BBC of the performances of some Ampico rolls demonstrate that at least these rolls can be brilliantly recorded with no concession whatsoever to the quality of either playing or recording. It is to be hoped that the Busoni Ampico performances may be given this royal treatment, although of course these rolls are really Hupfeld recordings (Triphonola, Phonola, Animatic, and/or DEA, were all various trade names for the Ludwig Hupfeld rolls, recorded in Leipzig). Hupfeld published an interesting and varied catalogue, but the rolls proved rather elusive and in all my searches I have been able to locate only few Hupfeld machines that play. But I am sure that this is merely a question of time: basically the Hupfeld rolls must be satisfactory, as some of the Ampico rolls—notably the Busoni ones—were originally recorded by Ludwig Hupfeld, reprocessed for Ampico, and therefore not as sensitive as the real Ampico recordings, which were a later development. Only one other current commercial release measures up to these Ampico performances. This is a scheme to record the Welte rolls by an American company—Recorded Treasures, featuring Busoni, among others. Given the fact that the Welte mechanism is the earliest and most primitive of the systems, the sound is on the whole quite good. In the rendition of the *Rigoletto Paraphrase*, however, there is a missing pedal near the end, and the dynamic range of the Busoni recording is, on the whole, rather limited.

5. Various catalogues of the Welte-Mignon rolls, published by the Welte company in Freiburg, Germany (August 1912).

6. Welte-Mignon rolls issued by the Deluxe Reproducing Roll Corp., U.S.A., 1927, p. 18.

7. *The International Piano Library Bulletin*, vol. 2, no. 1 (May 1968), pp. 13-14, reprints a letter from Harold Bauer dated 16 June 1922. In it he speaks of a visit to London: "I heard several rolls played when I was there two weeks ago, and found most of them good, with the exception of the Busoni records, which are all poor. The principal reason for this, however, is, I believe, that he made no corrections whatever himself, and as his recordings are liable to certain eccentricities, it has simply happened that the person who tried to reproduce his special characteristics from memory, failed."

8. A rather poor rendition when compared with other versions by Busoni.

9. My friend and roll specialist, Denis Condon, informed me that he had discovered, in first class order, 150 rolls under this label in a private collection. Some Busoni rolls were among these. Unfortunately, there was no machine to play them, and we have no way of assessing the worth of this discovery. Few collectors whom I have approached know anything about this label. Yet its production in Germany in the 1920s must have had some significance—by then the reproducing piano industry was well developed, and Busoni would not have recorded for an unknown inferior company. Yet another mystery and difficulty to be solved in connection with piano rolls. Research into this make of piano rolls is presently being conducted at the Musikwissenschaftliches Institut Der Johann Wolfgang Goethe-Universität in Frankfurt.

Appendix

We are not so rich in musical genius that we can afford to disregard totally the life work of so great and exceptional an artist as Ferruccio Busoni.

Hugo Leichtentritt

The following are, at the time of writing, previously unpublished. It was my original intention to publish both the *Notturni-'Prologo'* and the *Cadenza for Mozart's Two-Piano Sonata* complete in this Appendix. However, permission to do so was denied by the Deutsche Staatsbibliothek in East Berlin. I therefore present the opening bars only.

1.   Cadenzas to the Mozart d minor piano concerto

2. New ending to "All' Italia!"

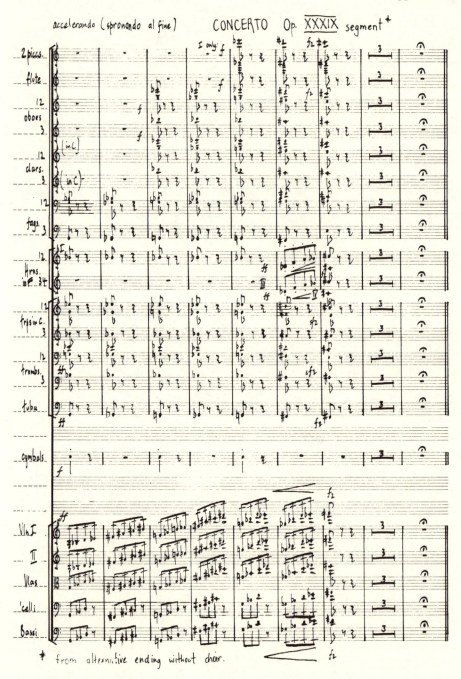

3. Segment from Piano Concerto Op. XXXIX. By kind permission, Deutsche Staatsbibliothek, Berlin.

4. "Notturni-'Prologo.'" By kind permission, Deutsche Staatsbibliothek, Berlin.

5. Cadenza to the Mozart 2-piano sonata. By kind permission, Deutsche Staatsbibliothek, Berlin.

DISCOGRAPHY OF RECORDINGS BY EGON PETRI AND OTHER PIANISTS

It may be pointed out that in a book on Busoni, it seems both unnecessary and irrelevant to include a complete listing of recordings made by Egon Petri. But in Petri we have a direct musical link with Busoni; he was his friend, pupil, and disciple for about 30 years. His interpretations of Busoni works must be regarded as authentic, and since Busoni did not record his own music, and then only a few rolls of his transcriptions, the Petri legacy is the only one we have that is on a large scale in direct tradition and in a similar style of approach to the keyboard that Busoni himself had. Some other pianists from the Busoni circle also left recordings, and I list them below; but none of these ever achieved international renown as virtuoso players.

Although there were musicians who claimed that Petri playing behind a screen could not be distinguished from Busoni, I doubt whether this is true. Petri, although confessing that "sometimes I do not know what is Busoni and what is Petri," also pointed out that Busoni's approach to the piano and his whole way of playing was unique and personal and could not be copied even if one desired to. Apart from all this, Petri was always underlining the fact that only the general concepts came from Busoni, the details were his own. Anyway, Busoni never really gave lessons, he did not have the temperament of a teacher. When Petri played music by other composers, therefore, what we have is not a copy of a Busoni performance (Petri was too great a pianist and musician for this to happen) but an overall similarity to what was a Busoni performance—the big approach, the massive effects, the sheer electricity of the playing, the complete authority and conviction.

I have not included any recordings of Busoni's music by pupils of Petri or other contemporary pianists. Such a list would be out of date as soon as it was written. The interested reader can easily discover such recordings by consulting any record catalogue.

ROLLS MADE BY EGON PETRI FOR WELTE-MIGNON

Paganini Etude No. 5 (Liszt) 514
Chapelle de Guillaume Tell (*Années de Pelerinage,I, No. 1*) (Liszt) 515
Mal du Pays (*Années de Pelerinage, I, No. 8*) (Liszt) 516
Canzonetta del Salvator Rosa (*Années de Pelerinage, II, No. 3*) (Liszt) 517
Les Jeux d'Eaux de la Villa d'Este (*Années de Pelerinage, III, No. 4*) (Liszt) 518
Capriccio a la Soldatesca, Op. 50 No. 1 (Alkan) 519
Ancient Melody of the Synagogue, Op. 31 (Alkan) 520
Melody in d minor (Gluck-Sgambati) 522
Abegg Variations, Op. 1 (Schumann) 525
Rondo in a minor (Mozart) 526
Thirty-two Variations in c minor (Beethoven) 527

ROLLS MADE BY EGON PETRI FOR HUPFELD

Andante & Variations (Schubert/Tausig) 53185
Years of Pilgrimage (3rd Year) *Nos. 1, 2* (Liszt) 53180 *5, 6,* (Liszt) 53181
   7 (Liszt) 53182
Ballade Op. 10 No. 3 (Brahms) 53183
Ballade Op. 10 No. 4 (Brahms) 53184
Caprices Valses No. 3 (Melancolique) (Liszt) 53186
Etude de Concert Op. 2 No. 7 (Henselt) 53192 *No. 10* (Henselt) 53191
Etude Op. 25 No. 4 (Chopin) 53190
Die Forelle (Schubert-Liszt) 53193
Liebesbotschaft (Schubert-Liszt) 53197
Paganini Etude No. 4 (Liszt) 53189
"Penitence" (Beethoven-Liszt) 53188

RECORDINGS MADE BY EGON PETRI FOR COLUMBIA

Carmen Fantasie (Bizet-Busoni) LX 462
Soirée de Vienne (Schubert-Liszt) LX 469
Mazeppa (Liszt) LX 483
Sonata Op. 111 (Beethoven) LX 491-3 (M263)
Orphee-Melodie (Gluck-Sgambati) LX 508
Three Menuets (Bach-Petri) LX 508
Faust Waltz (Gounod-Liszt) LX 520
Sonata Op. 90 (Beethoven) LX 544-5 (CX 71)
Sonata Op. 78 (Beethoven) LX 576
Sonata ("Moonlight") Op. 27 No. 2 (Beethoven) LX 602-3 (CX 77)
Concert Study in D flat Major (Liszt) LX 602-3 (CX 77)
Indian Diary (Busoni) LX 617
Variations on a Theme of Paganini (Brahms) LX 628-9
Fantasia nach J. S. Bach (Busoni) LX 640
Andante & Variations in b minor (Schubert-Tausig) LX 714
Variations and Fugue on a Theme of Handel (Brahms) LX 734-6
Albumblatt No. 3 (In der Art eines Choralvorspiels) (Busoni) LX 792
All' Italia! (from *Elegies*) (Busoni) LX 792
Sonatina ad usum infantis (Busoni) LX 806
Don Giovanni Serenade (Mozart-Busoni) LX 806
Ricordanza (Liszt) LX 846
Rigoletto Paraphrase (Verdi-Liszt) LB 39
Concerto in B flat minor (Tchaikovsky) with London Philharmonic Walter
   Goehr LX 681-4
Concerto No. 2 in A Major (Liszt) with London Philharmonic Leslie Heward
   LX 737-9
Gretchen am Spinnrade (Schubert-Liszt) LX 737-9
Fantasia on "Ruins of Athens" (Beethoven-Liszt) with London Philharmonic
   Leslie Heward LX 752-3
Der Lindenbaum (Schubert-Liszt) LX 752-3
Sonata No. 3 for Violin & Piano (Brahms) with Szigeti LX 699-701
Hammerclavier Sonata Op. 106 (Beethoven) ML 4479

Sonata Op. 10 No. 2 (Beethoven) ML 2049
Chaconne (Bach-Busoni) ML 2049
Preludes Op. 28 (Chopin) M 523
Polonaise Op. 53 (Chopin) Am. Col. 17377D
Prelude Chorale & Fugue (Franck) CX 176
E flat Rhapsody Op. 119 No. 4 (Brahms) & Rhapsodies Op. 79 CX 183
Viola Sonata (Brahms) with Lifschey M 487
Chorale Prelude "In dir ist freude; Ich ruf' dir; Nun freut euch; Wachet auf" (Bach-Busoni) 71463D
Adelaide (Beethoven-Liszt) Am. Col. 72163D
Rapsodie Espagnole (Liszt-Busoni) Mitropoulos Minneapolis Symphony Orchestra LX 891-2

RECORDINGS MADE BY EGON PETRI FOR H.M.V.

Die Forelle (Schubert-Liszt) GB 3508
Auf dem Wasser (Schubert-Liszt) EG 1579
Waltz Op. 42 in A flat Major (Chopin) GB 3791
Paganini Etude No. 5 "La Chasse" (Liszt) EG 1577
Gnomenreigen (Liszt) GB 3718
Liebesbotschaft (Schubert-Liszt) EG 1787

Some of the Columbia and HMV performances have been and are being re-issued on LP records.

LP RECORDINGS MADE BY EGON PETRI FOR WESTMINISTER

Toccata & Fugue in d minor (Bach-Busoni) XWN 18910
Toccata Adagio & Fugue in C Major (Bach-Busoni) XWN 18910
Prelude & Fugue in D Major (Bach-Busoni) XWN 18910
Prelude & Fugue in E flat Major (*St. Anne*) (Bach-Busoni) XWN 18910
Sonatas: "Moonlight," "Pathetique," "Appassionata" (Beethoven) XWN 18255
Fantasia Contrappuntistica (Busoni) XWN 18844
Christians Rejoice (Bach-Busoni) XWN 18844
I Call to Thee (Bach-Busoni) XWN 18844
In Thee Is Joy (Bach-Busoni) XWN 18844
Sleepers Awake (Bach-Busoni) XWN 18844
Sheep May Safely Graze (Bach-Petri) XWN 18844
Minuet (Bach-Petri) XWN 18844
I Step before Thy Throne, O Lord (Bach-Petri) XWN 18844
Now We Thank Thee (Buxtehude-Petri) XWN 18844
Midsummer Night's Dream—Wedding March and Dance of the Elves (Mendelssohn-Liszt) XWN 18968
Faust Waltz (Gounod-Liszt, with Busoni cadenza) XWN 18968
Adelaide (Beethoven-Liszt) XWN 18968
Mephisto Waltz (Liszt-Busoni) XWN 18968
Fantasie on Two Motives from Figaro (Mozart-Liszt-Busoni) XWN 18968
Hammerclavier Sonata (Beethoven) XWN 18747

LP RECORDINGS MADE BY EGON PETRI FOR ALLEGRO ROYALE (ALLEGRO ELITE, PACIFIC ALLEGRO ELITE)

Four Ballades Op. 10 (Brahms) 1630
Three Intermezzi Op. 117 (Brahms) 1630
Two Rhapsodies Op. 79 (Brahms) 1630
Hungarian Rhapsody No. 12 (Liszt) 1618
Spinning Song (Wagner, from the *Flying Dutchman*) (Liszt) 1618
Jeux d' Eau (Liszt) 1618
Ricordanza (Liszt) 1618
Petrarch Sonnets Nos. 1, 2, and 3 (Liszt) 1618
The Trout, Barcarolle, Margaret at the Spinning Wheel, The Linden Tree, The Erl-King, Love's Message, and *Soirée de Vienne* (Schubert-Liszt) C. 4436
Andante & Variations (Schubert-Tausig) C. 4436
Sonatas Op. 109 and 110 (Beethoven) LDA/D 150.5 *Pacific Allegro Elite*

LP RECORDING ISSUED POSTHUMOUSLY BY VERITAS (IN CONJUNCTION WITH THE INTERNATIONAL PIANO LIBRARY)

Fantasy Pieces Op. 12 (Schumann) VM 116
Venezia e Napoli (Liszt) VM 116
Perpetuum Mobile (Busoni) VM 116
All' Italia! (Busoni) VM 116

Various other concert performances by Egon Petri have been and are being issued on commercial LPs.

MISCELLANEOUS RECORDINGS MADE BY EGON PETRI

In the course of my research into recordings, the undermentioned curiosity was discovered. I immediately tried to trace these acetates in the hope that these historic performances would not be lost. However, it is most unlikely that these recordings exist any more. During the war, many such acetates were stored in air-raid shelters. Some of them are still there at this writing, unclassified, and probably gradually deteriorating. It is sad to contemplate what other treasures are being lost to posterity unless something can be done very soon.

FOR FRANKFURT-AM MAIN RADIO ORCHESTRA, CONDUCTED BY HANS ROSBAUD; MADE FOR GERMAN RADIO

Concerto Op. XXXIX (Busoni) 2 June 1932 ref. Frankfurt 2537 479-81 4th movement only 23 November 1936 ref. Frankfurt 6057 32627-46 Complete work
Totentanz (Liszt-Busoni) 23 November 1936 ref. Frankfurt 6478 32622-6
[Note that Petri recorded both works on the same day.]

SOME RECORDINGS OF BUSONI'S PIANO MUSIC BY VARIOUS PIANISTS WHO HAD SOME CONNECTIONS WITH HIM

Eduard Steuermann: *Elegies, Toccata, Sonatinas Nos. 1 and 6* (Contemporary M 6501)

José Vianna da Motta: *Elegy No. 4* (Pathé X5451) *Duettino Concertante after Mozart* (with Castello Lopes)   (Pathé X5453)
Michael von Zadora: *Sonatina No. 3* (Friends of Recorded Music 23)   *Sonatina No. 6* (Deutsche Grammophon 27171)   *Sarabande con Partite* BWV 990 (Bach-Busoni) (Deutsche Grammophon 27046)   *Sonatina No. 5* (1917) (Friends of Recorded Music 24)
Edward Weiss: *Indian Diary* (Circle Records L-51-104)

There is also a recording by Edwin Fischer of the Bach *Concerto* in d minor, with Fischer's own orchestra, conducted from the keyboard. (HMV DB4420-2; COLH 15) This has some elements of the Busoni version, but not all.

Fischer has also recorded the Bach-Busoni *Prelude & Fugue* in E flat (BWV 552; HMV DB1991-2).

Record collectors and musicians interested in the music of Busoni have no doubt come across these recordings in old catalogues and gramophone encyclopaedias: Alexander Borovsky, with the Lamoureux Orchestra conducted by Eugene Bigot—Concerto in d minor (Bach/Busoni)   Decca LY 6150/1   American Vox 12002/3, set 162   Polydor 566201/2; and Concerto in f minor (Bach/Busoni) Decca LY 6154   Polydor 566203.

I was naturally interested for a number of reasons. The d minor Busoni version is very rarely played, and this is the only recording of it. I was curious to hear it. But the second item, the Bach-Busoni *Concerto* in f intrigued me; as far as I know, Busoni did not play the f minor or edit it. Perhaps Borovsky had a hand-edited copy of this concerto by Busoni? After some detective work, I tracked down Alexander Borovsky in the United States. He very kindly and promptly replied:

Many thanks for your letter. I am happy that you will write about Busoni whom I admired and heard a few times in life. Although it was terribly long ago, but I remember his interpretation of the Sonata Op. 106—an enormous impression of his playing is still vivid in many details. He played it in St. Petersburg Russia—in 1912. . . . Your information of my records are not correct. I made the D Minor Concerto with Mr Eugene Bigot in Paris, but never played F Minor with him. As we had to make two records only, we played at a reckless speed. . . . I never heard of a Busoni transcription of the F Minor Concerto by Bach. . . .
    With best wishes for your endeavour, with my greetings,

Sincerely yours,

Alexander Borovsky

The reference to the "two records only" must mean the physical problem of fitting the concerto onto two 78s, but Borovsky negotiates the "reckless speed" admirably. Incidentally, there is a recording by Borovsky of the f minor, as I listed above—he has simply forgotten having made it. But the ascribing of a transcription of this concerto to Busoni is wrong. This is one piece he did not edit.

It is also interesting to read Claudio Arrau's reminiscences of Busoni's playing, particularly concerning the same Beethoven sonata. See "Arrau as Beethoven Cyclist," *The Music Magazine*, September 1962.

Catalogue

... if the musical historians of a later day come to regard our age as one of a "new spirituality," the influence which Busoni's masterpieces will exert on the formation of such a judgment will perhaps be decisive.

Roman Vlad

The Catalogue consists of two main parts. Busoni's published music is listed in the following categories: piano, piano four hands, two pianos, and piano and orchestra. These are followed by the published transcriptions, arrangements, editions, and cadenzas based on Bach, Liszt, Mozart, and other composers. Busoni's orchestral, chamber, vocal, and operatic works, being outside the scope of this book, are not listed. Furthermore, since a detailed publishing history of each work is given in the main body of the book, the catalogue restricts itself to the titles only.

The second part of the catalogue concerns itself with Busoni manuscripts. A complete numerical listing of the original *Busoni-Nachlass* is given, with the current distribution of these items in the East and West Berlin libraries, including items originally catalogued and numbered but now considered lost. Other known locations of Busoni manuscripts are also identified.

I. PIANO SOLO

Scherzo per Pianoforte tratto dalla Sonata in Mi Maggiore
Cinq Pièces pour Piano Op. 3
Minuetto per Pianoforte Op. 14
Suite Campestre. 5 pezzi caratteristici per piano-forte Op. 18
Preludio e Fuga in Do minore per Pianoforte Op. 21
Gavotta per Pianoforte Op. 25
Racconti fantastici. 3 pezzi caratteristici per Pianoforte Op. 12
Menuetto capriccioso (C dur) Op. 61 für das Pianoforte componirt
Danze Antiche per Pianoforte Op. 11 Nos. 1-4
Gavotte (F-moll) für das Pianoforte Op. 70
3 Pezzi nello stile antico per Pianoforte Op. 10

Preludio e Fuga per Pianoforte Op. 36

24 Préludes pour le piano (Op. 37)

Una festa di villaggio. 6 Pezzi caratteristici per pianoforte Op. 9

Danza Notturna per Pianoforte Op. 12

Marcia di Paesani e Contadine (Una festa di Villaggio) per Pianoforte Op. 32

Macchiette Mediaevali per Pianoforte Op. 33

Trois Morceaux pour piano. No. 1. Scherzo Op. 4 No. 2. Prélude et Fugue Op. 5
    No. 3. Scène de ballet Op. 6

6 Etudes pour le Piano Op. 16

Etude en forme de Variations Op. 17. pour piano

Zweite Ballet-Scene Op. 20

Variationen und Fuge in freier Form über Fr. Chopin's C-moll-Präludium (Op. 28
    No. 20) für das Pianoforte Op. 22 rewritten as: Zehn Variationen über ein
    Präludium von Chopin

Zwei Clavierstücke Op. 30a. 1. Contrapunctische Tanzstück. 2. Kleine (III). Ballet-
    Scene rewritten as: Zwei Tanzstücke für das Klavier Op. 30a.

Vierte Ballet-Scene in Form eines Concert-Walzers für Pianoforte Op. 33a
    rewritten as: Vierte Ballett-Szene (Walzer und Galopp) für Pianoforte
    Op. 33a. (1892) (1913). Neue veränderte Ausgabe

Stücke für Pianoforte Op. 33b

Elegien. 6 neue Klavierstücke (later published as: 7 neue Klavierstücke) the
    seventh elegy first published separately as Berceuse pour le piano

Nuit de Noël (1908). Esquisse pour le Piano

Fantasia nach Johann Sebastian Bach für das Klavier

An die Jugend. Eine Folge von Klavierstücken Nr. 1 Preludietto, Fughetta ed
    Esercizio Nr. 2 Preludio, Fuga e Fuga figurata. Studie nach J. S. Bach's
    Wohltemperiertem Clavier (D-Dur) Nr. 3 Giga, Bolero e Variazione. Studie
    nach Mozart Nr. 4 Introduzione, Capriccio (Paganinesco) & Epilogo

Gross Fuge. Kontrapunktische Fantasie über Joh. Seb. Bach's letztes unvoll-
    endetes Werk für Klavier ausgeführt

Fantasia Contrappuntistica. Preludio al Corale "Gloria al Signore nei Cieli"
    e Fuga a quattro obbligati sopra un frammento di Bach. Compilata per il
    Pianoforte. (Edizione definitiva).

Choral-Vorspiel, und Fuge über ein Bach'sches Fragment (der "Fantasia con-
    trappuntistica" kleine Ausgabe.) für das Klavier

Sonatina. Für Klavier zu zwei Händen

Sonatina seconda.

Indianisches Tagebuch. Erstes Buch. Vier Klavierstudien über Motive der Rothäute
    Amerikas

Sonatina ad usum infantis Madeline M* Americanae pro Clavicimbalo composita

Drei Albumblätter für Pianoforte zu zwei Händen, the first of these initially published
    separately as: Albumblatt für Klavier

Sonatina in diem nativitatis Christi MCMXVII für Klavier zu zwei Händen

Sonatina brevis. In Signo Joannis Sebastiani Magni in freier Nachdichtung
    von Bach's kleiner Fantasie & Fuge d moll, (BWV 905)

Kammer-Fantasie über Carmen für Pianoforte

Toccata. Preludio-Fantasie-Ciaccona

Perpetuum mobile (nach des Concertino II. Satze Op. 54)

Fünf kurze Stücke zur Pflege des polyphonen Spiels auf dem Pianoforte (later augmented to: Sieben kurze Stücke zur Pflege des polyphonen Spiels, as part of the second edition of the *Klavierübung*)

Prélude et Etude en Arpèges pour piano

Klavierübung (first edition in five parts, second edition in 10 books)

II. PIANO FOUR HANDS

Finnlaendische Volksweisen für Pianoforte zu 4 Händen Op. 27

III. TWO PIANOS

Fantasia contrappuntistica. Choral-Bariationen über "Ehre sei Gott in der Höhe" gefolgt von einer Quadrupel-Fuge über ein Bachsches Fragment für zwei Klaviere

Improvisation über das Bachsche Chorallied "Wie wohl ist mir, o Freund der Seele, wenn ich in deiner Liebe ruh" für zwei Klaviere

IV. PIANO AND ORCHESTRA

Concertstück für Pianoforte mit Orchester Op. 31a

Concerto per un Pianoforte principale e diverse strumenti ad arco a fiato ed a percussione. Aggiuntovi in Coro finale per voci d'uomini a sei parti. Le parole alemanne del poeta Oehlenschlaeger danese. La Musica di Ferruccio Busoni da Empoli Anno MCMIV. Opera XXXIX

Indianische Fantasie für Klavier mit Orchester Op. 44

Concertino für Pianoforte und Orchester. II. Romanza e Scherzoso Op. 54

V. TRANSCRIPTIONS, ARRANGEMENTS, EDITIONS, AND CADENZAS

(i) Works Based on Bach (see Chapter 11 for details)

There are two separate collections of J. S. Bach's works edited by Busoni:

Joh. Seb. Bach. Klavierwerke unter Mitwirkung von Egon Petri und Bruno Mugellini. Herausgegeben von Ferruccio Busoni

Bach-Busoni. Gesammelte Ausgabe. Bearbeitungen, Übertragungen, Studien und Kompositionen für Pianoforte nach Johann Sebastian Bach von Ferruccio Busoni. Vollständige und vervollkommnete Ausgabe

Works appeared in either or both of these collections, as well as separately. Chapter 11 gives detailed publishing histories and other specific information. Already listed above are other works with some debt to Bach (*Elegien* Nr. 3, *Fantasia nach Bach*, *An die Jugend* Nr. 2, *Grosse Fuge*, *Fantasia Contrappuntistica*, *Choral-Vorspiel*, *und Fuge*, *Albumblätter* Nr. 3, *Sonatina brevis*, and *Improvisation über Bachsche Chorallied*). There is also: Konzert für Klavier in D moll. Joh. Seb. Bach. Freie Bearbeitung von F. B. Busoni.

(ii) Works Based on Liszt (see Chapter 12 for details)

Busoni edited the complete etudes in three volumes:

Franz Liszts Musikalische Werke. Herausgegeben von der Franz Liszt-Stiftung. II. Pianofortewerke. Etüden für Pianoforte zu zwei Händen Bd. 1-3

Selections from this edition were also published separately. The etudes after Paganini, as well as being part of the above, were issued two more times:

Sechs Paganini-Etüden für Klavier. Revidierte Ausgabe von Ferruccio Busoni
Etüden nach Paganini-Liszt (published separately and also in *Klavierübung*, second edition. These are transcriptions, unlike the above, which are editions)
Rhapsodie Espagnole (Folies d'Espagne et Jota aragonese.) von Franz Liszt. Als Konzertstück für pianoforte und Orchester bearbeitet von Ferruccio B. Busoni
Fantasie und Fuge über den Choral "Ad nos, ad salutarem undam" von Franz Liszt. Von der Orgel auf das Pianoforte frei übertragen und Herrn Joseph Sattler zugeeignet von Ferruccio B. Busoni.
Episode aus Lenau's Faust. Der Tanz in der Dorfschenke (Mephisto Walzer) von Franz Liszt. Mit Anlehnung an die Orchesterpartitur für das Pianoforte neu bearbeitet und dem Grafen A. Rozwadowski gewidmet von Ferruccio Busoni
Heroischer Marsch in ungarischem Styl für das Piano-forte von F. Liszt. Neu herausgegeben und Egon Petri gewidmet von Ferruccio Busoni
Franz Liszt. Polonaise No. 2 E Dur. Nouvelle édition, augmentée d'une cadence finale, par Ferruccio Busoni
Franz Liszt. Fantasie über zwei Motive aus W. A. Mozarts Die Hochzeit des Figaro. Nach dem fast vollendeten Original manuskript ergänzt und Moritz Rosenthal zugeeignet von Ferruccio Busoni
Réminiscences de "Don Juan". Konzert-Fantasie über Motive aus Mozarts "Don Giovanni" für das Pianoforte. Grosse kritisch-instruktive Ausgabe von Ferruccio Busoni
Totentanz. Phantasie für Pianoforte und Orchester (Beendet am 21 Oktober 1849) von Franz Liszt. Erste Fassung nach unzweifelhaften Handschriften zum ersten Male herausgegeben von Ferruccio Busoni
Franz Liszt. Ungarische Rhapsodie Nr. 19 für Pianoforte zu zwei Händen. Zum Konzertgebrauch frei bearbeitet von Ferruccio Busoni
(*Klavierübung* also contains a cadenza to the *Valse de l'opéra Faust*, as well as three variations on a theme from *Venezia e Napoli*.)

(iii) Works Based on Mozart (see Chapter 13 for details)

Symphonies arranged by Busoni for piano two hands: No. 30 (K. 202), No. 32 (K. 318), and No. 37 (K. 444).
Original cadenzas by Busoni for the following piano concertos: No. 20 (K. 466), No. 9 (K. 271), No. 23 (K. 488), No. 24 (K. 491), No. 21 (K. 467), No. 22 (K. 482), No. 19 (K. 459), No. 17 (K. 453), and No. 25 (K. 503).
W. A. Mozart. Andantino. Aus dem 9. Klavier-Konzert Werk 271. Für Klavier allein frei übertragen und mit einer Kadenz versehen von Ferruccio Busoni
Mozart. Rondo Concertante für Pianoforte und Orchester KV. 482. Neu bearbeitet von Ferruccio Busoni
Duettino concertante nach Mozart für zwei Pianoforte
W. A. Mozart. Fantasie für eine Orgelwalze, Werk 608. Für zwei Klaviere bearbeitet von Ferruccio Busoni

W. A. Mozart. Ouvertüre zur Oper Die Zauberflöte. Übertragung für zwei
   Klaviere von Ferruccio Busoni

Already listed above are other works with some debt to Mozart. In *Klavierübung:
Variations-Studie nach Mozart* 1 and 2 and *Sieben Kurze Stücke zur Pflege des
polyphonen Spiels auf dem Pianoforte* No. 6, as well as the earlier edition of these
same pieces, in *An die Jugend: Giga, Bolero e Variazione.*

(iv) Works Based on Other Composers, Arranged Alphabetically

Zwei Cadenzen zu L. van Beethoven's Clavier-Concert No. 4, G dur. I.) Cadenz
   zum ersten Satze. II.) Cadenz zum Rondo
Beethoven's Cadenzen zu dessen Clavier-Concerten ausgewählt und herausgegeben
   von Ferruccio Busoni
Ecossaisen für Pianoforte von Ludwig van Beethoven. Für den Konzertvortrag
   bearbeitet und Fräulein Gerda Sjöstrand zugeeignet von Ferruccio B. Busoni
Kammer-Fantasie über Carmen für Pianoforte
Sechs Orgelchoralvorspiele von Johannes Brahms für das Pianoforte ausgewählt und
   übertragen von Ferruccio Busoni
Frédéric Chopin. Polonaise en la bémol. Oeuvre 53. Interpretée par Ferruccio Busoni
Frédéric Chopin. Prelude Op. 28 No. 3 (in *Klavierübung*)
Fantasie über Motive aus "Der Barbier von Bagdad," komische Oper von Peter
   Cornelius, für Pianoforte componirt von Ferruccio B. Busoni
8 Etudes de Piano par J. B. Cramer choisies des 16 nouvelles Etudes Op. 81 Nos. 85-
   100 révues et publiées par Ferruccio B. Busoni
Novelletten für Pianoforte, Violine und Violoncell componirt und Herrn Ferdinand
   Hiller gewidmet von Niels W. Gade Op. 29. Bearbeitung für zwei Pianoforte
   zu vier Händen von F. B. Busoni. (Unter Beibehaltung der Original-Piano-
   fortestimme.)
C. Goldmark. Merlino. Trascrizione di Concerto per pianoforte di Ferruccio B.
   Busoni. Sopra motivi dell' opera Merlino del maestro C. Goldmark
C. Goldmark. Merlin. Klavier-Auszug zu zwei Händen. F. Busoni
F. Mendelssohn Bartholdy. Symphonie Nr. 1 in C moll Op. 11. Für 2 Pianoforte
   zu 8 Händen bearbeitet von F. B. Busoni
Scherzo aus dem Streichquartett in E moll von Ottokar Nováček. Zum Concertvor-
   trage für Pianoforte bearbeitet und Fräulein Ragnhild Lund zugeeignet von
   Ferruccio B. Busoni
Introduzione e Capriccio (Paganinesco)
(Nach Offenbach) Barcarole. (In *Klavierübung*)
Klavierstück Op. 11. Nr. 2 von Arnold Schönberg, Konzertmässige Interpretation
   von Ferruccio B. Busoni
Ouvertüren und andere Orchesterwerke von Franz Schubert. Bearbeitung für das
   Pianoforte zu zwei Händen von F. B. Busoni (see Chapter 14 for details)
Konzert-Allegro mit Introduktion Op. 134. Bearbeitung für zwei Pianoforte zu vier
   Händen. R. Schumann Op. 134. Bearb. von F. B. Busoni
Marcia Funebre in morte di Siegfried nel Dramma musicale "Il Crepuscolo degli
   Dei" di Riccardo Wagner. Trascrizione per Pianoforte di Ferruccio B. Busoni
Polonaise. Rich. Wagner. (Not fully authenticated. See Chapter 14)
Frauentanz. Sieben Gedichte des Mittelalters für Sopran mit Flöte, Bratsche,
   Klarinette, Horn und Fagott von Kurt Weill Op. 10. Klavierauszug mit Text
   (No. 3 only was reduced by Busoni. See Chapter 14.)

Busoni-Nachlass, Listed Numerically, and Other Manuscript Sources

Staatsbibliothek Number	Piano Item	Non-piano Item	Fragment	Sketch	Deutsche Staatsbibliothek. East Berlin	Staatsbibliothek Preussischer Kulturbesitz	Lost during World War II	Title is given as on Busoni's manuscript. Author's comments and information are in parentheses.
1	X					X		Canzone op. 1
2	X					X		Berceuse, op. 2
3	X					X		op. 3 (Introduzione, Tempo di Walzer & Finale)
4	X					X		Cadenza, Esecizio, op. 4
5	X					X		Studio, op. 5
6	X					X		Tema con Variazioni, op. 6
7		X				X		Preghiera alla Madonna, op. 7
8	X					X		Marcia-Funebre, op. 8
9	X					X		Romanza senza parole, op. 9
10	X					X		La Canzone del Cacciatore, op. 10
11	X					X		Preludio per pianoforte, op. 11
12	X					X		Inno-Variato, op. 12
13	X					X		Scherzo, op. 14
14	X					X		Polka, op. 16
15	X					X		Scherzo in Si b magg, op. 15
16	X					X		Menuetto, op. 17 (identical to No. 28)
17		X				X		Preludio per Clarinetto e Pianoforte
18	X					X		Canzone popolare, op. 13
19	X					X		Preludio, op. 19
20		X				X		Preludio per Clarinetto e pianoforte, op. 18
21	X					X		Preludio per pianoforte solo, op. 20
22	X					X		Sonata
23	X					X		Fuga a 2 voci in stile libero
24	X					X		Studio in do magge: per pianoforte solo
25	X					X		Fuga a 3 voci
26	X					X		Gavotta
27	X					X		Inno
28	X					X		Menuetto, op. 17 (identical to No. 16)
29	X					X		Studio Contrappuntato
30	X					X		Presto (identical to No. 43)
31	X					X		Invenzione (identical to Nos. 44 and 46)
32	X					X		Capriccio (identical to No. 42)
33	X					X		Inno (identical to No. 45)
34	X					X		Mandolinata
35	X					X		Waltzer da Concerto. Momento Musicale (identical to No. 47)

Staatsbibliothek Number	Piano Item	Non-piano Item	Fragment	Sketch	Deutsche Staatsbibliothek. East Berlin	Staatsbibliothek Preussischer Kulturbesitz	Lost during World War II	Title is given as on Busoni's manuscript. Author's comments and information are in parentheses.
36		X					X	Fuga per Harmonium-Organo a tre voci
37	X						X	Scherzi in Si b
38	X						X	Marcia-Funebre
39	X						X	Fantasie-Impromptu
40	X						X	Il Dolore. Romanza senza parole
41	X						X	Menuetto
42	X						X	Capriccio in Do minore (identical to No. 32)
43	X						X	Presto in Do min (identical to No. 30)
44	X						X	Invenzione a due voci (identical to Nos. 31 and 46)
45	X						X	Inno (identical to No. 33)
46	X						X	Invenzione (identical to Nos. 31 and 44)
47	X						X	Momento Musicale per Pianoforte (identical to No. 35)
48		X					X	Lied
49		X					X	Lied
50		X					X	Wiegenlied
51		X					X	1° Quartetto
52		X					X	Sonata per Violino e Piano-Forte in do maggr
53		X					X	2° Quartetto
54	X						X	Fughetta
55	X						X	Gavottina, op. 3 No. 3 (identical to No. 56)
56	X						X	Gavotta (identical to No. 55)
57	X						X	Meditazione
58		X	X				X	Ouverture per Grande Orchestra
59	X						X	Studio
60	X						X	(There is no given title for this piece in c minor)
61	X						X	Fuga in Sol magg
62		X					X	"Waise und Rose". Lied für Mezzo-soprano mit Klavierbegleitung
63		X	X				X	(There is no given title for this a capella chorus)
64	X						X	Sonata No. 1 in Do magg, op. 7
65	X						X	Invenzione

Staatsbibliothek Number	Piano Item	Non-piano Item	Fragment	Sketch	Deutsche Staatsbibliothek. East Berlin	Staatsbibliothek Preussischer Kulturbesitz	Lost during World War II	Title is given as on Busoni's manuscript. Author's comments and information are in parentheses.
66		X					X	Menuetto (for string quartet)
67	X						X	Sonata No. 2 in Re magg, op. 8
68	X						X	Preludio
69	X						X	Sonata No. 3 in Mi magg, op. 9
70	X						X	Allergro fugato
71		X					X	Salve Regina für Mezzosoprano mit Klavierbegleitung, op. 4
72		X					X	(No title, No. 71 arranged for mezzo-soprano and string quartet)
73		X					X	Antifona per Soprano, Mezzosoprano e Baritono con accompagnamento d'Harmonium
74		X					X	(No title, Pater Noster for mezzosoprano solo, three-part male choir, and piano or harmonium accompaniment)
75		X					X	L'Invalido (Ballata) per Tenore con accompagnamento di pianoforte, op. 31
76	X						X	Menuetto, op. 4
77	X						X	Toccata, op. 4
78	X		X				X	op. 6 (unfinished sonata)
79		X					X	Klarinetten-Suite, op. 10
80	X						X	Studio in Do min, op. 12
81		X					X	Andante ed Allegro Vivace per Quartetto ad Arco. op. 13
82	X						X	Preludio & Fuga in Do magg: per la mano sinistra solo, op. 15
83	X						X	Fuga in stile libero, op. 16
84	X						X	Concerto per piano-forte con accompagnamento di quartetto ad arco, op. 17
85	X						X	Suite Campestre, 5 pezzi caratteristici, op. 18
86		X					X	Pater Noster a 3 voci, op. 20
87	X				X		X	(Solo piece in C Major)
88	X						X	Preludio in Fa min, op. 19
89		X					X	Tristezza. Parole di Vincenzo Baffi per Canto con accom. di pianof

Staatsbibliothek Number	Piano Item	Non-piano Item	Fragment	Sketch	Deutsche Staatsbibliothek. East Berlin	Staatsbibliothek Preussischer Kulturbesitz	Lost during World War II	Title is given as on Busoni's manuscript. Author's comments and information are in parentheses.
90		X				X		Antiphona a 4 voci senza accompagnam, op. 23
91		X				X		Ave Maria per Canto con accom. di Quartetto ad arco. (same work as the Ave Maria op. 1 with piano, published Spina)
92		X				X		Suite per Clarinetto in B e pianoforte, op. 10
93		X				X		Graduale delle Messe comuni della Madonna. Solo per Mezzosoprano e Quartetto a Voci obligate con accomp. d'Organo o Pianoforte, op. 27
94	X		X			X		Rapsodie Hongroise, op. 28
95		X				X		Salve Regina per Canto con accopagn: di Pianf., op. 29
96		X				X		Lied der Klage für eine Altstimme mit Begl. des Pianof., op. 38
97		X				X		Ave Maria quatuor vocibus cantanda, op. 11
98	X					X		Preludio e Fuga a 2 pianof, op. 32
99		X				X		"Solo dramatique" pour la Clarinette in Si b et pianoforte, op. 13
100		X				X		Menuetto per 2 Violini, Viola & Violoncello, op. 15
101		X				X		Missa I. Quatour vocibus Cantanda, op. 34
102	X					X		Capriccio per 2 Pianoforti, op. 36
103		X				X		Op. 16 (Benedicta et venerabilis est, in three parts, a capella)
104		X				X		"Des Sänger's Fluch" Gedicht v. Uhland. In Musik gesetzt und für eine Sing-Stimme mit Orchester-Begleitung, op. 39 (same work published with piano accompaniment by Cranz)
105	?	?				X	X	Scherzo, op. 17
106		X				X	X	Andantino per Clarinetto in Si b e Pianoforte, op. 18

Staatsbibliothek Number	Piano Item	Non-piano Item	Fragment	Sketch	Deutsche Staatsbibliothek. East Berlin	Staatsbibliothek Preussischer Kulturbesitz	Lost during World War II	Title is given as on Busoni's manuscript. Author's comments and information are in parentheses.
107		X				X	X	Serenade No. 2 pour la Clarinette en Si b et piano, op. 19
108	X					X	X	Op. 43 (for four hands)
109	X		X			X	X	Concerto, op. 46
110		X				X	X	Scherzo, op. 20 (for string quartet)
111		X				X	X	Variationen für Clavier und Violine über ein Minnesängerlied aus dem XIII. Jahrhundert, op. 22
112		X				X	X	Sternlied. Für eine Alt-Stimme mit Begl. d. Pianof, op. 23
113	?					X	X	D Moll Fuge. Dreistimmig, op. 26
114		X				X	X	Novellette für Clarinette in B und Clavier, op. 27
115	?	?				X	X	Scherzo, op. 28
116	?	?				X	X	A Moll Scherzo, op. 29
117		X				X	X	Stabat Mater zu 6 Stimmen mit Begleitung eines Streichquintetts, op. 55
118		X				X	X	Tragische Geschichte, op. 30 (this was for low voice and piano, presumably an alternative version of No. 202)
119		X				X	X	"Lieb Liebchen, leg's Händchen aufs Herze mein". Für Soprano mit Clavierbegl, op. 31
120		X				X	X	"Es fiel ein Reif in der Frühlingsnacht". Für Mezzosoprano mit Begleitung des Pianoforte, op. 33
121		X				X	X	Märchen für Violoncell und Clavier, op. 34
122		X				X	X	Kyrie, op. 64
123		X	X			X	X	(No title was given. A setting for voice and orchestra.)
124	X					X	X	(Presumably a very early set of cadenzas to Mozart's d minor concerto K. 466)
125	X		X			X	X	Ouverture in Mi Magg (for four hands)
126	?	?				X	X	Andante
127	?	?	X			X	X	Moderato
128	?	?				X	X	Andante con moto

Staatsbibliothek Number	Piano Item	Non-piano Item	Fragment	Sketch	Deutsche Staatsbibliothek. East Berlin	Staatsbibliothek Preussischer Kulturbesitz	Lost during World War II	Title is given as on Busoni's manuscript. Author's comments and information are in parentheses.
129	X					X	X	(No title was given. Solo piece in b minor.)
130	X					X		(No title given. Solo piece in d minor.)
131	X				X			Andante e Tarantella
132		X			X			Drittes Quartett
133		X			X			Allegretto (for string quartet)
134		X	X		X			Andante Sostenuto-Allegro Vivace (for string quartet)
135		X			X			Sonata in Re Magg. per Piano e Clarinetto
136		X			X			Novellett (for clarinet and piano)
137		X	X		X			(For clarinet and piano)
138		X	X		X			Andante Maestoso (for orchestra)
139		X	X	X	X			(Setting for voice and piano)
140		X			X			Heine (song setting with piano)
141		X			X			Per soprano (song with piano)
142		X	X		X			Preghiera alla Madonna (six-part setting a capella)
143					X			(Book of sketches)
144		X			X			Gloria (four-part setting a capella)
145		X		X	X			Op. 65 (song sketch)
146		X		X	X			Op. 67 (sketch for voice and string quartet)
147		X			X			Praeludium (for organ. Companion piece to No. 152)
148	X				X			Preludium Fuge D-Dur A 3 voci
149	X				X			Walzer
	X				X			Gavotte
	X				X			Invention
	X				X			Fuge
	X				X			Variationen
		X			X			(See text. Most of No. 149 consists of composition exercises.)
150	X				X			Preludio Fuge
151		X			X			Duo für 2 Flöten mit Begleitung des Pianoforte, op. 43
152		X			X			Doppelfuge zum Choral, op. 76 (companion piece to No. 147)

Staatsbibliothek Number	Piano Item	Non-piano Item	Fragment	Sketch	Deutsche Staatsbibliothek. East Berlin	Staatsbibliothek Preussischer Kulturbesitz	Lost during World War II	Title is given as on Busoni's manuscript. Author's comments and information are in parentheses.
153	X					X		Rondo, op. 45
154		X				X		Impromptu, op. 48 (for clarinet and piano. The piano part is missing.)
		X				X		(No title, sketches for *Il Sabato del Villaggio*.)
		X				X		(No title, piece for clarinet and piano.)
155	X					X		Sonate
156	X					X		Fuge, G moll, op 74 (same work as No. 157)
157	X					X		Praeludium Fuge g-moll (same fugue as No. 156, see also No. 213)
158		X				X		Wer hat das erste Lied erdacht. Lied für Mezzosoprano, op. 77
159		X				X		Op. 44 Frühlingslied (for male voices)
160		X				X		Op. 45 Der Wirthin Töchterlein (for male voices)
161		X				X		Missa (for a capella choir)
162		X				X		Motete für Chor mit Begleitung des Pianoforte
163		X				X		Motette Für Chor und Orchester (same work as No. 162)
164		X				X		2° Quartetto in Do magg (string quartet)
165	X					X		(Six miniature etudes, the last one incomplete.)
166	X					X		Studio in la min.
167		X				X		Suite per Clarinetto con accompagnam. di Quartetto. Ad arco
168		X				X		Introduction par Spohr Elegia di H. W. Ernst. Riduzione per Clarinetto con accompagn. di quartetto ad arco.
169		X				X		Abendlied di Schumann. Riduzione per Clarinetto con accomp. di Quart ad arco
170		X				X		3 Romanzen von Robert Schumann, op. 94 (arr. clarinet)
171		X				X		Requiem per Assoli, Coro ed Orchestra

Staatsbibliothek Number	Piano Item	Non-piano Item	Fragment	Sketch	Deutsche Staatsbibliothek. East Berlin	Staatsbibliothek Preussischer Kulturbesitz	Lost during World War II	Title is given as on Busoni's manuscript. Author's comments and information are in parentheses.
172		X				X		Andante mit Variationen und Scherzo für Clavier, Violine und Violoncell, op. 18
173		X				X	X	Notturno (for clarinet and piano)
174	X					X		(No title. Fugue in F major.)
175		X				X		I. Frühling, op. 40, No. 1 (first movement of *Primavera, Estate, Autunno, Inverno*. Complete autograph with Ricordi, Milan.)
176		X				X		I. Primavera. Frühling (No. 175 for male choir a capella)
177		X				X	X	(See Preussischer Kulturbesitz listing below.)
178		X				X	X	(See Preussischer Kulturbesitz listing below.)
179		X				X	X	(Nos. 177-81 have to do with *Il Sabato del Villaggio*.
180		X				X	X	Nos. 177 and 178 were the full score and vocal score, respectively.
181		X				X	X	Nos. 179-81 were parts, lost during the war. The scores re-appeared in the Preussischer Kulturbesitz.)
182	X					X		Introduction et Scherzo pour Piano et Orchestre
183	X			X		X		Machiette Mediovali No. 2/B. Cavaliere Reiter
184	X					X		Studio 18. in fa minore
185	X					X		Etude 15, en forme d' "Adagio" d'une Sonate
186	X					X		Etude 16
187	X					X		Sonate, op. 20
188		X				X		"So lang man jung". Männerchor mit Orchesterbegleitung, op. 16
189		X				X		Gesang aus Mirza Schaffy für eine Singstimme und Piano (copy)
190	X					X		Invenzione. (facsimile of the autograph)
191	X					X		Anhang zu Siegfried Ochs "Kommt a Vogerl g'flogen"

Staatsbibliothek Number	Piano Item	Non-piano Item	Fragment	Sketch	Deutsche Staatsbibliothek. East Berlin	Staatsbibliothek Preussischer Kulturbesitz	Lost during World War II	Title is given as on Busoni's manuscript. Author's comments and information are in parentheses.
192		X				X	X	Fughette (for violin and piano)
193		X				X		(Autographs and copies of the third and
194		X				X		fourth movements of the *Symphonische Suite Op. 25*.)
195	X					X		Fuge über das Volkslied "O, du mein lieber Augustin" (four hands)
196	X					X		Finnländische Volksweisen (four hands) (also an untitled etude)
197	X					X		Concert-Fantasie für Orchester mit obligatem Pianoforte, op. 29
198		X	X	X		X		Sigune. Oper in 2 Akten und einem Vorspiel.
199		X	X			X		No. I/A Introduzione e Fuga sopra un Corale di G. S. Bach (orch.)
200	X		X			X		Marche Funebre (piano and orchestra)
201		X				X		(No title. Work for four-part male choir a capella.)
202		X				X		Tragische Geschichte. Gedicht von Chamisso-für Männerquartett (presumably an alternate version of No. 118)
203	X		X			X		Der 18. Psalm von Franz Liszt für 2 Pianoforte bearbeitet
204		X	X			X		An der schoenen blauen Donau (copy of part of Strauss's waltz)
205		X				X		Tempo di Minuetto per Orchestra
206	X		X			X		Sonata I e Schizzi (two unfinished movements)
207		X		X		X		Ouvertüre zu einem gedachten Singspiele nach der Tradition des "Lieben Augustin"
208		X				X		"Eine alte Geschichte in neue Reime gebracht". Melodram
209		X				X		Chorlied der Deutschen in Amerika (four-part male choir a capella)
210	X					X		Übertragungs-Versuch eines sechstimmigen Orgelsatzes

Staatsbibliothek Number	Piano Item	Non-piano Item	Fragment	Sketch	Deutsche Staatsbibliothek. East Berlin	Staatsbibliothek Preussischer Kulturbesitz	Lost during World War II	Title is given as on Busoni's manuscript. Author's comments and information are in parentheses.
211	X			X	X			(On printed copy and related to Bach's Art of Fugue.)
212		X		X	X			Skizzen zu einer Orchestration von Bach's Violin-Chaconne
213	X				X			Preludio (transposed from No. 157)
214	X		X		X			Orgelfuge von Bach für das Pianoforte (not by Bach, unknown)
215		X	X	X	X			Introduktion, Marsch, Walzer für Orchester
216	X	X	X	X	X			(eighty pages of various unidentified fragments and sketches.)
217	X				X			Concertstück für Piano Forte mit Orchester
218	X				X			Concertstück für Pianoforte mit Orchester (copy of above)
219	X		X	X	X			Vorspiel zu einem Bach'schen Choral. Calvarium (also sketches of another setting)
220		X			X			Symphonisches Tongedicht für Orchester
221		X			X			Unter der Linden (for voice and orchestra)
222	X		X		X			5e Scène de Ballet
223	X				X			Finnische Ballade
224	X			X	X			Ballade (sketch of part of third movement of Piano Concerto)
225		X		X	X			Sonata quasi una Fantasia per Violino e pianoforte, op. 36a
226	X				X			Zwei Orgeltoccaten von Johann Sebastian Bach. Auf das Pianoforte übertragen
227	X				X			Konzert für Klavier in D moll. Joh. Seb. Bach. Freie Bearbeitung
228	X				X		X	Rhapsodie hongroise (this edition of the so-called Liszt twentieth rhapsody is now in the Preussischer Kulturbesitz. See below.)
229		X	X		X		X	By the Waters of Babel. For a Man's Voice and Piano.

Staatsbibliothek Number	Piano Item	Non-piano Item	Fragment	Sketch	Deutsche Staatsbibliothek. East Berlin	Staatsbibliothek Preussischer Kulturbesitz	Lost during World War II	Title is given as on Busoni's manuscript. Author's comments and information are in parentheses.
230				X				(Design for a title page.)
231	X			X	X			(nos. 231, 232, and 233 have to do with
232	X			X	X			the *Piano Concerto*. Nos. 231 and 232
233	X				X		X	are sketches; 233 was a full score, lost during World War II. No. 231 also contains materials relating to the ending of the *Concerto* without choir.)
234		X		X	X			(No title. Sketches for the *Turandot Suite*.)
235	X				X			Zwei Cadenzen zu W. A. Mozart's D-moll Concert
236				X			X	(A composition by Busoni's son, Benni, from 1907.)
237	X			X	X			(Sketches for the *Elegies*.)
238	X				X			6 Elegien 1907-1908
239	X				X			(No title. Autograph of *Fantasia nach Bach*.)
240	X				X			Fuga figurata (from *An die Jugend*)
241		X			X			Berceuse élégiaque
242		X			X			(Corrected proof copy of No. 241.)
243	X				X			Klavierstück. Schönberg-Busoni
244	X				X			(Corrected proof copy of No. 243.)
245	X				X			(These four items have to do with the
246	X				X			*Versuch einer organischen Klavier-*
247	X				X			*Noten-Schrift*, and contain Bach's
248	X				X			*Chromatic Fantasy* as well as other newly notated works.)
249	X			X	X			J. S. Bach's Kunst der Fuge herausgegeben
250	X			X	X			Sonatina
251	X				X			Sonatina
252	X			X	X			Studien zur unvollendeten Fuge aus J. S. Bach's Kunst der Fuge
253								(This item is a catalogue error; it does not exist.)
254	X				X			Kontrapunktische Fantasie (autograph of the *Grosse Fuge*. Nos. 249 and 252 are studies and sketches of the same.)

Busoni-Nachlass, Listed Numerically, and Other Manuscript Sources (cont.)

Staatsbibliothek Number	Piano Item	Non-piano Item	Fragment	Sketch	Deutsche Staatsbibliothek. East Berlin	Staatsbibliothek Preussischer Kulturbesitz	Lost during World War II	Title is given as on Busoni's manuscript. Author's comments and information are in parentheses.
255	X				X			Fantasia Contrappuntistica
256					X			(Items 256 and 257 are in the same binder
257					X			as No. 249. They contain some sketches and work on *Ricercare* from Bach's *Musical Offering*.)
258	X			X	X			(No title. Contrapuntal studies on fugue theme, C major, WK I.)
259	X		X		X			(No title. Arrangement for piano of the fugue from K. 546.)
260		X	X		X			All' Orchestra della Cooperative di Milano a Berlino
261	X			X	X			Für die Pianola
262					X			(No title. One hundred forty-five new scale formations.)
263		X		X	X			Einleitung zum Wunder des Hlg. Antonius
264	X				X			Preludietto Fughetta (from *An die Jugend*)
265		X		X	X			Die Brautwahl
266		X			X			Die Brautwahl
267		X			X			Die Brautwahl (corrected proof copy)
268		X			X		X	Die Brautwahl
269		X			X			Die Brautwahl
270	X			X	X			Sonatina Seconda
271	X				X			Sonatina Seconda
272	X				X			Sonatina Seconda
273	X				X			Choral-Vorspiel, und Fuge über ein Bach'sches Fragment (this is the so-called *Edizione minore* of the *Fantasia Contrappuntistica*.)
274	X				X			Fantasie über Mozart's Figaro. Franz Liszt
275		X		X	X			Nocturne Symphonique
276		X		X	X			Operetten Musik (meant for Wedekind's *Franziska*)
277	X				X			(Op. 33a, 1913 version)
278	X				X			Paganini-Liszt. Thema mit Variationen. Eine Transcrip. Studie

Staatsbibliothek Number	Piano Item	Non-piano Item	Fragment	Sketch	Deutsche Staatsbibliothek. East Berlin	Staatsbibliothek Preussischer Kulturbesitz	Lost during World War II	Title is given as on Busoni's manuscript. Author's comments and information are in parentheses.
279	X				X		X	(Edition of the first St. Francis *Legend* by Liszt)
280	X			X	X			(Various sketches and titles, all to do
281	X			X	X			with the *Indian Fantasy*.)
282		X	X		X		X	Su Monte Mario (see Preussischer Kulturbesitz listing below)
283		X		X	X			Tre Cadenze per il Concerto di Violino
284		X			X			di Beethoven
285					X		X	"Floh-Sprung"-Canon mit oblig. Bass (facsimile reproduced in *Zeitschrift für Musik*, 99. Jg., 1932, S. 1095)
286	X				X			(Op. 30a, 1914 version)
287	X				X			12 kleine Präludien (J. S. Bach)
288		X			X			Rondo arlecchinesco
289	X			X	X			Indianisches Jahrbuch (sketches for books 1 and 2, *Indian Diary*)
290	X				X			Indianisches Tagebuch. Erstes Buch.
291		X			X			Indianisches Tagebuch Zweites Buch.
292		X			X			Cadenza für Violoncello zu Beethoven's "Adelaide"
293	X				X			(Supplement to the second book of the WK.)
294		X			X			Beispiel eines poly-harmonischen freien Contrapunktes (themes from No. 255)
295	X				X			2 Kadenzen zu Mozarts Es dur Conc. 9
296		X	X		X			Arlecchino
297		X	X		X		X	Arlecchino (see Preussischer Kulturbesitz, below)
298		X			X			Arlecchino
299		X	X		X			Entwürfe zu Turandot
300		X			X		X	(Title page: "La nuova commedia dell' arte")
301	X				X			Improvisation über das Bach'sche Chorallied (for two pianos)
302	X				X			Liszt-Busoni. Andantino capriccioso (second Paganini etude)
303	X				X			Sechs Klavierübungen und Praeludien (*Klavierübung* Pt. 1, 1st ed.)

Staatsbibliothek Number	Piano Item	Non-piano Item	Fragment	Sketch	Deutsche Staatsbibliothek. East Berlin	Staatsbibliothek Preussischer Kulturbesitz	Lost during World War II	Title is given as on Busoni's manuscript. Author's comments and information are in parentheses.
304	X				X			Sonatina in diem nativitatis Christi MCMXVII
305	X			X	X			Sonatina quasi Sonata
306	X				X			Drei Klavierübungen und Praeludien (*Klavierübung* Pt. 2, 1st ed.)
307	X				X			(Jarnach's copy of the Liszt-Busoni *Todtentanz* autograph.)
308	X		X		X			Notturni. Prologo (only the prelude written to the cycle)
309		X		X	X			Eldorado (setting with piano, words by Poe)
310	X				X		X	(Annotated copy of Mozart Piano Concerto K. 482.)
311	X				X			Cadenzen Es dur Konzert Mozart (K. 482)
312	X				X			Rondo Concertante für Klavier u. Orchester aus dem 22. Concerto von W. A. Mozart
313	X				X			Duettino concertante d'apres Mozart pour deux Piano
314	X			X	X			(Sketches of Carmen Fantasy.)
315		X			X		X	Cadenza istrumentata all'Adagio nel primo Concerto per il Flauto di W. A. Mozart (K. 313, see Preussischer Kulturbesitz below)
316		X			X		X	Cadenza all'Andante nel Secondo Concerto per il Flauto di W. A. Mozart (K. 314, see Preuss. Kultur. below)
317	X				X			Fantasia da Camera Sur Carmen
318		X		X	X			(These three items have to do with cadenzas to the first and second movements of Weber's f minor Clarinet Concerto. No. 318 is in Busoni's hand, but the final versions of the cadenzas are copies in an unknown hand.)
319		X			X			
320		X			X			
321		X			X			Divertimento per Flauto e Orchestra, op. 52
322		X		X	X			(Sketches of Tanzwalzer, op. 53)

Staatsbibliothek Number	Piano Item	Non-piano Item	Fragment	Sketch	Deutsche Staatsbibliothek. East Berlin	Staatsbibliothek Preussischer Kulturbesitz	Lost during World War II	Title is given as on Busoni's manuscript. Author's comments and information are in parentheses.
323		X			X			Tanzwalzer
324	X				X			"Lo Staccato" (*Klavierübung* Pt. 3, 1st ed.)
325	X				X			Cadences (two cadenzas to Mozart's Piano Concerto K. 459)
326		X			X			Lied des Brander von Goethe (baritone and piano. See Nos. 327-28.)
327		X		X	X			(Nos. 327, 328, and part of 326 are
328		X		X	X			sketches for settings of Goethe for voice and piano.)
329	X				X			Zweites Blatt. Drittes Blatt (from *Drei Albumblätter*)
330	X				X		X	Albumblatt (See Preussischer Kultur-besitz below)
331	X				X			Concertino Romanza e Scherzoso für Klavier mit Orchester
332		X			X			Nachtrag zu Turandot- "Diese Zeichen von Trauer"
333		X		X	X			Nachtrag zu Turandot
334		X			X			Die Bekehrte. (Goethe setting for female voice and piano)
335	X				X			(Annotated copy of Mozart's Sonata K. 448 and Fugue K. 426 for two pianos including Busoni's Cadenza.)
336	X				X			Ricordo di Londra (*Elegie* for clarinet and piano)
337	X				X			Terzen Tonleitern (*Klavierübung* Pt. 5, 1st ed.)
338	X			X	X			(*Klavierübung*)
339	X			X	X			(two sketch books of Mozart cadenzas. See also No. 340.)
340	X				X			Cadenza del Pianoforte per il Concerto in Do magg. (K. 503, see also No. 339 above for sketches of same.)
341	X	X			X			W. A. Mozart, Klavier Konzert G dur. Bearbeitung der Solostimme von Ferruccio Busoni. Übertragung des

Staatsbibliothek Number	Piano Item	Non-piano Item	Fragment	Sketch	Deutsche Staatsbibliothek. East Berlin	Staatsbibliothek Preussischer Kulturbesitz	Lost during World War II	Title is given as on Busoni's manuscript. Author's comments and information are in parentheses.
								Orchesters von Egon Petri. Ausgabe für zwei Klaviere (K. 453)
342				X	X			(Book of sketches, including *Doktor Faust*.)
343		X			X			Grausige Geschichte vom Münzjuden Lippold. Vier Gedichte von Goethe. (for baritone and orchestra)
		X	X		X			Grausige Historie vom Münzjuden Lippold (This is 343a, for baritone and piano, and is a reduction of the above item. Both this and the above are from *Die Brautwahl*.)
344	X				X			(Proof copies of the first edition of the *Klavierübung*, with the Paganini-Liszt *Etudes* and the *Fünf kurze Stücke zur Pflege des polyphonen Spiels*, organized for the second edition of the *Klavierübung*.)
345		X		X	X			(Sketches for *Doktor Faust*.)
346		X			X			Doktor Faust (photocopy of the score, original lost in World War II)
347	X				X			(Printed copy of *Minuetto*, op. 14, with fingering.)
348	X				X			(Printed copy of *Danza Notturna*, op. 13, with fingering.)
349		X			X			(Printed copy of the *Album Vocale*, op. 30, with fingering.)
350		X			X			(Printed copy of *Kultaselle*, for cello and piano.)
351	X				X			(Printed copy of Busoni's edition of the Bach WK, book 1.)
352		X			X		X	(Printed copy of *An Babylons Wassern* with various inscriptions.)
353	X				X			(Printed copy of the *Indian Fantasy*, two-piano reduction.)
354	X				X			(Printed copy of *Improvisation über Bach'sche Chorallied*.)

Staatsbibliothek Number	Piano Item	Non-piano Item	Fragment	Sketch	Deutsche Staatsbibliothek. East Berlin	Staatsbibliothek Preussischer Kulturbesitz	Lost during World War II	Title is given as on Busoni's manuscript. Author's comments and information are in parentheses.
356	X					X		(Proof copy of *Fantasia Contrappuntistica*, for two pianos.)
357	X					X		(Printed copy of *Duettino Concertante*.)
358	X					X		(Proof copy of *Klavierübung*, Pt. 5, 1st ed.)
359		X				X		(Proof copy of *Zigeuner Lied*.)
360	X					X		Invention (c minor), Praeludium Fuge (a minor), (also a fragment of a work for two pianos)
361	X					X		Cadenz zu Mozarts C dur Concert (K. 467)
362		X				X		(Printed copy of *Primavera, Estate, Autunno, Inverno*.)
363	X					X		(Bound volume containing the printed music of *7 Elegien, Nuit de Noël, Fantasia nach Bach*, and *An die Jugend*.)
364		X				X		(Bound volume containing the printed music of *Symphonische Suite*, op. 25, *Symphonisches Tongedicht*, and two overtures: *Die Entführung aus dem Serail* by Mozart with Busoni's concert ending, and Busoni's *Lustspiel-Ouvertüre*.)
365	X					X		(Bound volume containing the printed music of *8 Etudes de Piano par J. B. Cramer choisies des 16 nouvelles Etudes Op. 81 révues et publiées par Ferruccio B. Busoni*, as well as the following Bach works edited by Busoni: *2 and 3-part Inventions*, d minor *Concerto*, 10 *Chorale-preludes*, D major and E flat major organ *Prelude and Fugue*.)

Staatsbibliothek Number	Piano Item	Non-piano Item	Fragment	Sketch	Deutsche Staatsbibliothek. East Berlin	Staatsbibliothek Preussischer Kulturbesitz	Lost during World War II	Title is given as on Busoni's manuscript. Author's comments and information are in parentheses.
366	X				X			(Bound volume containing the printed music of Busoni-Liszt *Fantasie and Fugue on "Ad nos . . . ,"* *Mephisto Waltz*, *Spanish Rhapsody*, as well as Busoni's fantasias on Cornelius' *Barber of Bagdad*, and Goldmark's *Merlino* and Busoni's arrangement of Nováček's *Scherzo* from his string quartet.)

The West Berlin Staatsbibliothek Preussischer Kulturbesitz also has the following Busoni manuscripts not included in the numbered series:

N. Mus. ms. 120   Der Schmerz   Lied ohne Worte für Klavier Allein (same as SB 40)

N. Mus. Nachl. 4, 71 and 4, 72   Il Sabato del Villagio

N. Mus. ms. 281   Zweite Sonate fuer Clavier & Violine, op. 36A

N. Mus. ms. 10 363 op. 38   Ouverture zu einer komischen Oper. (copy of the Lustspiel- Ouvertüre)

N. Mus. Nachl. 4, 71, 2 and 4, 71, 3   Il Sabato del Villagio (copies of the first and seventh parts)

N. Mus. Nachl. 4, 73   Su Monte Mario (fragment for baritone and orchestra)

N. Mus. Nachl. 4, 74 and 4, 82   (sketches and fragment from *Arlecchino*)

N. Mus. Nachl. 4, 83   (sketch from *Turandot*)

N. Mus. ms. 10 362   (copy of the parts of *Turandot*)

N. Mus. ms. 10   Sonatina brevis   In signo Joannis Sebastiani Magni in freier Nachdichtung von Bach's kleiner Fantasie & Fuge d moll

N. Mus. Nachl. 4, 76   Albumblatt (No. 2 of the *Drei Albumblätter*)

N. Mus. Nachl. 4, 84 and N. Mus. ms 11   (sketches for *Doktor Faust*)

N. Mus. 4625   (copy of the incomplete vocal score of *Doktor Faust*)

Neuer-Busoni-Nachlass   (copies of SB 315 and 316)

N. Mus. Nachl. 4, 77   Kadenzen zu Mozart's Klavier Konzert in G-dur (K. 453)

N. Mus. Nachl. 4, 87   Rhapsodie hongroise après d'une copie dans le Liszt-Museum de Weimar   (Busoni's edition of the twentieth Rhapsody)

N. Mus. Nachl. 4, 88   (Busoni's printed copy of the Liszt *Tarantelle d'apres la Tarantelle de la Muette de Portici d'Auber pour piano*, with written inscriptions and amendments)

N. Mus. ms. 215   Exercise pour la l'emploi de la troisième Pédale (from the second edition of *Klavierübung*)

N. Mus. Nachl. 4, 78   Tema fugabile   Tema Passacaglia (fragment for piano)

N. Mus. Nachl. 4, 79   Tema, in modo d'un esposizione di Fuga (sketch for piano)

N. Mus. Nachl. 4, 80   (sketch for an orchestral piece)

N. Mus. Nachl. 4, 81   (sketch on postcard)

N. Mus. ms. 31   (contrapuntal sketches and fragment)

N. Mus. ms. 82   (fragment of a fugue for piano)

The East Berlin Deutsche Staatsbibliothek also has the following Busoni manuscripts not included in the numbered series:

Sigune (libretto of the unfinished opera)

Die Brautwahl (libretto of the opera)

Johann Sebastian Bach   Chromatische Fantasie

Sechs Orgelchoralvorspiele von Johannes Brahms für das Pianoforte ausgewählt und übertragen

G. Ricordi in Milan owns the autographs of:

Scherzo, tratto dalla Sonata op. 8 in Mi magg

Op. 14 Menuetto

Op. 21   Preludio e Fuga, in Do min
Op. 25 Gavotta
Danze antiche   Minuetto, Gavotta, Gigue, Bourrée, op. 10
Menuett 28   Aufgabe   Das dreitheilige Lied mit Alternativ-Trio, op. 40
Sonatine, op. 46
Gigue, op. 44 (The last three items constitute the *3 Pezzi nello stile antico*, op. 10.)
Praeludium e Fuga, op. 36
24 Preludi per Pianoforte, op. 37
Una Festa di Villaggio   6 pezzi caratteristici per Pianoforte, op. 9
Primavera, Estate, Autunno, Inverno   4 Poesie Liriche   Poste in Musica per
   Assoli e Coro d'Uomini con accomp. d'Orchestra o Pianoforte, op. 40
Serenate per Violoncello e Pianoforte, op. 34
Trascrizione di Concerto sopra motivi dell' opera "Merlino" di C. Goldmark
   per Pianoforte
Marcia Funebre in morte di Siegfried nel Dramma musicale "Il Crepuscolo degli Dei"
   di Riccardo Wagner   Trascrizione per Pianoforte

The James D. Hoskins Library in the University of Tennessee, Knoxville, houses
the Galston-Busoni Archive, which contains the following Busoni manuscripts:

F.1   Tanzwalzer vom Orchester auf zwei Klaviere übertragen vom Komponisten
   (fragment only)
F.4.f   Die Sproede-die Bekehrte   Zwei Geschwister-Lieder von Goethe (fragment
   and sketches)
F.4.d   Preludio (No. 2 of the *Fünf kurze stücke zur Pflege des polyphonen Speils
   auf dem Pianoforte*)
F.4.a, F.4.c, and F.8 (manuscripts and proof copy of the *Prélude et Etude en
   Arpèges pour piano*)
F.3   Liszt-Busoni   "Tremolo"   I   Etüde nach Paganini
F.2   Liszt-Busoni   "La Chasse"   5   Etüde nach Paganini
F.5   Mozart, Fantasie für eine Orgelwalze, für zwei Klaviere bearbeitet
F.7   Mozart's Ouverture zu "die Zauberflöte," auf zwei Klaviere übertragen
F.9   Sechs Varianten zu Etüden und Präludien von Chopin (for the second edition
   of the *Klavierübung*)
F.4.e   Eine bunte Sammlung von Missgeburten aus dem lieblichen Monat Juni
   1923 von dem sonst geschätzten Autor des "Harlekin" (various fragments and
   sketches)

The Staatsarchiv in Leipzig has:

Berceuse (from the *Elegien*) and Indianische Fantasie für Klavier mit Orchester

Breitkopf and Haertel in Wiesbaden have:

Nocturne Symphonique
Sonatina in Diem Nativitatis Christi MCMXVII
Turandot (copy of the score; original autograph lost)

The Busoni disciple Gisella Selden-Goth has in her private library:

Die Bekehrte   Für eine Frauenstimme mit Klavier

Mrs. Hilda Tagliapietra, widow of Busoni's disciple Gino Tagliapietra, owned
two Busoni manuscripts:

Zehn Variationen über ein Präludiem von Chopin
Notturni   Prologo (fragment)
(Copies of these manuscripts are to be found in the Biblioteca Marciana di Venezia,
   Dono di Gino Tagliapietra, No. 233546 and No. 233547. Currently originals are
   in the hands of Ronald Stevenson and Gino Gorini, respectively.)

C. F. Kahnt in Lindau own:

Zwei Lieder für eine Altstimme mit Begleitung des Pianoforte (published as op. 24)

The Centro Studi Musicali "F. Busoni" in Empoli owns:

Finnlaendische Volksweisen für Pianoforte zu 4 Haenden, op. 27

VEB Breitkopf & Härtel in Leipzig have a copy of the original autograph of:

Concerto Coda supplementaria corrispondente alla Versione in quattro tempi omettendo il coro Finale (the *Concerto*, op. XXXIX ending without choir)

The Library of Congress in Washington has:

Rondeau harlequinesque (published as op. 46)

The Central Museum of Musical Culture in the name of "M. I. Glinka" has:

Cadenz zum I.   Satze des Conzertes N. 4 von Ludwig van Beethoven

The Pierpont Morgan Library in New York has, as part of its Mary Flagler Cary
Music Collection:

Tre Cadenze per il Concerto di Violino di Beethoven

The music archives of Yale University have:

Busoni's arrangement of No. 3 of Kurt Weill's *Frauentanz*

In the private collection of Daniell Revenaugh:

Nos. 1, 3, and 5 of the *Fünf kurze Stücke zur Pflege des polyphonen Spiels auf dem
Pianoforte*

Bibliography

BUSONI'S OWN WRITINGS

I have not included below the numerous prefaces, notes, and essays that accompanied almost each one of Busoni's editions and transcriptions. These appear in the main body of the book, in the relevant chapters. Neither have I given the many reprints of various articles; only the first publication is given. Some writings appeared for the first time in *Von der Einheit der Musik* (1922) or else in its posthumous edition retitled *Wesen und Einheit der Musik* (1956). Such appearances are indicated as 1922* and 1956*, respectively.

On Music

Articles by Busoni

Published in *L'Indipendente* (Trieste) 1884-1885 under the anagrammatic pseudonym of "Bruno Fioresucci"):

1. (no title) 13/1/84
2. (no title) 6/2/84
3. "Rubinstein a Vienna." 28/2/84, 3/3/84
4. "A. Rubinstein," "V. de Pachmann," "Stanford." 24/3/84
5. "All'Accademia di canto," "Arte italiana," "Il 'Matrimonio segreto,'" "La stagione del teatro italiano." 25/3/84
6. "Fine della stagione," "I critici a Vienna," "Gli ultimi concerti filarmonici," "Requiem di Berlioz," "Manfredi," "Stagione italiana," "Novità all'Opera," "La violinista Soldat," "Pittura," "La mia prossima corrispondenza." 18/4/84
7. "Carmen di Giorgio Bizet, eseguita a Trieste per la prima volta il 12 maggio 1884 el teatro Armonia." 14/5/84, 15/5/84
8. "Carmen (alcune note)." 20/5/84

9. "Della Carmen di G. Bizet e del posto ch'ella occupa nella storia dell'opera francese." 13/6/84, 14/6/84, 15/6/84
10. "Hans Bülow." 26/12/84, 27/12/84
11. "Dell'intelligenza musicale (Saggio Critico)." 5/7/85, 6/7/85, 9/7/85, 10/7/85
12. "Chiacchierata d'un musicista." 24/10/85

"Musikstände in Italien." *Grazer Tagespost*, XXXI, 31/8/86, 3/9/86, 20/10/86.

"Zum Don-Juan-Jubiläum. Ein kritischer Beitrag." *Neue Zeitschrift für* Musik, 26/10/86.

"Verdis 'Othello.' Eine Kritische Studie." *Neue Zeitschrift für Musik*, LIV, 12, 23/3/87.

"Giovanni Sgambati. Eine Studie zur Beleuchtung der heutige Musikzustände in Italien." *Neue Zeitschrift für Musik*, LVIII/25, 23/6/87.

Untitled letter in *Welches Werk Richard Wagners halten Sie für das beste?* by Ugo Tomicich, Trieste, 1889.

"Die Ausgaben der Lisztschen Klavierwerke. Bibliographisch-kritische Studie, als Grundlage zu der geplanten Gesamtausgabe entworfen." *Allgemeine Musikzeitung*, 1901.

"Zu den Orchesterabenden. I. Offener Brief." *Allgemeine Musikzeitung*. Nov. 1902.

"R. M. Breithaupt. Die natürliche Klaviertechnik." *Die Musik*, IV/22, Aug. 1905.

"Über Instrumentationslehre." *Die Musik*, V, Nov. 1905.

"Mozart-Aphorismen. Zum 150 Geburtstage des Meisters." *Berliner Lokal-Anzeiger*, XLI, 27/1/06.

"Von Auswendigspielen. Offener Brief." *Die Musik*, VI/15, May 1906-1907.

"Wie ich komponiere? Offener Brief." *Das Konzertsaal*, May 1907.

"Über 'Salome,'" *Die Zeit*, 142, 26/5/07.

"Aus der klassischen Walpurgisnacht von Ino-Sub-F." *Die Musik*, VII/9, 1907-1908.

"Zu den Orchesterabenden, Offener Brief." *Allgemeine Musikzeitung*, Jan. 1908.

"Die Affaire in der Meisterschule. An der Hand eines Briefmateriales von Ferruccio Busoni." *Wiener Zeitschrift für Musik*, Heft 5, March 1908.

"Offene Entgegnung an die 'Signale,'" *Signale für die Musikalische Welt*, 1909.

"Aphorismen zu Kunst und Technik." *Signale für die Musikalische Welt*, LXVII/35, Sept. 1909.

"Brief über Amerika." *Signale für die Musikalische Welt*, 1910.

"Man achte das Pianoforte." Part of "Galstons Studienbuch," 1910.

"Die 'Gotiker' von Chicago, Illinois." *Signale für die Musikalische Welt*, LXVIII/5, 2/2/10.

"Was Busoni vom Pianisten verlangt." *Signale für die Musikalische Welt*, LXVIII/14, 6/4/10.

"Neglected Details in Pianoforte Study." *Etude* 28 (Apr.-May 1910): 225-26, 310.

"Galstons Studienbuch." *Signale für die Musikalische Welt*, LXVIII/30, 27/7/10.

"Wert der Bearbeitung." Annotations to a program by the Berlin Philharmonic, conducted by Arthur Nikisch, 7/11/10.

"Wie lange soll das gehen?" *Signale für die Musikalische Welt*, LXIX/2, 11/1/11.

"Die neue Harmonik." *Signale für die Musikalische Welt*, LXIX/7, 15/2/11.

"Routine." *Pan*, I, Mar.-Oct. 1911, pp. 654-655.

"Schönberg-Matinée." *Pan*, Oct. 1911-Mar. 1912, p. 298.

"Selbst-Rezension." *Pan*, II Oct. 1911-Mar. 1912, pp. 327-33.
"Zum Turandotmusik." *Blätter des Deutschen Theaters*, I/6, 27/10/11.
"Futurismus der Tonkunst." *Pan*, III, Oct. 1912-Mar. 1913, pp. 11-12.
"Das Klaviergenie." *Allgemeine Musikzeitung*, XXXIX/10, 8/3/12.
"Von der Zukunft der Oper." *Vossische Zeitung*, 1913.
"Important Details in Piano Study." Chapter by Busoni in *Great Pianists on Piano Playing* (Study Talks by Foremost Virtuosos) by James Francis Cooke (Philadelphia, Theo Presser, 1913; reprinted 1976).
"Über die Parsifal-Partitur." *Vossische Zeitung*, 10, 6/1/13.
"'Englisch-Horn' oder 'Alt-Oboe'? Offener Brief." *Die Musik*, XIV/15, May 1915.
"Zur Frage musikalischer Eigenart. Offener Brief." *Allgemeine Musikzeitung*, XLII, 5/11/15.
"Geleitwort zur Bach-Ausgabe." *Mitteilungsblatt des Verlages Breitkopf und Haertel*, 1916.
"Rondo Arlecchinesco." *Zürcher Theater-, Konzert- und Fremdenblatt*, XXXVI/22, 22/3/16.
"Beethoven." *Zürcher Theater-, Konzert- und Fremdenblatt*, XXXVI/26, 8/4/16.
"Chopin." *Zürcher Theater-, Konzert- und Fremdenblatt*, XXXVI/26, 8/4/16.
"Jan Sibelius." *Zürcher Theater-, Konzert- und Fremdenblatt*, XXXVI/26, 8/4/16.
"Liszt." *Zürcher Theater-, Konzert- und Fremdenblatt*, XXXVI/30, 22/4/16.
"Offener Brief an Hans Pfitzner." *Vossische Zeitung*, 278, 3/6/17.
"Arrigo Boito." *Neue Zürcher Zeitung*, June 1918.
"'Junge Klassizität,' Offener Brief an Paul Bekker." *Frankfurter Allgemeine Zeitung*, 7/2/20.
"Um Liszt. Offener Brief an Rudolph Kastner." *Das Tagebuch*, I/38, 2/10/20.
"Entwurf eines Vorwortes zur Partitur des 'Doktor Faust' enthaltend einige Betrachtungen über die Möglichkeiten der Oper." *Faust*, I/1, 1921.
"Zum Entwurf einer szenischen Aufführung von J. S. Bach's Matthäuspassion." *Faust*, I, 1921.
"Zur Musikbeilage 'Die Bekehrte' von W. Vogel." *Faust*, I, 1921.
"An die Jugend." *Musikblätter des Anbruch*, III/1-2, 1-15/1/21.
"Aufzeichnungen und Tagebuchblätter." *Musikblätter des Anbruch*, III/1-2, 1-15/1/21.
"Arlecchino sein Werdegang." *Blätter der Staatsoper* (Berlin), I/7, 13/5/21.
"Künstlers Helfer." *Vossische Zeitung*, 238, 13/5/21.
"Zu seiner Deutung." *Blätter der Staatsoper* (Berlin) I/7, 13/5/21.
"Erinnerungen an Saint-Saëns." *Vossische Zeitung*, 609, 27/12/21.
"A propos 'Arlecchino.'" 1922.*
"Aufzeichnungen." 1922*
"Bemerkungen über die Reihenfolge der Opuszahlen meiner Werke." 1922*
"Die Champagnerarie." 1922*
"Skizze zum Vorwort des Wohltemperierten Klavieres II. Teil." 1922*
"Von den Proportionen." 1922*
"Was gab uns Beethoven?" 1922*
"Offener Musikbrief an Fritz Windisch." *Melos*, III/2, 17 Jan. 1922.
"Bericht über Dritteltöne." *Melos*, III, Aug. 1922.

"Später." *Berliner Tageblatt*, 1923.

"Unsentimentaler Rückblick." *Die Woche*, 1923?

"Zeitgemässe Nachwort zu der Bach Ausgabe von Ferruccio Busoni." *Der Bär*, yearbook of Breitkopf & Haertel Verlag, 1923.

"Aphorismen." *Blätter der Staatsoper* (Berlin), 1924.

"Franz Liszt Vorrede zur ersten Kollektivausgabe von Fields Nocturnes." *Die Musik*, 1924.

"Vom Wessen der Musik. Anbahnung einer Verständigung für den immerwährenden Kalender." *Melos*, IV/1, 1924.

"Zeitwelle, musikalische Betrachtungen." *Blätter der Staatsoper*, V/2, 1924. (Probably Busoni's last writing.)

"Über die Partitur des 'Doktor Faust.'" *Blätter des Dresdner Staatstheater*, I/5, May 1925.

"Zwei autobiographische Fragmente." *Die Musik*, XXII/1, Oct. 1929.

"Die Melodie der Zukunft." *Zeitschrift für Musik*, XCVII/2, Feb. 1930.

"Über Melodie." *Zeitschrift für Musik*, XCVII/2, Feb. 1930.

"Schnitzel und Späne." *Zeitschrift für Musik*, 1932.

"Der Virtuose," *Zeitschrift für Musik*, XCIX/12, Dec. 1932.

"Die Einheit der Musik." *Zeitschrift für Musik*, XCIX/12, Dec. 1932.

"Sozialismus vom Künstler aus geschaut." *Zeitschrift für Musik*, XCIX/12, Dec. 1932.

"Virtuosenlaufbahn." In *Ferruccio Busoni: A Biography* by Edward J. Dent (London, Oxford University Press, 1933), p. 106.

"Beethoven und der musikalische Humor." 1956.*

"Über Richard Strauss." 1956.*

"Die Unzulänglichkeit der musikalischen Ausdrucksmittel." 1956.*

"Zum Zeitgeschehen." 1956.*

Letter to Georg Häser about *Parsifal.* 1956*

"Musikland Amerika." *Musika*, 10:196-97, Apr. 1956.

"Ferruccio Busoni an Karl Straube." *Musica*, 23:492, n.5, 1969.

"Sobre la tecnica de las octavas." *Heterofonia*, 4:20-22, n.24, 1972.

"Das Plagiat in der Musik." In *Lo sguardo lieto* by Ferruccio Busoni. ed. Fedele d'Amico (Milan, Il Saggiatore, 1977), p. 83.

Books by Busoni

Entwurf einer neuen Ästhetik der Tonkunst (Trieste, Carl Schmidl, 1907; Leipzig, Insel-Verlag, 1916; Wiesbaden, Insel-Bücherei, 1954).

Versuch einer organischen Klavier-Noten-Schrift (Leipzig, Breitkopf & Haertel, 1910).

Von der Einheit der Musik, von Dritteltönen und junger Klassizität, von Bühnen, und Bauten, und anschliessenden Bezirken. Verstreute Aufzeichnungen (Berlin, Max Hesses Verlag, 1922).

Über die Möglichkeiten der Oper und über die Partitur des "Doktor Faust" (Leipzig, Breitkopf & Haertel, 1926).

Wesen und Einheit der Musik. Neuausgabe der Schriften und Aufzeichnungen Busonis revidiert und ergänzt von Joachim Herrmann (Berlin, Max Hesses Verlag, 1956).

On Other Subjects

"Eine Märchenhafte Erfindung," (signed: Aprilus Fischer) *Signale für die Musikalische Welt*, LXIX/13, 29/3/11.

"Zum Geleit von E.T.A. Hoffmanns Phantastischen Geschichte," for an edition of Hoffmann by Georg Müller Verlag, Monaco, 1914.

"Der Kriegsfall Boccioni," *Neue Zürcher Zeitung*, 31/8/16.

"Charles Baudelaire über Edgar Allan Poe. Fragmentarische Übertragung." 1922,* pp. 251-54.

"Die Zigarrenkiste." 1922,* p. 201.

"Gedanken über den Ausdruck in der Architektur. (Fragment.)" 1922,* p. 229.

"Nachteil des Sehenden." 1922,* p. 213.

"Projekt für eine dreifache Bühnenöffnung." 1922,* p. 268.

"Sonetto CXXIII" by F. Petrarch, translated by Busoni into German. 1922.* pp. 266-67.

"Traum." 1922,* p. 198.

"E. T. A. Hoffmann und Edgar Allan Poe." *Zeitschrift für Musik*, XCIX/12, Dec. 1932.

Librettos

Der mächtige Zauberer (The Mighty Magician), from a short story by Gobineau. Dedicated to Gerda Busoni (Trieste, Schmidl, 1907).

Die Brautwahl (The Bridal Choice), after a story by E. T. A. Hoffmann (Trieste, Schmidl, 1907).

Arlecchino oder Die Fenster, ein theatralisches Capriccio (Arlecchino or the Window) (Leipzig, Breitkopf & Haertel, 1919).

Turandot, after Gozzi's play. (Leipzig, Breitkopf & Haertel, 1919).

Das Wandbild (The Picture on the Wall). Dedicated to Philipp Jarnach. Set to music by Othmar Schoeck (Leipzig, Breitkopf & Haertel, 1920).

Doktor Faust (Berlin, G. Kiepenheuer, 1920).

Das Geheimnis (The Secret), three scenes after Villiers de l'Isle-Adam (Berlin, Blätter der Staatsoper, 1924).

"Der Arlecchineide Fortsetzung und Ende" (continuation and end of the Harlequinade). Unpublished manuscript.

"Die Götterbraut" (The Bride of the Gods), written for L. T. Gruenberg. Unpublished manuscript.

Letters

Witt, Militza V. "Aus Briefen Busonis." *Deutsche Allgemeine Zeitung*, 8/5/31.

"Brief an Guiseppe Verdi." *Zeitschrift für Musik*, XCIX/12, Dec. 1932, p. 1057.

"Brief an Marcel Rémy." *Zeitschrift für Musik*, XCIX/12, Dec. 1932, p. 1058.

Freundesbriefe (Berlin, Neue Rundschau, 1934), Juli-Heft, p. 71.

Briefe an seine Frau. Ed. Friedrich Schnapp (Erlenbach-Zürich-Leipzig, Rotapfel-Verlag, 1935).

Fünfundzwanzig Busoni-Briefe. Ed. Gisella Selden-Goth (Wien-Leipzig-Zürich, Reichner-Verlag, 1937).

"Briefe Busonis an Hans Huber." Ed. Edgar Refardt, in *Hundertsiebenund-zwanzigstes Neujahrsblatt der Allgemeinen Musikgesellschaft in Zürich auf das Jahr 1939* (Zürich-Leipzig, Verlag Hug, 1939).

Mahler, A. M., and Gustav Mahler. *Erinnerungen und Briefe* (Amsterdam, Verlag Albert de Lange, 1940).

A. N. Scriabin (an anthology) (Moskva-Leningrad, Muzgiz, 1940).

Klinckerfuss, M. *Aufklänge aus versunkener Zeit* (Postverlag-Urach, 1947).

Corte, A. D. *Arrigo Serato* (Siena, Casa Editrice Ticci, 1950). (Letters from Busoni to Serato appear in the Appendix.)

Wessely, O. "Fünf unbekannte Jugendbriefe von Ferruccio Benvenuto Busoni." *Festschrift Walther Vetter* (Berlin, 1961).

Busoni, F., "Briefe und Widmungen an Othmar Schoek." *Schweiz Mus.*, 106:132-35, n. 3, 1966.

Wis, R. *Terra boreale* (Helsinki, 1969), pp. 149-82.

"Briefwechsel zwischen Arnold Schoenberg und Ferruccio Busoni, 1903-1919 (1927)." Ed. Jutta Theurich, in *Beitrage zur Musikwissenschaft*, Berlin, (GDR) 19 Jahrgang 1977- Heft 3, pp. 163-211.

A number of Busoni's letters appear in *Von der Einheit der Musik* and in *Wesen und Einheit der Musik* (see above).

Letters are also quoted in writings by the following, to be found elsewhere in the Bibliography: Gerda Busoni, Dent, Giazotto, Selden-Goth, Stuckenschmidt, Debusmann, Pisk, Bekker, Kastner, Theurich, Stevenson, Szigeti, Prelinger, Sartori, and in the *Piano Quarterly*.

Many Busoni letters remain unpublished, and it is hoped that the numerous letters, now in private hands, from Busoni to Jakob Wassermann, Egon Petri, Gottfried Galston, Philipp Jarnach and Eduard Steuermann, and others, will eventually be released for publication.

There is an unpublished letter to the Marquis Silvio della Valle di Casanova in the *Busoni-Nachlass* (No. 234); the *Nachlass* should also be investigated for further unpublished letters.

The Gottfried Galston archives contain much Busoni material, including musical and literary manuscripts, many concert programs, photographs, newspaper items, and other memorabilia; letters from Busoni to Emil Gutman (11), to Professor Waldemar Meyer (10), to Herr Lienau, Musikverlag "Schlesinger" (12), and to Galston himself (54). There is also a personal diary of Galston's visits with Busoni in the last years of Busoni's life, dating from 14 October 1921 to 21 July 1924. (This diary consists of 256 handwritten pages.) The archives are now located in the Special Collections Department of the James D. Hoskins Library on the Knoxville campus of the University of Tennessee. See P. S. Bayne, *The Gottfried Galston Music Collection and the Galston-Busoni Archive* (Knoxville, University of Tennessee Library, 1978).

IMPORTANT TRANSLATIONS OF BUSONI'S WRITINGS

Sketch of a New Esthetic of Music. Trans. Th. Baker (New York, G. Schirmer, 1911; reprinted in *Three Classics in the Aesthetics of Music: Monsieur Croche, the Dilettante Hater, Claude Debussy; Sketch of a New Esthetic of Music, Ferruccio Busoni; and Essay before a Sonata, Charles Ives*, New York, Dover Publications, 1962).

Scritti e Pensieri Sulla Musica. Trans. Luigi Dallapiccola and Guido M. Gatti (Firenze, Felice le Monnier, MCMXLI-XIX). Contains an introductory essay by Massimo Bontempelli.

Letters to His Wife. Trans. Rosamond Ley (London, Edward Arnold, 1938; reprinted New York, Da Capo Press, 1975). Also translated into Italian as *Lettere alla moglie* by Luigi Dallapiccola (Milano, 1955).

The Essence of Music and Other Papers. Trans. Rosamond Ley (London, Rockliff, 1957).

Lo sguardo lieto: tutti gli scritti sulla musica e le arti. Ed. Fedele d'Amico. Trans. Laura Dallapiccola and Fedele d'Amico (Milano, Il Saggiatore, 1977). Contains an introductory essay by Fedele d'Amico plus a supplementary booklet, *Sulla trascrizione per pianoforte delle opere per organo di Bach.*

MAJOR WRITINGS ON BUSONI

Barinova, M.N. *Vospominaniye o Hoffmane i Busoni* (Moscow, Musika, 1964.)

Busoni, Gerda. *Erinnerungen an Ferruccio Busoni* (Berlin, AFAS Music Verlag, 1958).

Busoni, Gerda. *Il mio incontro con Ferruccio Busoni.* Trans. M. Lollini, MUS OGGI 3:8-20, Jan. 1960.

Dent, Edward J. *Ferruccio Busoni: A Biography* (London, Oxford University Press, 1933).

Giazotto, Remo. *Busoni: La Vita nell' Opera* (Milano, S. A. Editrice Genio, 1947).

Guerrini, Guido, with Paolo Gragapane. *Il Doktor Faust di Ferruccio Busoni* (Firenze, Casa Editrice Monsalvato, 1942).

Guerrini, Guido. *Ferruccio Busoni: La Vita, La Figura, L'Opera* (Firenze, Monsalvato, 1944).

Kindermann, Jürgen. *Thematisch-chronologisches Verzeichnis der musikalischen Werke von Ferruccio B. Busoni* (Regensburg, Gustav Bosse Verlag, 1980).

Kogan, G. *Ferruccio Busoni.* (Moskva, Vsesoyuzonoe izdatelstvo, Sovietskii Kompozitor, 1971).

Kosnick, Heinrich. *Busoni Gestaltung durch Gestalt* (Regensburg, Gustav Bosse Verlag, 1971).

Krellmann, Hanspeter. *Studien zu den Bearbeitungen Ferruccio Busonis* (Regensburg, Gustav Bosse Verlag, 1966).

Leichtentritt, Hugo. *Ferruccio Busoni* (Leipzig, Breitkopf & Haertel, 1916).

Meyer, Heinz. *Die Klaviermusik Ferruccio Busonis* (Wolfenbüttel, Möseler Verlag, 1969).

Nadel, Siegfried F. *Ferruccio Busoni* (Leipzig, Breitkopf & Haertel, 1931).

Santelli, Alfonso. *Busoni* (Roma, Carlo Colombo, 1938).

Selden-Goth, Gisella. *Ferruccio Busoni: Der Versuch eines Porträts* (Leipzig, E. P. Tal, 1922).

Selden-Goth, Gisella. *Ferruccio Busoni: Un Profilo* (Firenze, Historiae Musicae Cultores, 20, Leo S. Olschki-Editore, 1964).

Stuckenschmidt, H. H. *Ferruccio Busoni: Chronicle of a European* (Zürich, Atlantis Verlag AG, 1967; English translation by Sandra Morris, London, Calder & Boyars, 1970).

van Dieren, Bernard. *Down among the Dead Men (and Other Essays)* (London, Oxford University Press, 1935).

GENERAL BIBLIOGRAPHY

Aisberg, E. "Iz oblasti sovremennovo pianizma." *Muzika*, no. 157, 1913.

Altmann, Wilhelm. "Zu der Musikbeigabe." *Nord und Süd*, 34. Jg., o.J., S. 7.

Anniversaire Ferruccio Busoni, port. *MUS*. (Chaix) n.147:5-6, June 1966.

Anzoletti, Emilio. "Ferruccio Busoni quale compositore." *Il Giornale dei Musicisti*, 2. Jg. S. 122-26. 1909.

Backhaus, Franz. *"Arlecchino"—Ein theatralisches Capriccio von Ferruccio Busoni mit einem Beitrag zur Geschichte der Parodie in der Oper.* Msschr. Diss., Innsbruck, 1977.

Ballola, Giovanni Carli. "La 'Turandot' di Ferruccio Busoni." *La Rassegna Musicale*, 32, Jg. S. 132-42. 1962.

Balogh, E.: "The Universal Man," port *Opera News*, 24:12-13, 19 Dec. 1959.

Baume, I.: "Souvenirs," port *MUS* (Chaix) n.147:6-7, June 1966.

Bekker, Paul. "Busoni." *Neue Musik*. Ed. Deutsche Verlage-Anstalt Stuttgart, 1923. Vierte Auflage, Erich Reiss Verlag, Berlin, 1920.

_____. "Busoni." *Musikblätter des Anbruch*, 6. Jg. 1924.

_____. "Busoni." Gedenkrede zur Enthüllung seines Grabdenkmals." In *25 Jahre neue Musik*. Jahrbuch 1926 der Universal-Edition.

_____. "Busonis Bach-Ausgabe. 1921." In Paul Bekker, *Klang und Eros*. Zweiter Band der Gesammelten Schriften. Deutsche Verlags-Anstalt, Stuttgart und Berlin, 1922.

_____. "Ferruccio Busoni: 'Turandot'—'Arlecchino' . . . Offener Brief." *Klang und Eros*. Stuttgart und Berlin, S. 82-86. 1922.

_____. "Futuristengefahr? 1917." Appears in: Paul Bekker. *Kritische Zeitbilder*. Schuster und Loeffler, Berlin, 1921.

_____. "Impotenz oder Potenz? Eine Antword an Herrn Professor Dr. Hans Pfitzner, *Frankfurt Zeitung*, 15 und 16 Januar 1920"; also in Paul Bekker, *Kritische Zeitbilder*. Schuster und Loeffler, Berlin, 1921.

_____. "Nachruf für Busoni." *Musikblätter des Anbruch*. Oktober-Heft, 1924.

_____. "Neue Musik." *Tribüne der Kunst und Zeit*. Berlin, 1919.

_____. "Über Busoni 1921." In Paul Bekker, *Klang und Eros*. Zweiter Band der Gesammelten Schriften. Deutsche Verlags-Anstalt, Stuttgart und Berlin, 1922.

Berg, Alban. "Die Musikalische Impotenz der 'neuen Ästhetick' Hans Pfitzners." *Musikblätter des Anbruch*, 2. Jahrgang, Nos. 11-12, Wien, June 1920.

Berten, Walter. "Ferruccio Busoni." *Musik im Leben*, 5. Jg. 1929-1930.

Bie, Oscar. "Busoni." *Neue Rundschau*. Fischer Verlag, Berlin, 1921.

Boghen, Felice. "L'Italia di Busoni." *Arte Pianistica*, Napoli, anno XI, no. 10, Oct. 1924.

_____. "La Italianita di Ferruccio Busoni." In *Ferruccio Busoni da Empoli*, 1927.

_____. "L'Italianita di Ferruccio Busoni." Atti dell'accademia del R. Conservatorio di Musica "L. Cherubini." Firenze, anno LX 1938.

Bohmer, H. "Busonis Zukunftglaube." port *MELOS* 18:337-44, Heft 12, Dec. 1951.

Bonavia, Ferruccio. "Giacomo Puccini and Ferruccio Busoni," *ML* 6:9-109, 1925.

Bontempelli, Massimo: "Busoni teorico," *La Rassegna Musicale*, Torino, Gennaio 1940, XVIII, Anno 13, No. 1.

Breithaupt, R. M. *Die natürliche Klaviertechnik*, Leipzig, C. F. Kahnt, 1927.

Brendel, Alfred: "Busoni, Vollender des Klavierspiels," *Osterr. Musikzeitschrift*, 9(1954), S.238-242.

Briner, Andres: "Busoni zum Gedächnis," *Musikwoche*, Berlin, 1954.

_____. "Freheit und Bindung im Denken von Ferruccio Busoni," *Schweizer Musik-zeitung*, 96(1956) S.9-11.

Brugnoli, Attilio: "La Celebralita e il Paradossale Nell'Arte di Ferruccio Busoni," *Il Pianoforte*, Torino, Anno II, 15 giugno, 1921, pp. 172-175.

Ferruccio Busoni da Empoli. Publicato a cura del comitato per le onoranze al grande concittadino. Ditta R. Noccioli, Empoli, 1927. (Scritti di Cordara, Mantovani, Boghen)

"Busoni on Mozart" (aphorisms, trans. H. Zohn). *Saturday Review*, 39:56 27 Oct. 1956.

Busoni, "Rabochie pravila pianista" (trans. G. Kogan) port *Soviet Muz.* 23:127-28, Jan. 1959.

Busoni, Benvenuto. "Um Das Erbe Busonis." *Die Musik*, 27. Jahrgang. S. 187. 1935.

Busoni, F. Entwurf einer neuen Aesthetik der Tonkunst, mit Anmerkungen von Arnold Schoenberg. (Frankfurt am Main, Suhrkamp, 1974), p. 84. *Melos/NZ* 1:148-49, nZ, 1975.

"Busoni vu et entendu par Chantavoine apres un concert consacre a Liszt" (London, 1913). *Mus.* (Chaix) n.147:7, June 1966.

Cadieu, M. "Busoni visage du futur." port. *Musique*, n.19:2-4, Nov. 1974.

Cahn-Speyer, Rudolf. "Ferruccio Busoni." *Allgemeine Musikzeitung*, 1916.

Capellan, Georg. "Ferruccio Busoni: Versuch einer organischen Klaviernoten-schrift." *Die Musik*, 10. Jg. S. 41. 1910/11.

Caporali, Rudolfo. "Le Trascrizioni pianistiche delle opere di Bach." *La Rassegna Musicale*, 20. Jg., S. 241-42. 1950.

Casella, Alfredo. "Busoni Pianista." *Il Pianoforte*, Torino, 15 giugno, 1921.

Casella, Alfredo. "Busoni pianista." *La Rassegna Musicale*, Torino, XVIII, anno 13, no. 1, Gennaio 1940.

Cattaneo, Gulio. "Doktor Busoni." In *Gulio Cattaneo*. Esperienze intellettuali del primo Novecento. Milano-Verona, 1968, pp. 139-161.

Chantavoine, Jean. "Busoni," MQ 7:331-343. 1921.

_____. "Ferruccio Busoni." *Revue Hebdomadaire*, Paris, 17 April 1920.

_____. "Ferruccio Busoni." *Il Pianoforte*, Torino, anno I, no. 6, June 1920.

_____. "Ferruccio Busoni." *Musikblätter des Anbruch*, 3 Jahrgang, H.1/2, Wien, 1-15 Januar 1921.

_____. "Ferruccio Busoni." *La Revue musicale*, 1923/24, no. 11, Octobre 1924.

Chesterman, D. "Boult Remembers Busoni." *Mus. & Mus.*, 14:25 Apr. 1966.

Conze, Joh. "Erinnerungen an Ferruccio Busoni." *Signale für die musikalische Welt*, 94. Jahrgang. 1936.

Cordara, Carlo. "Il Mirabile Artista." In *Ferruccio Busoni da Empoli*, Empoli, 1927.

Corti, Mario. "Ricordi di Ferruccio Busoni." *La Rassegna Musicale*, Torino, anno 13, no. 1, Gennaio 1940. XVIII.

Coul, P. op de. "Ferruccio Busoni (1866-1924)." Facs ports. *Mens en Mel*, 29:194-99 Jul. 1974.

Cowell, Henry. "Busoni's opera 'Arlecchino.'" MQ, 38:134-36, 1952.

Crankshaw, G. "Busoni for Organ." *Mus. & Mus.*, 16:47, June 1968.

Creighton, U. "Reminiscences of Busoni." Il port. *Rec Sound*, 1:249-55, n.8, 1962.

Dalhaus, Carl. "Von der Einheit der Musik. Bemerkungen zur Asthetik Ferruccio Busoni." *Deutsche Universitatszeitung*, no. 10. S. 19. 1956.

Dallapiccola, L. "Pensieri su Busoni." *La Rassegna Musicale*, Torino, XVIII, anno 13, no. 1, Gennaio 1940.

Debusmann, Emil. *Ferruccio Busoni*. Wiesbaden, Brucknerverlag, 1949.

Demetriescu, Teophil. "'Beglückt und entwaffnet.' Erinnerungen an Ferruccio Busoni." *Musik und Gesellschaft*, Berlin, 7. S. 470-71. 1969.

Dent, E. J. Biography note on Busoni in program of Phillip Levi's recital, Grotrian Hall, 7 March 1930.

_____. "Busoni." *The London Mercury*, vol. II, pp. 488-91, Aug. 1920.

_____. "Busoni." *Truth*, 30 June 1920.

_____. "Busoni a Berlino et il Dottor Faust." *Il Pianoforte*, Torino, anno II, pp. 168-72, 15 giugno 1921.

_____. "Busoni and His Operas." Il port, *Opera* (London), 5:391-97, July 1954.

_____. "Busoni and the Pianoforte." *The Athenaeum*, 24 Oct. 1919.

_____. "Busoni—A Posthumous Paper." *Monthly Musical Record*, vol. LXII, pp. 99-100, June 1932.

_____. "Busoni as Composer." *The Athenaeum*, 28 Nov. 1919.

_____. Busoni entry in Grove's *Dictionary of Music and Musicians*. New York, St. Martin's Press, 1954.

_____. (trans. Lotte Dormann)," Busoni in Berlin." *Dresdner Woche*, 15 Apr. 1922.

_____. "Busoni on Musical Aesthetics." *Monthly Musical Record*, vol. XXXIX, pp. 197-98, Sept. 1909.

_____. "Busoni's Arlecchino." *The Listener*, 26 Jan. 1939.

_____. "Busoni's Pianoforte Music." *The Listener*, 25 Nov. 1936.

_____. "Busoni's Works." *The Nation and the Athenaeum*, 5 Mar. 1921.

_____. (trans. Rita Boetticher). "Busoni und das Klavier. Busoni als Komponist." *Musikblätter des Anbruch*. 3 Jahrgang, H.1/2, Wien, 1-15 Januar 1921.

_____. "Ferruccio Busoni." *ML* 14:186-87, 1933.

_____. "Ferruccio Busoni." *The Listener*, 16 Oct. 1935.

_____. "Ferruccio Busoni: A Fragment of Autobiography." Ed. F. Schnapp; trans. Dent. *The Dominant*, vol. II, no. 5, pp. 25-29, Nov. 1929.

_____. "Ferruccio Busoni-Italiano." *La Rassegna Musicale*, Torino, vol. III, no. 1, pp. 44-53, Gennaio 1930.

_____. "The Italian Busoni." *Monthly Musical Record*, vol. LXI, pp. 257-60, Sept. 1931.

_____. "Letter on Busoni's 'Dr. Faust.'" *Monthly Musical Record*, vol. LXVII, pp. 113-14, June 1937.

_____. "Letters from Germany III—The Return of Busoni." *The Athenaeum*, 17 Dec. 1920.

_____. "Mozart and Busoni." *Truth*, 22 Feb. 1921.

_____. "On the Interpretation of Chopin." *The Athenaeum*, London, 9 July 1920.

_____. Pages 11-20 on the Concerto Op. XXXIX, program at Queen's Hall, 21 Feb. 1934 (Petri was soloist).

_____. Translation of the libretto of Dr. Faust, including the Introduction and Epilogue. Published in the program of the BBC concert in Queen's Hall, 17 Mar. 1937. (Pp. 5-6 have an introduction to the opera by Dent.)

Diesterweg, A. "'Futuristen-Dämmerung.' Ein offener Brief und sein Widerhall." *Allgemeine Musikzeitung*, 49. Jg. S. 375. 1922.

Doemling, W. "Revolutionaer wider Willen: Ferruccio Busoni und sein 'Entwurf einer neuen Aesthetik der Tonkunst.'" *NZ*, 134:564-69, n.9, 1973.

Draber, H. W. "Busoni in Weimar." *Musikblätter des Anbruch*, 3. Jg. H. 1/2, Wien, 1-15 Januar 1921.

Dubitzky, Franz. "Ferruccio Busoni: Berceuse élégiaque." *Die Musik*, 9. Jg. S. 376-77. 1909/10.

Duse, U. "L'Estetica di Ferruccio Busoni." *Musica e Verita*, Padova, Marsilio Editori.

Dyment, C. "Ferruccio Busoni, His Phonograph Records." *Association for Recorded Sound Collections Journal*, vol. X, nos. 2-3, pp. 185-87, 1979.

East, Leslie. "Busoni and Van Dieren." *Soundings*, no. 5, University of Cardiff, 1975.

Eimert, H. "Vollender und Wegbereiter." Fac il port, *Mus u Szene*, 6:97-101, no. 9, 1961-1962.

Einstein, Alfred. "Busoni als Briefschreiber." In *Von Schutz bis Hindemith*, S.134-41. 1957.

Ermatingen, Erhart. "Busoni und wir." *Schweiz. Musikz.*, 90. Jahrgang. no. 2, 1950.

Ertei, Paul. "Ferruccio Busoni." *Neue Musikzeitung*, 19. Jahrgang. no. 11, 5 März 1908.

Fisher, E. "Busoni and Phillip." *Rec. Sound*, 1:242-48, n.8, 1962.

Fleischer, Oskar. "Ferruccio B. Busoni: Zweite Sonate für Klavier und Violine op. 36a." *Zeitschrift der Internationalen Musikgesellschaft*, 3. Jg. S. 31. 1901/02.

Friedheim, Arthur. "Busoni und Liszt—Interpretation." *Signale für die Musikalische Welt*, no. 6, 10 Februar 1909.

Fryer, H. "Celebrated Pianists I Have Known." *Music Teacher* 33:285-86, June 1954.

Ganev, K. "Ferucho Buzoni." Port *Bulgar muz* 17:39-42, Jul. 1966.

Gatti, G. M. "Busoni the Musician." *MM* 2:21-23. Apr. 1925.

_____. "Il mesaggio di Busoni." *Musica*, I, Firenze, 1943.

_____. "In memoria di Ferruccio Busoni." *Rivista Musicale Italiana*, Turin, XXXI, pp. 565-80, April 1924.

_____. "Opernkomponist Ferruccio Busoni" (trans. H. Schatz). Port *Melos* 25:189-94, June 1958.

_____. "The Stage Works of Ferruccio Busoni." *MQ* 20:267-77, 1934.

Gatti, G. M., ed. Special issue of *Il Pianoforte*, Torina, 15 giugno 1921. (Articles by Dent, Gatti, Brugnoli, and Casella.)

Georgii, Walter. *Klaviermusik*, 2. Aufl., Zürich, 1950.

Gerigk-Danzig, Herbert. "Bemerkungen über Busoni." *Die Musik*, 26. Jg. S. 807. 1934.

Gervais, T.W. "Busoni as a Contemporary Figure." *Chesterian* 34:69-75, no. 201, 1960.

_____. "Busoni's Continued Significance." *Chesterian* 27:63-67, Jan. 1953.

_____. "Busoni's Possible Influence." *Chesterian* 28:1-5, July 1953.

Goebels, Franzpeter. *Der Neue Busoni: Übungen & Studien für Klavier, zusammengestellt und eingeleitet von Franzpeter Goebels*. Wiesbaden, Breitkopf & Haertel, 1968.

_____. "Deutung und Bedeutung der Bach-Ausgaben." *Musik im Unterricht*, 55. Jg. S. 249-52. 1964.

_____. "Ferruccio Busoni als Musikerzircher." *Musik im Unterricht*, Mainz. 45. S.204-208. 1954.

Goetz, Bruno. "Erinnerungen an Busoni." In *Die Schlapperklange*. A. Meder, Donaueschingen, 1934.

_____. "Ferruccio Busoni." *Das Nationaltheater*. Buhnenvolsbunverlag, Berlin, 4. Jg. S. 81-91. Gennaio 1931.

_____. "Gedanken über Ferruccio Busonis 'Doktor Faust.'" *Die Schweiz. Illustrierte Monatsschrift*, 23. Jg. S. 433-37, 1919.

Goslich, S. "Das Wandbild; Othmar Schoek und Ferruccio Busoni." *Musica* 11:322-25, June 1957.

Gray, Cecil. *Predicaments, or Music and the Future*. 1936. Reprinted Books for Libraries Press, Freeport, N.Y., 1969.

_____. *A Survey of Contemporary Music*. Oxford University Press, London, 1924.

Grunfeld, F. V. "Ferruccio Busoni." Port *Musical America* 69:6, 15 Nov. 1949.

Guadagnino, L. "Busoni über Mozart." *Neue Zfm* 122:442-44, Nov. 1961.

Guerrini, G. "Ferruccio Busoni maestro." *La Rassegna Musicale*. Torino, XVIII, Anno 13, No.1. Gennaio 1940.

_____. "Ferruccio Busoni nei ricordi bolognesi di un discepolo." *Rassegna dell' Instruzione Artistica*, anno XIII, nos. 1-3, 1935.

_____. "La Turandot di F. Busoni." *Musicista*, Roma, anna 7, Marzo-Aprile, 1940.

_____. "Intorno al Dottor Faust di Ferruccio Busoni." *Il Musicista*, Roma, 8. Jg. S. 153-58. Stembre 1941.

_____. "La Turandot di G. Puccini e quella di F. Busoni." *Illustrazione Toscana e dell' Etruria* VIII, 18. Jg. S. 16. Aprile 1940.

Gui, Vittorio. "Arlecchino." *La Rassegna Musicale*, Torino, XVIII, anno 13, no. 1, Gennaio 1940.

Gunn, Glen Dillard. "Busoni's Lost Studies." *Musical Digest*, May 1948, pp. 30-32.

Günther, Siegfried. "Die Sonatinen Busonis." *Die Musikantengilde*, 1. Jg. S. 30-34. 1923.

Gutmann, Albert. "Eingesandt. 'Wie lange soll das gehen.'" *Signale für die Musikalische Welt*, no. 9, 1 März 1911.

Guttmann, Alfred. "F. B. Busoni." *Die Neue Zeit*, bd. 2, 1922.

Haeser, W. "Ferruccio Busoni, Eine Biographie." *Die Schweiz*, 23. Jahrgang. S. 465. 1920.

Halm, August. "Busonis Bachausgabe." *Melos*, 2. Jg. S. 207, S. 239. 1921.

Hamilton, D. "The recorded legacy of Ferruccio Busoni", port. *Hi Fi/Mus Am* 20:77-78, sec. 1, Feb. 1970.

Hanslick, Eduard. "Kritik über zehnjärigen Busoni." *Neue Freie Press*, Wien, 13/2/ 1887.

Hedwig, Abel. "Ferruccio Busoni." *Die Gegenwart*, Berlin, 1897.

Henderson, A. M. "Busoni as Artist and Teacher," *Music Teacher* 35:515, Nov. 1956.

Herrmann, Joachim. "Busoni oder die Schöpferische Unendlichkeit der Musik." In Ferruccio Busoni, *Wesen und Einheit der Musik*. Berlin, Max Hesses Verlag, 1956.

_____. "Mozart und die Musik der Gegenwart. Das Mozart-Bekenntnis Ferruccio Busonis." *Acta Mozartiana*. 3. H.2, S.2-8 (Augsburg: Deutsche Mozart-Gesellschaft) 1956.

Heuss, Alfred. "Ferruccio Busoni." *Zeitschrift für Musik*, 91. Jg. 1924.

_____. "Nachruf auf Busoni." *Zeitschrift für Musik* 91. Jg. S. 435. Aug. 1924.

Hilmar, Ernst. "Eine stilkritische Untersuchung der Werke Ferruccio Busonis aus den Jahren 1880-1890." Diss. Graz 1962.

Holl, Karl. "Erinnerungen an Busoni." *Auftakt*. Prag, 14. Jahrgang. S. 165. 1934.

Hove, R. "Apokryfferne II." Port *Dansk Mus.* 36:155-61, n.4; 231, n.6, 1961.

Il Pianoforte. Special issue. Torino, 15 giugno 1921. Articles by Leichtentritt, Casella, Dent, and Brugnoli.

Jacob, Walter. "Der Faust-Stoff in der Oper bis zu Busonis 'Doktor Faust.'" *Allgemeine Musikzeitung*, 61. Jg. S. 430-32. 1934.

_____. "Faust in der Oper." *Das Musikleben*. 6. Jg. S. 256-60. 1953.

Jacob-Loewenson, Alice. "Die Sonatina Seconda—Busonis Vorstudie zum 'Doktor Faust.'" *Melos*, 7. Jg. S. 194. 1928.

Jarnach, Philipp. "Das Stilproblem der Neuen Klassizität Im Werke Busonis." *Musikblätter des Anbruch*, 3. Jahrgang. H. 1/2, Wien, 1-15 Januar 1921.

Jarnach, Philipp. "Ferruccio Busoni." *Beilage des Berliner*, Börsen, n. 135.

_____. "Ferruccio Busoni." In: *Ferruccio Busoni, Wesen und Einheit der Musik*. Berlin, Max Hesses Verlag, 1956.

_____. "Ferruccio Busoni." *Zeitschrift für Musik*, vol. 12, S. 1050. Dec. 1932.

_____. "In memoria di Ferruccio Busoni." *La Rassegna Musicale*, XVIII, anno 13, no. 1, Gennaio 1940.

Jelmoli, Hans. "Ferruccio Busonis Zürcherjahre." In *Neujahrblatt der Allgemeinen Musikgesellschaft*. Zürich, Kommissionsverlag von Hug & Co., 1929.

Kammerer, R. "Philipp compares Pianists Past and Present." *Musical America*, 75:16, 1 Dec. 1955.

Kapp, Julius. "Einführung in das Werk (Arlecchino)." *Blätter der Staatsoper* (Berlin) 5. Jg. S. 14-15. 1924.

_____. "'Turandot' Die Dichtung im Wandel der Zeiten." *Blätter der Staatsoper* (Berlin) 1. Jg. S. 12-14. 1921.

Kastner, Rudolf. "Busonis Commedia dell' arte." *Das Tagebuch* 1. Jg. S. 695. 1921.

_____. "Offener Brief an Ferruccio Busoni." *Vossische Zeitung*, 1920.

_____. *Zu Busonis "Doktor Faust,"* Eine Einführung, Dresden, Katz-Verlag, 1925.

Kempff, Wilhelm. "Busoni." In *Wilhelm Kempff, Unter dem Zimbelstern*, Stuttgart, 1951.

_____. "Vstrechi s E. d'Alberom i F. Busoni," *Soviet. Muz.* 31:60-64, no. 1, 1967.

Kerr, R. "Arrau as Beethoven Cyclist," *Music Magazine* 164:13, Sept. 1962.

Kestenberg, Leo. "Busoni." in *Leo Kestenberg. Bewegte Zeiten*. Wolfenbüttel und Zürich, Möseler Verlag, 1961.

Kogan, Grigorii M. "D'Albert, Busoni i sovremennost." *Soviet Muz.* 31:58-60, Jan. 1967.

_____. *Rabota Pianista*. Moscow, Muzgiz, 1963.

Kosnick, H. "Busoni als Interpret." ZFM 115:403-5, July 1954; and *Schweizerische Musikzeitung*, 94. Jahrgang. no. 2. S. 59. 1954.

_____. "Busoni. Ein bahnbrechender Meister in der Geschichte des Klavierspiels."

Allgemeine Musikzeitung, 61. Jahrgang. no. 30-31. S. 429. 1934.

───. "Vier junge Pianisten: Gedanken zum Busoni-Wettbewerb." *Neue ZFM* 118:60-61, Jan. 1957.

Krenek, Ernest. "Busoni—Then and Now." *Modern Music*, 19 (Jan.-Feb. 1942):88.

Lafite, M. "Zur Aesthetik von Ferruccio Busoni und Hans Pfitzner." *Oe Mz*, 29:357-62 Jul.-Aug. 1974.

L'Approdo Musicale, special Busoni issue, 1966.

Lendvai, Erwin. "Busoni." *Sozialistische Monatshefte*, Berlin. S. 374-76. 1922.

La Rassegna Musicale, Busoni issue. Torino, Gennaio 1940. Articles by Bontempelli, Casella, Pannain, Gui, Guerrini, Previtali, Corti, Dallapiccola, Tagliapietra, Jarnach, Schnapp, and Sulzberger.

Leichtentritt, Hugo. "Busoni e Bach." *Il Pianoforte*, Torino, 2. Jg. S. 161-64. 15 giugno 1921.

───. "Busoni und Bach." *Musikblätter des Anbruch*, 3. Jg. H. 1/2, Wien, S. 12-16. 1-15 Januar 1921.

───. "Ferruccio Busoni." *Musical Review*, VI, 1945, p. 206.

Leitzmann, Albert: "Ferruccio Busoni: Sonatina," *Die Musik*, 10. Jg. S. 296. 1910-1911.

Lessmann, Otto. "Aus dem Conzertsaal (Kritiken über Busoni)," *AMZ*, 12. Jg. 1885, S.152 und 21.Jg. 1894, S. 606.

───. "Gibt es noch eine weitere Entwickelung des Klavierspiels? Betrachtungen nach dem jungstem Busoni-Klavierabend." *Allgemeine Musikzeitung*, Jahrgang 37, no. 1, 7 Januar 1910.

Lewinsky, W.-E. v. "Busoni-Mensch und Musiker der Grenze." *Das neue Forum*, Darmstadt, 8. Jg. S. 82. 1958-1959.

Limmert, E. "Arlecchino & Nachtflug." *Musica* 10:776, Nov. 1956.

Liuzzi, Fernando. "Busoni e la sua visione dell'arte." *L'Esame*, III, no. 8, 1924.

Lochmann, G. "Busoni-Bornefeld." *Mus und Kirche* 27:203-4 July-Aug. 1957.

Lombriser, Francis. "Studien über Ferruccio Busoni." *Musikalische Rundschau der Schweiz*, Fribourg-Bern, June 1955.

Longo, A. "Ferruccio Busoni." *Arte pianistica*, Napoli, agosto-settembre 1924.

Looyenga, A. J. "Over Busoni's pianotranscripties van orgelwerken van J. S. Bach." port *Mens en Mel* 29:84-87, Mar. 1974.

Lyck, Hans. "Artikel Busoni." *Atlantisbuch der Musik*, Zürich, 1953.

───. "Zehn Jahre später. Gedenkwort für Ferruccio Busoni." *Deutsche Zukunft*, Berlin, 2. Jahrgang. No. 30, S. 20. 1934.

Maine, Basil. "Some Busoni Recollections." *Musical Opinion*, London, S. 586. 1960-1961.

Malnev, S. "O sovremennoi virtuoznosti. K smerti Ferruccio Busoni." *Muzikalnaya kultura*, no. 2. 1924.

Mangeot, A. "Ferruccio Busoni." *Le monde musical*, Parigi, Agosto, 1924.

───. "Une nouvelle Notation Musicale par F. Busoni." *Le Monde Musical*, 22. Jg. S. 226-28. 1910.

Mantovani, Tancredi. "L'Ultimo dei grandi pianisti-compositori Italiani." *Ferruccio Busoni da Empoli*, Empoli, 1927.

Marcus, M. "Busoni revisited." *Mus & Mus*, 10:42 Jul 1962.

Martienssen, C. A. *Die individuelle Klaviertechnik auf der Grundlage des schöpferischen Klangwillens*. Ed. Breitkopf, Leipzig, 1930. kap. XVIII-XIX.

Martinotti, Sergio. "A proposito di un recente libro su Ferruccio Busoni." *L'Approdo Musicale*, n. 19-20, Rome-Turin, 1965, p. 227.

_____. "Coscienza e presagio nel primo pianismo di Busoni." *R Ital Mus* 1:218-36, n.2, 1966.

_____. "I Lieder: primi dati per la vocalità busoniana." *L'Approdo musicale*, n.22, Roma-Torino 1966, pp. 107-20.

_____. "Tavola rotunda di Studi Busoniani ad Empoli." *R Ital Mus* 1:313-14, n.2, 1966.

Mason, R. M. "Enumeration of Synthetic Musical Scales by Matrix Algebra and a Catalogue of Busoni's Scales." *Journal of Music Theory* 14:92-126, no. 1, 1970.

Mayer, Anton. "Aus Ferruccio Busonis Nachlass." *Antiquitäten-Rundschau*, 22. Jg. S. 438. 1924.

Mellers, Wilfrid. "The Problem of Busoni." *Music and Letters*, XVIII, 1937.

Mersmann, Hans. *Die moderne Musik, Handbuch der Musikwissenschaft*, bd. 2, Potsdam, S. 149. 1917.

_____. "Entwurf einer neuen ästhetik der Tonkunst." *Allgemeine Musikzeitung*, 44. Jg. S. 79, 95. 1917.

_____. "Pfitzner und Busoni," *NMZ* 38, Jg. 1917, S.447.

Mersmann, Hans; Hans Schultze-Ritter; Heinrich Strobel; "Musiker der Zeit. Ferruccio Busoni." *Melos*, 9. Jg. S. 420. 1930.

Moldenhauer, H. "Busonis Kritik an Beethovens letzten Quartetten." *Neue ZFM* 121:416-17, Dec. 1960.

Monod, Edmond. "Une nouvelle notation musicale." *La Vie Musicale*, 3. Jg. S. 353 1910.

Moser, Hans Joachim. "Ferruccio Busoni." *Musikgeschichte in 100 Lebensbildern*, Stuttgart, 1952.

Movshon, G. "Little Orchestra: Busoni's 'Turandot.'" *Hi Fi/Mus Am.*, 18:MA 13, Jan 1968.

Musikblätter des Anbruch. Special issue, 2 Jahrgang H. 1/2, Wien, 1-15 Jan. 1921. Articles by Chantavoine, Leichtentritt, Jarnach, Dent, Simon, Selden-Goth, and Draber.

Nagel, Willibald. "Busoni als Ästhetiker." *NMZ*, 38. Jg. S. 239, 253. 1917.

_____. "Neue Notensysteme." *Signale für die Musikalische Welt*, no. 47, 23 Nov. 1910.

Newman, Ernest. *More Essays from the World of Music*, London, S. 65-70. 1958.

Ohlekopf, R. "Ferruccio Busoni zu Gedenken." *Signale für die Musikalische Welt*, 99. Jahrgang. S. 108. 1941.

Oppenheimer, Max. Busoni Portrait on Cover of *Schweiz Mus*, July/Aug. 1964.

Paddack, C. "The Piano Art of Ferruccio Busoni." port *Etude* 71:13, Sept. 1953.

Palmer, L. "Harpsichord Repertoire in the 20th Century: The Busoni Sonatina." *DIAP*, biog., il. 64:10-11, Sept. 1973.

Pannain, Guido. "Ferruccio Busoni." *La Rassegna Musicale*, anno 1, no. 6, Guino 1928, pp. 352-64.

_____. "Ferruccio Busoni nei ricordi bolognesi di un discepolo." *Rassegna dell'istruzione artistica* anno 13, gennaio-febbraio-marzo 1935.

_____. "Il 'Dottor Faust'", *La Rassegna Musicale*, Torino, XVIII, anno 13, no. 1, Gennaio 1940.

_____. *Modern Composers.* Trans. Michael Bonavia. London, J. M. Dent & Sons, 1932.

_____. "Saggio su Ferruccio Busoni." *Rassegna Musicale,* Turin, June 1921.

Pascal, Roy. "4 Fausts: From W. S. Gilbert to Ferruccio Busoni." *German Life and Letters,* Oxford, 10. Jg. S. 263-74. 1956-1957.

Perrachio, Luigi. "Bach-Busoni." *La Rassegna Musicale,* 1. Jg. S. 415-18. 1928.

Petri, Egon. "Principles of Piano Practice." *Proceedings of the MTNA,* thirty-fourth series, 27-30 Dec. 1939, pp. 275-83.

Petzold, Richard. "Ferruccio Busoni in seinen Klaviersonatinen." *AMZ,* 61. Jg. S. 432. 1934.

Pfitzner, Hans. "Die neue Ästhetick der musikalischen Impotenz. Ein Verwesungs-symptom? 1919." In Hans Pfitzner, *Gesammelte Schriften,* Augsburg, Band 2, Dr. Benno Filser-Verlag, 1926.

_____. "Futuristengefahr. Bei Gelegenheit von Busoni's Ästhetick." In *Süddeutsche Monatschelte,* Leipzig, 1917. Also reprinted in Hans Pfitzner, *Gesammelte Schriften,* Augsburg, Band 1. Dr. Benno Filser-Verlag, 1926.

Pfohl, Ferdinand." Busoni und Bach." *Die Musikwelt,* 1. Jg. 4. Heft. S. 5-6. 1921.

_____. "Die Brautwahl." *Busoniheft der Blätter des Staatsoper* (Berlin), 1. Jg. S. 6-8. 1921.

Philipp, Isidore. "Ferruccio Busoni, Uneasy Spirit of the Keyboard." *Musical Digest,* June 1947.

_____. "Quelques considérations sur l'art du piano." *Le Courrier musical et théatral,* Paris, 15 novembre 1927.

The Piano Quarterly. Busoni issue, Winter 1979-1980, no. 108. (Articles by Franco Agostini, Larry Sitsky, Peter Armstrong, Anthony Beaumont, Daniel Raessler, Gunnar Johansen, Dolores Hsu, F. E. Kirby, and Guido Agosti.)

Pisk, Paul Amadeum. "Busonis offener Musikbrief." *Musikblätter des Anbruch,* 4. Jahrgang. S. 104. 1922.

Ponnelle, Lazare. *A Munich: Gustave Mahler, Richard Strauss, Ferruccio Busoni.* Paris, Librairie Fischbacher, 1913.

_____. "Ferruccio Busoni." *Pianoforte,* 1920.

Prechtl, Robert. "Zweig auf Busonis Grab." *Melos,* 4. Jahrgang. Heft 2. 1 Sept. 1924.

Preiburg, Fred. K. "Busoni." *Lexicon der neuen Musik.* Freiburg, 1958.

Prelinger, Melanie Mayer. "Erinnerungen und Briefe aus Ferruccio Busonis Jugend-zeit." *Neue Musikzeitung,* 48. Jg. S. 6-10. Oct. 1927. S. 37-40. Nov. S. 57-61. Dec.

Previtali, Fernando. "Sul 'Dottor Faust' di Busoni." *Musica* (Firenze), 2. Jg. S. 158-83. 1943.

_____. "Turandot." *La Rassegna Musicale,* Torino, XVIII, anno 13, no. 1. S. 38-46. Gennaio 1940.

Prinz, Ulrich. *Ferruccio Busoni als Klavierkomponist,* Heidelberg University, 1970.

Rattalino, P. "Scritti giovanili di Ferruccio Busoni." Il port *Mus D'Oggi* 2:405-11, Mar.; 152-58, Apr. 1959.

"Recalling Busoni." *Am. Rec. Guide,* 22:102, Mar. 1956.

Reger, Max. "Konzertstück für Pianoforte mit Orchester von Ferruccio Busoni." *AMZ,* 21. Jg. S. 401. 1894.

Reich, Willi. "Ferruccio Busoni. Anmerkungen zum 'Wohltemperierten Klavier.'" *Schweizerische Musikzeitung*, 92. Jg. S. 49-54. 1952.

Reimann, Hugo. "Busoni." *Musiklexicon*, Mainz, 1959.

Reinhart, Hans. "Ferruccio Busoni." In *Hermann Draber und andere. H. Reinhart und seine Werke*, Zürich, 1941.

Reuss, Eduard. "Ueber Busoni's Ausgaben und Bearbeitungen Bach'scher Werke." *IMGZ* 4:721-28, Leipzig, Zeitschrift der Internationalen Musikgesellschaft, 1903.

Reyle, K. "Wandlungen der Turandot und ihrer Rätsel." *Neue ZFM* 125, nos. 7-8. S. 303-6. 1964.

Righini, Carlo. "Un aspetto di Ferruccio Busoni." *Il Pensiero Musicale*, 3. Jg. S. 51-55. 1923.

Ringger, R. U. "Zu Busonis 'Entwurf einer neuen Ästhetick der Tonkunst.'" *Musica*, 14:715-18, Nov. 1960.

Roner, Anna. "Ferruccio Busoni: 'Turandot' und 'Arlecchino.'" *Neue Musik Zeitung*, 38. Jg. S. 275-76. 1917.

Rosen, Waldemar. "Zu Busonis 70 Geburstag. Schöpfertum zwischen zwei Nationen." *Allgemeine Musikzeitung*, S. 269. 1936.

Rothe, Friede F. "How Ferruccio Busoni Taught; An Interview with the Distinguished Dutch Pianist, Egon Petri." *Etude* 58 (October, 1940):657.

Russcol, Herbert. *The Liberation of Sound—An Introduction to Electronic Music.* Englewood Cliffs, N.J., Prentice-Hall, 1972.

Salzman, E. "Ferruccio Busoni's Monumental Piano Concerto." port *Hi-Fi R* 20:75-76, Apr. 1968.

Saminsky, Lazare. "More about 'Faustus'" *MM*, 5:38-39, Nov. 1927.

Sartori, Claudio. "Adolescenza ardente di Ferruccio Busoni e un suo primo ignorato progretto di opera lirica." *La Rassegna Musicale*, Apr. 1940.

Saul, P. "Busoniana." *Rec. Sound* 1:256-61, no. 8, 1962.

Schaefer, Hansjürgen. "Was leben wahr, will nachgeahmt erscheinen . . . Zum 100. Geburtstag Ferruccio Busonis." *Musik und Gesellschaft*, 16. Jg. S. 175-77. 1966.

Schlesinger, Paul. "Ferruccio Busoni." *Schaubühne*, Berlin, 1915.

Schmidt, C. Busoni entry in *Dizionario Universale dei Musicisti* and *Enciclopedia Treccani*.

Schmitt, Kurt. *Busoni als Pädagoge und Interpretdargestellt an seiner Bearbeitung der Klavierwerke J.S. Bachs*, Diss. Saarbrüchen, 1965.

Schmitz, Eugene. "Busonis 'Doktor Faust.'" *Die Musik*, 17. Jg. S. 760-64. 1925.

Schnabel, A. "My Life and Music." *Mus T* 102:489, Aug. 1961.

Schnapp, Friedrich. "Anekdoten um Busoni." *Zeitschrift für Musik*, Heft 12. S. 1094, Dec. 1932.

_____. "Busonis musikalisches Schaffen," *Zeitschrift für Musik*, 99. Jg. Heft 12. S. 1045. 1932.

_____. "Busonis persönaliche Beziehungen zu Anton Rubinstein." *ZFM*, 99. Jg. Heft 12. S. 1053. 1932.

_____. "Ferruccio Busoni e Antonio Rubinstein." *La Rassegna Musicale*, XVIII, anno 13, no. 1, Gennaio 1940.

Schonberg, Harold C. *The Great Pianists*. London, Victor Gollanz, 1964.

_____. "Recalling Busoni: Mitropoulos Remembers Teacher with Affection." *New York Times*, 100:7, sec. 2, 7 Oct. 1951.

Schuh, Willi. "Ferruccio Busonis 'Doktor Faust.'" *Schweizer Musikzeitung*, 95. S. 309-12. 1955.

_____. *Von Neuer Musik*. Zürich, Freiburg, S. 125-31. 1955.

_____. *Vorwort ze Busonis Briefen an seine Frau*. Erlenbach, 1935.

Schultze, Adolf. "Ferruccio Benvenuto Busoni." *Neue Musikzeitung*, no. 15, 18. Jahrgang. 1897.

Schulz-Dornburg, Rudolf. "Ferruccio Busoni, der Prophet." *Das Musikleben*, 3. Jg. Heft 10. S. 273. Mainz 1950.

Schweizer, Gottfried. "Ein wiederentdecktes Busoni." *Neue Musikzeitschrift*, München 3. Jahrgang. Heft 8/9. S. 238-39. 1949.

Schwers, Paul. "Ferruccio Busoni." *Allgemeine Musikzeitung*, S. 574. 1924.

Searle, Humphrey. "Busonis 'Doktor Faust.'" *Monthly Musical Record*, London, vol. 67, no. 785, Mar.-Apr. 1937, pp. 54-56.

Selden-Goth, Gisella. "Das Goethesche in Busoni." *Musikblätter des Anbruch*, 3. Jg. H. 1/2, Wien, S. 37. 1-15 Januar 1921.

Simon, James. "Busoni." *Das Feuer*, Saarbrücken, 1920.

_____. "Busoni Bühnenschaffen." *Schweizerische Musikzeitung*, 73. Jahrgang. S. 517-22. 1933.

_____. "Der musikalische Stil." *Musikblätter des Anbruch*, 3. Jahrgang. H. 1/2, Wien, S. 32-37. 1-15 Januar 1921.

Sitsky, Larry. "Busoni." *Dictionary of Contemporary Music*, New York, E. P. Dutton, 1974.

_____. "Busoni and the New Music," *Quadrant*, n. 33, vol. IX, no. 1, Jan.-Feb. 1965.

_____. "Ferruccio Busoni's 'Attempt at an Organic Notation for the Pianoforte' and a Practical Adaptation of It." *Mus. Rev.*, vol. 29, no. 1, Feb. 1968.

_____. "The Six Sonatinas for Piano of Ferruccio Busoni." *Studies in Music*, University of West Australia Press, no. 2, 1968; also in *Studi Musicali*, anno 2, n. 1. Accademia Nazionale di Santa Cecilia, Rome, 1973.

_____. "Transcriptions and the Eunuch." *Quadrant*, n. 43, vol. X, no. 5, Sept.-Oct. 1966.

Smith, P. J. "The Riddle of Turandot.'" *Mus Opera* 29:24-25, 16 Jan. 1965.

Sorabji, K. S. *Around Music*. London, Unicorn Press, 1932.

_____. *Mi Contra Fa*. London, Porcupine Press, 1947.

Spanuth, August. "Der verdächtigte Busoni." *Signale für die Musikalische Welt*, no. 9, März 1911.

Spink, G. W. "From Bach-Liszt to Bach-Busoni." *Mus Op* 89:601 Jul. 1966.

Spiro, Friedrich. "Bach und seine Transkriptionen." *Neue ZFM*, 71. Jg. 1904.

Stefan, Paul. "Bildnis Busonis." *Musikblätter des Anbruch*, Wien, 15. Jahrgang. S. 49. 1933.

Steinhauer, Werner. "Busoni als Wegbereiter." *Melos*, 13. Jg. S. 225. 1934.

Stevenson. R. "Busoni and Mozart." *Score* (London) 13:25-38, Sept. 1955.

_____. "Busoni e la Gran Bretagna. "*Bulletino Storico Empolese*, vol. I, anno 2, no. 1, 1958.

_____. "Busoni's Arlecchino." *Mus Times* 95:307-8, June 1954.

_____. "Busoni—The Legend of a Prodigal." *Score* (London) 15:15-30, Mar. 1956.

_____. "Ferruccio Busoni." *Mus. Rev.*, vol. 18, 1957, pp. 234-38.

Stuckenschmidt, H. H.: "Busoni." In: H. H. Stuckenschmidt, *Schopfer der Neuen Musik*, München Suhrkamp Verlag, 1962.

_____. "Busoni-Austellung in Berlin." *Schweiz Mus* 106:173, n. 3, 1966.

_____. "Busonis 'Brautwahl.'" *Schweiz Mus* 102:344-51, n. 6, 1962.

_____. "Busoni včera dnes zítra." Il port *Hud Roz* 19:259-61, n. 9, 1966.

_____."Ferruccio Busoni als Komponist. Die Schweizer und die letzten Jahre." *Schweizerische Musikzeitung*, 107. Jg. S. 191-98. 1967.

_____. Nachwort zu Busonis Entwurf einer Neuen Ästhetik der Tonkunst." In *F. Busoni. Entwurf einer neuen Ästhetik der Tonkunst.* 4. Auflage. Wiesbaden, Insel-Bücherei, 1954.

_____. *Neue Musik (Zwischen den beiden Kriegen II)*, Berlin, 1951.

_____. "Rede über Busonis 'Doktor Faust' Gehalten bei einer Matinee im Zürcher Stadttheater am 22. Mai 1955." *Schweizerische Musikzeitung.* 96. Jg. S. 3-9. 1956.

Sulzberger, H. S. "Ferruccio Busoni." In *Hunis-Musik-Jahrbuch.*

_____. "Ferruccio Busoni nel ricordo di un discepolo." *La Rassegna Musicale,* Torino, XVIII, anno 13, no. 1, Gennaio 1940.

Szigeti, Joseph. "Busoni." In Joseph Szigeti, *With Strings Attached.* London, Cassell & Co., 1949; also published in Germany, 1962, and in Russia, 1969.

_____. "Busoni—A memoir." In *Bromsgrove Festival*, 1966.

Tagliapietra, Gino. "Ferruccio Busoni trascrittore e revisore." *La Rassegna Musicale*, Torino, XVIII, anno 13, no. 1, Gennaio 1940.

Taubmann, Otto. "Ferruccio Busoni." *Mitteilungen der Musikaleinhandlung.* Breitkopf & Haertel, no. 77, 1904.

Theurich, J.: "Busoni-Ausstellung," *Mus. u. Ges.* 24:698-99, Nov. 1974.

_____. "Zum 50 Todestag Ferruccio Busonis—Gedanken zu einer Begegnung des Komponisten mit Arnold Schoenberg in unveroeffentlichten Briefen." Facs. *Mus. u. Ges.* 24:401-5 July 1974.

Thiessen, Karl. "Busoni als Erfinder einer neuen Notenschrift." *Signale für die Musikalische Welt,* 68. Jg. no. 45, S. 1685-88. 9 Nov. 1910.

Thurneiser, Leonhard. "Die Brautwahl, eine Berlinische Oper Busonis." *Melos,* 5. Jg. S. 22-28. 1925.

_____. "Doktor Faust." *Der Deutschen Spiegel. Politische Wochenschrift*, 23. H., S. 1091-97. 1925.

Trapp, Klaus. *Die Fuge in der deutschen Romantik von Schubert bis Reger.* Frankfurt, 1958.

Varèse, Louise. *Varèse: a looking-glass diary*, New York, Norton, 1972.

Vatielli, "Busoni a Bologna." *La Rassegna Musicale*, XVII, numero undici, anno undicesimo, Nov. 1938, pp. 417-26.

Vlad, Roman. "Bach e la musica moderna." *La Rassegna Musicale*, (Bach bicentenary issue), 20. Jg. S. 230-31. 1950.

_____. "Busoni's Destiny." *The Score*, Dec. 1952; also "Destino di Busoni." *La Rassegna Musicale*, anno 23, 1953.

Vogel, J. P. "Das Unproportionierte der Futuristengefahr—zwei Neuausgabe des 'Entwurf einer neuen Aesthetik der Tonkunst' von F. Busoni." *Pfitzner*, n. 33:25-7, Nov. 1974.

_____. "Der 'Progressive' Theoretiker und der 'Konservative' Komponist." *MF*

25:258-68, n. 3, 1972.

_____. "Pfitzner und Busoni—Eine aethetische Auseinandersetzung im Lichte der Gegenwart." *Pfitzner*, n. 33:10-22, Nov. 1974.

Vogel, Vladimir. "Aus der Zeit der Meisterklasse Busoni." *Schweiz Mus* 104:165-66, n. 3, 1964.

_____. "Ein Testament." *Musica Viva*, Zürich-Bruxelles, no. 1, Apr. 1936.

_____. "Eine begegnung." In *Ferruccio Busoni. Wesen und Einheit der Musik.* Berlin, Max Hesses Verlag, 1956.

_____. "Impressions of Ferruccio Busoni." *Pers New Music* 6:167-73, n. 2, 1968.

_____. "Über Busonis 'Doktor Faust.'" *Schweizerische Musikzeitung*, 106. Jg. S. 66-67. 1966.

Wasserman, J. "In memoriam Ferruccio Busoni." *Lebensdienst*, Berlin-Zürich, 1930.

Waterhouse, J. C. G. "Busoni into Focus: A Centenary Tribute." Port *Mus & Mus* 14:24, Apr. 1966.

_____. "Busoni: Visionary or Pasticheur?" Mus *RMA* 92:79-93, 1965-1966.

_____. "Weill's Debt to Busoni." Mus *Mus T* 105:897-99, Dec. 1964.

Weigart, M. "Busoni at Weimar in 1901." *Mus Rev.* 15:47-54, Feb. 1954.

Weill, Kurt. "Busoni—On the First Anniversary of His Death." *Berliner Boersen-Courier*, no. 345, Sonntag 26, Juli 1925.

_____. "Busoni und die Neue Musik." *Der neue Weg*, 54. Jg. no. 20. S. 282f. 16/10/1925.

_____. "Busonis Faust-Oper," *Der deutsche Rundfunk 5* (28 Oct. 1927):3028-29.

_____. "Busonis *Faust* und die Erneuerung der Opernform." *Jahrbuch Oper* (Jahrbuch 1926 der Universal-Edition), 9. Jg. S. 53-56. 1927.

_____. "Ferruccio Busoni—Zu seinem 60 Geburstag." *Der deutsche Rundfunk*, 4. Jg. no. 13. S. 872. 28/3/1926.

Weissmann, Adolf. "Busoni." In *Der Virtuose*, Berlin, Paul Cassirer, 1918, Zweite Auflage, 1920.

_____. "Der 50 jährige Busoni." *Schaubühne*, Berlin, S. 330. 1916.

_____. "Ferruccio Busoni." *Die Musik*, 16. Jg. S. 887. 1924.

Whitwell, D. "Hindemith, Blacher, Weill and Busoni—Their Music for Winds." *Instrument* 23:40, Feb. 1969.

Wimbush, R. "Busoni." *Gramophone* 43:486, Apr. 1966.

Wirth, Helmut. *Musik in Geschichte und Gegenwart*, bd. 2 Kassel, 1952.

Wis, Roberto. "Ferruccio Busoni and Finland." *Acta Musicologica*, 49. Jg. S. 258. 1977.

Yates, P. "Which music? The Notated Pattern vs. the Unique Sound Event." *Piano Quarterly* 16:14-15, no. 62, 1967-1968; 18-20, no. 63, 1968.

Yavorski, B. "Posli moskovskikh kontsertov Ferruccio Busoni." *Muzika*, nos. 104, 105, oktiabr-noyabr 1912.

Zadora, Michael. "Busonis Ausklang." *Vossischen Zeitung*, 3 Apr. 1931.

"Zeugene Kraft der Utopie: Zur 100 Wiederkehr des Geburtstages von Ferruccio Busoni." Port *MH* 17:43-44, n.2, 1966.

Zijlstra, M. "Jeugdherinnerungen van Ferruccio Busoni." Port *Mens en Mel* 29:389-90, Dec. 1974.

Zschorlich, Paul. "Ferruccio Busoni und die Deutschen." *Allgemeine Musikzeitung*, 65. Jg. S. 19. 1938.

Zweig, Stefan. "Bildnis Busonis." *Insel-Almanach*, 1925.

_____. "Busoni." In Stefan Zweig, *Begegnungen mit Menschen, Büchern, Städten*. Berlin und Frankfurt am Main, S. Fischer-Verlag, 1955; Zweite Auflage, 1956.

_____. "Busoni." In *Neue Freie Presse*, Vienna, 8 Apr. 1918.

_____"Über Ferruccio Busoni." Port *Musikleben* 7:280-2, July-Aug. 1954.

A list of newspaper articles and other published items regarding Busoni, not included in this bibliography, may be found in Bayne, Pauline Shaw. *The Gottfried Galston Music Collection and the Galston-Busoni Archive*. Knoxville, University of Tennessee Library, 1978, pp. 285-87.

BIBLIOGRAPHY OF BUSONI'S PLAYING

Those interested in reading contemporary accounts that describe the special characteristics of Busoni's playing are directed to the following, by no means a complete listing.

Books

Hanslick, E. *Konzerte, Komponisten und Virtuosen der letzten fünfzehn Jahre (1870-85)*. Berlin, 1886.

_____. *Am Ende des Jahrhunderts (1895-99)*. Berlin, 1899.

Weissmann, Adolf. *Berlin als Musikstadt*. Berlin, Schuster und Loeffler, 1911.

Leichtentritt, Hugo. *Ferruccio Busoni*. Leipzig, Breitkopf & Haertel, 1916.

Niemann, Walter. *Meister des Klaviers*. 8 Auflage. Berlin, Schuster und Loeffler, 1919.

Weissmann, Adolf. *Der Virtuose*. 2 Auflage. Berlin, Paul Cassirer, 1920.

Dandelot, A. *Francis Planté*. Paris, Ed. Dupont, 1920.

Selden-Goth, Gisella. *Ferruccio Busoni*. Leipzig, E. P. Tal, 1922.

Bekker, Paul. *Klang und Eros*. Stuttgart und Berlin, Deutsche Verlag Anstalt, 1922.

25 Jahre neue Musik, Wien, Jahrbuch der Universal-Edition, 1926.

Prokofiev, G. *Igra na fortepiano*. Moskva, Muzesector Gosizdata, 1928.

Martienssen, Carl Adolf. *Die individuelle Klaviertechnik auf der Grundlage des schopferischen Klangwillens*. Leipzig, Breitkopf & Haertel, 1930.

Nadel, Siegfried. *Ferruccio Busoni*. Leipzig, Breitkopf & Haertel, 1931.

Dent, Edward J. *Ferruccio Busoni*. London, Oxford University Press, 1933.

Cortot, Alfred. *Cours d'interprétation*. Paris, Legouix, 1934.

Casella, Alfredo. *Il Pianoforte*. Milan, Ricordi, 1937; 3 Edizione, 1956.

Debusmann, Emil. *Ferruccio Busoni*. Wiesbaden, Brucknerverlag, 1949.

Kempff, Wilhelm. *Cette note grave*. . . . Paris, Plon, 1955.

Zweig, Stefan. *Begegnungen mit Menschen, Büchern, Städten*. 2 Auflage. Berlin und Frankfurt, S. Fischer, 1956.

The Memoirs of Carl Flesch. London, Rockliff, 1957.

Fischer, Edwin. *Von den Aufgaben des Musikers*. Wiesbaden, Insel-Verlag, 1960.

Klemperer, Otto. *Erinnerungen an Gustav Mahler und andere autobiographische Skizzen*. Zürich, Atlantis-Verlag, 1960.

Schnabel, Artur. *My Life and Music*. London, Longmans, 1961.

Schonberg, Harold. *The Great Pianists*. New York, Simon & Schuster, 1963.
Barinova, M. N. *Vospominaniye o. I. Gofmane i F. Busoni*. Moskva, Muzika, 1964.
Selden-Goth, Gisella. *Ferruccio Busoni. Un profilo*. Firenze, Leo S. Olschki, 1964.
Stuckenschmidt, H. H. *Ferruccio Busoni*. Zürich, Atlantis-Verlag, 1967.
Conversation with Edward Weiss in booklet accompanying record titled "Ferruccio Busoni: His Complete Disc Recordings and Busoni Pupils Play Busoni." (IPA 104), 1976.
Novoe vremia (16, 18 avgusta 1890); 19, 25 oktiabria, 9 noyabria 1912; 20 noyabria 1913).
Den (19, 27, 31 oktiabria, 8, 11 noyabria 1912; 20 noyabria, 1 dekabria 1913).
Utro Rossii (21, 23 oktiabria, 2 noyabria 1912; 26 noyabria 1913)
Izvestiya (12 avgusta 1924)
Novosti (17 avgusta 1890)
Peterburgskaya gazeta (16, 18 avgusta, 7 sentiabrya 1890)

Journals

Die Musik (Jahrgang II, Heft 3; Jahrgang IV, H. 10; Jahrg. V, H. 6 und 11; Jahrg. VI, H. 10; Jahrg. VIII, H. 9; Jahrg. IX, H. 6; Jahrg. X, H. 11 und 13; Jahrg. XI, H. 1, 4, 5; Jahrg. XII, H. 7; Jahrg. XIII, H. 11; Jahrg. XVI, H. 12; Jahrg. XIX, H. 11)
Neue Musikzeitung (Jahrg. XXIX, H. 11)
Allgemeine Musikzeitung (1909, Nos. 3, 6; 1910, Nos. 1, 44; 1911, Nos. 44, 45, 48)
Signale für Musikalische Welt (1909, Nos. 2, 4, 6; 1910, No. 44; 1911, Nos. 45, 51; 1913, No. 21)
Melos (1924, September)
Musikblätter des Anbruch (1924, Oktober)
La Revue musicale (1924, octobre)
Le Courrier musical et théâtral (1927, 15 novembre)
Le Ménéstral (1931, no. 35)
Russkaya muzikalnaya gazeta (1903, nos. 7-8; 1905, nos. 3-4, 7; 1906, no. 9; 1910 no. 2; 1912, nos. 40, 45, 46, 48; 1913, no. 50)
Muzika (1912, nos. 101, 105; 1913, no. 158.)
Rampa i ghizn (1912, nos. 43, 44, 48; 1913, nos. 47, 48)
Tiatr i iskusstvo (1912, nos. 44, 47; 1913, nos. 47, 48)
Obozrenie tiatrov (1912, nos. 1884, 1888, 1896, 1904; 1913, nos. 2269, 2280)
Muzikalnaya kultura (1924, no. 2)
Ghizn iskusstva (1924, no. 33/1007)
Allgemeine Musikzeitung (12 Jg. S. 152 1885, 21. Jg. S. 606 1894, 22 Jg. S. 71 1895). 1895.)
Bayan (1890, no. 9)

Newspapers

Golos Moskvi (12, 20, 21 oktiabria; 1, 6, 7 noyabria 1912; 26, 28 noyabria 1913)
Russkoye slovo (12 oktiabria, 6 noyabria 1912; 27, 28 noyabria 1913)
Russkiye vedomosti (13, 20, 21 oktiabria, 2, 9, 20 noyabria 1912; 9, 28 noyabria 1913)
Moskauer Deutsche Zeitung (14, 24 oktiabria, 4 noyabria 1912; 29 noyabria 1913)

Vecherneye vremia (18, 21, 24, 30, 31 oktiabria, 7 noyabria 1912; 14, 19, 30 noyabria 1913)

Rietch (18, 25, 30 oktiabria, 2, 8 noyabria 1912; 20, 28 noyabria 1913)

Birzheviye vedomosti—vechernii vipusk (18, 30, 31 oktiabria, 7 noyabria 1912; 19, 30 noyabria 1913)

Index of Busoni's Works

For a list of the short unpublished works still in manuscript see pp. 13-15.

General Index

Alkan, Charles Valentin, 4, 40
Allan, Maud, 6
Arrau, Claudio, 6, 382
Auber, Daniel, 165, 168, 240

Bach, Johann Sebastian, 21, 34, 35
  n.3, 43-47, 52, 59, 65, 67, 72-74, 87
  nn.2, 3, 120, 137 n.2, 139-154, 160,
  165, 167-169, 171-172, 177-206,
  242-243, 257-262, 288-296, 300-308,
  309-312, 314, 321, 323, 325 n.11
Bartók, Béla, 4, 62, 67, 129, 131-132,
  155, 211, 213, 315
Beethoven, Ludwig van, 4, 28-29, 35
  n.3, 43-44, 46, 53, 78, 95, 120, 136,
  165-166, 168-169, 242-243, 245-246,
  248, 266 n.6, 268-275, 296
Beklemischeff, Gregor, 6
Bizet, Georges, 166, 169-170, 274. See
  also (in "Index of Busoni's Works")
  Kammer-Fantasie über Bizet's
  Carmen
Blum, Robert, 6
Borovsky, Alexander, 6, 351-352
Brahms, Johannes, 27, 47, 49, 57,
  59, 119, 125, 274-275, 288, 290 n.11,
  307, 312, 314
Busoni, Ferruccio: his duality, 3-4, 19;
  conducting, 4, 93, 127, 285; transcriptions, 5, 141, 180-181, 213,
  228-229, 243, 254, 283, 288, 295-298,
  300-313; hybrid works, 5, 141-152,
  181, 201-204; as outsider, 6;
  disciples, 6; location of manuscripts,
  11; question of opus numbers, 12;
  list of juvenalia, 13-15; early music
  for two pianos, 20-21; studies with
  Wilhelm Mayer, 21; first romantic
  style, 23-24, 34; unpublished sonatas
  and suites, 25-28; unpublished works
  for piano and orchestra, 28-34;
  major/minor fluctuation, 25-26, 37,
  43, 48, 54, 62, 100, 103, 111, 115,
  141, 201, 246; early published
  "character" pieces, 37-41; early
  published "baroque-classical" pieces,
  42-47; early published "formal-
  romantic" pieces, 47-49; ballet
  music, 46-47; miscellaneous roman-
  tic-style works, 51-60; ballet-scene
  works, 53-57; Bach-Busoni transcriptions, 52; semi-tonal alterations or
  instabilities, 55-61, 64, 120, 144, 154,
  156; revision of early works, 55-60,
  117 n.14; new style, 61-68, 81;
  impressionism, 66, 68, 73, 76, 81,
  315; major works, 71-174; re-use of
  material, 77; cellular technique,
  78-86, 97-99, 102, 105-107, 113, 124,
  181, 185-186, 194-195; works leading
  to Fantasia Contrappuntistica,
  142-152; architectural sketch of

About the Author

Larry Sitsky is Head of the Department of Composition and Musicology at Canberra School of Music in Australia and, as one of Australia's most prolific and commissioned composers, the winner of many prizes and fellowships. He is also a well-known pianist and has performed many of the Busoni works described in this book. His articles have been published in *The Music Review, Quadrant, Sydney Morning Herald, Reader's Digest, Studies in Music, Dictionary of Contemporary Music,* and *Soviet Encyclopedia,* among other sources. He is currently working on a book on the classical reproducing piano roll.

**Recent Titles in
Contributions to the Study of Music and Dance**